Fashion and Celebrity Culture

Fashion and Celebrity Culture

Pamela Church Gibson

London · New York

English edition
First published in 2012 by
Berg
Editorial offices:
50 Bedford Square, London W1CB 3DP, UK
175 Fifth Avenue, New York, NY 10010, USA

Berg is an imprint of Bloomsbury Publishing Plc.

Library of Congress Cataloging-in-Publication Data
A catalogue record for this book is available from the Library of Congress.

British Library Cataloguing-in-Publication Data
A catalogue record for this book is available from the British Library.

ISBN	978 1 84788 385 8 (Cloth)
	978 1 84788 386 5 (Paper)
e-ISBN	978 0 85785 231 1 (Institutional)
	978 0 85785 230 4 (Individual)

Typeset by Apex CoVantage, LLC, Madison, WI, USA
Printed in the UK by the MPG Books Group

www.bergpublishers.com

Contents

Illustrations

All photographs for plates and figures by Anne-Marie Michel, except Figure 18 by Alexei Daras.

PLATES

1 Fashion icon Alexa Chung, relaxed and at home in the front row, was given an award for her personal style by the British Fashion Council

2 The 'celebrity look' emulated by the high street—the glitter, the cling and the inevitable vertiginous heels

3 Embodying the possible origins of the glamour look—star of 'adult movies' Jenna Jameson dressed for an appearance at the Las Vegas Film Festival

4 How to negotiate a crash barrier with style—the elegant and truly glamorous Dita von Teese

5 Constantly chided for her bohemian style, English actress Helena Bonham-Carter resists pressure to change and sticks with Dame Vivienne Westwood, her favourite designer

6 One of the all-original supermodels, Naomi Campbell

7 Paris Hilton at the World Music Awards—celebrity guest rather than nominee

8 The celebrity as designer—Lauren Conrad accepts the applause

9 The designer as celebrity—Donatella Versace

10 Celebrity and director Sofia Coppola's new film is matched in billboard size and space by the commercial sponsors of the festival where it was first screened

11 The fans wait for the star at the premiere of *Salt*

12 The star does not disappoint them—Angelina Jolie's trademark look

FIGURES

Acknowledgements

It was Tristan Palmer who originally commissioned this manuscript and who helped me draw up a plan of campaign; I would like to thank both him and Anna Wright at Berg, who took over halfway through—it has been a pleasure to work with them both. I should also like to express my gratitude to the staff of the British Film Institute Library; their expertise is of as much value to those who work there as the holdings themselves.

I would like to thank various staff at the University of the Arts—Adam Briggs and Roy Peach, both benevolent and sympathetic managers; Helen Thomas in the Research Office; Alistair O'Neill; Agnes Rocamora, who kindly lent me a pre-publication draft of her manuscript; and Shaun Cole. My immediate colleagues, Jan Miller and Nik Mijovic, have both helped me in numerous ways, and I am incredibly grateful to both of them. Among the students, Kate Battrick provided a particularly helpful guide to the blogosphere, while the very talented Anne-Marie Michel took all but one of the extremely professional photographs which illustrate the book and adorn its cover. I would like to thank Alexei Daras for taking the photograph which now forms Figure 18 within the main body of the text.

I am also indebted to my interviewees, particularly to Terre Thaemlitz.

I should also thank those who have invited me to their institutions and so given me a chance to sound out responses to some of the ideas here. I would like to thank, in particular, Dorothea Mink and Andrea Sich of the Academy of the Arts in Bremen. Some of the material within Chapter One was presented at their conference, OUT OF ORDER, in Bremen in January 2010 and has appeared in the online version of the papers. There will be a publication in book form to follow (see endnote to Chapter One).

Andrew Hill read through early chapters and consistently encouraged me. Tamar Jeffers McDonald has provided support in many ways; she also offered me access to her DVD library, with suggestions for therapeutic viewing. Sarah Gilligan helped me throughout; whilst her frequent emails ensured that I never missed a new development in the field, she also provided an opportunity for informed discussion and gave me endless practical assistance.

Finally, I would like to thank Celia Britton, Roma Gibson and Gill Pengelly, and of course my family: my mother as always; my nieces Daisy, Grace and Ella, all as impervious as they should be to celebrity *diktats* and the eldest only too delighted to desecrate my 'research' copy of *Hello;* and lastly my sons, William and Thomas, to whom the material might be equally alien, but to whom this book is dedicated. Their father kindly read through the first two chapters, providing both moral support and sound stylistic suggestions, and I should not forget Eighty-Three.

Introduction, Rationale, Context

Fashion is the medicament that will console for the phenomenon of forgetting on a collective scale.

—Walter Benjamin: *The Arcades Project*

The biggest celebrity of the last decade? The designer handbag.

—Nilgin Yusuf, journalist: BBC 2 documentary

This book begins with the assumption that the relationship between fashion and celebrity culture needs to be carefully examined, and that this task is long overdue, since their new interdependency has arguably altered the workings of contemporary fashion—in quite significant ways. Whether these changes are irreversible, or merely superficial and temporary, is, of course, as yet unknown—and is as puzzling as the apparent lack of any real admission, anywhere, of their actual extent. Ironically, the celebrity phenomenon has brought about these modifications just at the very moment when, we could argue, cultural theorists have finally succeeded in establishing fashion as a legitimate academic discipline and have put forward different possible modes of investigation (see amongst others: Wilson 1985/2005; Gaines and Herzog 1990; Bruzzi and Church Gibson 2000; McNeil et al. 2009). There is still some cavilling from scholars who work within long-established areas (see McNeil 2010), but, by and large, the analysis of fashion has been accepted, if grudgingly, as an area of scholarship like any other. Now, however, the recent and palpable alteration of the 'fashion system' (Barthes 1967/1990) wrought by celebrity culture surely means that these same modes of analysis and explanation need to be amended. Certainly, the mechanisms and the day-to-day workings of that 'system' have subtly shifted.

It is this changed—and charged—relationship which is, arguably, both key feature and driving force in the new proliferation of celebrity culture as a global, collective and disturbing obsession. And I will suggest that it is not only the *fashion* landscape that has changed, but rather the entire topography of visual culture. However, it does seem that as yet no one has looked *across* the entire spectrum—to make the necessary links, to describe and try to comprehend the new geography.

As we enter the second decade of this new millennium, the cult of celebrity seems rampant as never before, both nationally and globally—and fashion consumption, too, is noticeably, defiantly triumphant. Furthermore, it seems almost impossible to avoid some level of engagement with the new phenomenon, whether or not it is welcome; the only way to shut it out is to avoid cities, shun the media—to adopt, in fact the kind of spartan lifestyle seemingly advocated by the late F. R. Leavis (1930), one of the cultural critics most antagonistic to mass culture. He would prefer that we avoid the media in all its most popular configurations; today, however, he would have to go further—to be more specific, forbidding the opening of any form of newspaper and certainly the use of most commercial e-mail providers, such as Hotmail and Yahoo, where the latest celebrity stories form a kind of border down the side of the main page. Whether we like it or not, celebrity culture has seeped into every conceivable nook and cranny within the public sphere.

It is difficult to disagree, here, or to quarrel with another assertion central to this book—that this new global celebrity culture is, in fact, in a worrying way, a major aspect of just one more configuration of Western imperialism, and possibly the most profitable yet. Although each continent—indeed, most countries where there is some form of profitable economic activity—have their own icons, there is no East–West traffic. Instead, the flow is in another, more established direction, just as it has been for so long—but now the Anglo-American dissemination of goods and images across the world has, simply, been reshaped.

When football superstar and fashion icon David Beckham visited Japan with his then team, Manchester United, in December 2002, he was greeted not only by thousands of screaming fans, but also with a giant chocolate statue, carved in his very own image ('Japan Unveils' 2002; Yu 2005). The statue has long since melted—perhaps some of it was actually eaten—though, as yet, Beckham's earning power remains strong and he has not, himself, been swallowed up. Indeed, after he ruptured an Achilles tendon in March 2010 and was pronounced unfit to play for several months (Fifield 2010), the British Football Association announced that he would still accompany their team to the World Cup finals in South Africa that summer—to act as ambassador, elder statesman, tribal fetish or even good luck charm, though, sadly, unsuccessful in this last capacity (see Burt 2010; Haywood 2010). They did not mention his strange iconic potency, nor the various valuable marketing opportunities for both star and team which this same tournament would provide.[1]

There is an interesting quasi-philosophical concern raised by the global infatuation with Beckham—who, like certain other celebrity superstars, will, inevitably, appear and reappear within the following pages—questions around *reality*, image, symbol and referent. For quite soon after this particular tour, the British artist Alison Jackson took the Beckham lookalike Andy Harmer to Japan on a 'tour' of her own.[2] Jackson's own artistic practice is made up of photo shoots and video narratives—all of which feature celebrity lookalikes (see Jackson 2007, 2003). Her own success was assured in 1999 by her controversial degree show at the Royal College of Art. There, the centrepiece was a simulated 'family portrait' of the dead Princess Diana and Dodi Fayed, now seemingly coexisting in a parallel universe and proudly showing off their mixed-race child.[3] On her trip to Japan with 'Beckham', Jackson found that the huge crowds who gathered around them everywhere they went were, in fact, quite delighted to discover that the man they at first took to be Beckham was just an imitation, for it gave them a freedom and a license they would not have otherwise possessed. They hovered around the artist and model, touching him happily (Johnson 2008; Finel Honigman 2007). Those who wish to might adduce the work of Baudrillard (1968/2005, 1970/1998, 1981/1994) to address questions of simulation, simulacrum and 'reality'; although doing so may be relevant in this one particular instance, it is of little real help in comprehending, and conceivably resisting, this extraordinary, unprecedented phase of late capitalism and consumer culture, characterised by excess consumption and within which the celebrity phenomenon plays such a central part.

Scholarship has certainly noted—and attempted to make some sense of—the extent and the significance of this new celebrity culture. After a few initial forays proved successful, academic books and articles are now increasingly appearing in print, while a new academic journal, *Celebrity Studies,* edited by Su Holmes and Sean Redmond, has been launched *solely* to examine this phenomenon (Routledge, launched 2010). Yet surprisingly, so far there has been little mention of fashion, surely so important to any understanding of this new phase, dominated as it is by consumption on an extraordinary scale. Today's fashion-centred consumption is not only, in part, a nightmarish reconfiguration of Veblen's notion of the 'conspicuous' (1899/1994). More disquietingly, it is now *continuous*, too, rather than merely seasonal. It is also wholly dependent upon built-in obsolescence taken to the point of 'instant throwaway'.

However, no fashion theorists are to be found on the editorial board of the journal *Celebrity Studies,* which first appeared in 2010, while a hunt through the indexes of existing academic books on the topic will yield, at the very most, half a dozen entries under 'fashion' (see Rojek 2001; Cashmore 2004, 2006; Austin and Barker 2003; Holmes and Redmond 2006; Redmond and Holmes 2007; Turner 2004; Turner, Bonner and Marshall 2000). In the first volume of the brand-new journal, there is much play with what contributor Emma Bell calls the 'C-word' (2010: 126) and the fact that for some—though not the editorial team involved—it has such negative connotations. However, a diligent and thorough scouring of its pages reveals not a single mention of what Valerie Steele, defending her own discipline, famously called the 'F-word' (1991); these scholars seem unaware that for many young women, 'celebrity' and 'fashion' are virtually synonymous.

In the second issue, however, Ellis Cashmore examines the way in which the singer Beyoncé has made herself into a brand—and, of course, it is primarily clothing and fashion-related products that she endorses. Since this article appeared, Beyoncé has danced both semi-naked and perhaps rather suggestively to promote her new fragrance, Heat; the commercial incurred a number of complaints. Cashmore is, of course, principally concerned with the way in which Beyoncé has seemingly toned down and carefully commodified her ethnicity; he argues that her 'ethnic ambiguity' can be taken to suggest that racism has somehow, magically, vanished from contemporary America, while her 'glamour', her high public profile and her place at the forefront of 'unrestrained consumption' seem to be constructed as what he calls 'a salve to the enduring effects of racism'. In 2008, when she was chosen to appear in the L'Oréal commercial with its infamous caption 'Because I'm Worth It', critics claimed that her face had been digitally whitened, a claim that was denied by L'Oréal. Certainly she looked much paler than when posing for the cover of *Essence,* the African American magazine, in that same year, where she wore her hair in an Afro style; normally, long blonde extensions adorn her head. Such reflections are vital to our consideration of fashion and celebrity—for, as we will see, the fashionable celebrity seems, invariably, to be pale in colour, except when fashion elects to fetishize blackness as 'other'. I would also add that the iconic potency of the singer is surely strengthened by her position as one of the very few *fashion icons* of colour. Her marriage to rapper Jay-Z, which Cashmore discusses, has meant that together they now form one of the very few *non-white* celebrity couples.

Most of the protagonists in these new academic debates are scholars working in the fields of television, cinema and cultural studies, or sociologists such as Chris Rojek, whose 2001 book *Celebrity* arguably opened up this field of academic enquiry and who in 2010 edited what must surely become the definitive anthology, running as it does to seven hundred pages (Rojek 2001; also see Marshall 1997, 2006). We can hardly ignore his horribly accurate observation in this seminal text that 'the grotesque, bloated cultural shape created by some of our celebrities is the development of the common constituents of social form' (Rojek 2001: 198).

Yet fashion scholars themselves—unlike fashion journalists—have been rather slow to investigate the precise workings of celebrity culture, which, as it has grown—or, rather, swollen gargantuanly—has become very obviously involved with economic and creative enterprises which fall squarely within the sphere of their own discipline. Jennifer Craik (2009) has a section in her latest publication on the particular phenomenon that is Kate Moss, and Tim Edwards finishes his latest book (2011) with a chapter on celebrity; but otherwise, very little work of this kind has so far been carried out. The journal *Fashion Theory,* which was set up specifically to investigate any and all relevant concerns, has so far published only three articles which investigate the relationship between celebrity culture and the world of fashion. One of these discusses the new fad for 'celebrity knitting' (Parkins 2004): Brad Pitt and Julia Roberts, it seems, are both skilled with their needles, knitting to while away the hours spent waiting on set.

Another article, more central to the ways in which celebrity and fashion are interlinked, examines the 'habitus' of Elizabeth Hurley (Barron 2007). In the third instance, Nicky Ryan considers 'Prada and the Art of Patronage' (2007). The art-celebrity nexus (see Stallabrass 2004) has arguably now evolved into an art-celebrity-*fashion* nexus and will be a central area of exploration in this book, whilst the artist's own creation of a celebrity persona to accompany and assist his or her actual creative activities will be examined, particularly in chapter 11.

Andy Warhol—to whom I shall return in this introduction and throughout this book—was of course a pioneer here; not only did he clearly perceive and therefore profitably harness the symbiotic relationship between art and fashion, but he introduced 'celebrity' into his different forms of artistic practice so as to create this now-familiar triangle, arguably doing so forty years ahead of anyone else. While the fashion industry is perhaps the real beneficiary of the recent consolidation and public recognition of this same triangulated relationship, acquiring a new cultural legitimacy along with its enhanced visibility and increased sales, celebrities too can nonetheless now take on associations with one form of 'cultural capital' or another; the art world simply receives ever-increasing financial support and, of course, maximum publicity. Meanwhile, the new link between celebrity and fashion provides unprecedented opportunities for marketing and retailing. Given the indifference thus far to Marx within the field of celebrity studies, it is perhaps unsurprising that no one has noted the grim relevance of his concept of the prostitute as both vendor and commodity to the field (see Marx 1844/1988: 100). Over seventy-five years ago, Walter Benjamin saw Marx's configuration of the prostitute as emblematic of modern capitalism (see Benjamin 2002: 40–1). However, it seems still more appropriate in this era of self-publicizing celebrities and their business ventures, their creation of the 'subject of fame' as a more or less lurid brand.

Rojek's concept of the contemporary 'celetoid' (2001), a figure who achieves initial fame through association, is perfectly illustrated through an essay to which I referred earlier (Barron 2007), which takes the figure of Liz Hurley as case study. Hurley has gradually built up a viable fashion business based solely upon the *habitus* of 'which she is both transmitter and subject' (Barron 2007: 444). Hurley's career as a model, and subsequently as the kind of 'designer' considered later in this book, began with one lucky red-carpet photo opportunity, upon which she then capitalized. The London premiere of the film *Four Weddings and a Funeral* in 1994 took place after the film had first been released in the United States, where it generated considerable interest. Hurley was at that time a little known and inexperienced actress, attended the screening as the then girlfriend of the film's star, Hugh Grant. Posing happily for the paparazzi in her borrowed and very revealing Versace gown, seemingly held together by a few shining, conspicuous and strategically placed 'safety pins', she attracted much media attention, and the resulting pictures made front-page news (also see Barron 2007, 2006).

The extraordinary manipulation of that moment created a pattern for others to follow (if they could). It meant, too, that by a nice irony, the 'star' Hugh Grant in some degree waned in the celebrity heavens, where his own place depended upon his acting ability, while that of his former companion, though predicated primarily upon her good looks and her commercial acumen, began to wax. She embarked on a new career, first as a model, becoming the highly paid face of Estée Lauder; she was soon featured on the covers of various prestigious magazines, culminating in the Christmas cover of British *Vogue* in December 1998. She was one of the first of the new celebrities to make this transition from celebrity (or *celetoid*) to fashion icon and is a perfect example of one type of activity within the new 'fashion system'. There is a full account of the means by which celebrity is, if not created, then certainly capitalized upon in Graeme Turner and colleagues' *Fame Games* (Turner et al. 2000). But while he describes the unseen workings of agents and PR agencies within the different strands of the media to ensure maximum publicity for their protégées (2000), he offers no investigation of specific fashion-related activity. Nor does he discuss the new role of the celebrity stylist, who not only dresses his or her employer but, in doing so, works closely with fashion houses, designers and magazines.

The journal article which examined 'the habitus' of Hurley (Barron 2007) focussed on her range of beachwear called, of course, Elizabeth Hurley Beach. However, since the article was published, Hurley has diversified further, becoming famous for her range of organic produce and the chic-rural lifestyle associated with her new 'habitus' deep in the Cotswold countryside. If this playing-at-farming might remind the reader of Marie Antoinette's faux-shepherdess antics in the gardens of the 'village' built for her beside the Petit Trianon in the grounds of Versailles, the comparison is both important and telling. For that same hated French queen, a central player in the drama whereby the Ancien Régime ceded control to the bourgeoisie, incurred her spectacular unpopularity not only through her alleged though unproven sexual shenanigans but, of course, through her famous sartorial excesses and her unparalleled extravagance, which helped to render Louis XIV's position utterly untenable (see Fraser 2001; Zweig 1933/2002).

Yet today we do not imprison, bring to trial or guillotine those who offend in these very ways. We rather follow both the sexual scandals and spending sprees, and do so with an extraordinary fascination, as they are carefully chronicled for us both in various strands of the reconfigured mass media and on the new Internet sites set up specifically for this purpose. Even respectable broadsheet newspapers across the world seem to have given up the unequal struggle to keep celebrity activities—and fashion itself—safely stashed away on their inside pages. The latest celebrity liaisons, divorces, deaths and unusual, spectacular appearances now regularly grace the front pages, even there. It is worth referring here to Guy Debord's notion of the 'society of the spectacle' (Debord 1968/2002); and perhaps we could take the notion of the delight in spectacle still further, suggesting that it evokes the 'bread and circuses'

Figure 1   A blonde Peaches Geldof relaxes in the front row. Photograph by Anne-Marie Michel.

atmosphere of the Roman Empire in its decadent death throes (see the work of Alain Badiou 2004, for instance).

So, in our particular phase of late capitalism, Hurley and her ilk have a popularity denied to the infamous fashion icon of the 1780s—even if, incidentally, Marie Antoinette did employ the first designer and hairdresser who we could perhaps describe as the first celebrity stylists (for a detailed account of their roles see Weber 2008). Today there is not only uncritical adulation, for the most part, of our visibly extravagant celebrities, but, paradoxically, press accounts of their lavish spending on clothes, houses and yachts garner yet more publicity and generate still more income. The presence of talent or skill—which mega-celebrities such as Beckham, Madonna and Beyoncé do of course possess—is no longer significant. Most recently, we have witnessed the 'uncoupling of celebrity from talent' (Holmes and Negra 2008; Negra and Holmes 2008; Holmes and Redmond 2010). For the nature of celebrity itself has now altered, and those venturing onto the screen in reality television programmes are as important to the press as those who have attained celebrity status through their abilities and achievements. So, too, are the sexual partners and children of those already in the public eye.

Although Rojek (2001) does have a category, 'celebrity by ascription', within which we would place Marie Antoinette, one does not necessarily inherit celebrity. There is, however, what could be called 'celebrity lineage', which can and does provide unparalleled career opportunities, the relevant careers invariably emerging within fashion. Many of today's models are the children of rock stars or other public figures: the Jagger and Richards daughters, for example.

Nevertheless, until very recently, celebrity lineage alone could not guarantee success as a fashion *designer*: Stella McCartney had to study at St Martin's for three years. Today, however, the notion of training and apprenticeship as the prerequisite for such a career seems to have disappeared completely, certainly where celebrities, their relatives or their offspring are concerned.

In March 2010, it was announced that Lourdes Ciccone, thirteen years old, would be launching her own range of designs, to be called Material Girl for Macy's (Thomas 2010; Moore 2010) and based, of course, on her famous mother's very first incarnation.[4]

Once a particular celebrity has been accepted as some form of bona fide fashion icon, it is not necessary for him or her to do any more actual work within their original sphere of employment (acting, singing, presenting and so on). Chloe Sevigny began her career as an excellent actress in small, often controversial independent films, of which *Boys Don't Cry* (1999, dir. Kimberly Pierce) was the most high profile: Oscar nominated, in fact. However, she was swiftly welcomed into the fashion world and was there lionized for her idiosyncratic, highly individual fashion sense: she is a very different form of fashion celebrity from Hurley (also see Barron 2007, 2006), whose own dress sense and 'designs' represent a more orthodox conception of glamour. We will look at these contrasting celebrity templates later in the chapter. Sevigny is currently photographed whenever and wherever she appears in public, but for her outfits alone; her film career is no longer mentioned.[5] Her quirky, slightly Bohemian look (see Adolescent 2008), so beloved of so many young designers, is exemplified in the style of other celebrity fashion icons, though not necessarily those celebrities of most interest

Figure 2   Celebrity-turned-designer Nicky Hilton. Photograph by Anne-Marie Michel.

to the majority of young women, who seem overall to prefer the more glamorous ideal offered by the other celebrity prototype.

The young actresses Ashley and Mary Kate Olsen, once well-known for their television career, now appear regularly on fashion pages and Internet sites, either to flaunt their latest quasi-goth look or to display their latest collections. *Bazaar* wrote of their spring 2010 collection for their line, The Row (see therow.com), that it 'nailed' the new trends, writing of the twins in the same paragraph and in the same register as established designers Phoebe Philo and Isabel Marant. Their original career is now almost forgotten, but their image remains one of great interest, and so they now appear in the press, not in connection with any thespian activity but simply *as themselves.* The resulting publicity helps with their two successful ranges of garments, The Row and Elizabeth and James, to which they have given their name and their backing. A third, the 'Brit-inspired' Olsenboye fall 2010 collection for JC Penney, is, at the time of writing, imminent (see DeSimmone 2010). There is even a coffee-table book, *Influence* (2008), given over largely to pictures of things the twins like and involving leading figures within the fashion world, with the additional cachet of photographs by Bruce Weber.[6]

But the celebrity fashion status of two young American television actresses, Whitney Port and Olivia Palermo, is even more of an index of the new 'system' and its *modus operandi;* unlike Sevigny and the Olsens, who had 'careers' as such, these two women starred in one single television show, *The City,* involving the 'real' world of fashion and designer Diane von Fürstenberg, itself a spin-off from *The Hills.* In 2010, their 'fashion capital' seems to be accepted as a given, and they are used repeatedly in fashion features (Palermo 2010; Friedlander 2010; Power and Kerr 2010; Cohen 2009). Furthermore, it is accepted that they will automatically be recognized by their intended audience, and their fashion credentials accepted as impeccable. The fact that both girls employ stylists is not widely publicized (see Friedlander 2010). It will be interesting to see whether, unlike Sevigny and Moss, who have styles of their own which have lasted, these two rapidly sink below the horizon (Gyben 2011). What is central to—and what has arguably helped to create—the new and all-pervading celebrity culture of the last two decades is in fact this very same relationship with fashion, this new interdependency which has changed the patterning of fashion-related consumption and altered so many other aspects of the fashion industry. In other words, the extraordinary prevalence of celebrity culture in this new millennium can plausibly be explained through these recent, carefully forged links with the marketing, promotion and production of fashionable goods, and this at both ends of the market.

Dominant within the new system is the luxury fashion brand, whose resurgence in the 1990s coincided with the burgeoning of the new phase of celebrity culture. The two speedily joined forces for their mutual benefit, just as the luxury brands themselves either joined—or were devoured by—one of the two powerful conglomerates, LVMH and PPR, who now control this end of the fashion business.[7]

Although the revitalization of Gucci that dated from Tom Ford's appointment as creative director in 1993 (see Hirschberg 1996; Sharkey 2000) depended on his shrewd deployment of already-established stars, particularly Madonna, subsequent luxury brand campaigns have used emerging and thus less expensive celebrities to the advantage of both parties. Madonna, incidentally, remains both a central figure within the celebrity pantheon and a favourite model of the fashion houses; just after her fiftieth birthday, she appeared in the Louis Vuitton spring 2009 campaign (see Johnson 2009; Singh 2009) and then featured in Dolce & Gabbana's winter 2009–2010 magazine advertisements, masquerading as a sexy Sicilian housewife, complete with black woollen stockings (see Wheeler 2009). Here we might see, again, echoes of the faux-pastoral of Versailles. It is interesting to note that Sofia Coppola, who features in the following pages in her various incarnations as fashion celebrity, the muse of designers and a successful film director (perhaps by 'ascription'), chose to make a film about Marie Antoinette (2006). Furthermore, she subtly modified the source she cited in the credits, Antonia Fraser's (2001) biography of the French queen. Like the biographer, Coppola portrayed the queen as a hapless victim of dynastic manoeuvrings. But, unlike Fraser's book, the film seems to suggest that her only outlet for her frustrated creativity was through fashionable excess. Well-known designer Manolo Blahnik provided some of the shoes seen on screen (Cannatà 2010), and the chic Parisian patisserie

Ladureé proffered the multi-coloured macaroons so often seen at contemporary fashion events (Owens 2007). The film came close to being a revisionist version of French history (also see Cook 2008) and was loudly booed on its first screening, in France, at the Cannes Film Festival of May 2006 (Waters 2006; Bamigboye 2006; Jacobson 2006). It may have been logical to launch the film at Cannes, but it was hardly likely that a French audience would greet it with acclaim there.

Meanwhile, at the opposite end of the economic spectrum, on high street, in shopping malls and street markets, we now find progressively cheaper clothes and accessories, copying celebrity looks. A particular tranche of the fashion industry worldwide—given the geographical location of so much garment production—is now concerned, most profitably, with the swift production and speedy distribution of cheap and disposable copies of designer clothes and accessories as seen and coveted in the endlessly circulating images of celebrities. The lower end of the market has profited just as significantly as the luxury fashion conglomerates. Both have strategically yoked themselves to and systematically exploited the celebrity phenomenon.[8] Chains such as Primark and New Look do not advertise, but they do have websites exhibiting the word *celebrity,* here used to signify one particular subcategory of style (Primark 2010; Flint 2009; 'Primark Goes Posh' 2007; Vernon 2005; Davey 2007).

CHANGES IN VISUAL CULTURE

The repercussions of this new cult of celebrity, and these recent alliances with fashion and with art, have, as indicated earlier in this chapter, affected and altered visual culture in all its manifestations. But this does not seem to have been widely acknowledged, nor analysed within the different, relevant areas of the academy—and indeed, scholars remain locked within their parent disciplines. A key element in my argument here is that an interdisciplinary approach is the only possible way to understand contemporary visual culture, for images now 'bleed' right across the whole spectrum of the media through its formerly discrete strands, from cinema and television to fashion shoot and advertising, and this process subtly alters and even devalues their original meaning. Thus, I stress the need to look *sideways* if we are to understand the full significance of the new visual currency.

Only those involved in different commercial forms of media production, from magazine journalism to film-making, together with those who work in the various overlapping spheres that form the universe of fashion, seem really attuned to what has happened, however unenthusiastic some of them may be about the celebrity component in contemporary culture and its new centrality. In the documentary film *The September Issue* (2009, dir. R. J. Cutler), which examines the production of US *Vogue* during a crucial four-week period, various members of staff are interviewed. Senior Fashion Editor

Grace Coddington muses, 'Perhaps I'm a bit of a Romantic—I think I got left behind somewhere.' She offers an explanation later in the film: 'I wouldn't care if I never saw another celebrity again,' a sentiment many might share. Those readers who want an uncritical celebration of celebrity here should perhaps stop reading now and look elsewhere.

Coddington continues, wistfully, 'That's the way it's going and you just have to go with it.' Although she had worked in the fashion industry for forty-odd years, she was virtually unknown outside that world; after the film's release and enthusiastic reception, ironically enough, she found that she was *herself* a minor celebrity—even receiving the Isabella Blow Fashion Creator award at the British Fashion Awards in December 2009 (Byrne 2010; Armstrong 2009; Alexander 2009).

In the previous quotation, Coddington is specifically talking about Anna Wintour's 'pioneering' work in getting celebrities rather than actual fashion models on to the cover of US *Vogue,* far ahead of the other fashion 'glossies'. However, Coddington's rueful acknowledgment of 'the way it's going' is not only true of fashion journalism, but also of popular print media in its entirety. Most manifestations of popular culture have adapted, chameleon-like, or reconfigured themselves completely in response to the phenomenon that is contemporary celebrity. Magazine journalism has altered radically, while most newspapers have changed in shape, style and content. Print journalism has changed across the past two decades in response to the new economic power of celebrity—we have only to look at a newsstand anywhere in the world—which we will consider further in a later chapter. It is worth noting that magazine journalists have beaten most scholars into print, even within the hard covers of books. Certainly Jennifer Craik has her chapter on Moss (2009), but a full year before her book appeared, fashion writer Angela Buttolph had already written and published *Kate Moss: Style* (2008b), a detailed analysis crossed with a how-to guide (also see Buttolph 2008a).

Meanwhile, in the art world, the boundaries between 'high art' and popular culture have been increasingly blurred over the last forty years, since the emergence of pop art and, in particular, the success of Andy Warhol. Here, too, over the past decade in particular, there have been further changes. We will scrutinize them in chapter 10. But while many who are aware of the changes would accept that they have affected the workings of television, journalism, popular music, the Internet and the art world, little account has been taken so far of the way in which the celebrity-fashion nexus has changed developments in and around contemporary cinema.

This I find troubling, and I will examine these changes in detail across three chapters, for cinema has mutated just as surely as has the art world. Indeed, celebrity culture has arguably affected every aspect of the spectacle that is postmillennial society. I would hope that this particular book will, if only by virtue of scrutinizing the extent of the changes, make possible a greater understanding of their scope and significance.

Spectacle and Scrutiny

Within the academy, those seeking to defend fashion itself have often argued that it can be subversive or confrontational—particularly those writers concerned with youth cultures who see subcultural style as a form of rebellion and resistance (see Hebdige 1979; Hall and Jefferson 1993; Fiske 1993, 1989a,b; Gelder and Thornton 1997; Muggleton 2000). More frequently, fashion's defenders have suggested that it provides us with a means of self-expression, a vital form of 'agency' (see Miller 2001, 1998; Slater 1997; Miles 1998). Some feminist writers, in particular, have championed the freedom and the creativity involved in self-adornment (Hollows and Moseley 2006; Hollows 2000; Moseley 2002; Stacey 1994; Church Gibson 2000).[9]

Maybe it is time for a moment of reassessment. For much of the subversive potential of street style has now been undermined; today, each new and fledgling youth culture is swiftly co-opted by the forces of commerce—as in the case of emo, for example—whilst any form of 'agency' is similarly threatened. What we should concern ourselves with is the way in which celebrity culture is increasingly driving the very machine of fashion and, in changing the workings of the system, has rendered our discussions of 'agency' problematic. Self-expression through dress is to some extent eroded, a fortiori subversion. More and more people actually seek sameness, and shop to create cloned looks inspired by the celebrity pantheon.

While there have always been fashion leaders and style icons, they did not possess the extraordinary power and influence, nor have the unprecedented earning potential connected with them, available at this juncture. Most significantly of all, they did not have professional stylists liaising with luxury brands. Fashion leaders, true style icons—of whom Moss is one—are still with us, but they are now arguably in a minority; those who look to celebrities for inspiration are not always aware that the look of so many is actually provided by anonymous stylists who happily use the expensive garments and accessories donated by designers and fashion houses to generate maximum publicity. These new patterns of consumption—which they are co-opted to encourage—now appear to flourish despite global economic problems and even in a fully fledged recession (see Roberts 2010; Oxbury 2010).

It should be noted here that in his book *Celebrity Culture* (2006), Ellis Cashmore does stress that, particularly in the last decade, the phenomenon has been deployed to, as he puts it, 'make us want more *stuff*'. But Cashmore doesn't really scrutinize the precise nature of the 'stuff', nor does he identify the relationship specifically between celebrities and fashion. For although he explores the ways in which celebrities from the worlds of sport and music have been used successfully for brand endorsement and in advertising, it is surely within the domain of the *fashionable* that the 'stuff' is really shifted—offered and accepted, in various forms, to men and women, young and middle-aged, rich or poor.

To return to Beckham: as one of the most successful sportsmen, he is of great interest to Cashmore (2004) and others (Cashmore and Parker 2003; Milligan 2010; Purohit 2008; Vincent, Hill and Lee 2009; Vincent and Hill 2007; Yu 2005). But his extraordinary appeal and financial success are explained not by his prowess on the field, nor by his good looks—no, they are due to the fact that he straddles the former divide between sport and fashion (also see Bruzzi and Church Gibson 2000), which he has helped to narrow, and, more significantly still, he has a famous wife, whose own appearance and fashionability are constantly photographed. I shall discuss the newly profitable phenomenon of the celebrity couple later, as well as the emergence of the celebrity-as-designer, where Victoria Beckham's career provides an interesting case study.

In the field of popular music, traditionally seen as the site of innovation in dress, the scene has changed in recent years to involve both the fashion designer and the luxury brand. In 2009, the extraordinary success of Lady Gaga was partly due to her idiosyncratic use on- and offstage of clothing and makeup. However, her extraordinary costuming, which has attracted publicity and helped significantly in the creation of her appeal, is a joint activity, although many within her legion of fans may be unaware of the names of her talented team of stylists. In China, in the spring of 2010, it was reported that—among the young—the expression which translates into English as 'Oh my God' had recently been supplanted by 'Oh my Lady Gaga', particularly online, in texts and in Twitter feeds (Macartney 2010). This worried those Chinese scholars who, like the Académie Française, are concerned with preserving the purity of their language; it also reveals the global power of the singer and the fact that her power may be based on her highly unorthodox manipulation of her appearance.

Lady Gaga's team of young designers, known as Haus of Gaga, may not be successful in always keeping their individual names in the public eye, although Nicola Formachetti, Gaga's leading stylist, was presented in autumn 2010 with the Isabella Blow award bestowed upon Grace Coddington twelve months before. It is the already-established designers, from Giorgio Armani to those less well-known, who provide the garments and accessories for her videos and stage performances (Robinson 2010: 139; Goodyear 2009; Chaban 2009) and make quite sure that their names and contributions are credited and acknowledged, as does the singer herself.[10] Lady Gaga has in fact appeared on stage and in video wearing the hoof shoes with twelve-inch heels which the late Alexander McQueen designed purely for use in his last complete show (Plato's Atlantis, autumn 2009, see Abraham 2009; Dana 2010). He created a pair especially for her, and when receiving one of her many awards at the Brit Awards ceremony in February 2010, in the week immediately after McQueen's death, she tearfully dedicated it to him (see Chilvers 2010; Moodie and Lawler 2010).[11]

The choice of his clothes—highly creative, hardly commercial—seems suitable for a singer as unusual in her self-presentation as Lady Gaga. But the mention of a designer as economically successful and aesthetically conservative as Giorgio Armani in this particular context is significant, and helps to provide a fuller understanding of the new landscape. He has been involved in costuming cinema since the welcome publicity provided by *American Gigolo* in 1980 (US, dir. Paul Schrader); the film generated an estimated $19 million worth of sales (Celant and Koda 2000; Bruzzi 1997: 26). But, more recently, he has come to understand that young musicians can provide healthy profits. He is not alone here. Karl Lagerfeld famously tried for both a new persona and a high profile in the southern hemisphere by dressing Kylie Minogue for her 2006 public rebirth. Armani dressed Lauren Hill for her *Miseducation* tour in 1998 and has worked in various ways with other figures in the music business; these changes are also the subject of a later chapter. Over the years, Armani has also successfully constructed *himself* as a celebrity, easily identifiable by a signature outfit; the emergence of the designer-as-celebrity, different from the celebrity-as-designer, is another of the radical changes in the fashion world during the past two decades, and again the subject of a later chapter.

In the art world where the luxury brands operate so successfully—backing individual artists, creating foundations and trusts, creating gallery spaces within their new shops, sponsoring exhibitions in leading museums—Armani has also been active. In 2001, he was granted the exhibition space of the Guggenheim Museum in New York within which to curate an exhibition of his designs; what he presented, however, was less an artistic retrospective and more an elaborate display, in notably splendid surroundings, of merchandise currently available in Armani shops across the world (Celant and Koda 2000; Leight 2000; Ennis 2000).

A more recent flurry of artistic activity, in another prestigious museum space, again brought Lady Gaga and a successful luxury brand together, but in a very different way; this later event suggests that the new art-fashion-celebrity nexus is being pushed to the very limits of its own extraordinary logic. Francesco Vezzoli, whose career will be discussed in chapter 10 and whose fame is based on his creation of various installations which all involve celebrities, has arguably gone still further down this particular path. Here, he has brought the luxury brand into his work in a new way, actually using the visual currency of the fashion logo itself. In November 2009, he staged an installation at the Los Angeles Museum of Contemporary Art entitled 'The Shortest Musical You Will Ever See' (see: Akerlund 2010; Winter 2009). This performance was sponsored by Miuccia Prada and attended by leading figures from the fashion industry— among them Carine Roitfeld, then the high-profile editor of French *Vogue*—together with artists, including David Hockney and Damien Hirst, and film stars, including celebrity couple Brad Pitt and Angelina Jolie.

At the centre of the catwalk-cum-stage was a Barbie-pink piano, decorated with a pattern of blue butterflies painted by Damien Hirst, at which sat Lady Gaga, wearing a dress designed—like all the costumes seen on the stage—by Miuccia Prada, with a

Figure 3   Celebrity designer who has always had a celebrity look—Donatella Versace. Photograph by Anne-Marie Michel.

floor-length skirt that resembled a vast chandelier of silvery glass beads. Her hair was streaked pink to match the piano, and she sported a heavy silver headpiece designed by architect Frank Gehry. While she sang the song 'Speechless', dancers from the Bolshoi Ballet arranged in pairs along the catwalk performed a sequence of brief pas de deux. Beside the singer, a masked man in black theatrically mimed the act of embroidery; in the frame he held before him was a petit-point portrait of the singer by Vezzoli. The Russian ballerinas and their partners were clad in black-and-white patterned outfits which were presumably intended to evoke and complement the other player in this spectacle: the Prada logo. It was to the fore in the documentary film commissioned to record the whole spectacle. The camera follows the large white carrier bags with their distinctive black logo as they are carefully carried onto the stage by the protagonists (see Akerlund 2010; Yablonsky 2009a,b).

In the chapters to follow in which I consider the effect of celebrity culture on contemporary cinema, I shall argue that, certainly within Hollywood cinema, the luxury brand has its very own on-screen presence in an entirely new and disturbing way, as it does in this gallery piece. As the Vezzoli–Lady Gaga–Bolshoi Ballet–Prada collaboration shows, the luxury brands now do not serve simply to *adorn* those who have—or aspire to possess—celebrity status, either on screen or on the red carpet. Now, they can be seen themselves 'performing', and they can even do so independently of the human body, fêted *as and for themselves,* starring alone on screen: bags, boxes, wardrobes and 'closets'; rails and racks of garments; distinctive logos and characteristic shop interiors, all these have their own place within recent cinema.

The films involved, which include *The Devil Wears Prada* (2006, dir. David Frankel), *Sex and the City: The Movie* (2008, dir. Michael Patrick King) and the sequel he directed in 2010, also remind us how 'designer literate' so much of the viewing public has become. People are now aware of, and knowledgeable about, both designers and brands in a new way; on the day following Alexander McQueen's death, many newspapers made it their lead story, while much Internet space was devoted not only to gossip and speculation but, significantly, to well-informed tribute (see amongst others: Knox 2010; Camber and Nathan 2010; Tran 2010; Wilson and Horyn 2010; Horyn 2010; Barrett 2010). This awareness of the designer, the brand, the characteristic style and the relevant logo is, again, among the recent changes which form both the backdrop to and the substance of this book.

Some have seen the 'new celebrity' as a way of creating—however briefly—the opportunity to transcend class boundaries and break down racial barriers, since many celebrities have come from impoverished homes, or belong to ethnic minorities, and have famously attained wealth and fame. This seems to be the impetus for the Miley Cyrus video which accompanied the release of her song 'Party in the USA' and the simultaneous launch of her own range of clothing (Duff 2009). In the lyrics of the song itself, Cyrus mentions both Britney Spears, who has talked of her own blue-collar origins, and, to show her desire to be as representative as possible, Cyrus namechecks rapper Jay-Z. In the video, Cyrus and her backing singers, a group of very young girls who represent some of the country's ethnic minorities, dance together onstage at what seems to be an impromptu rural gathering, where all the participants are blue-collared and cowboy-booted and the standard mode of transport is the flatbed truck. As the camera moves in on the singer for the closing minutes of her song, a massive American flag descends and unfurls behind her to form a backdrop (see Hollywood

Records 2009). Both song and video would seem to stress the plethora of opportunity offered to those from supposedly disadvantaged backgrounds growing up in contemporary America.

However, I will argue that not only is the supposed new equality-through-celebrity an illusion, even a dangerous one, but that among the many overlooked consequences of the new dominance of celebrity culture, we might in fact find some possible *reconfiguration* of class identities, particularly around issues of dress and style.

THE ORDINARY AND THE WOULD-BE FABULOUS?

An understanding of the perhaps unwitting elitism that has characterized academic writing on fashion is surely central to any future developments in the field of fashion scholarship, and indeed across the entire spectrum of contemporary cultural studies. With the notable exception of Diane Crane's work (2001), the notion of the 'ordinary' and the 'everyday' has never been properly examined within fashion scholarship. Of far more interest to fashion theorists are the two opposite ends of the spectrum: high fashion on the one hand, street style and youth culture at their most confrontational on the other. The reasoning behind this has never been articulated, but presumably there is an unspoken assumption in play that high fashion possesses more artistic merit (an assumption which defends the would-be theorist from charges of frivolity), and a further assumption that subcultural style, which is seen as synonymous with rebellion, is a legitimate subject for the left-wing academic.

I would suggest that not only does the fashion scholar deem the truly 'everyday'— which should be called 'dress' or 'clothing', perhaps, rather than 'fashion' and which could range from high street jackets and dresses through stonewashed denim to tracksuits made from inexpensive synthetics—unworthy of his or her attention, but that, more significantly, an insidious snobbery is at work. 'Everyday' clothes in the States, say, might come from Walmart, whose jeans are actually dismissed by Anna Wintour in the opening seconds of *The September Issue* since, she suggests, it would be logical to prefer J-Brand jeans, so much more pleasing both in cut and fabric—and currently retailing at $150 a pair. This preference, she implies, is at the very heart of 'fashion', which she is seeking here to defend; sadly, there is no mention anywhere in the film of the fact that there exist radical differences in income levels which just might affect our purchasing choices.

Cheap, ubiquitous clothes which lack artistic merit of any kind are consigned not only to landfills in the real world but also to hinterlands beyond scholarship. This is partly, of course, because they make a mockery of ideals of 'agency' and the concept of our endless 'creativity'. Yet the only existing scholarship that actually addresses this issue is an essay, 'People Dress So Badly Nowadays', in the anthology *Fashion and Modernity* (Hill 2005), where writer Andrew Hill sets out on a picaresque expedition in search of the individual 'style' supposedly found through the exercise of 'agency' but discovers no evidence of the exercise of creative individuality other than a gold-crested pheasant in Golder's Hill Park and Zippo the Clown busking on a corner. Perhaps what is needed to interpret contemporary dress is an elaborated version of Barbara Vinken's concept of 'post-fashion' that moves far beyond the world of the radical high-fashion designers discussed in her book (2005) and out into those realms where scholarship has yet to set foot.

Interestingly, at least three of her chosen subjects would probably abhor links with celebrity, and their designs are not likely to be worn by actresses-singers-models, nor craved by their followers—I am thinking of Yohji Yamamoto, Martin Margiela and Helmut Lang. In fact, Lang has now left the world of fashion design in order to work as a fine art dealer (Solway 2008).

However, since the publication of her book, both Karl Lagerfeld and Rei Kawakubo, each the subject of a chapter, have accepted offers to design for the ever-more-aspirational high street chain H&M ('Karl Lagerfeld for H&M' 2004; 'Lagerfeld's High Street' 2004; Barnett 2008; West 2008), while Lagerfeld continues to present *himself* as a celebrity, all the time working with existing superstars. Both Gaultier and Dolce & Gabbana (Vinken 2005: 91–9, 119–26), of course, are noted for their celebrity collaborations; Gaultier's famous designs for Madonna's *Blonde Ambition* tour of 1990 were followed by a general rush to work with the singer, and the costumes and mise en scène for her *Rhinestone Cowgirl* tour of 2005 were the work of Dolce & Gabbana. In 2009, this duo selected the actress Scarlett Johannson, a familiar sight on magazine covers, as the face of their new makeup line (Casciato 2009). The images chosen for their campaign show her, carefully styled to look uncannily like Marilyn Monroe, applying lipstick before a mirror.

The overlooking of the ordinary is a particularly worrying omission in this era of celebrity culture, simply because celebrity emulation has created *new* and different ideals of dress and self-presentation—and particularly of body shape and adornment—which significantly depart from the ideals advocated by fashion itself, or rather by high fashion. These new ideals not only coexist with, but even challenge, the high-fashion ideal, and arguably provide still further psychological pressure. In fact, the *new* body images might be seen as more insidious than the much-debated thinness of catwalk models, which suggests that the fashion industry should not be the only one castigated over issues of size, shape and the problems thus created for young women.

There has not yet been any real general acknowledgement of the fact that there are now two rather different ideals of feminine style and shape in circulation, or any proper discussion of them. A critical analysis is vital to a clear understanding of twenty-first-century fashion in all its complexities; more so, perhaps, since the celebrity look aspiring to glamour and sexuality is as influential as the high-fashion look, if not more so.

Figure 4   The catwalk look on a catwalk body—here at Pam Hogg. Photograph by Anne-Marie Michel.

This question of the double ideal must be defined, addressed and interrogated if we are really to comprehend and illustrate the true impact of celebrity culture on fashion. Only then can we fully comprehend the dilemmas around self-image—and the issues around the body—for a great many young women worldwide.

Figure 5 The possible origins of the glamorous ideal—Jenna Jameson, not just a pin-up girl but a star of adult movies. Photograph by Anne-Marie Michel.

THE TWO IDEALS: SEXY OR ÜBER-STYLISH?

Fashion, 'Glamour' and Crossover

In *Glamour* (2008), Stephen Gundle discusses the new alliance between fashion, celebrity and luxury brands. The book charts the history of glamour from Lord Byron to the present day. Glamour is not always synonymous with historical celebrity. Equally, many celebrities of the past had nothing whatsoever to do with style and its leadership. Gundle's book nevertheless must be read by all who wish to understand the ways in which we reached our current position, or more accurately, found ourselves in our present predicament.

We are all too familiar with the celebrity who puts his or her name to a particular scent, or what is now referred to in fashion journalism as a 'fragrance'. But most of us are unaware that the very first celebrity endorsement of a scent was provided by Liane de Pougy in the late nineteenth century; she was not the most famous of the Parisian courtesans who dominated the demimonde of the Belle Époque, but she was definitely the most commercially minded (Gundle 2008: 100).

I would argue, however, that Gundle's choice of the young American celebrity Paris Hilton to exemplify contemporary glamour actually acts as an extraordinary indictment of celebrity culture. Furthermore, it shows, despite Gundle's valiant attempts to argue otherwise, exactly how the notion of glamour has been irreparably tarnished by the contemporary lionizing of celebrity and the endless misattributions of the word *glamorous,* so that the term has become gradually stripped of meaning.

Hilton is nonetheless still important in these pages, but for quite other reasons. She epitomizes a certain kind of contemporary female celebrity. Her family connections originally helped her to obtain a role in the television reality show *The Simple Life* (2003–2007), where she was joined by Nicole Ritchie, the adopted daughter of singer Lionel, who herself is now successful as a 'designer'. Hilton's aptitude for self-publicity is extraordinary: she released her first album at the same time as a sex tape was leaked; swiftly accessed and much viewed in cyberspace, it showed off the activities of Hilton and her then-boyfriend (Genz and Brabon 2009: 103). She, too, has put her name to merchandise, and she possesses most of the physical attributes of the new would-be glamorous celebrity prototype: the mandatory possession of a slender body, long blonde hair, and Caucasian origins. Almost all of the young women whose images appear in celebrity magazines are white, though, perversely, their skin is invariably dyed so as to appear much darker.

However, it is important to stress that, as we have seen, celebrities now fall into two opposing camps where styling and dress are concerned. One group is made up of the devotees of high fashion, and they are much-favoured by designers. Chloe Sevigny, Madonna and the Olsen twins have already been mentioned, and there are many others, including, say, Alexa Chung from the world of music and television and Emma Watson, star of the *Harry Potter* films and the face of the Burberry campaign for autumn–winter 2009–2010 (Bergin 2009), who champion the fashionable ideal and eschew the overly sexual and would-be glamorous look to which Hilton aspires. Incidentally, in 2009, Emma Watson was the highest-paid actress in Hollywood (Topping 2010a), which says a great deal about the power of the franchise within contemporary cinema. I shall consider this further in a later chapter.

Celebrities who adopt the high-fashion look and who champion leading designers are welcomed into the coveted front-row seats at the seasonal couture shows, replacing the leading fashion journalists who traditionally occupied those seats, many of whom are now relegated to the second row (Cartner-Morley 2009; Stebbins 2010b). Sometimes, however, this welcome is extended to the wrong people—for example, the young actress Lindsay Lohan, who was never noted for her knowledge of high fashion, but rather for her skin-tight outfits, garish blonde hair and fast living. she was appointed Artistic Advisor at the House of Ungaro for a brief period. Widespread criticism of the collections she was involved with prompted Lohan's exit from the brand (Odell 2009a; Bumpus 2009).

Fashion as understood within the higher echelons of the industry is, as I have indicated, different from the *clothes* that most people actually wear on an everyday basis and from their chosen methods of self-presentation. For many people today, their ideals may be the women in the other camp, the glamour-oriented celebrities, who include the wives and girlfriends of the famous. Many of these women would definitely not be found in the pages of the upmarket fashion 'glossies', nor used by younger cutting-edge magazines such as *Nylon, Tank* and *Purple.* The fashion celebrity, however, is at home there; despite her 'teen-pic' role in *Bring It On,* Kirsten Dunst is now more closely linked to fashion than glamour; this was cemented by her casting as Coppola's Marie Antoinette, and so she was asked to guest-edit an issue of the magazine *Lula* in 2009.

But the contrasting look that aspires to the now-debased currency of contemporary glamour and to a perceived sexiness arguably has a more pronounced effect on the style of many young women and has shaped their everyday mode of self-presentation. Many would rather be seen as sexy than stylish; so endless polls, both online and in print, indicate and underline.

It is the manipulation of the female body that is at the centre of the size-zero debate centred on fashion—and this, as I have suggested, should have its parameters redrawn. While the size-zero look is certainly still central to the catwalk show and the pages of high-end fashion magazines, celebrity culture has seen the construction of new body ideals in a way that is seemingly ignored and inordinately oppressive.

The most popular of the two contemporary body types is that decorated by breasts far larger than would be allowable in a fashion runway show. In fact, the whole new twinning of fashion and celebrity possibly affects young women more than any other demographic. My focus on women here is entirely deliberate; I am quite aware that young men have been increasingly involved with and affected by fashion and its visual imagery since the sea-changes of the 1980s (Jobling 1999; Mort 1996; Nixon 1996; Edwards 2006, 1997; Simpson 1994a,b; Benwell 2003). There are certainly celebrity male images where dress and hair provoke interest and emulation, whether on screen, in boy bands, or within the more authentic indie music scene. The idea of the dandy, too—with a lineage traceable from Beau Brummell through the now-forgotten Bulwer Lytton, champion of head-to-toe black for daywear, to Jimi Hendrix, Mick Jagger, David Bowie and latterly leading fashion journalist Hamish Bowles—has retained its potency and power (Kelly 2007; Breward 1999, 2000; Mitchell 2003; Hawkins 2009; Rodriguez 2009). But although there is a strong male interest in celebrity figures, I would argue that the most widespread imitation of celebrity through body shape, dress and adornment which is central to this text is, for the most part, gender-specific, and that young women are most vulnerable here. Young men may indeed want a six-pack (see *Men's Health*), but not all of them see the need to set out on the arduous quest to achieve one, nor do they necessarily despair if they fail. There are cases of male body anxiety, but they are far outnumbered by its prevalence amongst young women (Tartakovsky 2010). Nevertheless, young men are increasingly seen as 'at risk'; Rootstein's 2010 range of fashion mannequins, based on the slender body shapes of teenage boys and blessed with a waist span of 27 inches, was swiftly condemned (Vernon 2010; Black 2010; Colman 2010).

Nevertheless, Internet sites are not dominated by men in search of masculine styles of celebrity dress to copy, and much of what seems to go on within cyberspace centres on the old-fashioned heterosexual 'look' or 'gaze', involving an unreconstructed and unapologetic focus on the female celebrity body. The question of gay fandom—which has different modes of operation—is a separate issue; different modes of looking at celebrity culture will be discussed within a later chapter.

Obviously, most of the young women who want a celebrity look cannot possibly afford the luxury brands and designer clothes seen on their idols, so there is an ever-expanding market for inexpensive copies of designer accessories and an ever-increasing growth in 'counterfeit' goods. However, girls who want to look sexy and glamorous—rather than to be admired for their style—may well select, from the garments on offer, those that show off their bodies, that are close-fitting or revealing. It is high fashion alone that does not necessarily seek to be form-fitting.

Jess Cartner-Morley, in a newspaper article analysing the undiminished power of the WAGS (a nickname for the wives and girlfriends of British footballers bestowed on them by the media in 2006), comments in an aside:

> Unlike, say, Agyness Deyn, they will never even consider wearing a dress that does not enhance their cleavage or shoes that are anything but leg-lengthening. Unlike the fashion

avant-garde, their status is dependent as much on looking attractive as in looking 'on-trend', and this makes them a truer reflection of real women's concerns. (Cartner-Morley 2010e)

As I have already suggested, journalists are seemingly far more aware of what is happening in the name of 'celebrity'—and its impact on the majority of women—than cultural theorists. She confines herself to this one observation, but it is very telling. The sight of the so-called WAGS on their daily spending sprees in Baden-Baden, where they were quartered during the 2006 World Cup and where they acquired this soubriquet, horrified the fashion avant-garde, who saw their dress sense and their ostentatious consumption as comical, vulgar or perhaps a mixture of the two; however, their bulging carrier bags, borne like trophies through the streets and full of new clothes paid for by their partners, were envied by many young women outside that avant-garde (Moodie 2006; Hyde 2006; Woods 2006; Battle 2006).

The overly sexual, curvaceous look is partly influenced by the look of the real glamour model herself, the so-called pin-up girl of men's magazines. This idea of glamour has, of course, very little to do with the old-fashioned version of glamour so lovingly and carefully charted by Gundle (2008) and Dyhouse (2010). Today's glamour model takes her visual cues from elsewhere; she displays, in fact, a toned-down version of the porn star look. While the size-zero debate continues to rage in and around the world of high fashion, the new and even harder-to-achieve body is now entrenched everywhere else within popular culture. This new body demands not just starvation, but even surgery. For though the fashion body is invariably flat-chested, the glamorous celebrity body so popular amongst young starlets and singers must also be very slim, but still boast a bosom which may range from the modest to the unbelievable in its contours and size.

The over-inflated cartoonish body, as exemplified by so many glamour models in men's magazines and tabloid newspapers, is found at the extreme end of this spectrum and has nothing at all to do with fashion. It does, however, have a lot to do with the way that many young women ('I'll Never Be Like Jordan' 2008; Heyes and Jones 2009) say they would like to look—whether they want to emulate Pamela Anderson in her *Baywatch* days, the 'reality soap star' Kim Kardashian or the British celebrity Jordan, herself a glamour model for men's magazines before she, too, became a star of reality television (Oliver 2007; Price 2006, 2007). Among the many significant features of this unprecedented and seemingly global desire for a body modelled on new celebrity ideals, there is the fact that Jordan's extraordinary image highlights the very question of what fashion is. In 2009, 85 per cent of the hits on her website were from women, for some of whom Jordan does indeed represent an ideal of female beauty.

In fact, in addition to her ghostwritten novels, Jordan has written a 'style' manual on dress, hair and makeup for her legion of female followers (Price 2009). Her 'rules' would of course horrify any true follower of fashion since they include the daily use of a sunbed and the liberal deployment of facial fillers, which she describes as 'far bet-ter than any creams' (Glover and Smith 2009). This returns us to the gulf between 'fashion' as understood in glossy magazines and in the academy and the 'style' that so many people actually choose to adopt: thus we encounter once more the idea that the subject matter of fashion theory might be too exclusive. Jordan herself accuses fashion designers of 'snobbery, pure and simple' (Price 2009; Glover and Smith 2009: 71). In a chapter actually called 'Celebrity Style', she explains how she tried to bor-row clothes from ten leading British designers in order to pose for the images that il-lustrate that chapter. Most recipients of her request did not bother to return her calls while the three who did refused outright. The high street shops, however, participated enthusiastically, lending her everything she wanted.

High fashion, then, is now no longer the only culprit where questions of body anxiety, dissatisfaction and dysmorphia are concerned, despite much feminist work on body image which has tended to focus on the fashion and beauty industries, seeing them as overlapping and interlinked (see Wolf 2002 and Orbach 2009). Instead, we must also put the blame on the new celebrity magazines and the constant images that flood the Internet. Orbach in fact seemed to have identified the real culprit and the danger-ous illusions it creates:

> Celebrity culture has brought us an invidious version of sharing. By creating internationally recognisable iconic figures, it appears to be inclusive and democratic. In reality the visual nature of our world sucks out variety and replaces it with a vision that is narrow and limited as far as age, body type and ethnicity are concerned. (Orbach 2009: 145)

However, when the reader consults the relevant endnote, he or she discovers that Orbach's criticism remains focused on high fashion; she writes of 'the catwalk and the covers of fashion magazines' as still a celebration of whiteness (2009: 163). There is no mention in her text of that other model of celebrity, whether singer, starlet, televi-sion presenter or trophy wife.

With the proliferation of body awareness around divergent ideals, the question of surveillance is central to a critique of today's relentless self-scrutiny. Many women are all too aware that the images of the fashion magazine and the advertising campaign are airbrushed and Photoshopped to create flawless, poreless faces and slimmer, longer limbs.

So, too, are many posed photographs of celebrities published with their consent to publicize their next career move or show off designer wares. But in paparazzi photo-graphs, and the pages of celebrity magazines given over to illicitly purloined *unposed* images, the stars shown, from whatever medium—film, music, reality television—are often stripped of their clothes and always of any mystique. No digital manipulation is used to create an impossible perfection; instead, we are invited to observe and note the flaws and imperfections thus revealed.

The British publication *Heat* gave the name 'Circle of Shame' to this particular phenomenon, whereby attention is drawn to particular bodily flaws or sartorial errors of judgement—an ill-fitting top, a too-tight skirt, a bulge of flesh, dimpled skin, sagging buttocks, facial wrinkles (Frith 2008). This might be defended as less threatening for women, since it shows the fallibility of the famous, the imperfection of the supposedly perfect (Feasey 2008, 2006). But arguably it may have quite the opposite effect, showing instead the negative effects of one single lapse in self-policing. The idea that we are all under twenty-four-hour scrutiny and that we cannot afford to gain an ounce, let alone reveal the effects of childbirth or the ravages of time, is damaging beyond belief. Endless paparazzi photographs of model Kate Moss show her getting off a long-haul flight or relaxing on a beach; the telephoto lenses scour her face and body, always seeking blemishes and thrilling at the sight of a wrinkle or sunspot. Although Moss is, after all, in her mid-thirties, there is a visible pleasure within these magazines if there are any changes, however slight, in the appearance of the woman who started her modelling career at fourteen. 'There is a God' crowed one tagline, scrawled across a close-up of her face which revealed fine lines around her eyes and mouth (17 July 2009; see Brooks 2009).

The issue of ageing within the public eye is another aspect of celebrity culture that should certainly be of concern to cultural theorists. For academic writings on the phenomenon of an ageing population have proved almost as unpopular as the physical effects of ageing itself—see Kathleen Woodward's (1991) account of the initial reactions to her work. Nevertheless, we should persevere—not only is ageing truly the last taboo, a fate seen as worse than death; it is now judged, within celebrity culture, to be avoidable. Celebrities must work hard to remain exactly the same, year on year. Demi Moore has predicated her recent career on her (so far successful) attempts to do exactly that.

In 2008, paparazzi pictures of hard-working, Oscar-winning actress Helen Mirren, who was then sixty-three years old, swimming and sunbathing in a red bikini and looking extremely attractive, were published across the world (Davis 2008; 'Helen Mirren the Bikini Queen' 2008). They signalled to all women that to look as good as this was their goal—their duty, no less. Yet every summer, there are other, less appealing pictures on offer of Jack Nicholson, her contemporary in age, also swimming and sunbathing, usually in female company. These latter images, however, are usually presented as sources merely of mild amusement, sometimes accompanied by a caption explaining that his girth reduces neither his entourage nor his sex appeal (e.g. 'After the Blob' 2009).

All these questions of self-policing—a self-policing largely for women—might suggest that one theorist whose work should seem relevant in any consideration of these new bodies and their overexposure is, of course, Michel Foucault (1979). Never, surely, have bodies been more disciplined and in certain senses punished than today, the

Figure 6   Helen Mirren's raising of the bar for style after sixty has ensured her continuing popularity. Photograph by Anne-Marie Michel.

regimes being diet, exercise, dress and, of course, cosmetic surgery. Foucault's notion of 'the panopticon' (1979: 203–4) is also peculiarly relevant. Never has there been a society so comprehensively subject to surveillance as ours in the early twenty-first century. The ever-waiting lenses of the paparazzi, the ever-ready coffers of the press barons, are distinctive if not the most conspicuous features of the world of watchers and watched.

Yet Foucault, of course, confined his work on the disciplining of the body to the sphere of the masculine. In 1990, feminist scholar Sandra Lee Bartky applied her theorizing to women in fashion as subjects of the patriarchal gaze. But Bartky only considered the preternaturally thin women created by high fashion (1988: 66). If now there are new pressures arising from the emergence of different ideals, it is clear some feminist re-evaluation of the debates around the body is logically necessary.

One of the problems with the proliferation of images of female celebrities within the celebrity magazines that have been rushed into print over the past two decades, and the endless circulation of less than flattering photographs of such women on the

Internet, is that they are invariably exhibited to invite criticism if not derision. The celebrities are either pilloried for being too thin or vilified for being too plump. The *Daily Mail's* daily celebrity coverage on its 'Femail' web pages provides a perfect example of these contradictory discourses. With rare exceptions, like those of the bikini-clad Mirren, photographs are rarely made public to garner admiration, but precisely in relation to their shock value, to chastise one celebrity for her jutting collarbones, another for her jiggling thighs and dimpled derrière.

The only celebrity bodies which pass muster are commonly those modified by surgical intervention. Silicone implants have given one ultra-thin celebrity ampler breasts, whilst liposuction has made another, larger celebrity woman look toned and smooth-skinned beneath the waist. Such interventions are described in detail, with commentators explaining the exact methods by which certain features were achieved. *Grazia* magazine in August 2009 published an article showing its readers which of the famous 'bikini bodies' on display that summer were 'Bought or Worked For', as the title proclaimed. The 'bought body' meant that there had been work carried out by a cosmetic surgeon, while the 'worked-for' body was the result of gruelling exercise regimes and drastic diets. In general, never have young women been presented with so many images of other young bodies or made so aware of their own shortcomings. This is the society of the spectacle—and the spectator, and the 'spectated'—on a new, unprecedented scale.

The late Princess Diana, so important within any history of celebrity culture, was partly of great interest to other women because of her radical physical mutations, which took place, of course, in the public eye. Originally a self-conscious and slightly plump teenager who famously described her legs as they appeared in one photograph as 'looking like the legs of a grand piano' (see Brown 2007), she became a victim of bulimia and her attenuated limbs the subject of horrified scrutiny. She conquered the disease, admitting in the famous 1995 television interview with Martin Bashir to both its ravages and her own need for therapy (Morton 1998; Brown 2007), and finally emerged, healthy and more athletic in build than most subsequent icons of fashion. The very fact that she acknowledged her eating disorder so openly only enhanced her popularity. Interestingly, many of the websites which show off the results of advanced anorexia—the so-called 'pro-ana' websites—feature the transposition, through digital manipulation, of recognizable celebrity faces onto virtually skeletal female bodies (Junor 1983), and this is perhaps another indication of the darker underside of celebrity culture.

If there are, then, different but equally demanding body ideals, it would seem, to judge from the extraordinary proliferation of plastic surgery worldwide and the recent popularity of 'cosmetic tourism' (Heyes and Jones 2009; Morgan 2009), that the glamorous look is probably more popular in the real world than the fashion look. So we need to pay careful attention to certain questions that critical theory has not so much as articulated, let alone raised. What exactly is this contemporary, rather de-based, ideal of glamour, how is it created and how does it differ from the high-fashion template? We have no real sources to consult, only images to study and journalistic asides to note: in other words, we enter altogether uncharted waters. Jordan's manual is of no help here, since she is still invited to pose semi-naked, where the average glamorous wannabe may lead a more conventional life. We must look at the two con-trasting body shapes and modes of self-adornment to devise and develop an original critical framework.

Perhaps we should start at the top—which here means the crown of the head, per-haps? The glamorous look invariably requires long, glossy hair, often a matter of exten-sions woven in to create the illusion of volume or to extend natural length. While the wannabes must be content with Dynel, the celebrity, whether celetoid, football wife or rock star girlfriend, will use real human hair. The most popular hair for the rich West-erner's extensions originates on the Indian subcontinent. The 'virgin hair' to be found there is undamaged by bleach or chemical dyes and, until in the end when it is sev-ered from its original owner, untouched by scissors. Those same impoverished Indian women who make up a significant part of the workforce deployed to create cheap cop-ies of celebrity clothes also provide the celebrity herself with these inordinately expen-sive extensions, which can cost her several thousand pounds and for which, of course, the Indian donor receives little or nothing. Here the notion of a new imperialism of fashion—of a postcolonial neocolonialism—is perhaps seen most clearly (see Edwards 2009). Glamorous celebrity hair is usually changed in colour; most frequently, it is dyed blonde or highlighted. It will rarely be cut short and never cropped. But high-fashion haircuts follow different agendas: the hard-edged bob synonymous with Anna Wintour, for example, or the radical, continuing tonsorial experiments of model Agyness Deyn.

Whilst the fashionable body may have a light tan, the deep mahogany colour which was once a sign of exotic travel and wealth has increasingly been devalued, first by the package tour and now by the obvious fake tan that seems an essential part of the celebrity ideal. Lindsey Lohan has even marketed her own range (Whitworth 2009). The glamorous celebrity body, though usually that of an ethnic white, is not only dyed much deeper in colour than the bodies displayed on the catwalk; it is differently 'ac-cessorized'. Hands are a clue here: the hands of fashionistas tend to have shorter nails and, if they are painted, may display either the latest seasonal colour or some shade which is not designed to look conventionally attractive. After the extraordinary success of Chanel's Rouge Noir varnish in the late 1990s, aided by its appearing on the short, square nails of the ultra-fashionable Uma Thurman in *Pulp Fiction* (US, 1992, dir. Quentin Tarantino), luxury cosmetic houses realized that they could profit-ably create a new climate of interest around 'this season's' nail varnish. Soon after *Pulp Fiction,* Chanel produced a dark navy blue varnish which was also widely copied and have since sold out of each new high-fashion colour, whether jade green, gunmetal grey or khaki. Each new colour is heavily pre-publicized, and thus waiting lists are created, precisely as they are for the latest handbag. Ironically, the founder of the house famously hated painted nails; they were, she decreed, 'vulgar' (Charles-Roux 2009).

It is with the hair and the hands that the glamorous celebrity look comes closest to that of the semi-naked glamour model. Long, even false hair and breasts that may be silicone-enhanced are invariably accompanied by overlong nails, often themselves false, painted pink, red, coral, or given a French manicure with exaggeratedly whitened tips. The ghetto-fabulous look of wildly coloured and creatively embellished synthetic nails is perhaps closer to the spirit of fashion than to that of glamour.

Thus, while many young women may strive for this glamorous celebrity style and mode of self-presentation, when they decide that they want to be accepted by the world of *high fashion,* if they do, they must obviously make changes. Victoria Beckham once exemplified the glamorous celebrity look, but when, in 2008, she launched her new range of high-fashion dresses, each of which cost around a thousand pounds, a change in image was de rigeur. No trace could remain of the footballer's wife at the World Cup of 2006, whose mane of hair and bare bronzed thighs meant she was always identifiable, and who was repeatedly photographed in her tiny hot pants and knee-length boots. The hair extensions now had to be removed, the hair cropped short and restored to its natural dark brown (see Thompson 2009). Her nails were visibly cut short, and her arms and legs, formerly so liberally fake-tanned, now grew pale. Finally, her breast enhancements were removed (see Nicoll 2009). She now conformed to the fashion ideal, and her new business venture has in fact proved, at the time of writing, eminently and correspondingly successful. The dresses are elegant and well-designed: would they have sold so well without their 'designer's' own makeover? Certainly the well-respected fashion writers who sang her praises might not have championed her as they did (Armstrong 2008; Cartner-Morley 2010c), nor would supermodels have chosen to be photographed at public functions wearing her dresses.

Always aware of how to manipulate the media, Beckham cleverly chose to show her fall 2010 collection in a penthouse in New York, in the very same vast apartment that had been used as a location for 2008's *Sex and the City: The Movie* (Armstrong and Leich 2010). In the film, this apartment was chosen by Carrie Bradshaw as her marital home, and thus, through association, the Beckham clothes showcased there acquired some of the accepted fashion-icon status of Carrie (and Sarah Jessica Parker). All Beckham's different decisions were triumphantly vindicated when three actresses chose to wear her dresses to the Oscar ceremonies in 2010; she has retained this location for her subsequent shows. In 1998, Alexander McQueen had complained that she would bring 'the wrong kind of publicity' to his catwalk show.[12] Even in 2007, Christopher Kane famously announced that he did not want to see her in his clothes (Freeman 2007a). By 2008, however, the woman disparaged by many in the fashion world was now being welcomed and accepted.

THE ULTIMATE CONSTRUCT: OR, 'THE IMPORTANCE OF BEING ANDY'

Andy Warhol is central to any consideration of the celebrity phenomenon, for if we re-examine Warhol's world, and the various modes of production he deployed, we find many features in common with the topography of visual culture today, especially in the construction of the Warhol persona, 'Andy'.

There is, of course, his frank, unabashed interest in the profit motive, his famous motto 'Good business is the best art' (Warhol 1975: 100–1; Bankowsky, Gingeras and Wood 2010) and his prefiguring, ahead-of-its-time construction of his own particular and completely new 'Warholian' world. This moved across different strands of the visual arts—prints, paintings, photography, films—and was peopled by the new 'stars' he found, many of whom swiftly became fashion icons; finally, of course, he founded the fashion-geared magazine *Interview,* still successful today, and frequently worked both *in* and *for* advertisements.

Here, in the introduction itself, we need to think about the centrality of Andy Warhol in a book that concerns itself with the relationship between celebrity and fashion, and we must examine the particular ways in which Warhol the star, the public figure, the celebrity, pre-empted in his own self-presentation and career virtually all the manifestations of today's celebrity culture. He had extraordinary prescience, particularly in his creation, manipulation and frequent reconstruction of his own image. We should think not only about his overly quoted remark, 'In the future everyone will be world-famous for fifteen minutes' (cited in Cashmore 2006: 211), but also consider carefully the construct, Andy, which he created; suggest why this is of such relevance today; and observe the different uses to which these changing manifestations of Andy were so cleverly put by their creator. It is also significant that, like so many later celebrities, he was referred to only by his first name.

Early in his life, having already changed his name from Andrew Warhola, he changed his appearance. He underwent cosmetic surgery, unusual in those days, to improve the shape of his nose and subsequently was quite willing to talk about it. He also shared his concerns about his poor complexion, his general dissatisfaction with his appearance and the courses of action he thought should be taken to remedy these different physical shortcomings. He also dyed his hair and his eyebrows blonde and silver at different times and wore a variety of wigs throughout most of his life in the public eye. He also *reinvented* his appearance on a regular basis—his first incarnation in chinos and simple long-sleeved shirts, during his days as a fashion illustrator in 1950s New York, was used in a Gap campaign of the 1990s, the strapline being 'Andy Warhol wore chinos'.

During his early success, in the Factory period of the 1960s, he adopted a second look, a uniform of tight black leather jackets, striped T-shirts, dark glasses and white-blonde hair, to match the style of his 'Factory Girl' and the star of his films, Edie

Sedgwick. She herself was swiftly picked out by fashion magazines because of this distinctive look and was the subject of a US *Life* magazine article and fashion spread, 'The Girl with the Black Tights' (1965: 47–8). Sedgwick—who, like so many of the people Warhol christened his 'superstars', died young—has in fact had an afterlife as a fashion icon; she is resurrected frequently by fashion writers and was most recently the subject of a feature film, *Factory Girl* (2006, dir. George Hickenlooper), which it-self starred a contemporary celebrity and another fashion-page regular, Sienna Miller. Finally, after the near-fatal shooting of 1968, Andy proceeded to don a third uniform of dark tailored suits, casualized through plimsolls, since this was the pre-trainer era, and completed by very spiked-up wigs.

Warhol, like so many since, was delighted to appear in advertisements as *himself* and did so most notably in a campaign for the infamous 'junk bond' dealers of the 1980s, Drexel Burnham, who were later to be prosecuted. He also provided artwork for advertising, long after he became rich and famous as an artist; he was the first of a series of painters to create new images for Absolut vodka. Predictably, the commer-cially minded Takashi Murakami is the most recent; he has also designed the bottles for Marc Jacobs's house scent, Daisy.

But above all, Warhol loved fashion, glamour and celebrity, and he perceived, as others around him did not, the various ways in which they could be woven into artis-tic practice. He did this quite literally in his endlessly reproduced 'Celebrity' series of paintings and prints, with their iconic simplified images of Marilyn, Elvis, Jackie Ken-nedy and Elizabeth Taylor.

Famously beginning life as a fashion illustrator, he actually worked as a model him-self in the later years of his life, and in fact, his very last public appearance was on a small catwalk in a Manhattan club.

He perceived the clear links between art, fashion and celebrity long before anyone else; he promoted his film stars as style icons, worked closely with fashion photogra-phers and, inevitably, founded the first real celebrity magazine, *Interview,* in 1972. It was, as its title would suggest, made up entirely of interviews, mainly with figures from the world of fashion: designers, fashion journalists, photographers and models. In this publication, he created the concept of the celebrity interview, whereby one celebrity interviews another. He surrounded himself throughout his later life with the rich and famous, while he always courted those who, if nothing else, were simply good-looking.

In the early 1970s, leading fashion photographer David Bailey was asked to make three television documentaries for ABC about noted 'image-makers'. He chose Cecil Beaton, film-maker Luchino Visconti and Andy Warhol. Interestingly, Warhol, always provocative, agreed to be filmed only if the interview could take place *in bed*. Bailey, equally provocative, agreed, and the two of them are seen on screen, interviewer and interviewee, tucked up together quite innocently under the covers, like Morecambe and Wise, Ren and Stimpy, or even Noddy and Big-Ears. However, in the opening minutes of the film, Warhol does ask Bailey what he's wearing. 'Well, I'm naked,' replies Bailey. 'How about you?' But Warhol, always shy and self-conscious, but especially so after the scars he sustained in the attempt to kill him, reveals that he himself is fully dressed and announces that his body is a mass of stitches, 'like a Dior dress'. Bailey was at that time slim and very attractive, presumably prompting Warhol's suggestion that the interview take place where it did; he looks, briefly, disconcerted. Possibly Paula Yates knew about this interview when, ten years later, she built her own career on a series of star interviews for the new Channel Four and its morning programme *The Big Breakfast,* which also involved interviewer, subject and double bed. But here, as befitted breakfast television, they lay fully dressed *on,* rather than in, the bed.

Lastly, Warhol appeared in the series that pre-empted reality television, *The Love Boat;* he was interviewed to mark the three hundredth anniversary of this, his favourite programme. But he also made his very own series, *Andy Warhol's TV,* and a one-off programme called, inevitably, *Andy Warhol's Fifteen Minutes.*

Many of his pronouncements, in his various writings, have a peculiarly prophetic quality. Together with the 'fifteen minutes of fame', we could cite his observations about the future and the new importance of the plastic and the mechanical. Of particular interest is his assertion that he often thought about the contribution of 'the ordinary people who built the pyramids' and that they were in his mind when he immortalized the dead woman who hangs from the car window in *Great American Disasters 37* (see Michelson 2001: 79).

In all these ways, Warhol was a *contemporary* celebrity, and one of great importance to this particular examination of the relationship between fashion and celebrity. He understood how fashion worked and how it could be deployed in other spheres; he was, of course, a perfect template for the artist-as-celebrity, and one who tried to dissolve the boundary walls between high art, popular culture—*and* the commercial. His 'Factory' paved the way for the working methods of Damien Hirst, among others.

But, most importantly, we need to follow his unique methodology. As I suggested earlier, we must move out of disciplinary confines, as he did, in order to comprehend the celebrity phenomenon and its workings within fashion. Moreover, to understand popular culture itself, we need to look as Andy did, right across the spectrum of visual culture, and make links rather than examine separate strands. Warhol, none more so, was aware of the movement of images across visual culture, something he actively encouraged within his own artistic practice.

But the continuing reluctance of and even refusal by theorists to look *sideways* has stymied much academic work around fashion, photography, film, adaptation theory, contemporary art and within cultural studies as a whole.

CONCLUDING THOUGHTS: METHODOLOGIES AND MORALIZING

In conclusion, I'd first like, tentatively, to bring in a quotation from the work of American queer theorist and post-Habermasian Michael Warner. In his essay 'The Mass Public and the Mass Subject', he talks of the new 'display of physical bodies' within the media and the way in which the bodies of the famous are observed in the processes of change; he sees their 'bloating, slimming, wounding, and general humiliation' as 'mutant prostheses of our own desirability' (1992: 394).

Cultural theorist Hal Foster, who invoked Warner in, interestingly, an essay on Warhol, 'Death in America', describes the 'breakdown' of the distinction between the public and the private and the creation of what he calls the 'pathological public sphere' with its 'strange new mass subjectivity' (2001: 76). He goes on to suggest that there is a 'new relationship' between private 'fantasy' and public 'reality' and that it is only, perhaps, Warhol in painting and J. G. Ballard in literature who have managed to convey this within their artwork. This perceived breakdown, this changed public sphere, the notion he advances of a 'mass witnessing'—all these are ideas that he advanced just as contemporary celebrity culture was taking shape and that usefully inform the more limited territory we will survey within this book. Both Foster and Warner were writing nearly twenty years ago; like Warhol himself, they seem to be prophetic.

Finally, while I may at the moment of writing safely claim that we need to examine these links between celebrity and consumption across the globe to understand both contemporary society and the changes in fashion, it may be that this phenomenon has at last peaked. During the period between the writing of this book and its publication, there could be both revulsion and a move away from celebrity dominance, sparked either by continuing worldwide recession or, more simply, by boredom. In that case, it may be that much of the text will seem curiously dated. I would argue, however, that it will still have a resonance, since it will constitute a historical curiosity, the recording of a hysterical moment.

On the opening day of a huge multi-storey store on London's Oxford Street, shoppers who had queued all night were whipped into frenzy by the rumoured promise of even cheaper clothes (Freeman 2007b). This resulted in a scene of such mayhem that vast pictures were printed on the front pages of the English red-topped tabloids. And in America, a Walmart employee was actually crushed to death when he became trapped behind the doors he was opening to the waiting public on a discount day (McFadden and Macropoulous 2008).

As the clothes on offer in these stores are manufactured in impoverished Asian countries, often by children, it is very difficult to celebrate such events as a triumph of 'agency'. And nothing could be more distressing than to contemplate the gulf between these same child labourers and their Western celebrity counterparts; one might

Figure 7   Chaperoned by her father, singer Billy Ray Cyrus, Miley waves to her fans at the premiere of the Hannah Montana film. Photograph by Anne-Marie Michel/London Entertainment.

look at the tiny Suri Cruise, whose designer wardrobe is celebrated in print journalism and online in a way that is baffling (for example see Suri Cruise Fashion Blog, suricruisefashion.blogspot.com). Valued at several million dollars, it includes shoes said to have been especially manufactured for this child fashion icon by Christian Louboutin, shoemaker of choice for the fictional Carrie Bradshaw, among so many others. He has made for this little girl, who is one of the most-publicized celebrity children, several pairs of high-heeled shoes that will fit a preschool 'lifestyle'.

Children are now involved from the very beginning in this new relentless cycle of craving and consuming, in so many different ways. The very young girls who idolize Miley Cyrus in her Disney incarnation as Hannah Montana and who seek to emulate her style should not be forgotten; her younger sister, Noah, has launched a range of clothes, targeted at six-year-olds, which many would regard as provocative; some items look like the clothes that might be worn by the Bratz dolls should they head for a night out in a fetish club. The Disney creation Hannah Montana herself is much more innocent in her self-presentation, and we look at the styling of Disney characters in a later chapter.

But I trust we are in agreement; there *are* concerns. We cannot simply discuss celebrity as an interesting phenomenon, whether we do so within the media or to further our careers in the academy; surely we should be prepared to be more critical and to share our reservations.

Within contemporary cultural theory, there is a curious reluctance to offer up judgment, let alone to moralize. I have suggested, however, that changed circumstances might provoke changes in stance. Many of us seemed in retrospect overly keen to stress our distance from the perceived puritanism of the Frankfurt School, from the anti-Americanism of Hoggart, Williams and Leavis, and their distaste for certain aspects of popular culture. Perhaps we should realize that the result may be the current predominance of apolitical scholarship. Far too many unsettling phenomena are discussed by academics as manifestations of 'postmodern irony'; worse still, others are casually and carelessly labelled 'post-feminist'. Maybe we should remember the highly political agenda of cultural studies in its early days. In this new phase of later capitalism, we have, though it is unfashionable to say so, a new responsibility, particularly if our feminism is to have any meaning at all. I have written elsewhere of the way in which the feminist project has, sadly, become sequestered within the walls of academic institutions (2000, 2004b, 2005a). This does not mean that it has failed (see Segal 1999) but rather that it needs to be reinvigorated, reoriented.

Lastly, it is customary within academic texts to invoke the key texts continually and to cite the main sources. But, as I have argued, here we are entering virgin territory. Texts on 'celebrity' there may be, but those which link it with fashion and examine that relationship have yet to be written; hence, my own particular move, here in these pages, towards some kind of rudimentary map making, with directions provided throughout to websites, newspapers and magazines, rather than to accredited works of scholarship. Hence, too, my reliance both on textual analysis, which I would always deploy, but also on primary material, provided through the many different interviews I have conducted. Lastly, the discursive writing, such as we might find in a journal, is deliberate, as are my occasional horrified exclamations as we move together through the newly reshaped landscape.

NOTES

A paper delivered in Bremen as a work in progress at the symposium Out of Order, in January 2010, was part of the genesis of this book and so contained some of the material found within this chapter. The conference proceedings can be found online and are to be published in book form, in Germany, as *Fashion—Out of Order,* by Arnoldsche.

1. For further discussion of Beckham and branding see amongst others: Milligan 2010; Purohit 2008; Cashmore 2004; Cashmore and Parker 2003; Vincent, Hill and Lee 2009, Vincent and Hill 2007; Yu 2005.

2. For details of Beckham lookalike Andy Harmer see: Beckham Lookalikes, www.beckhamlookalikes.com/www.beckhamlookalikes.com/Biography.html. Alison Jackson's video 'Beckham' featuring Andy Harmer is available online at www.youtube.com/watch?v=we0ePH_iXEg.

3. For details of Alison Jackson's work including interviews, videos and photographs see: Alison Jackson, www.alisonjackson.com/index.html.

4. For further coverage of the promotion and launch of the Material Girl range (3 August 2010 at Macy's New York City) and journalistic debate see: Reslen 2010; Thomas 2010; Price 2010; 'Madonna's "Material Girl" ' 2010; 'Material Girl' 2010; Brady 2010.

5. For examples of Chloe Sevigny's style see amongst others: 'Chloe Sevigny Photos', Style.com, www.style.com/peopleparties/celebritysearch/person272, 'Style Spotlight: Chloe Sevigny', WhoWhatWear, www.whowhatwear.com/website/full-article/style-spotlight-chloe-sevigny.

6. Also see Olsen and Olsen 2006.

7. See: 'Archive', LVMH Group, www.lvmh.com/lvmh-news/news#/archive, and PPR, www.ppr.com/en/brands.

8. Also see: 'New In', New Look, www.newlook.com/shop/womens/new-in_10013, New Look Group, www.newlookgroup.com, and My Celebrity Fashion, www.mycelebrityfashion.co.uk, for 'copy the look' tips featuring New Look and Primark garments.

9. This writer would count herself among them (see Church Gibson 2000). But this position is becoming increasingly problematic in the current climate.

10. Nicola Formachetti, the stylist who has worked most closely with Lady Gaga, did in fact receive public recognition for his work. At the British Fashion Council Awards of 2010, he received the award for 'Creator', given the previous year to Grace Coddington.

11. Lady Gaga's single 'Bad Romance' was premiered at Alexander McQueen's spring/summer 2010 collection Plato's Atlantis (autumn 2009). For footage of the show featuring the hoof shoe see: www.youtube.com/watch?v=pUvFTc2mlNY.

12. McQueen famously banned her from attending the particular show in which he used the Paralympic athlete Aimee Mullins as a catwalk model, making for her specially designed prosthetic legs (see Khan 2000: 119; Evans 2007: 177, 188; Pullin 2009: 29–35).

–2–

Celebrity and Fashion, Past and Present

During the American presidential election campaign of 2008, the Republican candidate John McCain funded a commercial which took Barack Obama to task for his celebrity status. He was clearly using the word *celebrity* pejoratively, implying that celebrities may have photogenic appeal but are also self-evidently trivial phenomena. The commercial began with a montage which included footage of Paris Hilton and Britney Spears and a voiceover which portentously intoned: 'He's the greatest celebrity in the world—but is he ready to lead?' Obama riposted by swiftly releasing a commercial portraying McCain as a 'Washington Celebrity' (see Falcone 2008). However, Paris Hilton herself also joined in the fray, with an altogether more entertaining production.

Her film (see Swaine 2008) began with an identical voiceover to that of the McCain production—but here images of McCain himself were substituted for those of Obama and then intercut with pictures of the Golden Girls and Yoda from *Star Wars* as the voice announced 'He's the *oldest* celebrity in the world.' Paris herself, recumbent on a white sun-lounger, then took over, informing us that 'the white-haired old dude' had mentioned her in his campaign commercial, so 'I guess I'm running for President...I'm *totally* ready to lead.' She outlines her energy policy and wonders if Rihanna would be the best choice of running mate. Hilton's commercial did her no harm and probably helped Obama a good deal; it also raised larger questions regarding leaders-as-celebrities.

Whilst genuinely successful political leaders have often possessed great funds of charisma (see Rojek 2001; Baudry 1986), a display of any fashion sense might customarily be seen as traditionally the provenance of their wives. However, Obama's own wife Michelle made it quite clear that she herself wanted to be taken seriously as a well-qualified lawyer with her own political ideas. Nevertheless, public interest in the new American first lady quickly became focussed on her clothes and appearance. As the new president and his family walked into the White House to take up residence there, they were watched by vast crowds and by millions more on television worldwide. It was an extraordinary and highly symbolic historical moment: a black family was taking possession of the most powerful 'home' in the world. Yet the awesome occasion was in some small measure marred by the seemingly interminable commentaries on the designer clothes chosen for the occasion by the president's wife and the possible provenance of the coats worn by her two daughters.

Later on, there was, of course, extensive worldwide coverage of the 'First Hundred Days' of Barack Obama's presidency. The *Observer*—after all, an English 'quality' broadsheet—chose to devote the cover of its colour supplement to 'Michelle Obama, Icon'. The second feature here was a two-page photo spread of the key outfits that the new first lady had selected for various public appearances. Her career as a lawyer, her impoverished upbringing on Chicago's problem-ridden South Side and her attempts to move rapidly into action as a role model for young women of colour were paid far less attention, tucked away as they were towards the end of the magazine (Cooke et al. 2009).

Journalistic coverage of a fashionable first lady is not new. But Michelle Obama's predecessor as 'fashion icon' was Jacqueline Bouvier Kennedy (Craughwell-Varda 1999; Tomer 2009), a woman born and brought up in the most privileged sector of American society, whose role as presidential consort was primarily one of ornament and display. Her academic credentials notwithstanding, her status was effectively comparable to that of the wives of the nouveaux riches American millionaires whom Veblen studied in the closing years of the late nineteenth century. Their couture-clad bodies, swathed in furs, bedecked with jewels and topped off by the lavish hats of the period, were offered up to the public gaze as visible proof of the wealth and taste of their husbands. So too were their new mansions, complete with carefully chosen antique furniture, ostentatiously displayed paintings and exquisitely manicured lawns (Veblen 1899). Indeed, Jacqueline Kennedy's apparently self-elected role in the White House was really not unlike that of a Veblen wife: to serve as a charming, decorative hostess, to oversee interior design and, in addition, to act as an 'ambassador for American fashion' (Jenkyn Jones 2002: 21; Craughwell-Varda 1999).

Michelle Obama, on the other hand, was quite rightly intent on using her own newfound celebrity status to champion more significant causes. But her ecological interests, for example, seemed abruptly to shrink in importance alongside the much-photographed organic garden she created on the lawn of the White House and that so preoccupied the media, a fact which would of course have fascinated Veblen, whose interest in swathes of well-tended greensward is conspicuous in his work (Veblen 1899). Meanwhile, her desire to help disenfranchised minorities has repeatedly generated photo opportunities in which more emphasis has been placed on her outfits than her work or what she has to say (also see Tomer 2009). She seems trapped and, by a weird irony—in her role as a new kind of celebrity fashion icon, the athletic, accomplished woman of colour—strangely disenfranchised *herself,* alienated in her image as though she were another. The US *Vogue* cover of March 2009 was designed to show off her athleticism and elegance through the precise way in which she was dressed, styled and posed. One was very aware of her arms, less so of her intellect. This hardly bespeaks the end of white supremacy in public life. It could rather be argued that the fascination with this first lady has swiftly dwindled to one more fetishization of 'otherness' (see Dyer 1997).

Sadly, in an interview with the first lady published in America's *Good Housekeeping* in April 2010, and then syndicated in the British edition of July 2010, she happily answered the question 'How has your Harvard education prepared you for parenting?' (Ellis 2010: 136). There was no mention of her own career nor of the new initiatives she had earlier discussed.

In the case of Michelle Obama's wardrobe decisions, all this is particularly troubling, since it suggests that the new relationship between celebrity and fashion has the power somehow to diminish political realities, to have the kind of flattening-out effect that we see in the pages of *Grazia* magazine and its regular feature 'This Week's Ten Hot Stories'. Here, a picture-story of, say, a devastating earthquake or an urban bomb atrocity is invariably sandwiched between two celebrity fashion stories. In that what politicians or their wives wear is now of more importance than what they may say or do, the Obama case also coincides with another recent trend. Alistair Campbell, former advisor to Tony Blair, tells us in his diaries that he and Peter Mandelson, his fellow publicist, actually came close to trading punches over the question of whether Blair should or should not wear a tie for his first broadcast speech as prime minister (Campbell 2007: 45–6).

Blair's successor, Gordon Brown, was mocked by the British press less for the fiscal policies he was pursuing in the summer of 2008 than for the fact that he chose a stuffy-looking grey suit in which to attend the mandatory beach photocall that is part of a prime minister's annual seaside holiday. His rival, the Conservative leader David Cameron, was judged to have won votes simply by being photographed in colourful, casual beachwear during the same week. The clothes chosen by the Cameron family were in fact those to be found in the Boden catalogue, which sells reasonably priced clothes to middle-class families with young children throughout that psychic and cultural territory popularly known as 'Middle England' (O'Sullivan 1998; Jones and Novak 1999: 185). The publicity-conscious Camerons, who, given their respective private and public incomes, could afford to purchase their clothes anywhere, had obviously made this choice in order to woo that particular tranche of the British voting public (see Woods and Flintoff 2008). Later, during the British election campaign of 2010, there was far more interest in, and coverage of, the clothes worn on- and off-duty by the wives of the party leaders than in most of the speeches made by their husbands (Jones 2010; McElvoy 2010). All this would be merely funny but for the clear implication that, in the new image-dominated world, political ideas are progressively disappearing into or behind appearances. In their article 'Celebrity Culture and Public Connection: Bridge or Chasm?' Couldry and Markham observe that, 'Such is the proliferation of celebrity culture that it can no longer be dismissed as external to the world of public issues' (2007: 404).

In 1962, Daniel Boorstin famously complained about the way in which the televised Kennedy-Nixon debate affected the outcome of the American election (see Boorstin

1962/1992). But back in those far-off days, it is at least conceivable that viewers were listening to what Kennedy said, rather than merely scrutinizing his haircut or choice of tie in the rather fuzzy black-and-white televisual images of the day, though his good looks and photogenic wife did give him a distinct advantage with the voters. His antagonist in the debate may famously have broken out in a sweat on screen and had a clearly visible five-o-clock shadow; nonetheless, the newspapers assiduously reported his every utterance. Today, by contrast, Carla Bruni-Sarkozy's outfits and her status as a former model insistently divert attention from the policies of her husband, Nicholas, currently the French prime minister (see Samuel 2010; Mower 2009; Fox 2008). Many members of the public will be aware that she dresses at Dior; far fewer know what her husband has to say about French immigration.

HISTORICAL CONSIDERATIONS?

'Celebrity culture' in a recognizably modern but still rudimentary form could be said to have emerged in the late eighteenth century. The period witnessed the new scientific discoveries and consequent technological developments associated with the Industrial Revolution. They would transform Western society from a predominantly rural one into one increasingly centred on urban and industrial life. Some of the new technologies also made possible the wide circulation of printed material—newspapers, broadsheets, pamphlets and so on. The combination of radical scientific changes and the tumultuous political events of that period—above all, of course, the French Revolution of 1789—mark the beginnings of modernity and the emergence of modern capitalism. This entailed a progressive transfer of power from the traditional aristocracy and the landed gentry to the more and more significant members of the bourgeoisie or middle classes, the 'captains of industry'. It also gave birth to our modern consumer culture and began its inexorable spread around the world.

The first 'celebrities' to be discussed in the broadsheets—soon caricatured in the new, popular form of the cartoon—were politicians, monarchs, leading members of the aristocracy and entertainers. Actresses were of great interest, given their supposedly questionable morals as well as their stylish dress, jewellery and hairstyles. Many were of course 'protected' by rich, prominent men, and some made advantageous marriages. Reynolds, Lely and other fashionable artists of the day painted leading English actresses (Postle et al. 2005). Such images were an early template for what would follow over the next two centuries. The canvases of these painters were a more elegant and durable forerunner of today's ubiquitous press photographs.

A detailed catalogue of the well-known 'fashion leaders' of the eighteenth and nineteenth centuries is unnecessary here. There are already histories of fashion which cover exactly this ground (see amongst others Breward 1995; McNeil 2008; Brooke and Laver 2000; Arnold 2009). Furthermore, although glamour and fashion are not always synonymous, Gundle's comprehensive and detailed book on *Glamour* (2008) provides a detailed overview of the history of 'fashion leaders' in Western Europe and the United States over the past two hundred years.

Gundle begins by instancing the poet George Gordon, Lord Byron as a central figure in the construction of the modern concept of 'glamour' (2008: 35). Not only a writer but a child of privilege who flouted the rules of society and left England in search of a more sympathetic way of life, he assiduously cultivated his persona of being 'mad, bad and dangerous to know', as his lover, Lady Caroline Lamb, famously described him. Such behaviour once again established a pattern for what was to follow over many decades to come. Byron helped to create or affirm a notion of the artist as one possessed not only of particular talents which set him apart, but one to whom special licence should be granted; the artist cannot or need not bend to the rules of conventional society. This assumption, fostered and even in some degree legitimated by Byron and some of his fellow romantic poets, had a lasting impact on popular conceptions of the artist.

But Byron was not a 'fashion leader' like his contemporary, the first proper dandy, Beau Brummell, who became the friend of and sartorial advisor to the Prince Regent, later George IV (Gundle 2008; Kelly 2007; Breward 1995, 1999). Significantly, Brummell created a career, a public persona and an international reputation for himself through his taste and style alone (Gundle 2008: 60). He came from a respectable middle-class family and had been educated at Eton and Oxford; however, his rise to social prominence and the highest echelons of Regency society was entirely predicated upon his fashion sense. This, too, was a pattern that could and would be frequently repeated. Brummell was like many modern celebrities in that he crossed class boundaries and made a career for himself in which the way he dressed was of integral importance.

There have been far too many celebrities involved in the history of fashion to list them here, particularly since chronologies can be found elsewhere. We should emphasise, however, that, like contemporary fashion, celebrity culture has always been firmly linked to technological change. The development of photography in the nineteenth century and the gradual emergence of techniques which made the printing of photographs a possibility, first in newspapers and then in magazines, were both significant in this context. But the growth of moving pictures and thus of popular commercial cinema in the early twentieth century was of still greater weight. The cinema has had a dominant, even central role in creating modern celebrities, effecting changes within fashion and connecting the two processes. It continues to play a central role today, if in new and different ways, and a significant portion of this book will thus be devoted to it.

It is also important to stress the way in which later technological changes helped to bring about the mass marketing of fashion and ensure its widespread availability.

If, in the contemporary world, we tend to take 'fashion for all' as a given, we might remind ourselves that, as late as the beginning of the twentieth century, fashion was still the prerogative of the few and the privileged, the aristocracy, the bourgeoisie and their wives. High fashion was not only inaccessible to the multitudes but also was not copiable, except perhaps through a few token gestures. If we look at newsreel footage from the earliest days of European or American cinema, we can instantly identify the social class of those on screen. In the famous Pathé footage of Derby Day, 1906, it is summer. Dressed in white garments, rich women hide beneath huge hats, their skirts billowing around them, while their male escorts are similarly white-clad: even on such an occasion, the poor, by contrast, wear dark, serviceable clothes and stout boots—markers, perhaps, of their simplicity and even honesty, but also of their relative abjection.

The years after the First World War saw radical changes in style, but also other, less visible changes, which brought about the mass production and distribution of fashionable clothes and accessories. The 'high street' as we now know it—in other words, as a place to go shopping—appeared only during and across the first half of the last century (Ewing 1997).

Before the twentieth century made high fashion both more democratic and more visible, it could only be admired at a distance; even in the press, only the relatively privileged were likely to get a look at it. Not only were the upper and middle classes the only ones who could actually afford fashion; they were the only people who could, quite literally, *read* about it. Mass literacy only became a possibility when, in the second half of the nineteenth century, new legislation in Western countries and subsequent moves to improve mass education gradually brought print culture to a much wider public.

Today's changed relationship between the public and private spheres is also linked to technological change. In *Celebrity Culture* (2006), Ellis Cashmore dates the birth of modern celebrity culture and the consequent disappearance of privacy to the advent of the telephoto lens in the early 1960s, specifically to the moment when it captured the clandestine embrace between co-stars Liz Taylor and Richard Burton as they sunbathed on the deck of a yacht while making the film *Cleopatra* in 1963. For Cashmore, the widespread publication of this image was a significant and seminal moment. Warhol, of course, chose Liz Taylor for his 'Celebrity' series; not perhaps surprisingly, since Andy was at first primarily interested in those who were, or might soon be, damaged or even destroyed by their own celebrity.

The telephoto lens was widely adopted; it not only made privacy impossible but no doubt fed a public need to know more and to want more. Certainly the titles of many celebrity magazines—*More, Now, Closer, Look, Reveal*—have a perceptibly urgent ring.

But Cashmore's technological determinism is to some extent problematic. We might compare the history of hardcore pornography, where technological innovations were successively and eagerly adopted by the industry and immediately put to profitable use: the still photograph, the moving image, the video cassette, digital technology, the Internet and webcams. But the photographers and directors within the world of pornography simply used these technological developments in ways that allowed them to respond more effectively to pre-existing demands. Surely technologies only effect changes in so far as these are embedded within pre-existing social and economic conditions. Certainly the telephoto lens made intrusion feasible, but we also need to consider why intrusion was deemed necessary in the first place; this would involve a scrutiny of the wider context of the early 1960s, the new modes of reporting, changes in sexual mores and in social attitudes, even perhaps the disappearance of deference and discretion and the new value placed on exploitation, 'letting it all hang out'.

Rojek (2001) lists other reasons for the new dominance of celebrity, citing the failure of parliamentary democracy, the breakdown of social communities and the decline of organized religion. But one need only look at the status of celebrities in India, or even in some degree America, to wonder how exactly far this last point holds. The collapsing or disintegration of the boundaries between what is private and what is legitimately part of the public domain is both complex and problematic; its proper consideration is outside the scope of this book. But it is clearly another significant factor. The work of Herbert Marcuse, now distinctly unfashionable, might be helpful in understanding our changed circumstances. Western culture has certainly moved in something like the direction *One-Dimensional Man* (1964) suggested it was taking; the question is whether its momentum is not by now out of control.

And while the mobile telephone has meant not only that we now become party to conversations of extraordinary intimacy in public, it also enables us to capture images immediately, to photograph anything and everything. Meanwhile, the Internet has rendered the seemingly impossible accessible, while the street today is a site of display and desire in a way undreamt of by Baudelaire or Walter Benjamin (Baudelaire 1863/2010; Berman 1980; Benjamin and Tiedemann 1999). Warhol complained that he would rather not go out to parties; he would prefer to stay at home and watch his own social life on television (Spigel 2008: 264). Today, the technological wherewithal is getting to a point where his wish could, almost, become a possibility.

THE RICH, THE FAMOUS, THE PRIVILEGED

Before we look at the representation and even the creation through new technology of contemporary celebrities, many of whom come from the ranks of those formerly destined for lifelong anonymity, we might mention a few interesting portents and precursors. A century before Princess Diana became a global superstar, the royal family had another fashion icon: the stylish Princess Alexandra. She was also married to a philandering Prince of Wales, who became Edward VII in 1901. Nicknamed Edward the Caresser, he counted other 'fashion leaders', such as the actress Lillie Langtry, amongst his high-profile mistresses (Weintraub 2001). Images of Alexandra and descriptions of her various outfits were ultimately restricted in their circulation and appeal (Jackson and Shaw 2006: 26; Norris and Curtis 1998: 147). She did not have the mass media following of the later 'Queen of Hearts'. Nevertheless, emulation of Alexandra amongst the upper-middle classes was pushed to extremes. It was understandable enough that women might want to tie black velvet ribbons around their necks, as she did, to create chokers, though she in fact originally did this to disguise a mark on her neck that worried her. However, bizarrely, when she damaged her leg in an accident, they then copied her subsequent limp and made it modish, a new fad, the 'Alexandra limp' (Rappaport 2004: 217).

In seeking to understand the radical changes in society and therefore in fashion brought about by the First World War and its legacy, an interesting shortcut suggests itself. Vita Sackville-West's quasi-autobiographical and commercially successful novel *The Edwardians* was first published in 1930 and thus considers that vanished era from the position of hindsight. The novel makes it abundantly clear that fashion and privilege were still tightly entwined in the first decade of the twentieth century. It may not be a cornerstone of literary history—Virginia Woolf suggested that Vita, her former lover and the main money-spinner for her own Hogarth Press, wrote with 'a pen of brass' (Caws 2003: 11)—but the author describes dress in unusual detail, while the plotline gives ample evidence of the way in which the celebrities of the day were venerated.

In the first chapter, through the depiction of the widowed Duchess, mother of the hero Sebastian, we witness the extraordinarily sumptuous and extravagant fashions of the period, which were dependent not only upon yards of expensive stuffs—silk, georgette, satin—but also on ornament, decoration, embroidery and jewels. Those lower down the socio-economic scale could never hope to emulate them. In fact, an elegant lady always needed to be dressed by her maid, an operation which took some time. In Sackville-West's novel, Viola, daughter of the Duchess, sits in the bedroom whilst, in the adjoining dressing room, the long-suffering maid, Button, prepares her mother for the evening:

> Viola knew well enough what was going on: her mother was seated, poking at her hair meanwhile with fretful but experienced fingers, while Button knelt before her, carefully drawing the silk stockings onto her feet and smoothing them nicely up the leg. Then her mother would rise and standing in her chemise, would allow the maid to fit the long stays of pink coutil, heavily boned, round her hips and slender figure, fastening the busk down the front, after many adjustments; then the suspenders would be clipped to the stockings; then the lacing would follow, beginning at the waist and travelling gradually up and down, until the necessary proportions had been achieved. The silk laces and their tags would fly out, under the maid's deft fingers, with the flick of a skilled worker mending a net. Then the pads of pink satin

would be brought, and fastened into place on the hips and under the arms, still further to accentuate the smallness of the waist. Then the drawers; then the petticoat would be spread into a ring on the floor, and Lucy would step into it on her high-heeled shoes, allowing Button to draw it up and tie the tapes. (Sackville-West 1930/1983: 39–40)

Only then can the Duchess emerge from the dressing room and be helped once again, this time into 'the billows of her dress', a 'mass of taffeta and tulle' (Sackville-West 1930/1983: 41). This dress has 'innumerable hooks at the back' which, again, can only be done up by her maid. The Duchess herself, however, may supply the finishing touches, 'the high dog-collar of rubies and diamonds, tied with a large bow of white tulle at the back', a 'knot of rubies' at her waist and 'long ruby earrings'.

Her son, Sebastian, swiftly moves through a series of disastrous relationships with women from different social spheres. The second of these, Teresa, is young, attractive and married to a kind-hearted doctor. She is interested in and even at first obsessed with high society and its fashionable luminaries:

She was quite frankly and childishly fascinated by high life; she had quite a collection of photographs which she had cut out of the newspapers and stuck into an album, so that she was confident she would be able to recognise any of these celebrities even though she had never yet seen them in the flesh. (180)

In order that she may do just that, her music-loving husband takes her to the opera at Covent Garden, even though he knows that she will be 'terribly bored' during the performance itself. Nevertheless, Teresa and the 'little London clerks who also give up their money' are all rewarded with a 'spectacle' that is, for them, 'as much a part of their evening's treat as the music itself', the sight of the opera house 'filled by the galaxy of London fashion' (179).

Suddenly, through a strange chance, Teresa actually finds herself amongst these very same people for a few days. The young Duke Sebastian has an accident in the street and so is carried into the house of the nearest doctor, who happens to be her husband. He is attracted by Teresa and returns to visit her; she is 'completely dazzled' by him (231). Eventually, in a plan to seduce her, he invites them both to his country estate, Chevron, for Christmas.

Poor Teresa is at first very worried, for her husband's gift of fifty pounds, though 'a generous cheque' (262) worth about £2,340 today, cannot begin to provide her with outfits like those she will see at Chevron. She is disappointed, however, with her fellow guests:

She was forced to admit that they did not seem to be saying anything worth saying...She had expected their conversation to rival their appearance...to be dazzled by their wit and thrilled by their revelations. (265)

However, Teresa found in fact that 'their conversation differed very little from the conversation of her own acquaintances; only the references were to people she did not know, and the general assumptions were on a more extravagant scale' (265).

She is outraged when Sebastian tries to seduce her, and so their unlikely friendship ends abruptly. His very last dalliance is, perhaps, a portent of the future; he takes up with Phil, an artist's model in Chelsea, where his now-rebellious sister is often to be found in the bohemian Café Royal. Phil's personal style foreshadows that of the post-war period—the makeup, the simple haircut, the loose comfortable clothes: 'her black hair cut square, her red generous mouth; her brilliant colours' (318).

Sebastian is finally rescued from an advantageous but loveless marriage by yet another chance encounter, this time with the explorer Leonard Anquetil, immediately after the coronation of George V. Anquetil had previously offered him the chance to join a long expedition and thus escape from a predictable future. Now he repeats the offer:

> After three years you may come back with a sense of proportion. Or there may be a war by then, which will kill you off. (349)

This time the hero accepts, and the novel ends. The 'sense of proportion' which Anquetil thinks Sebastian needs was not, of course, confined to titled Englishmen. Their way of life was seen as so attractive that many rich Americans with daughters of marriageable age would send them in hunt of just such quarry as Sebastian. Here again we may take an enjoyable shortcut: reading Edith Wharton's novel *The Bucca-neers* (1938), which recounts the stories of four young American heiresses who come to England in search of aristocratic husbands. The biography of a real-life buccaneer, Consuelo Vanderbilt, who married the Duke of Marlborough (Mackenzie Stuart 2007), is rather less enjoyable but nonetheless pertinent here. As her looks faded, Consuelo turned to new remedies; Sander Gilman tells us of her attempt to stave off old age by having paraffin wax injected into her cheeks, with disastrous consequences, which forced her to spend the rest of her life in a darkened room (Gilman 1997). There are more portents here: today, too, those who know that their material success depends upon their good looks are also willing to take drastic steps in order to sidestep the inevitable.

Interestingly, it was the very extent and horrific nature of the facial injuries that were sustained by soldiers during the First World War that crucially developed the skills of plastic surgeons. The particular nature of trench warfare meant that those soldiers who did survive often had such badly maimed faces that extensive surgical reconstruction was necessary. New techniques were swiftly acquired, and new experiments were carried out; only later did surgeons think to employ their newfound expertise on female patients simply unhappy with their looks (Gilman 1997). As early as the 1920s, plastic surgery was put to fresh uses, both feeding and battening on the growing sense of dissatisfaction with self which the new centrality of advertising was now producing. At this point, of course, it was only available to the rich. One of the more disheartening stories from this period concerns a leading New York newspaper's search for a 'homely' girl whose face, and therefore life, should she win the contest, would be transformed by plastic surgery. It is perhaps a mercy that the end of the story is lost to history (Gilman 1997, 2000).

The First World War also coincided with the screening of the first full-length narrative film, a 'three-reeler', made in Hollywood by director D. W. Griffith; *Birth of a Nation* was released in 1917. Although cinema had become increasingly popular as the new century progressed, and there were now in fact established film industries in a number of different countries, the creation of this form of Hollywood narrative at this precise moment was of extraordinary significance. Firstly, Griffith created a cinematic template, establishing the characteristic Hollywood style—including close-ups of the female face—which would now be repeatedly imitated by national cinemas worldwide. Secondly, the four-year war which paralysed Europe also gave Hollywood studios the chance to distribute their own films widely across that stricken continent, establishing a near monopoly. There would be no competition from indigenous cinemas for quite some time (see Thompson and Bordwell 2006).

American studios had already begun to sense the popularity, potency and economic potential of the stars who were under contract to them, the celebrities of the new century. In 1907, the possible fate of Florence Lawrence, the 'Biograph Girl' who vanished inexplicably, dominated the newspapers. There were stories that she had been kidnapped, together with rumours of sexual scandal and even of drug-taking: there were also more cynical suggestions that it was all a publicity stunt. Her discovery, like her disappearance and protracted absence, was front-page news (Brown 2007; Mann 2001; DeCordova 2001).

Although these stars of the cinema were to become new and democratic celebrities and fashion icons, interest in the more elegant or even outré aristocratic ladies nevertheless lingered on in the post-war period. The cosmetics company Ponds used 'Society Ladies' to advertise its products until they were gradually displaced and finally banished by the dominance and the ubiquity of screen actresses in the 1920s and 1930s (see Berry 2000b).

The period after the First World War brought about both the gradual democratization of fashion and an interest in the new categories of celebrity. However, the 'bright young things' of the Roaring Twenties, most of them aristocratic, rich or both, and their American counterparts, the flappers, were baptized as such and then closely followed in the press. The 'bright young things' mixed quite freely with jazz musicians, artists and 'bohemians'; before 1914, this would have incited censure (see Landay 2002; Hudovernik 2006).

Evelyn Waugh owed his successful career as a novelist to his highly critical yet fascinated descriptions of their behaviour in his first book, *Decline and Fall* (1928), and the subsequent *Vile Bodies* (1930). In the first of these novels, if incidentally, we see how Parisian couture, whose relationship with Hollywood we examine in the following chapters, maintained its place and its status at the forefront of fashion in this description of Margot Beste-Chetwynde emerging from her chauffeur-driven Hispano-Suiza in all her Parisian finery:

> So she stepped out, like the first breath of Spring in the Champs-Elysées: two lizard skin feet, silk legs, chinchilla body, a tight little black hat pinned with platinum and diamonds, and the high invariable voice that may be heard in any Ritz Hotel from New York to Buda-Pesth. (Waugh 1928/2003: 93)

But the bright young things and the flappers were gradually of less and less interest to those outside their world as the cinema gained in power and momentum. Now there were more accessible flappers on screen, culminating in the screen adaptation of *Flaming Youth* in 1923 (Ross 2000). On either side of the Atlantic, society gossip was confined to the black-and-white print of a newspaper. But the vast black-and-white images of the cinema were all-embracing. The largely forgotten sociologist of the media, Marshall McLuhan, differentiated between a 'cold' medium such as television, where the viewer is in control, situated in familiar surroundings and even able to stop the flow of images, and a 'hot' medium such as the cinema (McLuhan 1964/1994). The embrace of the screen was distinctly sultry and could be enjoyed once, twice, even three times a week. Cinema tickets were very cheap, and social class and lack of education were not barriers to participation and enjoyment. New celebrities and new fashion leaders could now be seen by everyone; the studios would very soon develop strategies to make the fashions they showed off widely available.

These strategies would also help to engender anxieties about appearance. As the Lynds suggest,

> Advertising is concentrating increasingly upon a type of copy aiming to make the reader emotionally uneasy...This copy points an accusing finger at the stenographer as she reads her *Motion Picture Magazine* and makes her acutely conscious of her unpolished fingernails. (Lynd and Lynd 1924, quoted in Addison 2000: 5)

We shall see more of these anxieties in the pages to come.

PART I

Fashion and Film

Film Stars as Fashion Icons

The intense interest in Hollywood stars, which combines a wish to emulate their style and possess their perfect bodies with the desire to know as much as possible about their private lives, has lasted for a hundred years. In the last ten years, however, the particular focus of that interest has shifted, rather as if a kaleidoscope has been turned. The same elements are there but now are rearranged to form different patterns. Until the early 1990s, there was still an interest in what stars wore *on screen*, just as in the heyday of Hollywood. Now, of course, it is far more likely to be their *off-screen* attire that is admired and copied. More significantly, their popularity, in the twenty-first century, is seemingly unrelated to the commercial success of their films. In fact, some cinematic celebrities can currently generate intense media interest and function as fashion icons quite independently of their on-screen roles, whereas traditionally their fans would go to the cinema to watch their films. And the popularity of a star today, their presence in the press or on the Internet, may in fact have little relationship to their actual earning potential. The antithesis holds true—for among the highest-earning stars of the last few years are Daniel Radcliffe and Emma Watson of the *Harry Potter* franchise (2001–2011), which was aimed largely at children.

Watson, as mentioned in chapter 1, has been chosen for a prestigious Burberry campaign and indeed has been given a seat in the front row at some fashion shows, but there are many other stars whose celebrity status and impact on current fashion are far more significant. The 'franchise phenomenon' will be mentioned later.

All this constitutes a radical and recent change in the 'star system'. The films themselves, formerly the site of study for both audience and academics, are now arguably less important than press and Internet coverage of the stars' outfits and their personal lives, together with their commercial deployment within 'the fashion system', in fashion features and advertising campaigns.

A further departure from tradition is the emergence and the equal status of two quite separate but equally important types of photo opportunity for stars. On the one hand, there is their appearance on the red carpet, 'dressed up' in the clothes of a named designer at the Oscars, the BAFTAs, the Golden Globes or the Cannes Film Festival: on the other, there are the dressed *down,* off-duty and invariably off-guard pictures showing the stars dressed casually in jeans and a T-shirt en route to yoga class,

Figure 8   The stars of the *Harry Potter* franchise pose outside the penultimate premiere. Photograph by Anne-Marie Michel.

or semi-naked sunbathing on a beach. Both are equally popular with the paparazzi; both influence contemporary fashion, perhaps in different ways.

The red carpet event is, of course, the new catwalk of the twenty-first century; for many top designers it has as much if not more importance than their own couture shows, and the stars pose happily, endlessly, to show off their borrowed outfits to best advantage. However, the off-duty shots, particularly those on the beach, in the sea or on the sundeck, where their privacy is invaded as never before, serve to show off their bodies in more detail; these are often the pictures that most help to generate the anxieties around 'body image' discussed in chapter 1.

During the years when the Hollywood studios were in control of their stars, which lasted until the very cusp of the 1960s, beach photocalls were carefully controlled. In Europe, too, they were also used to maximize publicity for a new film or star, as with the famous photographs of Brigitte Bardot posing in her bikini on the beach at the Cannes Film Festival in 1956. These pictures made her a star and ensured the success of her new film, *And God Created Woman,* directed by her then-husband, Roger Vadim.

Figure 9   The beach at Cannes during the Film Festival today—no longer the simple stretch of sand where Bardot posed in 1956. Photograph by Anne-Marie Michel.

As Vincendeau (2005) points out, Bardot had already featured in a dozen or more unmemorable films. More significantly for this particular book, these very pictures of this new celebrity made the bikini fashionable for the very first time. It was, in fact, created and publicized by a lingerie manufacturer in 1946 but had not achieved widespread popularity (see Vincendeau 2005: 136). The other effect of these particular photographs was the creation of an entirely new mode of female beauty which challenged the conventional glamour of Hollywood. Bardot's hair was unstyled, even rumpled, her eyes heavily made-up but her mouth seemingly free of lipstick, and she preferred to go barefoot rather than totter to the beach in a pair of mules. Bardot's style did not necessarily mean 'the end of couture' (Vincendeau 2005); it did, however, mean that traditional Hollywood glamour was now threatened and made to seem out of step with the youth and rebellion which Bardot seemed to personify both in that film and off-screen.

It is important to remember that not only has film had a greater influence on fashion than any other form of visual culture, but, as we shall see, the very shaping of consumer culture as we know it depends upon the cinema and its unique power to generate both demand and supply. Consequently, this chapter needs, at first, to look backwards in order to comprehend the full significance of the cinematic image and the uses to which it has been so profitably put. For the period following the First World War saw not only the birth of the star system, but also radical changes in advertising and spending patterns (Addison 2000: 3–10; also see Addison 2006). As industry developed and production intensified, consumption was encouraged: 'in pre World War I America the Puritan values of hard work and thrift predominated' (Addison 2000: 4). These same changes were gradually reflected across Europe, where 'Puritan values' were not part of the 'prevailing ideology'.

Film production in America began on the East Coast: the move across the country to Los Angeles and its environs was made not only in search of clement weather but, more significantly, in order to buy up the tracts of land still available there at very low prices, where studios might be built.

So the 'system' so familiar to film students was crystallizing in 1918 and was ready to harness not only the changes in the climate of consumption, but also the emergence of totally new styles of dress and modes of behaviour:

> During the 1910s and 1920s, the American motion picture industry flourished. Production became centered in and around Hollywood, California: the vertically integrated studio system emerged; and by 1928 attendance at movie theatres had reached sixty-five million people per week. (Addison 2000: 8)

The building of studios was followed by the building of homes for the stars themselves in the Hollywood Hills, carefully publicized when the studios realized the strength of public interest. The first celebrity couple of cinema, Mary Pickford and Douglas Fairbanks Jr, christened their splendid new house 'Pickfair' (see Charles and Watts 2000); this mixing of names has recently been revived, with the use of the nickname 'Brangelina' to describe the union of Angelina Jolie and Brad Pitt and the soubriquet 'Posh 'n' Becks' given by the media to England's former football captain and his wife. Pickfair, designed and decorated by the newly married Fairbanks and Pickford, was the first of the new star homes in Hollywood. Then, as now, the houses swiftly became a feature of any visit to Hollywood; maps were produced, as they still are today. The many pictures taken of Pickfair, and the publicity given to 'Mary the homemaker', took the sting out of the fact that their relationship had actually begun as an adulterous on-screen romance (see Anger 1975/1981). Again, there is a contemporary parallel, for the swift proliferation of children around Angelina Jolie's skirts possibly lessened the media accusations that she was predatory and destructive in her behaviour.

In 1920, Hollywood had its very first full-scale celebrity scandal. Olive Thomas, star of *The Flapper* (1920), was married amidst great publicity to Mary Pickford's brother Jack, so creating yet another popular celebrity couple: she was the first Hollywood star to be taken up by Condé Nast and featured in *Vogue*'s fashion pages. Very soon after the release of *The Flapper,* she was found dead on the floor of the royal suite in the Hotel Carillon in Paris; she was only twenty years old. Wrapped in a lavish sable opera cloak, she held a bottle of bichloride of mercury granules in one hand; it subsequently emerged that she was a heavy user of both cocaine and heroin. Ironically, the slogan of Selznick studios was 'Selznick pictures create happy homes' (Anger 1981: 151).

Whether 'happy' or not, the homes of the stars in the silent era fascinated their followers; they make today's Malibu Beach houses and even Mulholland Drive itself seem positively restrained. The public delighted in reading about the newly built swimming pools, maybe spanned by a marble bridge or even forming part of a living room, and the vast bathrooms, which might be made of black marble and onyx or perhaps crystal and glass. Some featured a sunken Roman bath, others a solid golden bathtub with matching taps. Outside the houses, in the formal gardens with their elaborate terracing and fountains, the shiny new motorcars were parked; these might be canary-yellow, purple or even upholstered with leopard skin like Gloria Swanson's Lancia (see Anger 1981: 73).

Female fans enjoyed even more the detailed information about the clothes, hairstyles and dietary regimes of the stars, provided in the new fan magazines quickly rushed into print by the studios (Fox 1995; Berry 2000b). It emerged that Gloria Swanson spent ten thousand dollars a year on lingerie and a further six thousand on her flaçons of scent (Anger 1981: 76).

Obviously the public did not want to match these excesses; but they certainly wanted to read all about them, and possibly to make their own modest, linked purchases. The sight of lingerie and negligées in the movies surely stimulated the growth of an entirely new market, while the average bathroom, though not black marble or onyx, became marginally less functional and possibly more pleasant. The bedrooms of the stars, as featured in these same magazines, together with those actually seen on screen and inhabited by the fictional characters they played, were invariably very lavish: canopied beds, vast gilded headboards, mirrored doors. These might be beyond the means of filmgoers, but the kidney-shaped dressing table with a triple mirror and possibly a flounced fabric skirt became a feature of many suburban homes in the interwar years. Anne Massey (2000) has written about the influence of the cinema on décor in the interwar years. However, she confines herself to the rich, who built extensively in the 'moderne' style so popular on screen. We should remember that the homes of the less fortunate could nevertheless in small ways try to reflect what their owners saw on screen, just as they might emulate the ways in which the characters dressed or combed their hair. The book on the full influence of the interior décor seen on screen across the years has yet to be written.

However, there is now a small but significant body of literature around the relationship of film and fashion in the narrower sense of the word, which began with the anthology *Fabrications: Costume and the Female Body* (Gaines and Herzog) in 1990. Here, the editors republished the seminal essay of 1978, 'The Carole Lombard in Macy's Window', in which Charles Eckert famously argued that 'cinema gave consumerism its distinctive bent' (1978/1990). The essay describes the loaded trains which snaked across America, loaded with clothes, cigarettes and cars, soon to be seen on screen and then made available in stores and garages—to coincide precisely with the release of the films in which they appeared (Eckert 1978/1990: 115).

I would suggest that these changes in the economic climate and spending patterns, encouraged by cinema itself, could in fact account for some of the ambivalence around the onscreen consumption of fashion in early Hollywood cinema by characters portrayed as foolish or misled. An overly developed interest in fashion may threaten to destabilize an individual or a marriage in long-forgotten films such as Mary Pickford's film *The New York Hat* (1912) or *Fools of Fortune* (1923), where a married couple are reduced to penury through their desire for the latest clothes and décor. Recently revived, Howard Hawks's *Fig Leaves* (1929), lavishly costumed by leading studio designer Adrian, makes the heroine solely responsible for the temptation; her desire for the latest outfits leads to her employment in the fashion industry and so threatens her marriage. But she comes to her senses and accepts the more modest life her husband can provide.

This ambivalence did not disappear completely. In 1956, Grace Kelly in Alfred Hitchcock's *Rear Window* has stylish, even stunning clothes and accessories to suit her employment in the fashion industry, while her Mark Cross overnight bag famously contains only an amazing negligée. Kelly told the designer of the garment, Edith Head: 'It makes me look like a peach parfait' (see Head 1959). However, if her character is to prove worthy of the rugged traveller-journalist hero, James Stewart, all these must be abandoned; her dresses become simpler as the film progresses, and her role more serious. Even then, we are shown that she is not fully redeemed; in the closing moments, sure that her fiancé is asleep, she opens *Vogue* in preference to the book on Patagonia she is dutifully reading. Such is the legacy of the Founding Fathers. In fact, the idea that fashion is still somehow synonymous with the frivolous and the feminine (see Church Gibson 1998; Wilson 1985/2005; Buckley and Fawcett 2002) is perhaps universal. Nevertheless, the screen became the place to find fashion and the means of facilitating, perhaps even dictating, changes in style. The literature in this new area of scholastic enquiry is still growing (see Gaines and Herzog 1990; Radner 1995; Bruzzi 1997; Desser and Jowett 2000; Bruzzi and Church Gibson 2000; Street 2001; Moseley 2005; Jeffers McDonald 2010; Gilligan 2000, 2009b, 2010a).

Moreover, the traditional role of the film star as image-maker and style icon is extensively discussed in less academic works—see in particular the recent books of Patty Fox (1995) and the classic Engelmeier and Engelmeier photo-essay of 1984 (revised 1997). It also forms a significant part of academic work on the phenomenon of stardom (Dyer 1978/1998; Stacey 1994). Rachel Moseley has not only written on the iconic potency of Audrey Hepburn (2002) but has edited an anthology covering a wide range of stars across different national cinema, all of whom have influenced mainstream fashion (Moseley 2005). This last anthology, together with the work of Stella Bruzzi (1997) and a few others (see Bruzzi and Church Gibson 2000; Babington, Davies and Powrie 2004; Reich 2004; Gilligan 2009b), has tried to redress the balance and to investigate European films, contemporary cinema and masculine dress; much of the new scholarship is still concerned with the feminine and with classic Hollywood.

The 'Hollywood effect', and the influences on mainstream fashion of stars working within other national cinemas, has also formed a staple part of fashion journalism across the decades. It features in published work on fashion (Breward, Evans and Ehrman 2004) and more recently in publications on glamour (Gundle 2008; Dyhouse 2010).

But while the academy took its time to understand and articulate the links between Hollywood and consumer culture, it must be noted just how speedily those with things to sell took advantage of this new relationship. This explains Eckert's observation (1978/1990). To see an image on screen was to create instant desire, for an overall image of beauty or for a single object: a car, a particular brand of cigarette, a dress, a hairstyle. The new cinematic close-up, the careful lighting, the generous costume budgets and the opulent sets all reinforced the glamour. Most of all, the appeal was in the presence of the stars, wearing these clothes, smoking their cigarettes, driving the new cars. They were, as celebrities still are, much more appealing to mass audiences than the haughty models who stared out from the pages of those glossy magazines which many of them would never read. Hollywood films actually had 'male models', too, in the form—or forms—of their leading men. The fashion industry would not follow suit until much later in the century, while full magazine coverage of men's fashion would have to wait until the 1980s (Church Gibson 2004b). Here the male stars, like their female counterparts, could showcase style to maximum effect, making it something to covet and emulate (also see Church Gibson 2005a; Gilligan 2009a,b).

Something not always acknowledged is the way in which Hollywood cinema and celebrity could and did make new silhouettes and other innovations of high fashion desirable at a mass market level, thus spurring both manufacturing and retailing into action. Eckert initiates this particular debate. However, he does not discuss the way in which, for women from lower socio-economic groups, cinema both compensated and acted as surrogate for the glossy high-fashion magazines read by the middle classes and so alien to their own lives—as Patty Fox puts it, 'the women who *don't* read Harper's Bazaar...the majority of women' (1995). Instead, for lower-middle-class and working-class women, an expedition to the cinema was possibly not unlike consulting their very own fashion magazine, in a number of different ways.

Firstly, the trip might showcase actual Paris couture through the medium of the short documentary fashion films shown before the main feature (see Bruzzi 1997). These formed a staple of cinematic fare across America and Europe from the first years of the twentieth century until well into the 1960s. They are often overlooked (see Pathé shorts for many examples, now digitized and so easily accessible). These short films also featured new accessories—gloves, shoes, furs, hats—and helped to make lingerie and nightwear decorative and desirable rather than merely functional. They showed off new hairstyles—one of the very last instances to be found on screen is a British documentary showing how the Vidal Sassoon 'five-point' bob was created in 1964.

And when the main programme of feature films began, women could then see exactly how attractive all these new fashions could look, through studying the newly created and highly appealing stars, whose dress, hair and makeup tricks, the work of the studio experts, so excited them. Star emulation and worship pervaded not only the new forms of journalism initiated by the studios; existing magazines, too, began to show off the stars' clothes, makeup, and homes (Berry 2000b; Stacey 1994; Moseley 2002; Möttölä 2007; Sheridan 2010).

Some cinema foyers even featured actual fashion-related products in glass display cases: perhaps cosmetics, scent or scarves. All cinemas would certainly have, hanging on the walls of the entrance hall and propped in their corridors, those large backlit studio portraits of the stars which epitomized the glamour of Hollywood (focus group work, Church Gibson 2008–2010; Stacey 1994). In the special displays sometimes seen in larger cinemas, which changed as did the programmes, the leading ladies in feature films could be seen wearing clothes which might take their inspiration in overall outline from Paris but which could be currently found in department stores as part of the 'tie-in' retailing campaigns, developed in the 1920s, arranged to coincide exactly with the opening of particular films (see Eckert 1978/1990). Men, too, were involved in this process; the portraits included the male stars of the moment, all looking very suave in their suits with the sharp white handkerchiefs folded carefully so as to be visible in the top pockets, and their beautifully coiffed hair.

The 1920s and later the 1930s brought new magazines, targeted at the lower-middle-class housewife, in which there were features showing ways to achieve fashionable styles and Hollywood looks on a limited budget (see Ferguson 1983). Here, we should remember, if we are fully to understand how celebrity style was circulated and copied in the twentieth century, that the majority of women across all social classes could sew properly and so were able, if they wished, to make their own clothes (see Ewing 1997). While women with higher incomes did not, of course, do this, and local dressmakers were used even by those of more limited means, most women were nevertheless taught to sew and could thus copy Hollywood looks for themselves, using paper patterns: these were often especially issued as part of the studio licensing processes (see Turim 1984/1990).

Many women continued to make their own clothes until the 1950s and 1960s, when radical changes in women's education meant that sewing skills were no longer an automatic part of the average school curriculum. So when the women interviewed by Jackie Stacey for *Star Gazing* (1994) and Rachel Moseley for her work on Audrey Hepburn (2002) talk of wanting and therefore copying a suit or dress, they mean, of course, that they made it for themselves (also see Moseley 2001). And since fashions became far simpler in outline and structure from the 1920s onwards, they were not only easier to copy at home but also to mass produce in emulation.

So couture designers were—in some ways—indebted to the designers and stars of Hollywood cinema. Many Paris-produced silhouettes were translated by studio designers and then 'modelled' by the stars on screen, so that film, in fact, acted as a form of international fashion show. Thus, the new styles became first desirable and then accessible as copies at different market levels were produced. Chanel herself famously said, 'What Hollywood shows today, you will wear tomorrow' (Bruzzi 1997: 3). She showed her appreciation of this new force within fashion when she accepted studio boss Sam Goldwyn's invitation to work in Hollywood, even though their liaison was short-lived (Bruzzi 1997).

She was thinking of clothes when she talked of the power of Hollywood; but there were other things to be copied. Sarah Berry describes the way in which the new market for cosmetics and other beauty products was totally dependent upon Hollywood celebrity; makeup, of course, owes its very ubiquity to its use onscreen (2000a,b). Chanel's observation also ties in perfectly with the studio designer Adrian's seemingly self-deprecating remark that 'Hollywood cannot create: it can only imitate' (see Simms 1974; Esquevin 2008; Gutner 2001). This statement can be fleshed out; *imitate* could be replaced by *popularize.* For instance, Adrian was responsible for taking the bias-cut evening gowns of Madeline Vionnet, something mass audiences would never have seen, and using them as inspiration for the dresses worn to such effect by Greta Garbo and Jean Harlow in, say, *Dinner at Eight* (1933) and *Grand Hotel* (1934). Meanwhile, costume jewellery, marabou-trimmed slippers, new kinds of hat, all were now paraded before ordinary women for whom high fashion was inaccessible and inconceivable. Not only could they now see it for themselves, but the studios would help them find it (Gaines 1990; Esquevin 2008).

The precise emulation of star behaviour was not, of course, confined to women. In 1933, as most readers will probably know, American men famously abandoned their vests after seeing *It Happened One Night.* Clark Gable was, it seemed, bare-chested beneath his shirt (Richards 1973: 232; Lehu 2007: 146).

Chanel's loose dresses and short skirts of the 1920s were translated into the clothes worn by the screen flappers such as the 'It Girl', Clara Bow (Ross 2000). She did far more to popularize bobbed hair, the cupid's-bow painted mouth and short skirts than any Paris fashion plate. Meanwhile, it was, of course, Marlene Dietrich's and Katherine Hepburn's wearing of trousers on screen (and off) that led to their widespread adoption. At first they were worn only by the rich and fashionable in the late

1920s and early 1930s—see for example the pictures of Chanel and her friends at the Lido or of society belles in their 'beach pyjamas' (Charles-Roux 2009). Their place within the wardrobe of the ordinary young woman was ensured during the Second World War, when women, now working in large numbers, found their comfort and practicality invaluable. In 1945, Nancy Mitford could write spitefully of her fictional character, the Bolter, seemingly frozen in time with her 'shingle' and her 1920s slang that 'she wore trousers with the air of one flouting the conventions, ignorant that every suburban shopgirl was doing the same' (Mitford 1945/2000: 134).

So the screen succeeded where journalism often failed; it made many designer fashions into global styles, simply through the medium of screen celebrity. Dior's New Look of 1947 might never have succeeded at a mass market level without its swift adoption by Hollywood costume designers. Edith Head helped to make the New Look popular for so long that a modified version of it, with longish pencil skirt, remained fashionable throughout the 1950s (Bruzzi 1997). The studios of Hollywood and their global reach took unattainable images and styles; not only did the studios place these where everyone might see them, but Hollywood provided—directly or indirectly—ways in which they might, to use Simmel's expression, 'trickle-down' (Simmel 1904).

The star celebrities may have acted as conduits, making high fashion interesting to the mass market and stimulating the industry into making copies; but they also started other more home-grown fashions, popularizing garments which, like Hepburn's trousers, quickly found their way into stores. Betty Grable's endless legs, famously insured for thousands of dollars (Wanamaker 1984: 76), made shorts fashionable for young women while Lana Turner, after her first film *They Won't Forget* (1937), was instantly christened the 'Sweater Girl', so making this simple garment newly fashionable. It was worn to great effect in the next decade by Marilyn Monroe, who like Turner showed that it could be sexy; Audrey Hepburn, by contrast, made the bohemian black turtleneck (see Koenig 1973: 198) seem both elegant and extremely versatile.

Hollywood stars had a consistent signature style; it was expected. When studio designer Edith Head took the traditional sarong of the Polynesian islands and adapted it for the exotic-looking Dorothy Lamour, she inadvertently trapped her forever, whilst also creating a staple part of beachwear then and now. In 1937, Lamour hopefully asked her fans, 'Wouldn't you like to see me in a film that wasn't a sarong film?' Sadly for her, they replied overwhelmingly that no, they would not (Chierichetti 2004; Calistro 2004: 284).

As early as 1923, Salvatore Ferragamo, founder of the family shoe firm, realized the potency of this new medium as a means of advertising his own products on a grand scale. He provided, free of charge, the sandals for every single man and woman who appeared onscreen in Cecil B. de Mille's version of the *Ten Commandments*. That meant the shoeing of hundreds of extras for the lavish crowd scenes, with no mention, as might be negotiated today, of his name in the credits (see Ferragamo 1987: 27;

Pedersen 2005: 66). However, the thought of the word-of-mouth publicity that would be generated was presumably enough, and indeed his name has been linked with film stars and celebrities ever since, his shoes very often their brand of choice, until the recent advent of the shoe-designer-as-celebrity, as discussed later in the book. In the 1950s, Ferragamo named a strapped ballet pump after Audrey Hepburn, and they are still available in stores such as Saks. He made over forty pairs of shoes for Marilyn Monroe, including a famous pair of red rhinestone pumps with stiletto heels; these were sold in 1999 for $42,000 at Christie's and then bought in 2010 for an undisclosed sum by Johnny Depp as a present for his partner, Vanessa Paradis (Barron 1999; Lomrantz 2010).

The naming of accessories after superstar celebrities still continues; contemporary shoe designer Jimmy Choo named a grosgrain loafer 'Diana' after the late princess, who was fond of this style off-duty (Brown 2007). In 2010, Ferragamo launched the 'Elise' stiletto-heeled shoe, named after the character played by Angelina Jolie in the film *The Tourist,* released in the same year. And, of course, most people with any interest in fashion will know that the Hermès handbag used by Grace Kelly to hide her pregnancy was christened for her, starting a trend within the firm that has continued up to the present day (see Tolkien 2002: 44; Haughland 2010: 78).

As the film industry developed, the stars of Hollywood films could and did help to sell anything and everything, at home and abroad. This was noted at the very highest levels, not merely by the studio moguls. In 1945, when the US Department of Commerce was looking for its chance to dominate global trading activity as it renewed itself in the post-war era, it chose to commission a series of studies on viewing habits worldwide in order to understand putative spending patterns in different countries across the globe. These reports included the analysis of differing tastes in film genres across the world, whether romantic comedies, musicals or melodramas. They also examined existing national patterns of spending, consumption and taste. This was not, however, solely confined to fashion purchases, although these featured prominently in the survey. Handbags were the subject of one report, with plastic popular in China, while crocodile skin was preferred in Argentina (see the Congressional Economic Reports analysed in Church Gibson 2007).

But the remit of the reports and the surveys involved went much further and looked at very different ways of using Hollywood cinema in a post-war economic climate ravaged by six years of war, with so many industrial infrastructures in ruins and much of Europe dependent on the American financial aid provided by the Marshall Plan. There was an investigation into how to use the cinema in order to sell the new fitted kitchens, while another looked at how to manipulate film narratives so as to showcase farm machinery for use in developing economies (Church Gibson 2007).

But if film actually helped to democratize fashion in the past, today the new relationship is partly that between the screen celebrity and the luxury brand. Once, the studios of Hollywood and their global reach took the unattainable images and styles of haute couture and placed them where everyone might see them. They acted as a showcase for 'alternative' styles, too, through a different, less conventional type of cinematic celebrity, before the appearance of television and the growing power of popular music in the 1950s. Black leather jackets and white T-shirts, originally marketed for and worn only by aircrew and GIs, were made desirable for young men by James Dean and Marlon Brando in their screen roles of the 1950s. They have remained wardrobe staples for the past sixty years (Springer 2007: 45). Brando explains in his autobiography that the origins of what he calls the 'slob look' were in his own preferred personal style of dress. He sought out workwear and army surplus stores for reasons of comfort and economy; he rather begrudges the way in which the iconic image of Dean has in fact taken the credit (Brando 1995).

Although cinema may have created new styles and helped to make high fashion less frightening, this was, of course, not done through some kind of altruism. In fact, some designers elected to become directly involved and so benefit financially, rather than simply have their styles copied. So they dressed the leading lady—and later on, like Armani and Cerruti in the 1980s and 1990s, the leading man—using films to show off their clothes, just as Ferragamo had done with his shoes. The first fashion designer to create a star wardrobe was, in fact, Paul Poiret, in 1912; he was invited by Sarah Bernhardt to dress her for her role as Elizabeth I. But it was in the second half of the last century that the relationship really developed—Bruzzi has a comprehensive chapter on this in *Undressing Cinema*. Since its publication in 1997, however, things have changed and new ties have been created; we will examine the new 'fashion films' in chapter 5. But it is enough here to remember that film can actively parade high design as well as serve to demystify.

The traditional relationship between designer and star—including, of course, the famous pairings of Givenchy and Hepburn, Yves St Laurent and Catherine Deneuve—was replaced by the proliferation of ready-to-wear on American screens from the 1980s onwards. The opportunity for fashion 'product placement' has been used in many different ways (see Church Gibson 2004b; Gilligan 2009a,b).

But cinema did not merely serve to show off products and generate revenue. From its beginnings, film also helped to create or reinforce dissatisfaction with self. Many cinemagoers were all too aware that they did not have the 'face of Greta Garbo' that so intrigued critic Roland Barthes, nor the long slim legs of Betty Grable and the tiny frame of Clara Bow. The perfect close-ups on screen and the carefully backlit pictures in the foyer also helped to fuel dissatisfaction, just as the results of digital manipulation and airbrushing may demoralize women today.

Heather Addison describes quite graphically the way in which the new advertising techniques of the 1920s coincided with the growing power of cinema to create the industry that she calls 'body shaping', which was of course predicated upon self-doubt, as it is today

Figure 10 Catherine Deneuve, a star since the 1960s and famously dressed for forty years by Yves St Laurent. Photograph by Anne-Marie Michel.

(Addison 2000). Eighty years on, 'body shaping' requires measures that are much more drastic; nevertheless, she shows us some worrying advertisements for thyroid pills, stout rubber garments and contraptions which include a 'chin reducer' available for six dollars (Addison 2000: 13), all marketed in the early years of the 'reducing craze' (27).

THE NEW RELATIONSHIP?

Cinema's new 'celebrity' stardom, within a Western context, is qualitatively different from previous forms of fandom or star emulation. In consequence, the existing theories of stardom (Stacey 1994; Gledhill 1991), sometimes co-opted from film studies to explain modern celebrity culture, are not really sufficient, although, as this book will suggest, Richard Dyer's idea of 'the ordinary' has a new relevance in this rather different context (1978/1998). Film studies within the academy must somehow address the very different circumstances of film production and its reception in the new century.

Today, when fans admire a star's style, they will usually be talking of the clothes that he or she wears *off* screen; in the past, they would be referring to what the star wore on screen, within the diegesis, the fictional world. Christine Geraghty (2000) has referred to the phenomenon of the 'star-as-celebrity' when writing about Keira Knightley's role in *Pride and Prejudice* (UK, 2001, dir. Joe Wright). This is a start; since then, that phenomenon has developed at an alarming rate, certainly within Anglo-American cinema. Today, the presence of the star-as-celebrity arguably determines whether or not a film can actually get made at all, and certainly whether or not it will receive proper distribution.

Figure 11 The commercial sponsors of the Venice Film Festival get their prominent billing. Photograph by Anne-Marie Michel.

The use of stars, or possibly celebrities-who-act, within fashion shoots and on magazine covers complicates things still further; it increases the flattening-out effect, the interchangeability of images that I have mentioned as a central feature of contemporary visual culture. Images already segue seamlessly from cinema screen to magazine cover to advertising campaign; now, with the recent move towards employing well-known film directors to make commercials, and the subsequent emergence of the celebrity-as-director, cinema *itself* is changing swiftly. This we need to address in subsequent chapters; it cannot simply be described as 'intertextuality'. We need, also, to address the ways in which this is driven directly by the desire to sell fashion through celebrity, something not yet discussed or even acknowledged.

Within the case studies that make up the following chapters, some of these questions will be raised; finding answers is much more difficult.

−4−

Changes in Cinematic Culture:
Some Celebrity Cover Girls

The new millennium is marked by an enhanced public knowledge of designer names and hallmarks, of luxury brands and, of course, the whereabouts of cheap copies, for the industry has been swift to respond; all this has been reflected within contemporary cinema. This new widespread craving for fashion, the increasing speed of change and the advent of shopping as mass leisure activity arguably began in the boom economies of the 'greed is good' decade of the 1980s. Back then, the new-look high street was ready to provide the necessary slew of faux-Armani suits and inexpensive flying jackets for those young men who might not have seen Ray Petri's 'seminal' Buffalo stylings in the new style magazines (see Jobling 1999; Barthel 1992) but who had probably seen Richard Gere in *American Gigolo* and had certainly watched the 1986 box office success *Top Gun* (1986) starring Tom Cruise (Church Gibson 2004a; Bruzzi 1997).

As we have seen, what we have to examine two decades later is not the power of cinematic narratives to show off the spectacle of celebrity, but rather the new potency of the cinematic celebrity *off screen*. And ever cheaper, faster methods of garment production assist seemingly impossible forms of emulation. Julia Roberts wore a vintage black-and-white Valentino dress to collect her Oscar for *Erin Brocovich* in 2002; the very next day, copies were advertised on websites such as edressme.com for as little as $120. While designers of couture, of course, fight over who they can dress for the Oscars and work with the endless stylists now involved (Fox 1995), the cheapest retail outlets use the phrase 'celebrity style' as a header on their websites (see New Look). In spring 2010, London Fashion Week joined forces officially with the BAFTAs, thus giving formal recognition to the fact that today high fashion and award ceremonies are inextricably intertwined.

During the 1970s and 1980s, it could be argued that the 'star' image was being replaced by the 'character' image (Epstein 2000: 184). But what may have been true in the past, with Faye Dunaway as Bonnie Parker or Diane Keaton as Annie Hall (see Bruzzi 1997: 177), does not hold good in the era of Angelina Jolie and, after her television career as Rachel ended, Jennifer Aniston.

Figure 12 Newly fashionable cover girl and celebrity 'face' Natalie Portman in a photocall for her film *Black Swan* at the Venice Film Festival. Photograph by Anne-Marie Michel/FeatureFlash.

JEN, ANGELINA, MARILYN AND KEIRA

Some of the films made by the new celebrity stars may not actually be seen by their fans; they will, however, have seen stills in magazines or on the Internet. When their films are commercially successful, the image of the star seen on screen often matches their most popular off-screen image. Jennifer Aniston in *Marley and Me,* made in 2009 and more successful at the box office than her previous string of romantic comedies, looks exactly like the off-screen Jennifer Aniston, so often photographed near her home on Malibu beach. The simple, casual clothes, the long bare legs...the looks seen within the film are completely interchangeable with the endless paparazzi shots of this celebrity star (see Sherrow 2006: 38–39). Aniston's popularity began with her ten-year television stint in the series *Friends,* which after it finished was endlessly rerun; the characters seemed to become part of popular mythology.

Aniston is popular partly because she seems, despite her good looks and enviable figure, to be unthreatening to female audiences while still attractive to young men. The phrase 'girl next door' has been used, which we could link to Dyer's (1998) notion of the extraordinary 'ordinary'. Despite posing semi-naked for *GQ* (UK, December 2005), nude sans a tie for the January 2009 edition of US *GQ* or styled exotically as the young Barbra Streisand in *Harper's Bazaar* (September 2010), Aniston does not intimidate (interviews and focus groups, Church Gibson 2008–2010). The fragrance she launched in 2010 is as wholesome and outdoorsy as the image she projects; her personal difficulties and problems with men only help to generate sympathy. She is used frequently on the covers of fashion magazines precisely because of this perceived relationship with the women who will be motivated to lift the magazines down from the shelf.

By contrast, the perfection of Angelina Jolie's perceived image does seem to alienate or at least frighten some young women (focus groups, Church Gibson). Since achieving celebrity status, this has also affected her on-screen mode of presentation. When Jolie starred as the tomboy Crash in *Hackers* (1995, dir. Iain Softley) or as a very disturbed young woman in *Girl, Interrupted* (1999, dir. James Mangold), for which she won an Oscar, her striking physical beauty did not interfere with her on-screen roles. At that time she was unknown and even anonymous. Since she became the partner of Brad Pitt after his divorce from Aniston, their relationship has had a consistently high media profile; consequently, she now seems to be a celebrity rather than an actress, despite her very considerable on-screen talent (also see Barron 2009). When she starred in Clint Eastwood's Oscar-nominated film *The Changeling* in 2008, the director had to bow to the potency of her *off-screen* image. The film was remarkable for its fidelity to period detail in the way that it recreated the Los Angeles of the 1920s—the clothes, the cars, the houses, the interiors, the public transport system. But though Jolie, like the other female characters, wears authentic 1920s dress and has her hair fashioned in the style of the earlier period, her wide mouth, so often commented upon in the press and perhaps her most striking feature, is painted an extraordinary, anachronistic pink. In *The Tourist* (2010, dir. Florian Henckel von Donnersmarck), she is given a highly spectacular on-screen wardrobe of great elegance, but with no real relationship either to her on-screen character or to the narrative of the film. The fitted dresses and strategically placed diamonds all seem designed to emphasize her extraordinary, even unreal, beauty—but at the expense of the film. Designer Colleen Atwood explained that she herself was inspired by the clothes worn by Kim Novak in *Vertigo* (1957, dir. Alfred Hitchcock) and that one of the dresses was actually a vintage offering, created by Charles James, leading American couturier of the 1940s and 1950s. This film, however, is supposedly set in 2010, and Jolie plays an undercover agent, rather than the supposed trophy wife portrayed by Novak. This particular agent, it seems, is never seen without four-inch stiletto heels, a clutch bag and long leather gloves. The leading Italian designer Alberta Ferretti is credited, but only for dressing the other guests at the ball which forms the film's denouement.

Of course, this is not completely new, this strategy of separating the star from the *corps de ballet.* In *Some Like It Hot,* made in 1959, which is set in the late 1920s, the girl musicians who make up the members of the jazz band all wear historically correct loose dresses. However, Marilyn Monroe, the film's star, as 'Sugar Kane', the singer who fronts the band, wears extraordinarily revealing, form-fitting dresses more suited to the period of the film's making and its release date and especially designed by William Travilla to showcase both her star image and her celebrity status.

Marilyn as star and celebrity is a seminal figure; a leading fashion icon of the 1950s, it is interesting to consider how she might differ from some of the contemporary celebrity figures of cinema. If we think of her as a cover girl, we might think of her frequent appearances on the front of *Life* magazine or remember that she posed for *Playboy.* The only time she was used by a fashion photographer was in the shoot she did with Bert Stern just before her death, now referred to as the 'Last Sitting' and often visually referenced—most recently by Lindsey Lohan for *New York* magazine (see Fortini 2008). Yet she definitely influenced fashion in the 1950s (see Lewis 1979) but, I would suggest, in a particularly democratic way.

Her image, once created, remained utterly consistent throughout her career on and off screen. Her hairstyle, known as the Italian demi-wave, was the most popular style of the 1950s. Marilyn's favourite earrings were little tiered diamond drops; these, copied in crystal or even glass, could soon be found on the high street. Her pencil skirts and tight sweaters were also easy to find and copy, as were her arched eyebrows and red lipstick. Versions of the simple white sundress printed with red cherries which Hollywood designer Jean-Louis created for her in 1956 were quickly made available, and the style has been consistently revived. Morgan, for example, sold a version in the summer of 2002. And the photographs taken of Marilyn on the set of *The Misfits* in 1961, by Eve Arnold, made blue jeans finally as desirable for women as they were for men (Arnold 2005).

Celebrities, of course, promote not only ways of dressing and making up, but also have been instrumental in creating the desirable body shapes of each decade. Marilyn's hourglass figure and strategically emphasized breasts led to a string of blonde, curvaceous lookalikes within the film industry, together with massive sales of conically stitched or padded bras, and finally to a search by plastic surgeons for some form of reliable implant material which took twenty years to find (see Gilman 2000). And, of course, her signature look was so strong that Warhol could represent her simply through heavily simplified and stylized eyes and red lips; these trademarks never really varied, whatever role she played.

Once her particular persona was established, the films in which she appeared were carefully constructed around it. In *Some Like It Hot* (1959), her penultimate film, the director Billy Wilder actually wrote the dialogue for the character 'Sugar Kane' with Marilyn's own past life in mind. So when 'Sugar' tells the disguised Tony Curtis of her disastrous personal life, there are deliberate reminders of Marilyn's own troubles. Despite her glamour, they helped to make her seem somehow 'accessible' (Dyer 1986/2004). The most-photographed woman of the 1950s, she acted out her personal tragedies—her illnesses, her miscarriage, her divorces—in front of her adoring public. Her suicide became a global news item, while to date there are no less than twenty-six books in print on the subject of her life and the circumstances of her death (see McCann 1988). Like Princess Diana, Marilyn is central to any consideration of celebrity; in fact, she seems to have foreshadowed Diana in certain ways. She had the same uncanny ability to pose perfectly whenever she found herself in front of the lens (Arnold 2005; Brown 2007), while her endless mistakes and her unhappy personal life, even her disastrous liaisons with married men, did not lessen the affection of the public. Although the scenes at her funeral were in no way comparable to the massive display of public mourning in 1997, the comparison is instructive. It was not only that both women possessed, in different ways, an ability to convey Dyer's idea of 'the ordinary' (1978/1998); more significantly, since this book looks at fashion, both had elements within a characteristic look that could be emulated by their fans.

But Angelina Jolie, ranked by *Forbes* magazine in 2009 at the top of 'the world's most powerful celebrities' (Pomerantz and Rose 2009), offers, by contrast, nothing that can really be copied. Jolie's exotic face and slender body are shown off by form-fitting couture clothes for public appearances. The leather dress at the European premiere of *Inglorious Basterds* in 2008 was designed by Michael Kors; the flesh-coloured, thigh-revealing floor-length dress worn at the Cannes Film Festival in the same year was lent by Versace. There is nothing ordinary about Jolie.

Whilst other actresses appear in endless advertisements, she has so far agreed to participate in only two major campaigns: the first for an American luxury brand, St John, in a campaign where the black-and-white images are carefully styled to remind us of the traditions of classical portraiture and of early-twentieth-century society photographs. She is posed here in formal settings, outside country houses, gloved and

Figure 13   No one can compete with her; there is nothing 'ordinary' about Angelina Jolie. Photograph by Anne-Marie Michel/London Entertainment.

flanked by pedigree dogs. Interestingly, in January 2010, Jolie was dropped from the St John brand. *Women's Wear Daily,* the *Huffington Post* and *Glamour* reported that Glen McMahon, chief executive officer for St John, had made the following decision:

> [Jolie] overshadowed the brand. We wanted to make a clean break from actresses and steer away...and cleanse the palate. (McMahon cited in 'Glossy Karlie' 2010)

It appears that Jolie's celebrity-as-commodity status had become too much for the exclusive brand; for the spring 2010 print campaign she was replaced by British model Karen Elson. Having previously modelled for Louis Vuitton, Chanel and Versace, Elson was used for the campaign in an attempt to 'show a modern point of view of St. John' and evolve the brand (Bumpus 2010). Two years earlier, Jolie had already lost her other source of advertising revenue; she was the face of the Japanese makeup brand Shiseido from 2006 to 2008, when she was replaced by the gamine, unconventional and even androgynous English model Agyness Deyn.

THE *W* SHOOT—FASHION, CELEBRITY AND CONTROVERSY

The July 2005 issue of leading fashion magazine *W* can be seen as instrumental in the formation of Jolie's celebrity power, which was later to overwhelm the St John brand. The *W* cover image and a series of fashion photographs feature celebrity couple Jolie and Pitt, who were to become in the following year the 'Most Powerful Couple in America' according to *Forbes* magazine, commanding, for instance, $4 million for the US rights to publish six photographs of Jolie, Pitt and baby Shiloh. By 2008, Jolie and Pitt's celebrity commodity status was such that they were able to command $14 million for photographs of their newborn twins to be published in *People* magazine ('Source: Jolie-Pitt Baby Pics' 2008).

The 2005 *W* cover and the fashion spread (see Bagley and Klein 2005) were designed to evoke various films of the past, but at the same time reflect a perceived present reality, the leading Anglo-American celebrity story of the moment. In this particular shoot, Jolie and Pitt agreed to pose for the magazine to publicize their recently completed film *Mr. and Mrs. Smith* (2005). Leading fashion photographer Steven Meisel, helped by Pitt himself, who provided all the cinematic references, created a series of images based on scenes from other films; the shoot, as presumably he had intended, provoked far more controversy than most issues of *W* magazine and has appeared as a collector's item on eBay. For, at the time of publication, although Jolie and Pitt were appearing in public together in connection with their recently completed film, they were carefully quashing all rumours that their relationship could be anything other than professional, since Pitt was still married to Jennifer Aniston.

However, the photo shoot contained a contradictory narrative, where the actors were shown as very much a couple. Some of the images were explicitly erotic; in the black-and-white shots they are presented as illicit lovers. Embracing passionately in anonymous hotel corridors, or locked together in stylish modern rooms dominated by pools of shadow, these pictures evoke Antonioni films of the early 1960s, particularly *La Notte* (1961) and *L'Eclisse* (1962). Another black-and-white photograph showed the couple lying together on a hotel bed, this time with a revolver clearly visible next to his head on the pillow. This instantly calls to mind a sequence in the French New Wave film *À bout de souffle* (1960) where Jean Seberg and Jean-Paul Belmondo, as a petty thief on the run, spend the afternoon on a similar hotel bed. The retro feel and filmic references continued in the contrasting, brightly coloured pictures within the shoot, which presented a pastiche of affluent married life in a mythical American suburb of the past, with more than a nod towards *The Stepford Wives* (US, 1975, dir. Bryan Forbes) and certainly a feel of David Lynch's later film *Blue Velvet (*1986).

The most interesting picture, perhaps, is the cover image, where the couple in 1960s-pastiche casual clothes sit in a large garden surrounded by their 'children'. I have described this particular shoot in such detail because it seems to me emblematic of the current relationship between fashion and the new form of cinematic celebrity. The crossing of boundaries in so many different ways is sly but explicit: *W* magazine's knowing use of the new celebrity couple increased its sales and gave far more potency to the designer clothes glimpsed on the couple, and carefully listed, than is usual in a fashion shoot. Aniston herself, in fact, posed for a similar *W* cover in 2010 to publicize her new film *The Bounty Hunter,* but sadly it did not have the back story which made the first shoot so salacious.

In an article in the *Times* (2009), Joan Collins, who herself was trained by Hollywood after her initial education in the Rank Studios 'Charm School', wrote of the changes in the self-presentation and media portrayals of contemporary film actresses. 'Screen goddesses', she argued, were a thing of the past, while elegance and glamour were now the exception rather than the rule. Collins, in fact, cited Angelina Jolie as one unusual example still capable of old-fashioned glamour and suggested that singers like Beyoncé and Rihanna were now more representative of the well-groomed, perfectly turned-out look of classic Hollywood. Interestingly, she mused briefly on the protective powers of the studio moguls, suggesting that today, Marilyn Monroe might find herself appearing before a congressional committee to explain her rumoured relationship with President John F. Kennedy.

All this has resonance and relevance here; it also perhaps conjures up indelible images of Marilyn, of the black-and-white newsreel footage of her at Madison Square Garden. Wearing a dress created for her by Jean-Louis composed seemingly of glittering paillettes and little else, she sings 'Happy Birthday, Mr President' to Kennedy, who is seated at the head of the table with his wife. There is no contemporary image with such complex levels of meaning for any current Hollywood star; if there were, the rules of the new celebrity culture mean we would want instantly to pick over the bones, to know all the intimate details.

Unwittingly, Collins also picked up on the continuing 'whiteness' of Hollywood; both the women of colour she mentions work within the music industry. There is, in theory, now some representation of other ethnic groups, but, in fact, the longstanding

Figure 14   Joan Collins shows off what is meant by 'old-fashioned glamour'. Photograph by Anne-Marie Michel.

sanitization of otherness continues. Halle Berry, the only woman of colour to win an Oscar, and who appeared on the significant September issue of US *Vogue* for 2010, is, in fact, mixed-race.

British celebrity and star Keira Knightley was not even mentioned by Collins. But she needs to be discussed here because she is a cover girl of fashion magazines who plays leading roles on screen. Knightley received an Oscar nomination for her role in

Pride and Prejudice (UK, 2005, dir. Joe Wright) and was nominated for a Golden Globe and a BAFTA when she made a second film, *Atonement,* for the same director in 2007. It was perhaps her casting that led to both films being made, well-funded and widely distributed.

Her first film, *Bend It Like Beckham* (UK, 2002, dir. Gurinder Chadha), in which she played the tomboy Jules, ensured Knightley's popularity through her extraordinarily photogenic qualities. Whatever the verdict on her acting ability, she has the kind of face that is naturally at home on magazine covers, and she was swiftly deployed as cover girl across a range of publications including *Vogue, Vanity Fair, Interview, Esquire* and *Elle.*

In *Pride and Prejudice,* Knightley stood out amongst the other Bennet sisters. If they all look very much 'of the period' in their dress, hair and deportment, she is resolutely modern. With a plaid shawl thrown across her shoulders, at times it can seem as if she had strayed in from a fashion shoot. Rosamund Pike plays her sister Jane and is as modest and demure in her deportment as Jane Austen would wish. But although Knightley plays the most outspoken sister, Elizabeth, she makes her into a thoroughly modern heroine in every way.

By the time this particular film was distributed, magazines across the spectrum were even more frantic in their courtship of Keira; later, she would be offered advertising campaigns. The process I have described as 'bleeding', as seeping sideways across the different strands of the media, is perfectly illustrated by the continual recycling of her image. Over the past decade, there has been a blurring of boundaries between the real and the imaginary, between fact and fantasy, which characterizes contemporary visual culture. And as I have argued earlier, images now move sideways across feature films, magazine covers, advertisements for luxury brands, newspaper stories and Internet sites. A photograph of Knightley, showing off her ultra-slim figure and fashion-model style while posing in a backless gold Gucci dress on the red carpet outside the British premiere of *Pirates of the Caribbean: Dead Man's Chest* (US, 2006, dir. Gore Verbinski), made the front pages of the papers and could be found circulating in cyberspace. It was almost indistinguishable from the publicity still, released a year later, of the actress posing in a green backless dress of identical cut for *Atonement* but which was, in fact, a costume worn by her within the film itself. This latter image was featured heavily in fashion magazines and again cropped up everywhere online. Perhaps in a similar way to Gwyneth Paltrow, Knightley comes to exist 'as a ceaseless flow of images' (Gilligan 2000: 248). There is not a single image that 'is' Knightley, but instead, like Paltrow, in the multiplicity of images 'past and present, character, stars and the "real" merge into something ever recognisable yet, somehow never stable' (Gilligan 2000; also see Gilligan 2009b).

Film and fashion segue seamlessly into one another; Knightley as herself and as the heroine of *Atonement* are indistinguishable, while her face is also the face of Chanel. As the new decade moved on, she might be seen, say, on a magazine's cover, then appear within its pages in a still from her latest film or in a paparazzi shot, and finally could even bookend the magazine, appearing half-naked on the back cover to advertise Coco Mademoiselle. Her styling in these advertisements seems designed to evoke images of Liza Minnelli as Sally Bowles in *Cabaret* (1972, dir. Bob Fosse). This blurring of boundaries, this use of a face or an image across different strands of the media, epitomizes the way in which the new celebrity culture works and shows us just why it is so deleterious to cinema as a formal medium.

The film *The Duchess* (2008, dir Saul Dibb), in its casting, construction and clever publicity, deliberately blurred all these boundaries still further. Based on the best-selling biography *Georgiana: Duchess of Devonshire* (Foreman 1999) and an eighteenth-century celebrity, the film chose to play up in every possible way not only the fact that the duchess had a famous descendant in Princess Diana, but that there were other parallels within their lives. This was perhaps most notable in the way that Georgiana, carefully married off by her mother to one of the richest dukes in England, found herself at first with a cold but philandering husband and then in a ménage à trois.

The film carefully played this up. The posters had as their strapline 'There were three people in her marriage'—designed, of course, to remind potential viewers of how Diana famously told her television interviewer, Martin Bashir, that in her life with Charles, 'Well, there were three of us in that marriage, so it was a bit crowded' (Bashir 1995). These posters were used as in-store advertisements and window displays in the chain of Laura Ashley stores, where mock-antique furniture and fabrics are on offer.

To make the links still more explicit to sell the film through the celebrity status of both the dead Diana and the living Knightley, the beautifully costumed film—it won both an Oscar and a BAFTA for costume design—showed us scenes of the young duchess at Althorp. This was chosen as a location because it was, in fact, Princess Diana's own childhood home. Here we see the threatened young heroine running happily around the gardens with her friends, all symbolically clad in white, completely unaware of the dynastic plotting taking place inside the house.

Ralph Fiennes, as her new husband, seems to have modelled his performance on the public appearances of Prince Charles—the mannerisms, the voice, the expressions. When the real Georgiana's marriage foundered, she took a proactive part in contemporary politics, championing and even campaigning for the Whigs. In the film, Knightley as the fictional Georgiana does so ravishingly dressed; this seems again designed to evoke Diana, who famously embraced good causes after her divorce, culminating in her ultimately successful campaign against landmines.

Knightley then filmed *The Edge of Love* (2008, dir. John Maybury) with Sienna Miller, who is herself a celebrity actress and a definite fashion icon, being credited along with Kate Moss for the success of the 'boho look' in the late 1990s. Miller was also the notoriously Photoshopped 'celebrity cover girl' (see Odell 2009b) for US *Vogue* during the filming of *The September Issue* (2009, dir. R. J. Cutler).

Even though this John Maybury film about the private life of Dylan Thomas did not do particularly well at the box office, it was nevertheless fully covered in fashion magazines, with stills of Knightley and Miller wearing 1940s-style print frocks and hand-knitted jumpers with knee-length Wellingtons. One of the shots from the film, used as a publicity still, showed the two young women sitting on a railing beside the sea, seemingly intended to evoke Bert Hardy's Box Brownie photograph famously used on the cover of *Picture Post* in 1951 (Hardy 1985).

Lastly, we might cite Keira's role within the incredibly successful *Pirates of the Caribbean* films. This is the most financially lucrative franchise ever created, easily trumping the *Lord of the Rings* trilogy and kept from the all-time top spot only by the blockbusters of James Cameron (see Box Office Mojo, boxofficemojo.com). This is interesting casting because, as in *Bend It Like Beckham,* she seems to have been asked quite simply to play herself, a high-spirited young girl with ideas of her own about her future. The films are lavishly costumed, and she looks spectacular; she swiftly casts aside her petticoats and adopts breeches, shirt, and cutlass to fight alongside Orlando Bloom and Johnny Depp (also see Gilligan 2009b). Later she appears in the fantastic robes of an Asian despot. Her tomboyish, even androgynous heroine perhaps explains the popularity of these films with young girls.

These same young girls should be mentioned in conclusion; there is still one arena of production where stars and fashions are created on screen through and within the diegesis. That is in the enormously lucrative films increasingly offered to the very young. The Disney phenomenon is more successful than ever—the Hannah Montana film with Miley Cyrus and *High School Musicals* 1, 2 and 3 have had a huge impact on the tween market. The stars of these films appear on the covers of magazines (*Glitter, Teen Vogue, Sugar*) targeted at that age group while endless merchandising lines use the names of both films. More recently, as the stars such as Zac Efron and Miley Cyrus have grown older, they have appeared on the covers of *Vanity Fair, Interview, Nylon, GQ* and *Wonderland.*

When Miley Cyrus, as the then fifteen-year-old star of Hannah Montana, was photographed by Annie Leibovitz for the June 2008 edition of *Vanity Fair,* semi-naked and smiling provocatively, there was an outcry (Handy 2008; Martin 2008; Roberts 2008). It wasn't just because she was photographed naked but for a sheet, with tousled bed head, and this in a high-end publication. Rather, it was because she had upset her young audience—and, more significantly, the studio executives, who need her to remain young and innocent in order to continue their own successful exploitation of the very young (see Greer 2008).

I would suggest that the new tween stars must, to please their audiences, remain forever young and child-like. When the cast of *High School Musical 3* are dressed for their prom, theoretically now ready to leave school and move on to university, they are still presented as physically prepubertal. There is no cleavage, and there are very few curves. The only star to possess a notable bosom keeps it carefully covered up; on prom night, she wears a dress with a bib front not unlike a young girl's party frock.

Figure 15 Teen star and fashion icon—Miley Cyrus of Hannah Montana fame. Photograph by Anne-Marie Michel/London Entertainment.

Perhaps part of the appeal for young audiences is a warding-off of what they see as the over-sexualized older body, seemingly on display everywhere.

These films have been successful worldwide; the magazines oscillate between calling the stars by their on-screen names and their 'real' names. The youth market is also responsible for another extraordinary franchise success, but this time the fans are slightly older, in the twelve-and-upwards age range. The *Twilight Saga* films, based on a series of novels about a young girl who becomes involved with a handsome high

Figure 16   Maybe a sharp suit will ensure a career after *High School Musical* for its star Zac Ephron. Photograph by Anne-Marie Michel.

school vampire, have made stars out of Robert Pattinson, nicknamed R-Patz or R-Pattz, and Kristen Stewart. These films, too, ward off adult sexuality through the plotline itself—for, if the heroine sleeps with the vampire, she will die and be reborn, herself, as a vampire. Furthermore, the vampire hero lives by the codes of conduct with which he grew up a hundred years earlier. He believes in courtship, engagement and in formally asking a father for his consent to the marriage of his daughter.

R-Patz became so popular by 2010 that he had to have extra space created for his waxwork figure in Madame Tussauds. To accommodate his many young fans, Brad Pitt and Tom Cruise had to be moved much closer together and crowded into a corner (see 'RPattz Waxwork' 2010). Meanwhile, two ranges of DuWop *Twilight* makeup went on sale: the Volturi range for the teen market and the more upmarket Luna Twilight range, together with a Nox Twilight nail polish range (all available via Twilight Beauty, twilightbeauty.com). The tie-in still lives, but now it is linked to a different demographic.

Lastly—ironically, as we will see in ensuing chapters—the medium of cinema is being used to show off entirely new fashion stars, people who are already celebrities within the fashion industry and who have now entered the public domain—Anna Wintour, Patricia Field, Valentino and Coco Chanel.

–5–

'Fashion Films': From *Prêt-à-Porter* to *A Single Man*

Product placement can operate most effectively and in quite new ways within our changed celebrity culture. The case studies that make up this chapter consist of films where the fashion presence is central and celebrity-linked in a completely new way. In fact, fashion, somehow personified and here walking hand-in-hand, if not hand-in-glove, with the luxury brand, is perhaps the real star of this new, and so far seemingly unrecognized, cinematic category.

Prêt-à-Porter, directed by Robert Altman, was released in 1994. Its several storylines were set against the background of Paris Fashion Week, while the film was made with the cooperation of many leading figures within the industry, who presumably thought it would provide them with positive publicity in a way that would guarantee artistic respectability. The late Robert Altman, a talented and maverick director who operated for more than a decade outside the American studio system, had recognized art-house credentials and acclaimed auteur status, particularly in France. Furthermore, the film's cast included a small number of well-established Hollywood stars, including Julia Roberts, the best-paid actress of the early 1990s. Also involved were old-style European stars Sophia Loren, Marcello Mastroianni and Anouk Aimée, together with Richard E. Grant from *Withnail and I* (1987, dir. Bruce Robinson). Finally, given Altman's reputation for quirky casting choices, the American country singer Lyle Lovett also appeared as a Texan boot manufacturer and millionaire (also see Bruzzi 1997: 31–33).

Lastly, the script involved the on-screen presence of various leading couturiers as *themselves,* plus the extra promotional opportunity provided by the garments they provided for the *fictional* Paris designers of Altman's story to show, as if their own, on the catwalk. Most notable were the Vivienne Westwood clothes shown on the catwalk and 'designed' by Richard E. Grant's character, English designer Cort Romney, who is himself dressed in full Westwood regalia throughout, his look completed by bright red lipstick, heavily gelled hair and a kiss curl.

The film failed dismally at the box office, grossing $5,860,483 in the United States and £1,120,302 in the UK (IMBD, imdb.com). This, I would suggest, is because it was in fact ahead of its time in a commercial sense and thus it was only cinéastes, those who were already aware of Altman as auteur, who liked the film. Yet recently we have seen the commercial success, worldwide, of what are arguably less interesting and innovative American films, but which similarly both showcase and rely upon both the fashion industry and top luxury brands. The first ten years of the new millennium have seen *The Devil Wears Prada* (2006, dir. David Frankel), *Confessions of a Shopaholic* (2009, dir. PJ Hogan) and *Sex and the City: The Movie* (2008, dir. Michael Patrick King), together with its sequel, *Sex and the City 2,* released in 2010 and also directed by King. *Confessions of a Shopaholic* met with quite respectable box-office returns (US gross $44,277,350), but the other three films earned enormous sums of money across the world. *The Devil Wears Prada* grossed $124,732,962 at the US box office and *Sex and the City: The Movie* still more—$152,647,258, in fact (see IMDB). The impressive financial rewards meant that the first feature-length film of *Sex and the City* was followed by the second, rather less successful, film (US gross according to IMDB: $95,328,937).

It seemed that *Prêt-à-Porter* had unwittingly set up a series of tropes which would to come to characterize these later films: the appearance of real designers as themselves, the shots of their runway shows within the cinematic narrative, the appearance of recognizable supermodels and other fashion-friendly celebrities, the use of fashionable locations and settings, the interiors of well-known shops and finally the centrality of luxury brand names and their now-recognizable logos as reference points, even as characters in their own right. The only thing which *Prêt-à-Porter* lacked was the presence of Patricia Field, who organized the costuming of all the other films.

The real designers who participated in *Prêt-à-Porter* are interviewed on camera after each show, as are the film's fictional couturiers, by the film's equally fictional television reporter, Kitty Potter (Kim Basinger). But this first film was made rather too soon to attract large audiences; it appeared just before the ballooning of celebrity culture and the linked growth of designer literacy. Were it to be remade today, with fashion once again as the leading lady and luxury brands in the same supporting roles, but with younger Hollywood stars cast in the parts then played by Julia Roberts and Tim Robbins, it might fare quite differently at the box office. Today, there would be no need to change the title to *Ready to Wear* in order not to confuse American audiences; it was, however, thought necessary in 1994.

In 1994, anxious to garner publicity, the leading fashion houses and luxury brands were very happy to participate. To read the credits as they scroll endlessly up the screen in the closing moments of the film, to the strains of *La vie en rose,* sung by Edith Piaf, is, in fact, to read a 'Who's Who' of contemporary fashion designers and desirable brand names, most of which would were to be acquired in the next decade by the mega-conglomerates LVMH and PPR. The credits of all the later, Field-styled films work in exactly the same way, with a list funnelling up the screen of those whose fashionable products and locations have been shown; *Sex and the City 2* is the only exception.

In *Prêt-à-Porter,* the fictional fashion editors from New York and London, together with leading American buyers, arrive at the Ritz with full sets of Louis Vuitton luggage, while within the narrative, carrier bags proudly show off the names of well-known designers, and they crop up endlessly within the dialogue. One seminal scene involves a Bulgari jewellery show as backdrop to a disastrous dinner party.

The world of fashion we see here is perhaps slightly demented; certainly intrigue and treachery dominate—but it is also, through its very on-screen presence under the direction of a very skilled filmmaker, both alluring and visually fascinating. Kitty Potter eventually walks out, saying she has 'had it with this fucking fruitcake scene', and hands both her job and microphone to Chiara Mastroianni's ingénue journalist. This reaction is prompted by the last fashion show of the film: the fictional designer, Simone Lo (Anouk Aimée), whose own son has sold her business behind her back to the Texan boot manufacturer, sends a host of naked models down the runway in revenge, with a pregnant, naked bride wearing only a veil to round off the show. Yes, the silly fashion flock stand up to applaud this 'Emperor's New Clothes' moment; but this image is not the most resonant of the closing shots. For they include the stunning sight of Sophia Loren, wearing vintage Dior, as she does for much of the latter half of the film, while the very last image is that of a spinning dancer, a mime artiste with painted face and top hat, who, as the fashion-loaded credits scroll up the screen, twirls across the catwalk to the closing song, which for many of the fashion literate might evoke the Paris of Audrey Hepburn.

As the newly chic, Givenchy-clad chauffeur's daughter in *Sabrina Fair* (1954, dir. Billy Wilder), Hepburn sits at a desk on her last night in the city, writing a letter which she reads aloud. Behind her, the open window is a frame for the silhouette of the cathedral of Sacré Coeur, and we can hear the accordion music from the street below. She explains that the unseen busker is playing *La vie en rose*; this, she rather liberally translates to us, the audience, is 'a song that means we should always look at life through rose-coloured spectacles'. Today, to use a Hepburn reference of any kind, however indirect, is always to invoke the ultra-fashionable. But at the time of *Prêt-à-Porter*'s release in 1994, the public weren't as designer-aware, or as fashion-hungry, as they now seem to be—or as they were when the next 'fashion film' came along, *The Devil Wears Prada* in 2006. It seems ironic that Altman, always proud of his outsider status, should have unknowingly created what could be described as a new genre, and one far more commercial than any of its predecessors. He died before the second film was made; we do not know whether or not he would have agreed with this hypothesis.

The Devil Wears Prada was an adaptation of the novel of the same name by Lauren Weisberger (2003), who had been a personal assistant to Anna Wintour at US *Vogue*: although denied by the author, it has been speculated widely that the central character was modelled on the author's experiences of her former employer (also see Mitchell and Reid-Walsh 2008: 230). For the film, however, a number of significant changes were made to make the portrait of the fashion world more seductive—or, as Patricia Field says in the DVD feature, 'more respectful to fashion'.

Field, once a marginal player who owned and ran two shops in New York, had become a household name with *Sex and the City,* the HBO series (see Bruzzi and Church Gibson 2004), which ran for eight years and made Sarah Jessica Parker into both a fashion icon and a celebrity; we will examine the franchise, so central to the fashion-celebrity alliance, in the following chapter. Field and Parker together helped to make a whole generation aware of luxury brand names and so created a demand for these new fashion films, partly to fill the void left by the demise of the television series.

The director of *The Devil Wears Prada,* David Frankel, had worked on multiple episodes of the *Sex and the City* series; the cameraman was Florien Bauhaus, whose characteristic style, developed on the series and marked by mid-shots of young women criss-crossing the streets of Manhattan, now instantly evokes that television show. It also rekindles the relationship between fashion and the city of New York first created in *Breakfast at Tiffany's* (1961, dir. Blake Edwards). The brownstone in which Carrie lives evokes that of Audrey Hepburn's character, Holly Golightly, while the sidewalks she strolls, and the yellow cabs she hails, were first made visually memorable by Hepburn in the opening moments of that film. Very soon, they were as much in demand for international fashion shoots as Parisian boulevards or Italian squares (Church Gibson 2006b). The camera, in both the *Sex and the City* series and *The Devil Wears Prada* film, also moves down the female body to show off designer shoes; Frankel calls this movement the 'Florien tilt' in the DVD feature 'NYC and Fashion'.

When this particular film was first screened on British TV, in February 2010, it was instantly followed by the very first television screening of the behind-the-scenes documentary made at US *Vogue* in 2009, *The September Issue.*

In the fictional world of *Runway* magazine, Meryl Streep plays the fashion editor referred to by her staff as the Dragon Lady or the Ice Queen. Here, Streep, like Wintour, has a trademark bob and dark glasses, a clipped manner and a slight interrogative inflection to her speech. Her white office, crisply modern and full of black-and-white photographs, seems deliberately designed to evoke the real editor's office which we see in *The September Issue.*

The casting of Meryl Streep was central to the commercial and critical success of *The Devil Wears Prada,* not only because of her unparalleled acting ability but also because of her particular form of celebrity status. Streep is not usually associated with off-screen glamour, but rather with excellent performances, and so she bestowed upon this mythical fashion editor the cultural capital accrued across her long career, thus giving the fictional Miranda Priestly a gravitas that might otherwise have been absent. Her on-screen image and voice have changed radically from film to film, so as to inform and inhabit each of the parts she has played over the last twenty years.

However, not only does her unquestionable talent give a serious edge to any project with which she is involved; it is also significant that she had already managed to make two very different commodities instantly desirable. After her performance in *Out of Africa* (1985, dir. Sydney Pollack), the sales of that year's 'safari look' fashions were guaranteed (also see Mayer 2002), while in a completely different commercial sphere, Kenyan tourism suddenly boomed quite dramatically. This phenomenon was intensified after the commercial and critical success of *The Devil Wears Prada.* The Greek island of Skopelos used as the location for *Mamma Mia!* (2008, dir. Phyllida Lloyd) instantly became a popular holiday destination; the mountaintop church where the film's wedding takes place received endless requests from couples anxious to marry there (also see Moir 2008; Brabant 2009). Finally, a repackaged Julia Child cookbook (Child 2001) entered the American bestseller charts after Streep played the 1950s chef in *Julie and Julia* (2009).

With Streep as the villainess, Field as costume supervisor and a clever screenplay that made the rather irritating self-pity of the novel far more palatable, the film seemed destined to trump the book. Frankel's clever direction ensured this by making sure that, in every single way, the visual allure of the fashion world was emphasized from start to finish. The film may pretend, as it shows us the havoc wrought in the heroine's life by her new job, that it disapproves of *Runway* magazine, of its terrified stick-thin assistants, their tyrannical editor and the overall ethics of the fashion world. However, all this is completely undercut by the visual style: the way the camera lingers on and even caresses the beauty of both heroine and supporting cast, the endless parading and voyeuristic glimpses of desirable clothes, the glamour of the settings throughout and finally their slick, stylish, highly polished portrayal through clever camerawork and cinematography. The film's narrative does depict all the problems created for the heroine by her new job in this alien environment, but it also emphasizes through the seductive work of the camera the splendid changes wrought in her appearance. Already a very pretty girl when she starts her job at *Runway,* though padded out and wearing what seems to be a tousled wig, the star looks completely stunning once the fashion world has transformed her (see Jeffers McDonald 2010: 166–197; Sheridan 2010: 2).

The film begins with a montage of the *Runway* girls dressing for work, intercut throughout with shots of the heroine's rather more casual toilette, which Jeffers McDonald discusses in some detail (2010: 178). I would suggest that the shots of the *Runway* staff, in which we see glimpses of black lace underwear, sheer black stockings, leopard-print knickers, and where eyelash curlers are wielded with such extraordinary efficiency, are in fact crafted so as to resemble a commercial for some fashion-related product. The interwoven footage of our heroine, by contrast, is seemingly intended to look like French New Wave footage, even cinéma-vérité. Andy, played by Anne Hathaway, is seen carelessly pulling on a thick woolly jumper, picking up a nondescript satchel, chomping inelegantly on a bagel. The cleverly adapted screenplay has a number of in-jokes and fashion references that are actually missing from the original novel, including the casting of supermodel Gisele as editorial assistant Serena. It also now includes a French fashion editor, whose style of dress and self-presentation are obviously intended to suggest, to the initiated, Carine Roitfeld, then the fashion-celebrity editor of French *Vogue*. For Jacqueline Follet (Stephanie Szostak), the fictional editor of French *Runway* and part of this new plot strand developed specifically for the film, is in appearance and dress seemingly modelled on Roitfeld—funky, punky, slightly rock-chick—completely opposed to the classic elegance of Streep's Priestly. And the Manhattan writer and columnist who pursues our heroine, threatening her relationship with her long-term boyfriend, here has his name emblazoned along the side of a bus, just as Carrie Bradshaw/Candace Bushnell's name is displayed in the opening credits of the *Sex and the City* television series.

In the film, Anne Hathaway as Andy is beautiful but basically good-natured, put-upon and largely silent. However, the narrator within the novel tends to forfeit our sympathy by constantly reminding us that what she really deserves is a job on a 'proper' publication, the *New Yorker,* where she would actually write, rather than run endless errands for her boss. Weisberger's wish was granted—she did, in fact, land the post she coveted. But the critics of the *New Yorker* hated the book, calling it 'trivially self-dramatizing fiction'; they went on to praise the film:

> Bright, crisp and funny, the movie turns dish into art—or if not quite into art, then at least into the kind of dazzling commercial entertainment that Hollywood, in the days of George Cukor or Stanley Donen, used to turn out. (Denby 2006)

In the film, Andy eventually instigates her own fashion makeover, asking the art director Nigel (Stanley Tucci) to help her fit in, whatever it takes. She is told at her interview with Miranda: 'You don't read *Runway*—you have no style or sense of fashion—no, that isn't a question'. She did not, luckily, hear what Nigel had to say when she first appeared in the office: 'Who is that sad little person? Are we running a before and after piece that I don't know about?' But at first she doesn't care, thinking herself superior to the rules of fashion and quite able to function through her talent alone. Her supercilious giggle of derision during a lengthy staff deliberation about the best belt to use in a shoot prompts a caustic but informative lecture from Streep's character—again, not in the book—about the way in which the fashion system actually works. It has, in fact, dictated the very colour of the cerulean-blue jersey she is herself wearing, 'no doubt...fished out of some clearance bin'. But finally, chided for her seeming incompetence, she is driven to seek help and asks Nigel what she must do. The answer, of course, is to adapt and conform.

Nigel marches her through 'the Closet', and, as they walk through this Aladdin's Cave, where the clothes called in for shoots are kept, he enunciates the names of the designers clearly and carefully—for the audience as well as for Andy—as he selects garments and accessories from the treasure trove (for a very detailed description of this makeover see Jeffers McDonald 2010: 181–3). The camera—and the audience—can follow her awed, newly reverent gaze as she studies the luxury brands with new interest. Nigel's very last pronouncement before he hands her over to the beauty department is, 'Chanel—you're in dire need of Chanel.' When we see her again, both she and the cameraman display their delight in the work that has been done; she swishes her newly cut hair proudly, even smugly, as she strides back into her office in her over-the-knee Chanel boots. But the most significant moment is perhaps that when the world's best-paid model—Gisele, of all people, masquerading here as Serena—tells her approvingly and truthfully, 'You look good', as she appraises the boots, the Chanel jacket and jewellery, the transformed hair and expertly applied makeup.

However, in the original novel, the heroine clings stubbornly to her own clothes. Finally, the embarrassed young man who looks after 'the Closet' surreptitiously hands her a bag of clothes and shoes. This is an ultimatum, as he explains: 'Um—people, like, aren't very happy with this *Gap* thing you've got going on' (Weisberger 2003: 132; italics added). In the film, the best friend of the novel is turned from a white 'grad student' into a black artist, who grows to distrust her friend, finally berating her for her new indifference: 'I don't know you—this *glamazon* you've become.' Earlier, however, she has squealed with pleasure, naming and pricing the Marc Jacobs handbag from the Closet that Andy gives her. In the novel, this same best friend ends up in a coma and so brings the heroine to her senses; here, the young journalist simply decides to leave Paris and to abandon the job.

The cinematic montage that marks the editor's arrival in the office every morning, as she throws a variety of coats across Andy's desk to be hung up (the credits thank Dries van Noten, Prada, Oscar de la Renta, Bill Blass and Calvin Klein among others), not only marks the passage of time; it also shows off these garments to great advantage. A similar montage is again used to suggest Andy's new life across a period of time, through a display of different designer outfits, all equally becoming to the heroine and shown off as she moves through and across the streets: the sidewalk-as-catwalk concept so familiar from *Sex and the City* is here reworked to great effect.

Here, there is a new celebrity ingredient in the 'fashion film' recipe, for we hear a member of the *Runway* team mention 'Gwyneth's second cover' and we see all those staples originally, inadvertently created by Altman and arguably reinforced within the television series of *Sex and the City:* the verbal designer namechecking, the surfeit of visual product placement, the authentic fashion locations of studio and catwalk. At Valentino's show, Valentino appears as *himself;* he was the only real designer to do so.

The ending is changed to make it cinematically more palatable. Here, Andy has the job she always wanted, but her estranged boyfriend does, in fact, suggest, 'I'm sure we could work something out.' In the book, however, she has her new career as a writer but no chance of any reconciliation with him. In the film, Emily (played by Emily Blunt), Miranda's first assistant, whose longed-for visit to Paris was stolen from her by our heroine, is slightly mollified; Andy gives her every single garment and accessory she has acquired there. In the novel, Andy sells them all to help finance her new, fledgling career.

Interestingly, the outfit Andy puts together for herself at the very end of the film, where we see her start a serious journalistic career, bears no relation *either* to her very first look or her ultra-fashionable *Runway* outfits. There is a parallel here with the costuming at the end of *Pretty Woman* (1990, dir. Garry Marshall), the ultimate transformation-through-shopping film, where Julia Roberts seems to have created for herself her very own look of blazer-over-jeans and crisp white T-shirt, with a possible nod to Princess Diana's off-duty look. Here, Roberts as Vivienne has rejected both her original how-to-attract-the-punters garb of miniskirt and patent boots and has also spurned the chic clothes which Richard Gere's billionaire helped her to select. Andy also has a seemingly original and self-created, smart-casual style. But like Julia's final look, it's not anti-fashion. For in this film and others like it, fashion itself has become a star, indeed a celebrity—and so must be placated.

The real Anna Wintour and the real world of the high-fashion magazine will appear in a later chapter, but a line of dialogue might be quoted here to close this critique:

> She saw the pictures and she doesn't want Chanel or Hilary. So I think we're done with Chanel *and* Hilary.

This is a snippet of nonfictional conversation from the fly-on-the-wall documentary of 2008 and *not* from the feature film of 2006, showing that it can be very difficult, where the fashion industry is concerned, to distinguish between its own hyperbole and fictional attempts at parody. This was another difficulty which Altman faced. But, as I have argued, Altman was ahead of his time; where his film failed, *The Devil Wears Prada* triumphed. It can be found towards the end in a list of the two hundred top-grossing films of all time (see IMDB). Streep was nominated for various rather prestigious awards.

At this juncture, the idea of the fashion film as a safe money-spinner was finally understood by Hollywood power brokers; the next to be made, again styled by Field, was *Sex and the City: The Movie* in 2008. The stylist is, of course, still best-known for her work on *Sex and the City*: the television series made her well-known and successful, even a celebrity herself, while the move to the big screen no doubt made her extremely rich. This transfer I would like to discuss in the following chapter, since *Sex and the City* is not only the best-known fashion franchise, making its four stars into fashion celebrities; more significantly, the franchise in its entirety also affords a chance to look at the different ways in which television and film showcase, or create, fashion and celebrity (also see Bruzzi and Church Gibson 2004).

So here, then, we must move on to the wardrobe Field assembled from the now-always-available pool of designers for *Confessions of a Shopaholic,* directed by P. J. Hogan in 2009. Here, the plotline again involved the world of magazine journalism. But this time, we are in the offices of a small, very serious financial magazine whose aim is to guide the consumer and where the heroine, rather like her predecessor in *The Devil Wears Prada,* reluctantly accepts a job just because it may get her closer to her ideal. Here she actually *wants* to work for the fashion glossy *Alette,* here presented as another *Runway;* she is at her happiest in the cathedrals of consumption, the chic stores along New York's Fifth Avenue, spending money she does not have on designer clothes and accessories she does not need.

This film—as the title would suggest—shows us the fashion world from a rather different perspective. It was, again, an adaptation, this time of the 'chick-lit' novels written by Sophie Kinsella (2001, 2002, 2004, 2009). But as it was directed by Hogan, who achieved fame with *Muriel's Wedding* (1994), it is an equally dark, ambivalent 'comedy'. He employed the indefatigable Field to give the film both fashion credibility and box-office appeal, and although there was no Streep, Hathaway or Emily Blunt, it made quite a respectable showing financially (see IMDB).

This film is peculiarly obnoxious because Becky (Isla Fisher), the shopaholic of the title, has run up several thousand pounds worth of debt on her various credit cards. So, too, have many young women in 'developed' countries, where unsecured personal debt is on the increase; the figures are alarming (Hickman 2006). This is important within the particular context of this book; it is the new fashion-yoked and label-dominated celebrity culture that has worked to speed up change and accelerate *constant,* as well as conspicuous, consumption through its relentless magazine and Internet presentation of fashion stars strutting along in their Louboutins, the new season's Louis Vuitton scarves around their necks, proudly toting the latest Fendi bags.

However, here the humour of the film is actually based on the many situations where the heroine tries to avoid the debt collector who has been assigned the impossible task of collecting all the money she owes. The actor Robert Stanton, who plays the noxiously named Derek Smeath, is styled to look as unappetizing and unattractive as possible. He is not to gain any of our sympathy—that must stay with spendthrift Becky. Eventually, she does, in fact, pay her debts, but she is seen as somehow the victim during their lengthy cat-and-mouse games. We are, it seems, intended to be firmly on her side as she fabricates yet another ludicrous lie, or scampers down back alleys to avoid him.

Finally, he traps her. But although she loses her job, the man she loves and her long-suffering best friend, in the closing scene everything is magically restored to her. Although briefly penniless, friendless, loveless and unemployed, she finally triumphs—but not, however, within the world of fashion, which she has learned to treat with caution. She is actually offered her ideal job, the opportunity to write a column for *Alette,* by Kristin Thomas's

Figure 17 The elegant actress Kristin Scott Thomas was cast as the fictional editor of a top fashion magazine in *Confessions of a Shopaholic*. Photograph by Anne-Marie Michel.

waspish fashion editor, who again has both bobbed hair and frosty manner. However, Becky turns her down and instead sells all the clothes she owns, so settling all her debts.

She ends the film instead with the love of the hero and the goodwill of her best friend, whose trust she consistently abused and whose bridesmaid's outfit she managed to lose through her wish to wear a St Laurent dress in a television interview. The bridesmaid's dress recovered, she turns up at her friend's wedding; all is instantly for-given. As she walks away from the Fifth Avenue church after the service, cured of her addiction, the mannequins in the store windows, who have whispered to her through-out the film, beckoning her in, holding up objects with which to entice her, now try for one last time to gain her attention. But sensibly she averts her eyes, and they all break into applause as she walks past them without stopping to look or enter the shops, completely reformed. Only then does the boss/boyfriend whom she formerly deceived, played by Hugh Dancy, suddenly appear before her—with a brand-new job to give her.

Earlier in the film, she visits a luxury brand shop with him. Finding that he, in fact, understands exactly what is on offer there, and could actually afford all these expen-sive, flattering clothes, she turns to him in surprise: 'You talk Prada?' Yes, he does, he explains, but he doesn't want to be defined by labels; she is bemused. But once again, although both heroine and storyline seem finally to reject the temptations of fashion and the lure of the brand name, we have by then seen enough stylish clothes and extravagant outfits to have had our fashion cake and so be sated. The film bears all the Field trademarks; the outfits are often quirky, mixing up styles, colours and pat-terns, combining different designers throughout, sometimes adding a dash of vintage. There is the now familiar dropping of designer names and the endless sightings of their clothes in all the shops she visits. This film follows the patterning set up by the earlier fashion films; however, the precise long-term future of this particular template is rather difficult to predict.

I would like now to move from what I have suggested is a novel, possibly transient genre to a study of the director—the auteur—in this new cinematic landscape, and to examine various developments there, many of which combine fashion and celebrity in new and still evolving ways.

FASHION, CELEBRITY AND A NEW AUTEURISM?

> Tom Ford has a huge loyal following. Any *Vogue* reader, *GQ, Elle, Vanity Fair*...they all know who he is, and there's always hot anticipation for the next thing he does. I thought he was very marketable.
>
> —Hugo Grumbar, head of Icon Distribution in the United Kingdom
> (Clark 2010: 9)

Before the era when celebrity culture joined forces with fashion, young would-be film-makers, particularly in England, learned their craft through the making of television commercials. Ridley Scott was one of these young men; he took what he had learned in the demanding field of the two- or three-minute sell and set off on a twenty-year Hollywood career, from *Alien* (1979) to *Gladiator* (2000) and beyond. Today, however, with the financial power of the luxury fashion houses, there are new ironies; now, it seems, fashion commands and film dutifully follows. Director David Lynch has some credible art-house credentials; his career began with the extraordinary, surreal and disturbing low-budget movie *Eraserhead* (1976), and he became much better known with the critical success of his film *Blue Velvet* (1986), which exposed the underbelly of American suburbia long before *Desperate Housewives.* This film opens with the sight of a brightly coloured fire engine moving slowly past a white picket fence. Lynch then went on to make prime-time television both innovative and unsettling with the very successful series *Twin Peaks* (1990–1991).

He then returned to making films and was, it seems, gradually seduced by fashion. He worked with his then-partner, the model Isabella Rossellini, on *Blue Velvet;* she subsequently accepted a multimillion-dollar contract to be the face of Lançome. She was one of the first celebrity faces chosen by a makeup firm to front a major international advertising campaign.

Lynch has since worked with the designer Agnès B. Her clothes were first seen on screen when Quentin Tarantino, without consulting the designer herself, bought outfits from her shop for his film *Pulp Fiction* (1994). Uma Thurman donned a simple black trouser suit and a classic white shirt for her date with John Travolta in a lurid 1950s-themed diner; discarding the jacket to enter a dance contest, the simplicity of the clothes was visually striking against the extraordinary backdrop and the ice-cream-sundae colours that dominated the décor. In Tarantino's next film, *Jackie Brown* (1997), the designer was made an official part of the team, and her name was shown in the credits. She later worked with Lynch on the film *Mulholland Drive* (2001) and then on his rather less successful *Inland Empire* (2006).

Agnès B was proud of this collaboration, putting blown-up stills from the second film in the interiors of her shops across Europe during the period of its release and distribution—though, unlike the classic Hollywood tie-ins, the pictures were not of striking outfits worn by the stars. Instead, they showed the giant rabbits who inexplicably haunt the screen throughout.

For whatever reason, Lynch is aware of the power of and willing to accept the rewards promised by fashion. In this new era, he has been seduced into making scent commercials for Gucci and Dior. He has also worked with the Oscar-winning French film star Marion Cotillard and designer John Galliano to publicize the Lady Dior handbag. The Hong Kong director Wong Kar-Wai—whose sensuous flooding of the screen with colour infused in *In the Mood for Love* (2000)—has also been persuaded to make scent commercials for Dior, one of which starred Sharon Stone (2005), and another for Lançome in 2007. Kar-Wai is not shackled by puritan scruples; he has also made commercials for cars (BMW), for a flat-screen TV and has directed a mini-film for 'Soft Finance' starring Brad Pitt.

The director Baz Luhrmann followed the success of his 'Red Carpet Trilogy', *Strictly Ballroom* (1992), *Romeo + Juliet* (1996) and the musical *Moulin Rouge* (2001), with an extremely expensive commercial for Chanel No. 5. Here, he employed Nicole Kidman, the star of his film *Moulin Rouge,* to portray a reluctant celebrity, briefly fleeing the paparazzi to join her lover on the rooftops of Paris. She is seen clinging to two vast interlinked neon letters atop a building; here, the Chanel logo, rather than the Moulin Rouge windmill, dominates the night sky. The House of Chanel obviously believed that this tie-in between feature film and commercial was worth repeating. They employed the director Jean-Pierre Jeunet to make a mini-narrative set on the Orient Express and starring Audrey Tatou, who had become famous in Jeunet's film *Amélie* (2001). Through yet another irony, the making and release of the No. 5 commercial overlapped with Tatou's role as Chanel herself in the film *Coco avant Chanel* (2009). Meanwhile, the highly avant-garde director Kenneth Anger was actually tempted out of retirement to make a commercial; he accepted an invitation to make a short promotional film for Missoni in 2010.

But all this is dwarfed by the most recent mode of collaboration between fashion house and film; now the power of celebrity and fashion combined can create between them a new director for feature films, *not* merely for commercials; designer Tom Ford can, it seems, change career. He has always been very much a designer-as-celebrity, always pictured in magazine coverage at social events—openings, launches, parties, shows—and has carefully courted publicity. He greatly enjoyed the fuss generated by the Gucci advertisement of 2003 (see Cozens 2003), in which model Carmen Kass pulls down her pale blue knickers to reveal that her pubic hair is shaved into the shape of the Gucci logo. A young, rather androgynous-looking boy kneels on the ground before her, his face bent to kiss this logo. Ford claimed that he had not simply come up with both the idea and the final image, but that he had actually shaved the model's hair for the shoot himself. Two years earlier, when working as the creative director for Yves St Laurent, he had quite literally stopped traffic with vast billboards that showed off another provocative image, this time the one he had created for the new and notorious campaign for the house scent, Opium. The huge posters showed the alabaster-white, statuesque body of model Sophie Dahl, lying on her back, naked but for silver-strapped high heels and gently caressing her own nipple (see 'Offensive Opium Posters' 2000).

He went on in March 2006 to guest edit an issue of *Vanity Fair* and to place himself on the cover, seated behind Keira Knightley and a prone Scarlett Johansson. Whilst Ford was fully clothed, both women were totally naked, and the tableau was quite clearly designed to evoke Manet's controversial painting *Le déjeuner sur l'herbe* of 1863, banned by the Paris Salon and subsequently exhibited elsewhere.

His advertising campaigns became still more outrageous. One poster image showed a huge bottle of Tom Ford scent, sandwiched between the large silicone-enhanced breasts of a headless, naked model, as she is somehow managing to hoist the bottle skywards with her own hands. Another showed a similar bottle, this time held tightly between the thighs of yet another headless, naked woman, thus hiding her own genitals and rising up her stomach to play-act a gender swap.

Ford, who parted company with Gucci in 2004, went on to become the director of his own worldwide group of inordinately expensive menswear shops. Now enormously rich, he decided that he wanted to fulfil his lifelong ambition of being a film director (see Blanks 2009). He therefore secured the rights to Christopher Isherwood's 1960s novel *A Single Man,* which he adapted for the screen. He cast, directed and in every way oversaw the subsequent film, which was quite well-received, for the most part, and which saw his star, Colin Firth, nominated for a slew of awards. The screenplay Ford wrote involved a very liberal interpretation of the original book in order both to glamorize the text and to make a fashion film; the novel describes what may, perhaps, be the last day in the life of its protagonist, George, an English professor now living in California and mourning the recent death of Jim, his partner of sixteen years.

For a start, Ford shaved more than a decade from the hero's age in order to cast a much younger man. Also gone from the novel is a long sequence in which George visits a woman in hospital who is dying of cancer. This woman, Doris, once had a brief affair with his dead partner. This scene, where the now-skeletal Doris calls out for morphine, does not suit Ford's purposes; it is replaced by a short, striking sequence, invented by Ford, involving a Spanish rent boy who looks exactly like a male model.

The film is punctuated throughout by verbal and visual references to the Cuban missile crisis, even though the novel makes it quite clear that the crisis is now over (Isherwood 1964/2010: 81). Ford adds further drama to the film by introducing George's decision to shoot himself rather than live without Jim; we see him retrieving a handgun from the safety-deposit box of a bank, writing a number of farewell letters to friends and setting out the clothes in which he wishes his own body to be dressed for his funeral. But in the novel, George is proud of the very fact that he is a 'survivor' (83). His regular gym workout, intended to sustain this quality and described in detail, is also banished from the film. The last chapter of the novel suggests that, on that night or any other, he will nevertheless fall victim to a fatal heart attack. This we actually see on screen.

The novel has passages of great humour—George's interior monologues as he drives along the freeway to the university, for example. This is banished, though there is instead some gallows humour around the sleeping bag George sets out in preparation for his suicide and his tentative rehearsals in both bag and shower cubicle. But overall, the pathos is enhanced in every way—for example, George is invited to Jim's funeral in the novel but firmly excluded in the film. And the film's George is now firmly fashion-aware, not only in his own dress—mentioned perhaps twice in the book and then *en passant*—but in other, new ways. In the film, as he compliments a pretty secretary on her new upswept hairdo, he inhales her scent and asks 'Arpège?'

Of George's own clothes, Isherwood simply tells us that at his lecture, unlike the student audience, he wears 'neat dark clothes, a white shirt and tie—the only tie in the room' (Isherwood 1964/2010: 41). In the film, of course, Firth looks incredibly stylish throughout in his Tom Ford menswear.

Most significantly, to make the kind of film Ford wants, Charley, the divorced, heavy-drinking Englishwoman who is George's near neighbour, great friend and confidante, has undergone a transformation so total that only her name and her marital status remain unchanged. In the novel, Charley is overweight, with untidy hair and, indeed, an untidy home. Once, George suggests, she must have been 'adequately pretty'; now her 'cheeks are swollen and inflamed' (Isherwood 1964/2010: 96). She has a pronounced limp, the result of chronic arthritis (97). She is also far from rich—she came to America as a GI bride and her husband, Buddy, has abandoned her; she now lives alone in a house George describes as a 'small box' (95). Her home is 'more than somewhat oriental gift shop in décor' (95) with 'a small, cluttered, none-too-clean kitchen' (98).

As for Charley's dress sense, George thinks to himself that her ill-fitting peasant skirt and blouse make her look even more plump and solid; nevertheless, they do have 'a grotesque kind of gallantry' (96). But he does despair of her general slovenliness: 'If she must wear sandals with bare feet, why won't she make up her toenails?' (96).

In the film, toenails, fingernails and face are most carefully made up; we see this task being carried out across most of the film's fictional day. Everything about Charley's much younger, totally transformed cinematic incarnation is polished, buffed and shining. In the film, she—and her home—are stylish beyond belief. Her prefab, that simple rectangular box, becomes a sizeable neocolonial mansion. Absentee husband Buddy has also been substantially altered, becoming the very affluent Richard, just as Jim has become a successful architect rather than an amiable man whose main interest was his home menagerie, which includes a mynah bird, a raccoon, some skunks and several king snakes. They, too, have been replaced, in this case by a pair of pedigree English fox terriers.

Ford cast Julianne Moore as Charley, and, for their dinner à deux, in her own home, he dressed her in a black-and-white vintage-looking dress created with his initial guidance by the costume designer Arianne Phillips. Charley and the black-clad George now stand out boldly against the silks and sofas of her home, where all is taupe, cream and beige, even the piled, subtly patterned cushions. There are gilt-framed mirrors, elegant lamps, floor-length curtains of heavy silk and tasteful abstract art on the walls; there is no 'clutter' or 'oriental gift shop décor' here, only very expensive, rather bland good taste.

Ford makes everything as visually pleasing as possible, even the student Kenny. In the novel we are told that he 'might have been conventionally handsome if he didn't have a beaky nose' (43); here, he is portrayed by the good-looking, even-featured

Nicholas Hoult. Kenny's explicit desire to explore his sexuality and even seduce George is also absent from the novel; there is definitely a frisson there, a flirtation, but the novel's Kenny is not on the same overt mission that Ford creates for him. There is, too, a suggestion in the film that Firth's George and Kenny might have a future together; when George wakes up, he finds Kenny fast asleep on the sofa, clutching the gun he must have secretly confiscated. Seemingly redeemed, George burns his suicide notes and returns, smiling, to bed—only to be struck down by death. The novel's Kenny disappears into the night while George is asleep, and after his romantic and sexual involvement with Lois has been firmly established. Ford has made all these changes so that the film may be not only less distressing—no cancer-ridden patients, no overweight arthritic women, even the glimpse of a positive future—but also infinitely more stylish and better adorned in every way, from houses to cars to women to young men. The architect-designed home in which George lives, all amber, glass and golden wood, is Ford's invention: Isherwood's George lives in a small house, 'shaggy with ivy and dark and secret looking' (10). The cinematic living room is spacious and has enormous windows; the living room in the novel is 'low, damp, and dark' (9).

Ford set about casting his film with the same piratical abandon he displayed in his successful 'fashion' career. He has been relatively modest about the film's success, saying he owes a huge debt of gratitude to the 'great team' with whom he worked (Pulver 2010; Blanks 2009). But he has not been overwhelmed, either, by the fact that the film has been nominated for various prestigious awards; his main actor, Colin Firth, won a Golden Globe and was nominated for a Best Actor award at the Oscars. Ford did not seem especially humble—rather, he congratulated himself on his own foresight in seizing Firth and likened it to 'closing a fashion deal: I just jumped on a plane, meal handshake boom boom—just like fashion—Julianne Moore the same' (Pulver 2010). An alternative narrative has Ford meeting Firth quite by chance, at a party hosted by Madonna, after he had already completed the casting of his film—and instantly changing his mind (Clark 2010).

In fact, Firth's performance was extraordinary, but what should we make of this overly stylish film? Is it possible for fashion, brand potency and celebrity status to overwhelm all notions of apprenticeship? In fact, the film is so visually sumptuous as to be curiously sterile. Ford's approach seems more akin to that of a stylist; every period detail is accurate, right down to the pink Cocktail Sobranie cigarettes smoked by Charley. In interview (Clark 2010), Ford stresses this particular need for exactly the right detail—for example, he made sure that Firth was wearing Creed's Bois du Portugal aftershave, created in 1957 and apparently favoured by Frank Sinatra, since that was the scent 'his' George would select. Isherwood's hero seems to eschew such things; he is a traditional academic, rather than a world-famous performer. But when Ford organized George's wardrobe, the jackets he created had sewn inside them 'labels from the right Savile Row tailor, with the date' (Clark 2010).

This kind of elaborate, unseen preparation is also familiar to us from the work of contemporary Method actors, including Daniel Day-Lewis, Dustin Hoffman and Robert de Niro, who famously rejected the Armani suits worn by the cast of *The Untouchables* (1987, dir. Brian De Palma). For his very brief cameo as Al Capone, he insisted on going to Capone's own tailor to be provided with his pinstriped suit (Bruzzi 1997: 28). And having read in some biography that Capone always wore pure silk underwear, de Niro allegedly went to Bloomingdale's and purchased some for himself in order properly to inhabit the role.

Ford's approach is not, then, that of a traditional film director. The finished film rather resembles a series of commercials; it contains a number of different vignettes, each with a particular visual feel. The sequence with Carlos, the strikingly good-looking Spanish hustler, with his quiff and immaculate white T-shirt, takes place in the parking lot of a liquor store and looks very like the famous retro-styled Levis commercials, made in the mid-1980s but set in a mythical early 1960s America. They increased the sales of the brand by an extraordinary 200 per cent; interestingly, they were not screened in America, only in Europe, but they are certainly known to all with any knowledge of the history of fashion-related advertising. Here, Carlos's rolled-up jeans expose black boots, just in case we miss the references to James Dean in the film's dialogue. As the sequence develops, the screen finally becomes suffused with a deep pink as the sun sets.

The lighting and the colours change from sequence to sequence; the attention to the details of filmmaking is there—but it is Tom Ford's own luxury brand detail. Tom Ford menswear is shown off throughout, while the scent bottles on Julianne Moore's dressing table are vintage Estée Lauder *Youth Dew* bottles of the period; now the brand is owned and has been reinvigorated by Ford (see Turin and Sanchez 2008).

Nicolas Hoult's Kenny is fascinated in a personal rather than in a more detached, intellectual way (as in the novel) by a professor he correctly assumes to be gay. He is very taken with the lecture we see as we move through this day in George's life; Firth/George abandons any attempt to control the rambling discussion around Aldous Huxley's novel *After Many a Summer* and substitutes, as in the novel, his own polemic on 'difference'. But when we first see the *cinematic* Kenny, before the lecture, the camera and George's eye catch him, sprawled on the grass, next to his blonde friend, Lois. She looks exactly like 1990s supermodel Claudia Schiffer, who herself has deliberately recreated as her trademark look the style of the young Brigitte Bardot—just part of the film's knowing visual self-referentiality; Isherwood's Lois is, in fact, Japanese. And Kenny is wearing a white angora sweater and tight white slacks, definitely gay signifiers of the period (Cole 2010), but here part of a Tom Ford range. We notice not only his greenish-blue eyes and youthful good looks, but also the soft texture of this white Tom Ford sweater, just as we later notice the texture of the wooden dashboard and the leather seats in George's Mercedes. We have our attention caught throughout by design details and by surfaces. Richard Dyer famously said, in a *Sight and Sound* review of *The Remains of the Day* (1993, dir. Merchant Ivory), that he knew the film was flawed when he found himself more interested in Emma Thompson's patterned teacup than in the words she was saying (1994). But at least Merchant Ivory were not marketing the china seen on screen in the film.

As suggested, Ford's careful product placement and, too, his stylist's eye for detail are visible throughout. As a feature film director, however, rather than a fashion designer and a stylist of commercials, he is still finding his own authorial style. In his debut here, there is a good deal of what fashion journalists call 'channelling'. Here, the authorial styles and visual trademarks channelled by Ford are often ones we recognize. The couple who live opposite Firth/George remind us in their presentation of the characters in the television series *Mad Men.* And when their daughter suddenly appears before him in the drab brown-and-grey infused interior of his bank, and the camera pans up her body, from her shoes and white socks up her lurid turquoise dress to her blonde hair, the shot itself and the overall incongruity are reminiscent of the camerawork in Lynch's *Twin Peaks.* A black-and-white flashback to George and Jack sunbathing on rocks silhouetted sharply against the sky evokes the work of fashion photographers Bruce Weber and Herb Ritts. There are, too, slow-motion sequences which call to mind Sofia Coppola's debut, *The Virgin Suicides* (1999).

Above all, Ford seems to be influenced by the later films of director Wong Kar-Wai. In the mise en scène of Kar-Wai's film *In the Mood for Love* (2000), dress and décor seem to seep seamlessly into one another across the frame. The leading actress, Maggie Cheung, is dressed throughout the film in cheongsams which Kar-Wai had specially made from bolts of furnishing fabric he found in a warehouse in Hong Kong; they had been stored there since the early 1960s, the precise period when the film was set. He then filmed her, in some scenes, standing against patterned walls or curtains, also seemingly from the same period. In other sequences, he—and his cinematographer— saturate the screen with colour, just as Ford does: the shocking-pink sunset of the car lot sequence, the amber-coloured light that suffuses the screen in the flashback sequences in which we see Jack and which also permeates the very last scene, with Kenny, in George's home.

Perhaps the loving recreation of period detail—the cars, the clothes, the interiors, the products—rather dominates this film, made as it is by an inexperienced director, at the possible expense of in-depth motivation and portrayal of character. Only Firth, as George, is really successful here; without his strong central performance, the film could be rather slight. But is this perhaps overly puritan, to criticize the fact that a fashion designer has made a film that looks rather like a sequence of commercials? Or is it acceptable, since the designer has used the cinema to display many of his own products? The use of film as fashion showcase seems to have reached its logical conclusion; now, rather than put his or her products on screen in a film directed by somebody else, the fashion designer, if sufficiently celebrated, can simply set out to make his very own film-as-showcase. Here, Ford is not just letting us admire 'Tom Ford' style, to be fair; he is also showing off the physical beauty of his cast, the décor and design of the early 1960s and the acting ability of Firth, whose extraordinary performance somehow welds this film together.

Interestingly, there is one historical error—and it concerns menswear. Ford's George sets out his funeral attire carefully and puts a note on the garments, topped as they are by his tie of choice: 'Tie in a Windsor knot'. This would certainly be in keeping with the character Ford creates here, though not for Isherwood's George. But the stylist-director then makes a faux pas, sending George off to the university wearing a tiepin more in keeping with *Mad Men*'s Don Draper. A man who, in the grip of complete despair, could still be fastidious about the need for a Windsor knot would never, however long he had lived in America, adopt something as transatlantic as a tiepin.

The lasting impression, then, is a memory of the individual sequences and of a style best suited to the display of dress, décor and beauty; Ford is not yet an auteur. Afterwards, we might remember, too, the differing uses of light and colour—in George's grieving present, it's drained away almost to sepia as he dresses, drives to class, clears his office—but this convention is not wholly original. We might recollect the liquor store two-hander, the pinks and violets, the backdrop of the billboard advertising the forthcoming film *Psycho*. But overall there is a sense that Ford is learning, trying things out, making experiments. It seems not to matter, since he can certainly experiment on, in and with film when he himself is paying the bill. Yet he can only meet the costs *because* he is a famous fashion designer, and furthermore one with acknowledged celebrity status. This presumably encouraged those who became involved, in whatever way, with this project. But if undisputed auteur Wong Kar-Wai is happy to make Gucci commercials, can former Gucci supremo Tom Ford not direct a feature film? This would certainly be logical in the new, changed cinematic landscape.

Ford is very happy to link this feature film to his own real-life commercials; his summer 2010 eyewear campaign featured none other than Nicholas Hoult—now familiar to us as Kenny—modelling the new season's designer sunglasses. There are crucial differences, however, between the 'then' and the 'now'. In 1923 (see chapter 3), shoe designer Salvatore Ferragamo would never have envisaged replacing Cecil B. de Mille behind the camera. What he wanted was a talented director in whose film his shoes might make their appearance. He would never have thought of trying to replace him.

As I have said, film, more than any other medium within contemporary visual culture, is yoked to and reshaped by the different forms of celebrity and the new relationship between film and fashion. Ford is now working on another film. While the box office takings for *A Single Man* were modest in comparison to some of the other fashion films discussed in this chapter, sales of Tom Ford Menswear—and eyewear—have risen. When Ford returned to womenswear design, in October 2010, he could surf the wave of publicity created by the film; there was no runway show in a public venue, rather an intimate, invitation-only show in a luxurious private home, from which the press were banned. He did, however, participate in a photo shoot with Steven Meisel for US *Vogue* which featured the collection. And it is surely significant that he chose celebrities to participate, together with well-known models; Julianne Moore was joined on the catwalk by Beyoncé and Lauren Hutton (see Alexander 2010). Ford has created new spheres of opportunity for himself and, it seems, his friends.

It might, therefore, be appropriate to end this chapter with a quotation from Colin Firth's speech when he accepted his BAFTA award:

> To encounter Tom Ford is to come away feeling resuscitated, a little more worldly, better groomed, more fragrant—and more nominated—than one has ever been before. (see Roberts, L. 2010)

6

Sex and the City: From Small Screen to Big Screen

DIARY ENTRY: 8 July 1976

Harold 'reading' children for Miles and Flora in Henry James' *The Turn of the Screw,* adapted for a stage play. A crowd of eager tots and chaperones around the stage door...A minute flaxen haired doll called Sarah, so small she could hardly read the script, proved to be the most brilliant actress.

   NOTE: Years later, I was amused to realise that that 'minute flaxen haired doll' had become famous as Sarah Jessica Parker.

This—later annotated—diary entry written by Antonia Fraser was published in her memoir, *Must You Go? My Life with Harold Pinter* (2010: 60). It somehow seems rather unlikely that Lady Antonia, socialite and historian, and her husband the celebrated playwright, sat down eagerly each week to watch the next episode of *Sex and the City.* Consequently, her awareness of Sarah Jessica Parker's later-life fame seems to show exactly how far the HBO television series seeped into the public consciousness.

   Possibly the most interesting television phenomenon ever in terms of fashion, celebrity and sales of fashion-related products, the series did not set out, originally, to create celebrities, nor to create and sell fashion. Its subsequent move into film was, at first, phenomenally successful, if only in financial terms; the second was ultimately disastrous since it seemed, at first, to have terminated the franchise forever. Stella Bruzzi and I have written elsewhere about the costuming and fashion currency of the television series (Bruzzi and Church Gibson 2004). In fact, we were among a small number of contributors to that same book, *Reading Sex and the City,* who actually had any reservations about the series; the dominant tone was one of unreserved academic fandom.

   Later events, and the consideration here of celebrity culture, not then a part of our remit, mean that it is vital to revisit what would go on to become a phenomenal global franchise, yet one that seemingly overreached and arguably self-destructed; all future plans were swiftly shelved, at least for the time being. It is necessary to examine the transfer from television to film, the films themselves and the subsequent collapse, or possible implosion, of this franchise—even if the DVD sales of the second film seem healthy, and rumours about plans for yet another film actually resurfaced after a few

Figure 18 A provincial shop window tells us that the 'tie-in' is still with us. Photograph by Alexei Daras.

months. For never before have a series and its subsequent cinematic forays become quite so fashion-linked, so brand-aware, nor created such an iconic fashion heroine of its central character, managing so completely to blur her identity with that of the actress who created her (also see Gilligan 2009b). The name Carrie Bradshaw soon became synonymous with a particular eclectic mix of luxury brands, recognizable accessories and thrift shop finds. By the time the final film was released, in May 2010, the fashion-related selling power of the franchise and of Carrie/Sarah Jessica Parker was vast. It failed the final test, however, through a combination of hubris, an execrable script and the fact that those now in control had forgotten exactly why female audiences had originally taken to Carrie (see Jermyn 2004, 2006, 2009). And if her appeal perhaps lay partly in her disaster-prone personal life and hand-to-mouth existence, then once Carrie Bradshaw had become an affluent Upper East Side maven, addressed by a fawning doorman as 'Mrs. Preston', as in the second film, there might well be problems. We will return to these pitfalls later and try to understand the initial fashion success of a series with another agenda, and the emergence of its boho-waif narrator as a celebrity with enormous appeal to women.

The HBO series was based on the original column of the same name by writer Candace Bushnell. She eventually published these columns in book form and went on to write three other novels. But her other work, though clever, well-plotted, often very funny and at times quite dark, has never met with the same success. Like the columns which were the basis of *Sex and the City,* it purports to be satirical yet is ultimately sympathetic to the world of the rich and successful denizens of Manhattan, a world Bushnell herself inhabits. However, these other fictional recreations have not touched a nerve in the same way. Of the other novels—*Four Blondes* (2001), *Trading Up* (2004), *Lipstick Jungle* (2006) and most recently *One Fifth Avenue* (2009)—only *Lipstick Jungle* has been adapted for TV.

NBC's version of *Lipstick Jungle,* which starred Brooke Shields, was heavily promoted in the United Kingdom in autumn 2008 as a flagship product for Virgin Media's digital channel Living; there was an intensive marketing campaign, complete with cinema adverts and 'strategic partnership' product tie-ins with Coffee Republic and *Heat* magazine (Sweeney 2008). Attempting to build on the Bushnell brand, where the main characters 'juggle their families, sex lives, affairs, high-powered business deals and scandals while still looking fabulous' (Sweeney 2008), the series attempts to emulate *Sex and the City* in other ways—for instance, through its tie-in website that includes 'featured clothes' and 'shopping guide' pages (NBC, 'Lipstick Jungle', www.nbc.com/Lipstick_Jungle). Despite the promotional activities, the programme was cancelled in the United States in March 2009, after only two seasons (Gibson 2009).

Bushnell, it seems, is yoked to Carrie, just as Sir Arthur Conan Doyle was forever tied to his fictional creation Sherlock Holmes. Like him, she may not have wanted this. Although Carrie has the same initials as her creator, she is very different in style; Bushnell herself is as conservatively dressed as her character Charlotte York. But whereas Conan Doyle took the drastic step of trying to kill Sherlock Holmes at the Reichenbach Falls, Bushnell has been more inclined to accept the inevitable and the profits that accrue thereby. She subsequently penned yet another novel, *The Carrie Diaries* (2009), which described her heroine's teenage years. Until the critical antagonism which greeted the release of the second film, and which we will examine later in the chapter, there were plans to film this book; Miley Cyrus, teenage fashion celebrity, was, it seemed, to play the young Carrie (Malkin 2010; Child 2010). This scheme was seemingly dropped after the negative reviews of the second film. However, after several months—or what might seem a decent interval—they were revived. *Grazia* magazine ran an enthusiastic article (18 February 2011) about the revival of the project, but in these new rumours, Blake Lively had now replaced Cyrus as the putative teenage heroine.

The original series, from the very beginning, had an extraordinary resonance with female audiences (also see Jermyn 2004, 2006, 2009). The pilot episode (1998) was directed by Susan Seidelman, best known for exacting from Madonna her only credible screen performance in *Desperately Seeking Susan* (1985). Madonna's presence—and her styling (see Street 2001: 55–72)—in this film both coincided exactly and fortuitously with her first musical foray and her initial success; so all she had to do for Seidelman was be herself, no more.

Seidelman's indie background suggests that at first there was no notion of the slick fashion-and-celebrity behemoth to come. The very way in which she filmed the *Sex and the City* pilot was completely different from the way in which the series would develop. Here, the main characters, with captions across the foot of the screen to identify them, talk directly to the camera; they include the interestingly titled 'Miranda Hobbes, Esq. Corporate Lawyer—Unmarried Woman'. There are plenty of 'vox pops' where seeming passers-by are asked for their views on the topic in question, posed by Carrie: 'Why are there so many great unmarried women and no great unmarried men?'

The way in which Carrie's 'question' shaped the episode that followed did, of course, remain a constant as the series became more and more successful. The first two or three episodes included some of the terms used in Bushnell's original column; there were 'toxic bachelors' and 'modelizers.' But Bushnell's authorial voice gradually disappeared as Carrie developed her own clear identity. Sarah Jessica Parker's now-familiar interrogative voiceover was there from the very start, but in seasons one and two, she speaks directly to camera, rather as if she were hosting a show.

Gradually, the style of filming changed; the subject matter did not. Although the central quartet of close female friends was not established straightaway, the very fact that the series was a frank study of the personal and professional lives of thirty-something single women in a hostile urban environment gave the series its unique appeal and attracted a strong female following. The commodity fetishism would come later.

The pilot sets the tone, using Bushnell's own words from the original book:

> This is New York, where instead of breakfast at Tiffany's, we have breakfast at seven a.m.; instead of affairs to remember, we have affairs we try to forget as quickly as possible. (1996: 2)

As the series developed and it became clear that its audience base was made up of young and 'middle-youth' women, so the clothes which defined the four different women, particularly those worn by Carrie, became integral to its appeal. And, increasingly, fashion designers sought out this extraordinarily effective weekly show-case, as Field explained in the book eventually produced to accompany a now-very-successful series (Sohn 2004). Sarah Jessica Parker/Carrie not only launched her own line of clothing, Bitten (Gilligan 2009b: 75); she had her own fragrances by the time the series ended. Her appeal, her style, was seemingly something to which women re-sponded and was also overtly promoted on the British high street. Debenhams hosted cardholder copy-the-look evenings tied to the movie, and even Marks and Spencers teamed with Field to create the thirty-five-piece *SATC*-inspired 'Destination Style: New York' collection of party wear and accessories (Gilligan 2009b: 266). But as her popu-larity increased, male perplexity was replaced by a most unpleasant misogyny. She was named by *Maxim* magazine in 2007 as the 'Unsexiest Woman Alive', the 'Ugliest Female Celebrity', while the mean-spirited website Sarah Jessica Parker Looks Like a Horse (sarahjessicaparkerlookslikeahorse.com) juxtaposes shots of the star with images of horses.

Over the years, the four actresses somehow became completely synonymous with the characters they played. Sarah Jessica Parker, though a talented lifelong actress, made a number of romantic comedies after the series ended. None met with much success, since in the public eye the actress is now Carrie Bradshaw and must remain so. Kim Cattrall, who plays Samantha, has acted in a number of stage plays and has made a film, *The Ghost* (2010), for no less a director than Roman Polanski. But she nevertheless has remained identified with Samantha, a character now seen as the first prime-time 'cougar' ('Don't Call Kim Cattrall' 2010). Cynthia Nixon and Kristin Davis did very little after the HBO series ended in 2004.

According to *Vogue* writer Plum Sykes, who would subsequently appear as *herself* on the big screen, the decision to create the full-length feature film was the result of director Michael Patrick King's dissatisfaction with the subsequent televisual offerings that sought to fill the vacancy left by the series' demise. Michael, 'himself a fashion fiend', was apparently 'not liking the bad TV fashion, like *Ugly Betty* and *Project Run-way*' (Sykes 2008). His move was also, presumably, impelled by the success at the box office of the other fashion films discussed earlier. The original series had several scriptwriters and directors. But King now assumed sole control.

The first film he directed outdid the other fashion films in box-office takings, netting over $400 million; it falls just outside the hundred top-grossing films of all time (see IMDB, imdb.com), and the DVD sales alone netted over $85 million (The Numbers, the-numbers.com). And, as with the series in its later years, designers were delighted to be involved and to have their wares showcased so profitably. The film used a number of ideas found in the other fashion films to great effect.

The impressive production budget presumably helped to secure the services of new fashion celebrities who had not appeared on screen before. US *Vogue* staff members André Leon Talley, a veteran columnist, and leading feature writer Plum Sykes appear as themselves during the US *Vogue* shoot which forms part of the film's storyline, and for which the pictures were taken by real-life fashion photographer Patrick Demarchelier, also new to the world of cinema. He and Talley would go on to feature, also as themselves, in *The September Issue.* The list of thanks at the end far exceeds that of *The Devil Wears Prada;* designers Bill Blass, Calvin Klein, Oscar de la Renta, Chanel and Valentino are joined by Ralph Lauren, Dior, Fendi and—from the rival luxury groups— the leading names of Louis Vuitton and Gucci. The prerelease publicity was efficient and relentless; the four 'girls' were put on four separate *Marie Claire* covers in the same month, a device the magazine has used before, but with double rather than quadruple cover shots on issues for the same month.

The fashion shoot, involving real US *Vogue* staff for an imaginary article in US *Vogue* about the fictional Carrie's forthcoming nuptials and showing nine designers' wedding dresses, formed the basis of an article, 'Rebel Romance', in the real US *Vogue* written by Sykes (2008) about this curiously incestuous affair. Here, she praised the original series, its fashion sensibility and, too, the forthcoming film. A central feature like this—with an especially commissioned photograph of a passionate embrace between Carrie and Big by leading American photographer Annie Leibovitz, best known for her *Vanity Fair* cover shots of celebrities—appearing in the style 'bible' shortly before the film's release, could not be bettered for high-fashion publicity. Sykes's article included not only her in-depth exploration of the series' appeal and thoughts on the forthcoming film, but also described her visit to both a location shoot and the film studio and, finally, focussed on the fashion-celebrity status of Sarah Jessica Parker *the actress,* whom the *Vogue* writer described as a 'powerhouse phenomenon'. She also analysed Carrie's fictional style of dressing in some detail and discussed the extraordinary difficulty of managing to separate the actress from the character seen on screen. Lastly, she asked some highly pertinent questions of the leading actress, trying to ascertain how far she approved of this particular style and how and where it diverged from her own mode of self-presentation. Sarah Jessica Parker gave an honest answer: 'In real life I never dressed the way she did, nor would I.' But she went on to suggest that what she and her fictional *alter ego* did have in common, when it came to fashion, was their desire to go 'all the way' (Sykes 2008). The actress is, of course, firmly accepted within the world of high fashion. She famously accompanied Alexander McQueen to the prestigious Met Ball in 2006, wearing one of his designs, and she was selected to present the posthumous trophy to the same designer at the Council of Fashion Designers of America Awards in 2010—even after the critical debacle of the second film. She is, after all, not Carrie.

The last interesting point raised by Sykes in this *Vogue* article is the similarity between Carrie's lifestyle—her modest income, her capacious clothes-filled closet, her numerous pairs of Blahnik shoes—and that of Candace Bushnell, as described in her early columns. Sykes (2008) tells us: 'She (Bushnell) didn't have any furniture in her flat, so she never invited anyone in...whatever clothes she could afford, she bought, the rest she begged and borrowed.'

This invites comparison with the sparsely furnished flat and lavish designer wardrobe of Audrey Hepburn's character, Holly Golightly, in *Breakfast at Tiffany's.* She, too, was an urban nomad; she kept only ballet slippers, cat food and champagne in her fridge. But whereas Holly had to earn her money by 'trips to the powder-room' subsidized by rich middle-aged businessmen and by visiting a Mafia don in jail, Bushnell and Carrie could earn their money by writing, and both knew where, and how, to borrow clothes. In the television series, as in the film, Carrie herself is an occasional contributor to US *Vogue;* one episode involved her being allowed into the famous, real-life 'Closet' and provoked the line: 'Manolo Blahnik Mary Janes—I thought they were just an urban myth.'

The film deployed a new and still more knowing use of fashion locations, as did the other fashion films. In an early scene in the movie, Carrie talks to boyfriend Big on her mobile whilst standing inside the Diane von Fürstenberg shop. Not only is the logo on the window carefully held in shot for some time, it is followed by a leisurely cinematic glance along the racks of clothes behind her. There is a new *visual* prominence of known designers in the film where they were mainly namechecked in the series, or seen on screen, but without the disclosure of their provenance. Designer names did, however, form the storyline for two episodes; one of these involved a stolen pair of Manolo Blahnik shoes and the other the purchase by Samantha of a 'fake Fendi' bag, which took on a highly symbolic role within the televisual text (Bruzzi and Church Gibson 2004: 127).

In the film, on a much bigger screen and in a text lasting far, far longer—five times as long as an episode in the series—there is a rather bewildering array of designer clothes. At odd moments, the usual attempts by Field actually to match the designer offering with the fictional character portrayed seem to disappear. At one point, the hard-headed lawyer Miranda walks with Carrie through Central Park, wearing an extraordinary outfit of white high-heeled knee boots over trousers and thigh-high socks, decorated with yellow pompoms, that are just the sort of ensemble likely to be chosen by her companion. Kim Cattrall described the extensive wardrobe provided for the film as resembling 'a fabulous trunk shop' (DVD extra), and at times the rummaging seems uncontrolled and uncoordinated. Usually, however, Miranda's character is still seen reinforced by more sober dress, following the conventions first set up in the series.

It is Carrie, always adventurous, whose outfits now become quite extraordinary; the opening moments of the film provide a knowing parody of her earlier incarnation in the television series. In the very first scene, she wears a short, tight white dress with a foot-wide corsage on one shoulder, a reference to one of her sartorial trademarks in the series, inexpensive copies of which had translated into highly profitable retail activity. Thus attired, she walks past four young girls who fan out across the sidewalk in a line, again parodying the 'catwalk' moments associated with the quartet of actresses/celebrities; these moments increased in number as the series acquired its distinctive format. The implication is that these girls are younger versions of our four protagonists, who have also come to New York, as Carrie puts it, 'in search of labels and love.' The order of the nouns here is worrying, and there are no less than three hundred costume changes in this first film.

The labels are most obviously to the fore in the previously mentioned wedding dress shoot for *Vogue*. Carrie is persuaded to take part in it by her editor, Enid (Candice Bergen), who promises '*Vogue* styling—*Vogue* makeup—*Vogue* airbrushing'. Carrie tells us the provenance of each dress she wears for these photographs in the narrative voiceover. This, too, has remained intact from the television series, and indeed, at one point, Carrie sits down behind her familiar Apple laptop to type up one of her trademark questions.

The pictures from the shoot result in Carrie being given the dress designed by the real Vivienne Westwood, so that she may wear it not only in the pages of *Vogue* but on her wedding day. It arrives, to her surprise, in a vast box with a handwritten note from Westwood herself saying 'The dress is yours.' For the actual wedding, however, Carrie personalizes this garment with an extraordinary blue feathered headdress. When her groom gets cold feet about the massive ceremony she has arranged in the New York Public Library, and so fails to enter the building, she briefly undercuts the emotion generated on screen by telling her friends 'I put a *bird* on my head for him.' This styling is redolent of some of her more eccentric sartorial decisions within the television series and has the same effect as her earlier whimsical and visually distracting choices, that of somehow undermining the emotional impact of the relevant scene and disrupting the narrative (Bruzzi and Church Gibson 2004). The designers, of course, have a field day. Patricia Field suggests that 'it's fun for them to see their clothes on Sarah, who is in fact a supermodel' (DVD extra).

But the transfer to a feature-length film creates various problems. Many could have been easily avoided; a team of scriptwriters, as used on the series, could have forestalled certain serious errors of judgment. Within the film's diegesis, Carrie hires an assistant to help her rebuild her life after her aborted wedding; worryingly, her hired helpmeet is a young black woman, so that the only non-white character in the film is cast as a servant. The series had tried to answer the endless questions around its 'whiteness' by introducing characters more representative of the ethnic diversity of New York in prominent roles. Samantha had a protracted liaison with a younger black man, and there was fierce resistance from his sister over this, while later in the series, her lesbian lover, Maria (Sonia Braga), was of unspecified but certainly Latina descent.

There are no difficulties around one aspect of the assistant's role, and this reinforces the selling power of both series and film. Louise–from–St Louis, played by Jennifer Hudson, not only organizes Carrie's website and correspondence, but helps, too, as her employer redecorates the famous flat; this provoked lively discussion on the Internet and so proved to any who might doubt it not only that celebrities can affect all forms of taste-making choices, but that, as Patricia Field claimed, 'These girls are part of everybody's living room—they're part of everybody's lives' (DVD extra). There were those who demanded online that the old décor be retained and others who asked where they themselves might purchase armchairs, coffee tables or wallpaper like those Carrie had installed in the new flat.

Louise is herself an avid fan of designer labels, but as she is of limited means, she belongs to an Internet rental site which enables its users to borrow designer bags for a short period of time. To show Louise her appreciation, Carrie gives her a Louis Vuitton patent-leather bowling bag for Christmas. Lest we are in any doubt as to its origins, the box is firmly in shot for several moments. And when Louise finally goes home to marry her former sweetheart, Carrie tells her, 'You really are St Louise—you gave me my life back.' To which her now ex-assistant replies, apparently without a trace of irony: 'And you gave me *Louise Vuitton.*'

This particular relationship is not the only troubling factor in the film. To watch the earlier series again, after seeing the feature film, is to stifle most previous criticisms—the short, often well-written episodes now seem, by contrast, subtle, moving and even to exhibit moments that resemble some kind of reality. For the situations encountered by the protagonists in the television series present them with difficulties that are real enough. Not only is Carrie's love life disastrous, but she very nearly loses her flat through her extravagance and financial incompetence. Miranda finds she has contracted an STD and then falls unwittingly pregnant; later, she tends a mother-in-law with Alzheimer's disease. Charlotte is badly let down by her first husband and then has to confront her own infertility. Samantha has breast cancer and undergoes a course of chemotherapy.

Throughout the television series, the women look after one another: it is Charlotte who rescues Carrie from the consequences of her incompetence and so saves her flat, Carrie who nurses a sick Samantha. Here, the women also have jobs that they value: Carrie is a successful journalist, Miranda a lawyer, Charlotte works in the world of art galleries and Samantha has a PR business which seems to flourish, despite one or two unwise decisions such as getting seriously involved with a client and dallying with the FedEx delivery boy.

It was this particular combination of strong, supportive female friendship with the depiction of personal and professional difficulties particularly relevant to women in their thirties that endeared the characters to an ever-growing fan-base (Akass and McCabe 2004). However, the transfer to full-length film proceeds to short-change these fans in a number of ways. On the professional front, Carrie seems now to be writing best-selling self-help books, rather than a pithy column, and using her three friends as case studies, while Charlotte long ago abandoned the art world to be a full-time mother to her adopted daughter. Her original decision to leave work for married life when childless was the subject of some wrangling between the characters in the original series. Miranda, however, has stuck with her career whilst bringing up her young son, and, despite the presence of her faithful Ukrainian housekeeper, the narrative suggests that it is Miranda's professional ambition which all but destroys her marriage. Samantha is still working, but her new LA-based business not only mysteriously allows her to leave for long periods of time, but also fails to dispel her growing boredom.

Even the friendship between the women is somehow sentimentalized when transferred to the big screen. In a long sequence, Carrie crosses New York in a snowstorm so that she and Miranda, both otherwise doomed to loneliness, can spend New Year's Eve together. This scene is hijacked from *When Harry Met Sally* (1989, dir. Rob Reiner); far more worrying, however, is the glutinous folk version of *Auld Lang Syne* offered to us as its soundtrack. However, Kate Stables in *Sight and Sound* sees things differently; she finds this 'the film's only really moving moment' (Stables 2008: 77).

The wit and humour that could often be found within the series—not in Samantha's dreadful puns, but rather through Miranda's sassy one-liners, retorts and reflections (see Merck 2004)—seem to have disappeared. There are now, by way of replacement, crude, situation-based gags; one involves Charlotte's inability to control her bowels after inadvertently drinking contaminated water, another involves Samantha's purchase of a small dog whose untrammelled sex drive leads her to simulate sex with cushions and other inanimate objects.

The spectacle provided by the lavish costume budget, the fashion parade it provides and the growing celebrity power that the four actresses now possess, all seem to have swamped the other elements that were central to the original appeal of the series. The problems faced here are easily surmounted. Miranda forgives her errant husband, whose one-off infidelity was, after all, apparently the result of her neglect. Carrie is reconciled with Big, who had remained true, sending her uncharacteristic love letters by email which languished undiscovered in cyberspace. Charlotte finds that she is, almost miraculously, pregnant, and Samantha abandons her attempt at monogamy for the single life she knows and prefers. Dialogue is at times minimal, replaced by a good deal of shrieking and jumping. I would disagree with Kate Stables and suggest that there is possibly only one moment of attempted emotional reality in the film, but not the one she proffers. When Carrie arrives in the supposed honeymoon villa with her friends, the day after she has been abandoned at the altar, she makes straight for the bathroom; she locks the door and carefully studies her gaunt face in the mirror. It is bare of makeup for possibly the first time in the franchise, and the lighting is harsh. Parker is a skilled actress, and the scene is genuinely affecting; it is notable simply because the remainder of the film is so lacking in emotional substance. Tamara Mellon, the director of Jimmy Choo, was more incisive than she knew when she suggested that 'the movie's kind of the dessert of the TV show' (DVD extra).

It ends with the now-obligatory roll call of designers, and, as I suggested earlier, the list is longer and more prestigious than in any previous fashion film. *Vanity Fair* actually listed all the designers and the other beneficiaries of this film; they were horrified at the size and extent of their list, which included soft drinks manufacturers and well-known restaurants used for location shooting ('Sex and the City: A Product Placement Roundup' 2008).

Yet the film was a financial triumph, successful worldwide. It provided the female audiences who had been saddened by the disappearance of the programme with a chance to see what the characters did next, and also, finally, to tie up loose narrative threads. Its huge box-office takings, the DVD sales and the various different forms of spin-off persuaded all those involved to return for a sequel two years later. It was unimaginatively entitled *Sex and the City: The Sequel*. This time there were far more frocks, and still more sponsors, including SKYY Vodka, Moët et Chandon and Hewlett Packard ('SKYY Vodka' 2010; Elliott 2010b). There were old-fashioned tie-ins (see Gaines 1990): in England, the middle-market department store Debenhams 'themed' its windows around the film when it opened, just as in the early years of Hollywood (Eckert 1978/1990). Sales of turbans, seen in the prerelease publicity, were reported to have risen sharply, while magazines once again provided fashion 'trailers', with cover stories such as 'See Carrie's New Wardrobe!' (*Grazia,* March 2010).

In December 2009, Carrie/Sarah Jessica Parker was the celebrity cover girl for US *Elle,* and an interview with her again provided a magazine's main feature article. Although she was supposedly interviewed to publicize her new film *Did You Hear about the Morgans?* with Hugh Grant, the interviewer assumed, rightly, that all her readers were really far more interested in the second *Sex and the City* film. The relentless hype around the new film continued to build.

Now confusion around character, celebrity and actress became intensified. There was growing activity on the Internet around the film, the actresses and possible storylines. Internet postings proliferated throughout the location shooting in New York; details of the next day's shooting were provided, together with a report on the past day's activities, and the four stars were always described by the names of the fictional characters they portray. The maps showing the sites scheduled for filming the following day meant that huge crowds gathered; there were frenetic shouts to the actresses, but always in the names of their characters: '*Samantha*—over here'. Chris Rojek describes Carrie Bradshaw and James Bond as 'celeactors' (2001), but subsequently her status seems to have shifted. Sarah Jessica Parker may still be trapped by this role, even though the franchise is finished, whereas Daniel Craig can and does take other parts quite freely, just as Pierce Brosnan did during his stint as James Bond (also see Gilligan 2010a).

The leaked pictures and stolen shots on the net showed off not only the 1980s outfits worn in the flashback sequences, but, far more significantly, they often named the designers whose clothes were worn in the display. For display is what the franchise ultimately became—the street, whether site of filming or scene within the narrative, no longer just a catwalk, but part of a continuing commercial. One blog showed the outfits worn for one particular day's filming, but with the garments all named and priced. Meanwhile, Parker was reportedly paid a million dollars to front the Halston Heritage campaign and promote this new company, formed to rerelease the clothes originally created by the 1970s designer: she is on the board of directors and wears a Heritage dress in the film's 'leaked' poster, together with Raybans also especially provided for the film (Sells 2010). The launch of the Heritage range was organized to coincide with the opening of the film. There were Internet sightings and magazine pictures, too, of Parker in a vintage ballet-length skirt and a T-shirt emblazoned *J'Adore Dior,* which Field described as her favourite outfit from the forthcoming film (also see Field 2010).

The actresses appeared in a very few Internet images wearing their own clothes— jeans, T-shirts, Ugg boots—but these pictures were of far less interest, or the bloggers might have posted more of them. So, after the months of frenzied speculation, the film opened. Just as the HBO series now seems extraordinarily subtle when set against the first film, so that cinematic exercise appears quite competent if set against the ill-advised sequel. If the 2008 film was a 'dessert' (Mellon, DVD extra), then this film resembles the solitary chocolate which causes the hugely fat Mr Creosote to explode after his massive indulgences at the restaurant table in *Monty Python's The Meaning of Life* (1978). Or perhaps it is more like the emetic which the ancient Romans swallowed after each gluttonous banquet, hoping that they could thus create room for yet more food. For there was now carefully orchestrated talk of a third film, a prequel, based on the new book by Candace Bushnell telling the story of the teenage Carrie. King and the cast were happy to endorse the new film, the build-up and the rumours of a third. They, like Mr Creosote and the Romans, seemed unaware of the perils of overindulgence. The cast were stalked, the spoilers leaked, while other stars such as Penelope Cruz, Liza Minnelli and Miley Cyrus spoke of their pleasure at being invited to appear in the second film.

But, however impressive and skilful publicity may be, obviously the product itself must always be able to meet the expectations it has created. Here, the response to the film, which failed to do this, was instant and indignant. *Entertainment Weekly* wrote a widely quoted and scathing review in which it stated, '*SATC 2* transformed four once mildly likeable characters into rancid, obliviously over-entitled grotesques' (Harris 2010). As the chorus of protest grew louder, box-office returns were disappointing; the film foundered in the wake of the fourth instalment of yet another franchise, *Shrek Forever After.*

The reviews and a number of related articles in the press and online (see Freeman 2010) objected to many things about this overinflated costume parade and the empty show of celebrity lifestyle now offered up by way of 'sequel'. Firstly, there seemed no longer any pretence at the presentation of a recognizable world, even one of Manhattan affluence and aspiration. The disappearance of an idealized but somehow still recognizable city was noted. So, too, was the equally worrying disappearance of ideas

Figure 19   Kristin Davis signs autographs—some in the crowd have dressed in a style intended to echo that of the characters, as with the large red hair bow. Photograph by Anne-Marie Michel.

around consistency of character and cinematic narrative. The second film is a compilation of set pieces; bewildering, unmotivated costume changes; and near-racism.

It begins with an extraordinary parody of a gay wedding. Antony, the wedding planner, caustic and catty, marries Carrie's great friend Stanford Blatch. On their first meeting, in the original series, he had turned away from Stanford without a word. This encounter

Figure 20   There is still off-screen evidence of the strong female friendship that made the franchise so popular. Photograph by Anne-Marie Michel/London Entertainment.

had been carefully stage-managed by Charlotte in the hope of somehow bringing the two together. Stanford, recognizing the sexual disdain exhibited, commented sadly and seriously on his own unappealing bald persona, at such a disadvantage in a world where appearance counts for everything. Here it is as if that moment of contemplation were a chimera. The huge wedding involves a performance by Liza Minnelli, an indoor lake graced by gliding swans and the most extraordinary outfits. Miranda is wearing a dress which her character in the series would have rejected instantly; slit down to the waist, it is heavily embellished with silver and sequins. Field said in interview that 'it was originally intended for Samantha' (DVD). It seems that demarcation of personality through costume is now unimportant; the dress parade is paramount. Interestingly, this dress is nowhere to be namechecked, nor are the hundreds of outfits we see in the film, apart from one group of Louis Vuitton outfits in the cartoon chase that concludes the trip to 'Abu Dhabi'.

For here there is, for the first time, no roll call of credits, both notable and bizarre in a film designed to showcase clothes, products and settings. So the fact that this particular dress Miranda wears was created by Julien Macdonald is something we have to hunt out for ourselves. In a second set piece, a film premiere for her former boyfriend Smith, Samantha chooses a tight, low-cut, short and heavily embellished dress, despite murmurs from the shop assistant that it might be 'too young'. She finds herself standing on the red carpet next to Miley Cyrus, who is wearing an identical dress. The British designer, Matthew Williamson, must presumably be pleased—but, once again, his name is nowhere in the cinematic text. Perhaps the filmmakers assume that the viewers will hunt out the frock's source as if participating in some sort of quiz? It may be, however, that as all the clothes have been blended together into a parade not unlike a burlesque show, so, in consequence, normal considerations of any kind around their function and provenance have also disappeared.

For many critics, the most disturbing element of the film was the trip to 'Abu Dhabi', which is offered to Samantha in order that she may publicize the country and in which she manages to include her three friends, who are seen as all in need of a vacation and a break from their difficult lives. For very good reasons, the authorities in Abu Dhabi objected to the script, and so the relevant scenes had to be shot on location in Morocco. The explanation for the location shooting is part of a very weak plot line and shows up the paltry nature of the 'problems' from which 'the girls' now need to escape. Carrie is upset because Big puts his feet on the sofa in their new and opulent apartment (the wallpaper was featured in decorating magazines and online). This misbehaviour is compounded by his present to her on their second wedding anniversary; she gives him a lovingly inscribed vintage Rolex, while his gift to her is a vast flat-screen television set on the bedroom wall on which, he suggests, they can watch black-and-white films. Meanwhile, Charlotte's longed-for baby is proving to be a difficult, ill-tempered two-year-old. Charlotte has a full-time nanny, but this doesn't prevent her feeling angry. The nanny, although hampered by her ludicrous 'Irish' accent, is not similarly impeded by underwear; her slender, braless young body irritates Charlotte still further.

Miranda, meanwhile, is finding the partnership in the law firm for which she has worked since the very beginning of the HBO series to be problematic, since her boss obviously dislikes her and prevents her from speaking whenever he can. Her husband Steve suggests, again with no irony, 'Why don't you give up the job? Stay at home—you could help around the house'. Instead of shaking newly sexist Steve, or pointing out that they do actually have a full-time housekeeper and their child is now at school, Miranda does in fact hand in her notice.

Now, in one of the many ludicrous and improbable moments in this film, Samantha persuades the sheikh who has employed her to extend his hospitality to her friends, who can thus briefly forget their problems. On the flight, travelling in great luxury, Charlotte and Miranda drink a champagne toast to those who have to deal with their children unassisted: 'the women without help—to them'. On their arrival, each woman is given her own butler, her own chauffeur-driven white Mercedes, and a room in the vast Jewel Suite in perhaps the most expensive and certainly the most tasteless hotel ever seen on screen. In both the series and the earlier film, Carrie's quirky taste extended to a declared interest in interior décor and the ability to create an environment as characteristic as her dress; Charlotte's background in art and design and her excellent yet understated taste in clothes were both mirrored in her perfectly presented Upper East Side apartments. Yet now, all their aesthetic sensibilities have seemingly vanished, like so much from the earlier fictional offerings.

So, too, have questions around correct behaviour and cultural imperialism. Here the film really does unravel. Arab men are seen as imperious and lustful, and women as their victims. To inspire the oppressed women around them, the four visitors perform a karaoke version of Helen Reddy's 'I Am Woman'. It is as if director and scriptwriter Michael Patrick King has actually *read* something, somewhere, about *Sex and the City* being championed for its feminism, or maybe its post-feminism; he can't quite remember, but he decides to reinforce these claims, or at least to try. This is part of the queasiness induced in this section of the film. The treatment of Islamic customs is equally distasteful. Carrie has somehow managed never to see a burqa before and therefore has to be told what it is. She then laughs as she watches a woman discreetly eating french fries while thus attired. And although they are well aware of the strict dress code and the rules around public behaviour, the girls nevertheless cheerfully flout them. Samantha finds a middle-aged Danish architect and at an *al fresco* meal openly simulates fellatio with a hookah, to the horror of the other diners; she is subsequently arrested. Miranda, remembering momentarily that she is a highly qualified lawyer as well as a vacuous freeloader, quickly secures her release, but they have to leave the country; their hotel bill is now their own responsibility.

They rush to the airport, having secured a first-class flight; to miss it would mean the horror of travelling Coach. An enforced deviation to the souk finds them pursued by an angry mob, at first appalled by the sight of Samantha's shorts and then whipped into a frenzy when she drops her handbag, scattering condoms across the pavement. They are rescued by a group of burqa-wearing women who remove these outer garments to reveal, as Carrie tells us in one of the few voiceover moments left, 'Louis Vuitton's spring collection.'

At home, Miranda finds a new job in what seems to be some patronizing Rainbow Coalition, Carrie accepts the television together with a black diamond ring and is forgiven for having a holiday kiss with an ex-lover, while Charlotte discovers that her nanny is a lesbian, so now, she decides, her plump, bald husband will be quite safe. Samantha consummates her relationship with the architect, in a scene involving, once again, her distasteful little dog.

Reviews were critical. Philip French (2010) went so far as to say that any reasonable person might elect for death by stoning in Riyadh rather than sit through the film again, a remark as questionable in its taste as the film itself, while many fans were vocal in their distress. Internet activity picked up again. Some bloggers and journalists discussed one fascinating and grotesque piece of product placement, again a complete denial of character and motivation. Carrie, a self-confessed technophobe, has since the start of the series used a Mac. When her first computer expired, she was appalled, but she grew to love her new MacBook. A recurring image in each episode was her thoughtful gaze at its screen as, clad only in camisole or vest, she typed the week's question in her strange pale blue font. And in the first film, although Carrie changed the entire décor of her flat, she remained faithful to her Mac. Here, however, we are asked to believe that she has suddenly abandoned it for a PC; Hewlett-Packard helped to sponsor the film (Elliott 2010b; Warren 2010). We also see their logo on the brand-new desktop equipment in Samantha's new office. Carrie's unexplained conversion provoked articles in the press and a spoof on YouTube (Elliott 2010b; Warren 2010; Williams 2010).

Most interesting were the journalistic features that expressed a sense of profound personal betrayal—a disappointment not with the celebrity actresses, but with the *characters*. Writing in the *Guardian,* Hadley Freeman (2010) articulated these feelings, asking how Miranda, of all people, could have become so feather-headed and greedy. She described how those who had followed the series from the start felt as if a group of friends, with whom they had grown up and to whom they had been close for ten or more years, had violated their trust in some very basic way. This conflation of character and actress, this fusion of the two, is, as I have suggested, absolutely fundamental to the appeal of the series; it was the motivation for the making of the films and for the massive endorsements by the many sponsors. They trusted that the transition to the cinema screen would be successful and that there would be a continued appeal to the female audience. Certainly the strong fan interest in the characters guaranteed the success of the first film.

But with the second, the voice of the single male writer/director faltered; it would appear that his desire to claim the franchise was not matched by a correct understanding of its modus operandi. Patricia Field (DVD extra) was right to talk of the way in which 'these girls...are part of the living room', but it was risky to move them out of the home and into the multiplex. The fact that women did feel some sense of ownership, as Field implied, meant that they demanded consistency of behaviour. To offer them only 'a fabulous trunk shop' (Field, DVD extra) was not enough; in fact, it seemed to compound the sense of betrayal. The fact that Field, too, misjudged her audience is clear; in the film, an unexplained trip into the desert seems simply an excuse to show off four extraordinary, unbecoming outfits which verge on self-parody.

There are various conclusions that can possibly be drawn here about the workings of fictional characters within the public imagination and the relationship between fiction, celebrity and the marketplace. Writer-director King failed, quite simply, to understand his product, and the now monstrous, bloated franchise seemed to have committed hara-kiri. It will be interesting to see what happens to the actresses, and to their celebrity status, so intimately bound up with the luxury brands seen in the series.

After the film was completed but before its release, the main protagonists, King and Sarah Jessica Parker, were confident about both its reception and the future of the fictional characters: however, as early as 29 June, it was reported in the press that 'Carrie and Co are to hang up their Manolos' ('End of an Era' 2010). The short article went on to say that 'Sarah Jessica Parker was in tears; she never expected this.' All of the articles referred back to one sole article, for some reason not available online but only to be found in the (at that point) due-to-be-published hard copy of British *Grazia* (1 July 2010). That magazine has been very involved with the franchise since its own first issue in 2003; both films have received massive coverage in the magazine, and there have been several fashion spreads devoted to 'sneak wardrobe previews'. Whether they, too, were taken by surprise may perhaps be disclosed in the future. However, the selection of Sarah Jessica Parker to present the award to McQueen at one of America's most select fashion events would seem to be an indication that she, at least, is still persona grata in the world of high fashion. Perhaps, too, it was a move to try and separate the icon from her alter ego.

It seems important to reinforce the arguments in this chapter which explain the possible demise of *Sex and the City* by calling on an article written in quite another register, for the trade press. Bonnie Fuller, in a piece published in *Advertising Age* (2008), examines Carrie's appeal to women from a practical, pragmatic marketing perspective:

> It is because Carrie has always had so much of the loveable loser inside her, despite her label-clad appearance, that she has become such a hit with women.

She published this article in 2008, after the first film but before the critical failure of the second, and she concluded:

> Here was a woman who real women could totally identify with—a truly authentic female . . . she was a woman who was cute but not too pretty, funny and smart but not too brainy, great buddies with her close girl-friends but repeatedly a loser in love—so much so that she endured the ultimate humiliation: being left at the altar. (Fuller 2008: 6)

Figure 21   At the London premiere of the *Sex and the City* film, the catwalk-inspired four-abreast manoeuvre. Photograph by Anne-Marie Michel.

Leaving aside her use of such phrases as 'real women' and 'truly authentic female', which are vague, ill-defined and highly problematic, we have here a set of criteria which seem highly germane to any consideration of popular female celebrity, from Marilyn Monroe and Princess Diana to Jennifer Aniston. King ought to have been more careful, given the huge power here ascribed to his superstar. Perhaps if David Frankel, direc-tor of *The Devil Wears Prada,* who had also worked on the series, had gone on to write and direct these films, then the onset of middle age and marital difficulties might have been properly dealt with in the context of a deft and stylish film. He might have under-stood how to make the transition from small screen to wide screen successful. On the evidence of his first film, he would certainly have been able to sustain the stylish and the fashionable which had become an expected part of the format, while still present-ing credible characters; not for him the insatiable Yorkshire terrier, nor the ill-advised desert foray.

Perhaps this autopsy has been conducted too soon. However damning the critical and fan-base response, the second film still made nearly $3 million (see IMDB, imdb.com), and the DVDs, as I suggested, are selling well enough. We may see the *Carrie Diaries* appear on screen after all, as *Grazia* joyously announced (18 February 2011). Blake Lively has a different demographic fan base and one that seems highly respon-sive to skilled marketing: we will discuss her status as fashion icon in a later chapter.

PART II

Fashion Media and Culture

7

The Changing Face(s) of the Fashion Magazine and the New Media Landscape

> Where printed public discourse formerly relied on a rhetoric of abstract disembodiment, visual media—including print—now display bodies for a range of purposes; admiration, identification, appropriation, scandal and so forth. (Warner 1993: 242)

I have argued both here and elsewhere (Church Gibson 2007, 2008) that images 'bleed' across the media; in this chapter, we now need to address the fact that the traditional boundaries between the different media institutions and strands within the media have themselves broken down, partly through the new power of the Internet. Not only does content now seep across these boundaries, but the different forms of media text are taking on new configurations and creating new relationships.

Traditional fashion magazines and women's magazines still exist, though they have changed their appearance and their format quite drastically in this new era of celebrity. But they now depend increasingly on television for their content, together with their longstanding reliance on cinema, and, more significantly, they have their own websites. With the increasing proliferation and power of fashion blogs over the past few years, whose authors can challenge, compete or corroborate, fashion journalism has been forced to cooperate with the bloggers. Overall, there is an interdependence in the presentation of contemporary fashion which is very new; a recognition of mutual needs has helped to created this reconfigured media landscape. Helen Warner, writing on the television series *Gossip Girl,* which we will discuss in the following chapter, talks of 'a framework of discourses':

> Shows like *Gossip Girl* are increasingly reliant on fashion to attract viewers, and as such, magazine articles, internet blogs and websites contribute to promoting onscreen fashion outside of the text and can...affect the reception of the text. (Warner 2009: 185)

This shows quite clearly a recognition right across the media of the changes, their significance—and their potential. Many of the best-known fashion bloggers display on their sites a border that lists their powerful sponsors, who might include, say, *Vogue* magazine and a number of leading luxury brands. Susie Lau, who as Susie Bubble writes the leading blog Style Bubble (stylebubble.typepad.com), is among those most assiduously courted. In 2009, she explained in an interview that she was now invited to special bloggers-only shows by leading designers (interview with Agnes Rocamora on 21 January 2009). But since then, her photogenic appearance, combined with the adventurous styling seen on her person and on her blog, have widened her profile much further. A typical post will show Lau in an outfit she has created from garments and accessories by new young designers. Although she is employed full-time at the magazine *Dazed and Confused,* founded by Jefferson Hack in collaboration with photographer Rankin, the blog, she explains, gives her the chance to 'write about stuff I like' (Uhlirova 2009: 60). Since 2009, Lau has been invited to the more traditional fashion shows rather than bloggers-only previews and photographed sitting in the front row as befits her new celebrity status (also see Stebbins 2010b). Another celebrity blogger, Bryanboy, is a regular feature there; he has his blog sponsored by Chanel, while Marc Jacobs has named an ostrich-leather bag after him. However, many fashion bloggers keep their amateur status and the independence it brings. Many of them are also preoccupied with celebrity style, and we will return to the blogosphere at the close of this chapter.

In this new mixed-media climate, shaped and even inspired by the new culture of celebrity and its close links with fashion, all magazines where fashion is a key element have completely changed, chameleon-like, to adapt to and reflect the world of celebrity dominance. If, once again, we look back across the years, we will find that there was a time when the 'woman's magazine' saw its role as that of straightforward everyday helpmeet (see Ferguson 1983; Gough-Yates 2003); it is significant that certain very successful blogs have now taken on this particular role (see Make Do Style, makedostyle.com; Economy of Style, economyofstyle.blogspot.com; The Budget Babe, thebudgetbabe.com). Today, the airbrushed images of celebrity perfection offered up in the pages of a magazine are, simply, daunting; but at the other end of the spectrum, a magazine's parading of celebrity bodies blighted by cellulite as images of complete abjection are not necessarily helpful, either.

Perhaps it is here, in this chapter, that we might try to investigate the question of 'looking'. For, in an era of endlessly circulating images of young women, largely presented directly *to* and *looked at* by other young women, the traditional theoretical arguments around 'the gaze' (Berger 1972; Mulvey 1975; Doane 1982) are no longer relevant; they depend upon the presumed dominance of the male gaze behind a camera, the idea of scopophilia and on different modes of address. Tim Edwards argues that:

> Mulvey's original argument that men look and women are looked at—while battered by a barrage of critique...still stands, albeit with a few bullet holes through it, in the world of fashion. (2010: 156)

I would contend that the changes within the world of fashion have rendered this argument increasingly problematic, dominated as it now is by *women* looking—and looking in new ways, perhaps. The anthology *The Female Gaze* (Gamman and Marshment 1988) is also rendered superfluous, for there is nothing in its pages which can help us to disentangle the difficulties around today's proliferating images of women, celebrity and fashion, addressed to a largely female audience.

I would venture to suggest that the gaze in the changed world of fashion is, in fact, *homosocial* (see Sedgwick 1985, 1990, 1993), as is so much of the dedicated space within the new world, not only of fashion but of the fashion-celebrity alliance. As yet, no one appears to have articulated this idea with regard to fashion and celebrity, but it does seem to provide one way of understanding the workings of contemporary visual culture. In Western societies of the past, the sexes in the upper echelons of society were segregated for the greater part of the day, just as they still are in other cultures, and only permitted to meet under the watchful eye of their elders. Young women, corralled together for long periods of time, would often engage in what anthropologists call 'homosocial grooming behaviour' (see Castle 1993): combing, brushing and dressing each other's hair; assisting each other in their toilettes; trying on each other's clothes, necklaces, earrings. The correspondence of Jane Austen provides us with ample evidence, as do so many nineteenth-century novels, letters and diaries (also see Church Gibson 2004a).

I would put forward the viewing of these new images as a modern variant on such activity. The habit of reading celebrity magazines in pairs or in groups, and of invariably discussing the latest images with other female readers, would seem to validate this suggestion (interviews, Church Gibson 2008–2010). The magazine *Grazia,* which has so successfully addressed the new twinned interest in fashion and celebrity, did so after a good deal of research prior to its launch in 2003. This involved the use of numerous focus groups within the targeted demographic of the new publication (interviews, Church Gibson 2008–2010). This focus group work showed that the prospective readers wanted these two ingredients alone, fashion and celebrity, within the proposed new magazine; the other traditional staples of a magazine for women were of far less interest and were, indeed, best avoided. Since the launch, the magazine has primarily addressed these two areas, and its sales reflect the validity of its new editorial policy.

MAGAZINES CHANGE SHAPE

Magazines directed at women alone first appeared in the eighteenth century: the purveying of information about the latest fashions was part of their remit, but they had other tasks to perform. The earliest magazines on both sides of the Atlantic were serious publications, often with an educational element (Ferguson 1983; Gough-Yates 2003). Nevertheless, they always contained line drawings and perhaps coloured plates of the latest fashions from Paris. The idea that the function of the magazine included the provision of both information and pictures to show and explain changes and new trends in fashion has remained a constant ever since.

The early magazines were targeted at women in the upper middle classes; so too were *Vogue, Harper's Bazaar* and similar fashion-led publications which appeared at the end of the nineteenth century (Hughes 2008). More down-to-earth magazines, created for middle- and working-class housewives, were launched in the 1920s and 1930s—titles such as *Good Housekeeping* and *Woman and Home* are self-explanatory. However, the information about running a home was nevertheless accompanied by that concerning the personal appearance of the 'homemaker', telling her how to look her best, often on a limited budget, and providing information on the latest trends in dress, hair and makeup. As we saw in the chapters on cinema, film stars rather than fashion models were of most interest to those of more modest means, and the new magazines of the 1920s and 1930s—including *Woman,* still on the market in 2010—responded to this fact by purveying information and images of the stars (see Ferguson 1983; Berry 2000a,b). Magazines for *young* women—for teenagers—in fact did not appear until the late 1950s and early 1960s, when the 'teenager', first identified and named in 1945 (Savage 2007), was suddenly targeted. As the demographic patterning of society changed radically and the effect of the baby boom phenomenon began to be understood, so the new spending power of the young was now pursued (Lewis 1978). Magazines like *Seventeen* and *Mademoiselle* made their appearance in the United States; *Honey* and *Petticoat* followed in Britain.

To read through these magazines now is to find that, even for young girls, advice on how to find and then to keep a boyfriend was part of the package. So, too, were stories and serials, traditionally on offer in magazines for older women, that were unashamedly romantic. The novelist Jilly Cooper began her career writing such serials for teenage magazines. Although a good deal has been written within the field of cultural studies and feminist scholarship about women's magazines (see Ferguson 1983; McRobbie 1991, 1997; Hollows 2000), the very recent and radical changes in their content wrought by celebrity culture surely, as with cinema studies, create a need for further work. The most recent magazines do not attempt to show, as did their more traditional, more humble predecessors, 'how to please a man'.

Up until and even after the socio-sexual upheavals of the 1960s and 1970s, this was very much a part of the magazines' remit, and it involved different modes of 'pleasing'. Before the watershed of the supposed sexual revolution, the more domestic, middle-market magazines traditionally told their readers that this involved maintaining a slim figure and youthful look, dressing as well as possible on whatever budget might be available, creating a pleasant, comfortable home and cooking the best possible meals using ingredients within the means of the reader. The magazines targeted at the young tended to ignore homemaking; more significantly, the changed mores of the

1960s and 1970s meant that there were other ways to please a man. Helen Gurley Brown, author of the best-selling self-help book *Sex and the Single Girl* (1962), married magazine publisher David Brown; she took one of his titles, *Cosmopolitan,* a staid and unsuccessful monthly magazine, and created a revolutionary publication.

Cosmopolitan, often parodied but widely imitated, took the notion of pleasing a man into the bedroom and made it quite clear that here women could not rely on their skilled wielding of furniture polish, duster and vacuum cleaner alone. There must be more varied activity in this domain, not merely the weekly changing of the sheets and the daily plumping up of the pillows (see Radner 1995; Radner and Luckett 1999).

If the new magazines of the 1920s and 1930s took the new interest in Hollywood stardom and built it into the world they were carefully creating, that world has changed once more, so radically that existing magazines across all market levels have had to adjust if they are to survive. Interestingly, some of the less glossy publications first began to modify their approach in the late 1980s and early 1990s; they used popular soap operas and their stars, often for their covers and usually for one or two of their main stories (*Bella, Best,* et al.).

However, with the dominance of celebrity culture, what is significant within magazine journalism is not just the way in which existing publications have now utilized the celebrity factor to ensure that they remain in print. More significant is the raft of completely new publications, created to reflect a new and radically changed world order. These changes, incidentally, are not confined to women's magazines; men's magazines now feature near-naked celebrities on their covers rather than using anonymous glamour models. This state of undress is not always deployed to satisfy the presumed male heterosexual gaze. In August 2010, Jennifer Aniston, having earlier in her career posed for the cover of *GQ* wearing only a tie, issued a series of photographs and conducted interviews with women's magazines in order to publicize the scent she was endorsing; in these pictures, she seems to be wearing nothing but another strategically placed piece of material, this time of unspecified function and origin (see for example *Grazia,* 10 August 2008).

Things started to change and to reflect the new interest in celebrity with the launch and success of *Hello* in 1993 and the similar magazines that followed it into print, all of which combined celebrity coverage with fashion. It is interesting now to look at the early issues of *Hello,* for there was a clear attempt to focus on the higher end of the social spectrum. Its photo spreads featured the homes and lifestyles of the rich, famous and well connected. As celebrity culture took hold, these extended to the homes of footballers, musicians and television stars. However, *Hello* now covers the weddings of lesser soap stars while showing off the homes of those in manufactured boy or girl bands. Of course, they still have an interest in the opposite end of the social spectrum and devoted half an issue to the wedding of Peter Phillips, son of Princess Anne; but they have dropped what Jordan called 'snobbery pure and simple' (see Price

2009). Nevertheless, they baulked at her own wedding to Peter André, the rights for which went to *OK* magazine; so did the rights for her later marriage to a television cage fighter named Alex Reid.

The US fashion magazine *In Style* was originally unique in that it offered the usual mix of fashion, beauty and interior décor, but here all of these features were celebrity-driven from its first appearance. Appearing in England in 1999 with Julia Roberts on its cover, its sales were spectacular, and other magazines swiftly adopted its formula. At the lower end of the market, a whole new group of celebrity magazines joined the successful gossip-driven *Heat.* The titles themselves are interesting and indicative— *Closer, Reveal, Look, Now, More.* None of the existing scholarship on women's magazines can be used to analyse these new magazines, while *Grazia,* now syndicated across the world wherever there is a developing market for luxury brands, does not conform to any pre-existing models. There is some very interesting work on 'gossip magazines' as female domain by Joke Hermes (1995) and Rebecca Feasey (2006, 2008), but these modes of exploration cannot be used to analyse shopping-driven, luxury brand–showcasing magazines like *Grazia.*

As the new magazines increased in number and popularity, so the paparazzi photographs which formed their content were invariably accompanied by often uncharitable comments on their new staple ingredient, the celebrity body. Relentlessly scrutinized in their pages, it obviously affected readers in their own endless quest for perfection and fuelled their feelings of dissatisfaction. *Heat* magazine was originally intended as a weekly publication which would provide television listings and act in a 'what's on' capacity. However, its first editor, Mark Frith, had the idea of making it into a forum for a particular mode of celebrity gossip and pictures. As it became more successful, some of its features were copied by other new publications. After ten years, Frith resigned, complaining that the magazine was now indicative of the way in which celebrity gossip of the very nastiest kind had come to dominate public life. This seemed odd coming from the magazine editor who had invented the 'Circle of Shame' described in chapter 1 (see Frith 2008).

One interesting characteristic of *Grazia* was its very *glossiness.* Traditionally, weekly magazines have been matt in appearance; the cost of producing a glossy magazine weekly was seen as prohibitive (interviews, Church Gibson 2008–2010). The glossiness, closer to the appearance and appeal of *Vogue* and *Harper's Bazaar,* helped to set it apart from the gossip magazines.

Not only the 'face' but also the faces featured within the glossy magazines have changed. In the 1980s, of course, fashion models were automatically used on most magazine covers and for the large-scale advertising campaigns of luxury brands and fashion-related products. But the first *Vogue* of the new decade was in some ways a portent. Normally *Vogue* has one single female face on its cover, but on the front of the January 1990 issue, it was felt that there was a need for five. They were selected from among the supermodels, created and then lionized as celebrities in the 1980s. They were photographed here by Peter Lindbergh, famous for making these powerful, long-limbed athletic women look almost Amazonian. The cover featured Linda Evangelista, Cindy Crawford, Tatjana Patitz, Naomi Campbell and Christy Turlington, all dressed alike in Levis and body hugging jersey tops, clustered on a grainy New York street. Some of these models are still with us, and the phenomenon of the model-as-celebrity will be discussed in a later chapter. But magazine covers and fashion advertising campaigns now depend for their success upon their exploitation of the celebrity factor and have recently tended to feature a fashionable celebrity in preference to an anonymous model.

In 1993, the year of *Hello* magazine's launch, the supermodels had their most famous fashion moment. Gianni Versace sent Campbell, Turlington, Evangelista and Claudia Schiffer down the catwalk together. Walking abreast with their arms around each other's waists and shoulders, they arguably set up an image of seemingly powerful femininity that would be exploited endlessly throughout the television series of *Sex and the City,* analysed earlier, and in reworkings for the screen of the 'catwalk moment'. This moment is mentioned here because it shows clearly how potent images can start their move across the media to feature in different ways within its various strands.

Magazine covers have now moved on beyond the heroines of the screen. US *Vogue* has featured Hilary Clinton, Oprah Winfrey and Michelle Obama on its covers. Anna Wintour, fashion celebrity, has yet to choose a solo shot of Victoria Beckham for her cover; however, in January 1998, Victoria was featured together with her fellow band members, the Spice Girls. She has now been seen on various different international fashion magazine covers; she has graced the covers of British, Indian, Russian, Spanish and German *Vogue,* also appearing with husband David in a special issue of *Italian Sport Vogue,* photographed by Steven Klein (July 2003). In addition, Ellen von Unwerth chose to photograph her for the cover of Turkish *Vogue* (August 2010) in a provocative manner. Although Beckham is fully dressed, she is nevertheless conspicuously holding both a cocktail and a lighted cigarette. Given that Turkey is a predominantly Muslim country, this is insensitive or, perhaps, given some of von Unwerth's past images, was in fact intended to provoke maximum controversy.

Victoria, at the time of writing, despite appearing on numerous international magazine covers, is still anxious to receive the supreme fashion accolade, to be chosen for the cover of US *Vogue.* At Nicole Farhi's London Fashion Week show in September 2010, Wintour allegedly told *Daily Mail* reporter Katie Nicholl, 'We're big fans of Victoria so it's not beyond the realms of possibility that we will put her on the cover' (Wintour cited in Nicholl 2010).

This leads us into an examination of the extraordinary symbolic power of *Vogue,* and US *Vogue* in particular, which has little to do with its sales figures but has given unquestioned celebrity status to its current editor, Anna Wintour.

ANNA AND THE NEW CELEBRITY: THE BIBLE ON SCREEN?

In the 1980s and even the 1990s, whilst a few photographers might be recognized within the public domain, the editors of glossy fashion magazines were not exactly household names, nor were they the subject of tabloid gossip and documentary film-making. In the past, even editors as well known as Diana Vreeland and Carmel Snow were not familiar, except of course to those especially interested in fashion. Most of

Figure 22 Anna Wintour returns the gaze.

Figure 23   Wintour in her traditional front-row seat—the blonde two seats to her right is Tonne Goodman, her senior fashion editor, who also appears in *The September Issue*. Photograph by Anne-Marie Michel.

those who saw the film *Funny Face*—now such a favourite with fashion cognoscenti— when it was released in 1955 would not have known that the overbearing fashion editor played by Kaye Thompson was intended to illustrate certain characteristics of both these women. One line of dialogue, 'My message to the women of America is— think pink!' used as the basis for a song-and-dance number, was apparently inspired by something Vreeland herself had once written, that 'pink is the navy blue of India'. And the fashion editor portrayed here never follows her own diktats; she has evolved her own unchanging style, a kind of uniform. This, too, is true of Vreeland herself (see Vreeland's advice throughout *D.V.,* her autobiography, 1984/2003).

The audiences who enjoyed *Funny Face* in 1955 had perhaps gone to the cinema to see Audrey Hepburn; some might have been aware that she had now formed a famous collaboration for Givenchy, who designed the 'Spring Collection' seen in the film. But very few would have automatically recognized the visual style of Richard Avedon, who not only took the photographs we see in the film but acted as overall visual consultant and who is named as such in the film's credit sequence.

Now, it seems, we are all much more aware not only of designers and of brands, but of key personnel within the industry. Anna Wintour is understood to have been at least partly the inspiration for a fictional cinematic narrative; she has also figured conspicuously within a successful documentary. It is important in a consideration of fashion and celebrity to consider how this has happened; it also mirrors the changed profile and role of the fashion designer, analysed in chapter 11.

Initially, she appeared as the purported inspiration for Miranda in *The Devil Wears Prada,* discussed in the earlier section on the new fashion films. However, in *The September Issue* (US, 2009), she appeared as herself. This documentary, filmed over a number of weeks, showed the creation of an issue of US *Vogue,* foregrounding not only Wintour herself but also the creative director, Grace Coddington. Just as with the new cinematic narratives of chapter 2, such a film would not have met with much success ten years earlier, and might not even have been made. As we saw earlier, the film not only cemented the status of Wintour as celebrity, but also made a star of Coddington. *Grazia* magazine actually asked its readers, 'How cool can a sixty-eight year old woman BE?' (*Grazia,* April 2009).

The most interesting thing in this film is perhaps the relationship between these women, and the extraordinary contrast between them. Wintour is impeccably groomed throughout, even while 'relaxing' at home in Lacoste polo shirt and slacks; at work, she seems to wear a uniform of designer dress, cardigan, heavy necklace and slingback Manolo Blahnik shoes. Her hair, however, is never off-duty; it seems to be blow-dried into her trademark angular bob even for a day at home in the Hamptons. Coddington, by contrast, is always casually dressed, her long red hair loose over her shoulders in a much simpler uniform of long white shirts or loose black linen dresses, always worn with flat sandals.

She is seemingly quite without any worries about ageing or thinness, and this is interesting, given that she works at the very centre of an industry deemed by some to have caused the size-zero obsession and to be responsible for our fears around the disappearance of youth. Coddington has said, 'Everybody isn't perfect in this world. I mean, it's enough that the models are perfect' (Block 2009), and she is not moved to visit the gym, or indeed the tennis court, as is her more compliant colleague, André Leon Talley.

Coddington's beautifully styled, even painterly fashion spreads provide aesthetic pleasure and showcase *clothes,* not celebrity bodies. But the cover girl for this issue and for the central shoot, not styled by Coddington, is the celebrity Sienna Miller, taken to Rome to be photographed by Mario Testino. She has a hard time. Her hair is deemed unsatisfactory and so a wig is specially made but then discarded because it's 'not working out'. Finally, the offending hair, described on screen as 'lank and lifeless', is tied up in a knot on top of her head. Even then, the cover image, when presented, is met with criticism: 'Look at her teeth,' murmurs Wintour.

The senior staff of the magazine are again an interesting phenomenon; like Grace and unlike their editor-in-chief, they are casual and relaxed, in linen shirts with long, tied-back, even rumpled hair and flat shoes. They form a sharp contrast to the pin-thin, carefully styled Wintour. It is she who demands that the paunch of a cameraman whom Grace had decided to include in a fashion image, quite spontaneously, be airbrushed out. Grace merely laughs and tells the man: 'You don't need to go to the gym—the stomach stays.'

This documentary joins the other fashion films discussed in chapter 5 as part of the new cinematic discourse I have outlined, using their familiar images and tropes. These films perhaps make good the deficiencies of television outlined in a later chapter. Here, we see Demarchelier at work, as in Sex *and the City: The Movie,* while we once more meet André Leon Talley. This time, he is seen learning tennis at Wintour's behest, he explains, as part of an effort to get him fit and perhaps a tad slimmer; there's no one to protect him, no airbrushing possible and no chance of Grace intervening. He mops his sweating brow with—what else?—a Louis Vuitton towel. There are, too, special Vuitton boxes, presumably customized, which contain tennis balls, while still others hold his supplies of Evian water.

Talley keeps a diary which is published; the final section of this chapter will look at those 'diarists' who are transforming fashion coverage and much more besides—the fashion bloggers.

BLOGGERS, FASHION AND CELEBRITY

The Internet was once conceived of as an information superhighway; however, the information it carries today is not quite that implicit in the phrase coined by former British prime minister Tony Blair. Much of the Internet is now used for hardcore pornography, and the rest for different forms of selling and gazing; just as there is no policing in cyberspace, there is no editing, no deferring to superiors, no worries around copyright. Anyone can access images; anyone can create a site or set up a blog. Arguably, the net has wrought changes in fashion coverage that are still not fully acknowledged in the press. Part of the appeal of blogs, perhaps, is the fact that they are interactive; with a few clicks, a reader can become a part of the fashion text and a participant in the dialogue.

The first fashion blog appeared in May 2003 (see Rocamora and Bartlett forthcoming). As time has passed, just as fashions themselves evolve and diversify, so too have blogs. There are now very different modes of fashion blogging, though most follow the visual-diary format. Some simply focus on the blogger's own purchases and activities, but others see it as their task to comment daily on celebrity fashions, while still others are what Rocamora and O'Neill describe as the 'straight-up street fashion blogs' (2008). Here, the term 'street fashion' is open to different modes of interpretation, as we will see.

Where once bloggers bypassed the official system and short-circuited it, and while many still try to work independently, the industry has noted their extraordinary appeal and, particularly with the luxury brands, adapted accordingly. There are the bloggers-only previews and other events mentioned earlier (interviews, Church Gibson 2008–2010). As suggested at the start of this chapter, some bloggers have themselves become celebrities. The youngest to have a high profile, the thirteen-year-old American girl Tavi, was invited to all the couture shows in the winter of 2009, and also to the Prada–Vezzoli–Lady Gaga installation in Los Angeles described in the first chapter. Most notably, in the press coverage of the Paris collections in the spring of 2010, Tavi was given a front-row seat at Dior and appeared in more photographs of the show than did the clothes paraded down the catwalk. She also featured in the Twitter feed for the day filed by the enraged journalist who was sitting behind her and whose view of the proceedings was completely obscured by the vast bow perched atop Tavi's grey-tinted head (Wiseman 2009; Rawi 2009).

The bloggers who evaluate celebrity style are now multitudinous; but because there is no redress, they can say whatever they wish, as can those who respond to their posts. The pictures they upload may be those seen in the press; the comments may be more blunt. Some, like the two women who write the blog Go Fug Yourself (gofugyourself.com), write only on celebrity, but do so critically. Other bloggers, for example Disney Roller Girl, disneyrollergirl.net, and Coco's Tea Party, cocosteaparty.com, combine comprehensive coverage of fashion shows and new ranges mixed with celebrity photographs and commentary, sometimes critical, sometimes not. Of course, fashion-conscious celebrities may have their own blogs, their own sites, their own space within cyberspace (also see Fairclough 2008).

However, there are those whose blogs have more in common with the spirit of the earlier women's magazines, who see their function as giving helpful and financially sound fashion advice and information across a range of topics. They link up with like-minded bloggers and create a virtual community; they can then refer their readers to other helpful blogs. Kate Battrick told the author of this book that she started Make Do Style (makedostyle.blogspot.com) when she found herself living in a new area with a small child; she had previously worked in fashion journalism and as a stylist. Her blog, both down-to-earth and practical, has won a number of awards; there are ceremonies in cyberspace. There are, too, blogs and sites to provide alternative eco-friendly information for those who want to be fashionable (for example, www.ecofashion.com) and are mindful of waste. Bloggers swap information and images, undercutting the official voices of the fashion journalists and creating a subversive subtext for fashion that arguably influences buying habits more than anything else. Fabulously Broke in the City (fabulouslybrokeinthecity.com) is actually written by a young woman whose former spending habits drove her to declare herself bankrupt, and who is now managing to be stylish with very little outlay.

NOTASTREETBLOGGER.COM? THE SUCCESS OF THE SARTORIALIST

'In the spirit of Walter Benjamin's flâneur, and armed with their digital cameras, street-fashion bloggers cruise the streets of Stockholm, Moscow, Buenos Aires Seoul—the cities of the fashion blogosphere are numerous—and offer to a huge audience of virtual flâneurs the real-life images of their city and its stylish citizens' (Rocamora and Bartlett forthcoming).

The street bloggers can and do make passing fashion celebrities of the stylish unknowns who people their posts. What is rather disconcerting is when something that masquerades as a street blog not only makes a celebrity of the blogger involved, but also goes beyond the pleasure of what he or she sees and captures as stylish into very rigorous judgments about the taste of others. The cultural critic Pierre Bourdieu (1984) would be most interested in Scott Schuman, whose blog The Sartorialist (thesartorialist.blogspot.com) is so influential that images from it have been published in book form. Schuman has a background in the fashion industry, and this is apparent in the cityscapes of his blog; many of his apparently random photographs are taken on streets near the sites of the major fashion shows, and he also positions himself carefully on the Rue St Honoré very near Colette, one of the most exclusive shops in Paris. There is nevertheless a deep-rooted belief that he takes photographs of 'ordinary people' (Stebbins 2010a; Olins 2009). In fact, he takes photographs of those who fit his particular ideas around style, which are curiously rigid. The consistency of the content is fascinating; it led to the creation of a blog post which pretended to be a game: 'Step-by-Step Guide on How to Get Shot by the Sartorialist' on FlowingData.com (flowingdata.com/2009/08/04/step-by-step-guide-on-how-to-get-shot-by-the-sartorialist). Those women who moved onto the map that formed the mock game were asked: 'Girls—are you model pretty? Do you own some killer accessories? Can you borrow some?' Men were simply asked: 'Are you middle-aged and Italian?'

He does indeed have a clear typology; on 7 July 2010, his post, headlined 'Italian men and the "back-dart" in their shirts', asked us to examine exactly that, to see how beautifully their shirts fit as a result. This may be a very accurate observation, but his tone can become waspish, or perhaps more accurately WASP-y:

The Sartorialist 28 July 2010

'Thea, New York'
   (Picture of young girl in long-sleeved cotton shirt and simple white shorts)
   'I thought it was great to see a 16 year old girl looking like this, as opposed to the media parade of Britneys and Lindsays: this is the anti-"Jersey Shore" look.'

*Jersey Shore i*s a reality television show featuring young Italian-Americans who presumably have not brought with them to the New World any inherited wisdom concerning back darts. This post shows how the blog can confer a dangerous sense of power, particularly when that blogger has acquired celebrity status. It is clear that, for him, most celebrities in the 'media parade' are automatically *without* style. It also makes for a comparatively seamless transition to the next chapter, where we will consider the relationship between fashion, celebrity and television. For soon after this particular post by Schuman, rumours started to circulate on the Internet about 'negative product placement'; these involved handbag companies carefully ensuring that their rivals' latest models would be toted by the young women appearing in *Jersey Shore.*

8

Contemporary Television: So Many Celebrities, So Little Fashion?

Chapter 6 examined the most successful link between fashion, celebrity and television ever made, but, of course, created by a series which did not set out with that particular objective in mind. Since television first found its place within most homes and people proceeded to rearrange their furniture around this new household god rather than the erstwhile fireside, there have been television stars and televisual celebrities. Some have had a style which has spawned emulation and where there might be marketing potential.

Music programming, speedily introduced to entertain the newly discovered teenage consumer, showed off radical new images to that particular demographic, from quiffed hair and 'brothel-creeper' shoes to men in makeup. The relationship between music and fashion is a complex phenomenon (see Miller 2011; McLaughlin 2000), and we will look at its relationship to celebrity in the following chapter.

Honor Blackman and Diana Rigg in the 1960s series *The Avengers* (1961–1969) made knee-length boots widely desirable for the very first time, and they became the high street retailing phenomenon of that first winter season; they have never since been out of fashion (also see Radner 2000). In the 1970s, Farrah Fawcett's 'flicked-up' hairstyle from *Charlie's Angels* was widely adopted (Sherrow 2006: 128–30; Mansour 2005: 152), while the unstructured men's tailoring of the 1980s was arguably popularized at mass market level by *Miami Vice*. In the 1980s, *Dallas* and *Dynasty* enjoyed extraordinary popularity, generated an inordinate amount of publicity and influenced the way in which many women dressed: padded shoulders, large earrings, bright colours, shiny fabrics, bouffant hair (see Cunningham, Mangine and Reilly 2005 for a detailed overview of this decade).

Dynasty not only chimed exactly with the zeitgeist of the 1980s, but it spectacularly revived Joan Collins's career and gave her a new celebrity status which she has worked hard to keep intact. She, like her then co-star Linda Evans, produced a book containing fashion tips and advice on how to keep fit. Both Collins and Evans—in character as Krystle Carrington—gave their names to the inevitable fragrances.

The Rachel haircut shown off by Jennifer Aniston in *Friends* was, according to the trade paper *Hairdressers' Journal,* the 'style of the decade' (also see Cox and Widdows

Figure 24   Now in her seventies, Collins still presents herself as elegantly as in her *Dynasty* days. Photograph by Anne-Marie Michel.

2005: 114). Aniston, in 2003, was voted number one on the *Forbes* magazine 'Celebrity 100' list. The female stars of youth-targeted situation comedies and soap operas have an important place within this consideration of celebrity culture and fashion. For the young female stars of such programmes as *Friends* and *The OC* stayed in the public eye after the demise of each series and continued to feature on the 'how-to' pages in the magazines that now link celebrities and fashion directly, in features like 'Her Style and How to Get It' and 'Get the Look'.

Postmillennial television figures used to offer celebrity style for young women include Mischa Barton from *The OC* (2003–2006), Paris Hilton and Nicole Ritchie from *The Simple Life* and more recently Olivia Palermo and Whitney Port from *The City,* all of whom have appeared not only in the celebrity slots that are now a journalistic feature, but also on the fashion pages. In June 2007, Hilton and Ritchie were featured on the cover and in the main fashion feature of the US edition of *Harper's Bazaar* (Brown 2007). The feature headline read 'Partners in Crime?' At the time, journalist Laura Brown had no idea that both would actually fall foul of the law, appear in court and be sentenced.

But the creation of new celebrities who could be used as fashion icons, and who could be wooed with luxury brands, was not enough, though these particular young women did make a fashion celebrity out of the stylist Hilton, Richie and Lindsay Lohan all shared. This stylist, Rachel Zoe, went on to publish her own book of fashion advice (Zoe 2007; also see Abrams 2009). But it was the extraordinary success of *Sex and the City*—its unique quality as fashion text and its creation of four extraordinarily durable celebrities from the raw material of relatively unknown actresses—that generated envy and has subsequently led to a number of attempts to emulate its patterning. *Ugly Betty* (2007–2010) was one of the shows which tried hard to fill the fashion vacuum. It only met with modest success, and America Ferrara never really achieved mainstream prominence as a celebrity commodity. Yet her unusual, 'geek-tastic' clashing outfits have created both fan and fashion appeal (Cochrane, L. 2010). As Lauren Cochrane (2010) in the *Guardian* suggests:

> Marc Jacobs and Miuccia Prada—both fans of a clashing, seventies style print—have created similar designs, and Suarez wore Marc by Marc Jacobs in the show.

Ironically, as the heroine Betty became, in theory, more fashion-aware, so her clothes became actually rather dull and smacked of middle management (also see Warner 2010). The show did, however, feature Victoria Beckham in a cameo role, playing herself and parodying her public persona as fashion victim and limelight-hogger (see Freeman 2008).

The *New York Times* reported that not only was the later series *Gossip Girl* (2007–) a deliberate attempt to target the 'daughters' of the *Sex and the City* audiences, but that it was the first show to operate quite so openly as a fashion-marketing feature (La Ferla 2007; Warner 2009). The writer talked of young girls entering shops with tear sheets showing outfits worn in the programme. It has a vast costume budget that provides a 'cavalcade of fashion' (La Ferla quoted in Warner 2009), and, once again, designers have happily offered their wares, while luxury brands can be glimpsed throughout. But the series does not seem able to attain the quasi-mythic status of *Sex and the City* in its televisual heyday. Nevertheless, it does have its followers:

> My mentality when I first began watching it was similar to that of the *SATC* viewers where everyone related to the specific characters' wardrobes...because they were so unique to each personality. When it first came on the air I had already been living in Manhattan for three years. I secretly emulated/pretended to relate to the absurdities in the plot and adopted some styling tips into my personal wardrobe. Granted, I'm not part of the younger high school demographic that watches, but if I were I definitely think I would have mimicked the costumes as closely as possible...I also admit that I am a true product of my generation—I have the Britney paraphernalia to prove it. (American MA student, twenty-five years old, interviewed by Church Gibson, 2009)

The programme is quite nakedly commercial: a website with style pages, 'shop Gossip Girl' and 'shop the looks' e-commerce sections (see CWTV Store, store.cwtv.com) enables viewers to bypass magazines and shops to go directly from character and scene to object of desire. Possibly some semblance of serendipity is needed for a show to become truly populist.

Nevertheless, there has been a strenuous PR campaign to promote its star, Blake Lively. She featured twice on the cover of US *Vogue* in 2010; she has also been taken to important fashion events by Anna Wintour herself. Certainly, as I write, Lively and her co-star Leighton Meester are being pushed to replace Carrie and the 'girls' as new fashion icons. Two pages in *Grazia* magazine (August 2010) showed off at least thirty outfits worn by Lively *off-screen,* not on, and provided both the sources and the prices of her designer garments and accessories; these were not high street copies. But whether this strategy will work is questionable. Although Christian Louboutin announced in September 2010 (Talarico 2010) that a new shoe would be named after her, in the same month she appeared in the 'Down' section of the familiar 'Up' (in) and 'Down' (out) column that is such a familiar feature of new-millennial journalism. The one-line entry read: 'The phrase "as worn by Blake Lively" Yeah, So what?' (Cartner-Morley 2010b). Her styling for the July 2010 US *Vogue* cover was very curious; she looked as if she had somehow strayed there from a *Cosmopolitan* cover from the 1970s (see the previous chapter).

There is a sharp contrast here with the far more fashionable and creative styling by US *Vogue*'s fashion director Grace Coddington of actress Carey Mulligan on the October 2010 cover; despite her vocal dislike of celebrity culture (see chapter 1), Coddington was obviously happy to work with this more quirky and original celebrity, who wears difficult and fashion-friendly frocks by Prada on the red carpet rather than the easy, glamorous creations proffered by the more popular designers.

When *The Hills* finished in 2010 after four years, there was the conscious creation of a fashion spin-off through *The City,* set around the storyline of two mythical fashion interns working in the real-life businesses of Diane von Fürstenberg and a PR supremo who has worked with Madonna. Its stars, Whitney Port and Olivia Palermo, have already been mentioned in these pages. Port and Palermo have also been promoted by clever PR agents and have thus become firm staples of both celebrity and fashion pages. But their fashion stardom does not rest on what they wear on screen, as is true when a series acquires a strong fashion identity. Not only is *The City* also desperate to fill the fashion void, but, just as in the early *Sex and the City* days, designers and others in the industry are delighted to cooperate. Again, its success is muted, despite the fact that Olivia Palermo was named *Tatler* magazine 'Girl of the Year' in October 2010. Like *Gossip Girl,* this show has not really caught the imagination of the general public through its placement on digital/satellite channels (*The City* airs on MTV, *Gossip Girl* on ITV2), though it is impossible to gauge exactly how many young people actually watch it online; the official viewing figures are no longer any real guide, perhaps by the time this book goes on sale, the void will be filled and a new fashion series will have mass appeal; *Mad Men* at the time of writing still has some cult status.

Historian and socialite Antonia Fraser would have absolutely no idea who any of these young actresses are (see chapter 6). Nor are they front-page regulars, as were the *Sex and the City* 'girls' and Joan Collins in her *Dynasty* days. Meanwhile, other shows such as *Project Catwalk, Project Runway* and *America's Next Top Model* try to offer at least a glimpse of the real workings of fashion and so satisfy the new audience cravings in a different way. *Project Catwalk* is a competition for aspiring designers that might not have been created before the recent growth of fashion literacy and interest in the design process suggested in this text. It may have helped some young people to find a temporary foothold within this fiercely competitive business; it has not, however, influenced fashion, nor has it created celebrities of any kind. Nevertheless, its very existence and survival is interesting, even if fashion journalist Plum Sykes (2008) cited *Project Runway* as an example of the bad fashion that prompted Michael Patrick King to take the most successful fashion franchise and rework it for the cinema.

The series that has sparked the most genuine viewer interest, and has also generated a response from the fashion pages, online and even from within the depths of the industry itself, is, of course, *Mad Men.* Part of its appeal is its period setting and its meticulous recreation of period detail; as chapter 5 suggested, Tom Ford is presumably a fan since he employed the production designer from the first series, Dan Bishop, to act as his set designer on *A Single Man.*

Part of the show's interest for cultural critics is surely the way that, unlike so many films set in the past, there is no attempt to glamourize the period; we see its sexism, casual racism, anti-Semitism and homophobia, all in operation, all in the very first episode. However, the task of this particular book is to determine whether it has created *celebrities* who have themselves influenced fashion. Its stars, with the exception of January Jones, who plays Betty Draper, did not become fashion celebrities, though there is an argument to be made for Christina Hendricks, who plays the incredibly voluptuous Joan Holloway. Jones, who is slim and blonde, has been photographed for men's magazines; in her own choice or her stylists' choice of clothes, for these shoots and for the red carpet, one thing is immediately apparent. Her *fashion* appeal only seems to last if she is in character as Betty Draper, while there seems to be no link at all between her own star persona and her series character, as was the case with Sarah Jessica Parker. The 'Betty Draper look' has passed, however, into journalistic parlance, while the premiere of the fourth series was screened outdoors—in Times Square—and drew large crowds ('Times Square' 2010). If the series depends for its appeal on perceived cult status, then perhaps mainstream success will be disruptive. There are, of course, Barbie Fashion Model Collection dolls by Mattell of the four main characters; these are not for children (Elliott 2010a).

The retro styling, the accurate and unsettling portrayal of gender politics and the sight of social change in process all seem to be an intrinsic part of the show's appeal, so it is unsurprising that the fashion designer who has most carefully invoked the series should be Miuccia Prada, supposedly one of the more cerebral figures in the industry. The Prada collection for autumn 2010 seemed deliberately designed to suggest the series; the clothes had small waists, full skirts and fabric and patterns that set up echoes of the late 1950s and early 1960s. The other designer who showed similar silhouettes that season was Marc Jacobs, designing for Louis Vuitton: like Miuccia Prada, he presumably wished to align himself with the series while it retained its cachet and its chic.

The Vuitton advertising campaign set out to reinforce this, showing three smart, ladylike young women with high, sleek ponytails and elbow-length gloves. One of them, the supermodel Christy Turlington, was provided with a new and generous décolletage, seemingly styled to suggest Joan Holloway.

In the UK, it was assumed that actress Christina Hendricks, who plays Joan, would, in fact, be familiar to the public. The new equalities minister Lynne Featherstone in the coalition cabinet created after the election of May 2010 suggested that this actress should be championed for her womanly curves and be put forward to offset the overly slender forms of fashion models; she might somehow help to end the size-zero obsession (Topping 2010b). This would be a viable move only if Hendricks's superb figure resembled in any way that of the average size-sixteen-and-upwards woman. Unfortunately, most women who carry superfluous weight do so around their hips, buttocks or abdomen, making them triangular in shape. She, by contrast, is the triangle inverted, giving her an extraordinary hourglass figure redolent of 1950s film stars, as difficult to emulate as the size zero against which she is offset (see Elsworth 2010). Her face is beautiful, her skin perfect; she is not really a role model for those with body dysmorphia.

REALITY TELEVISION: CREATING GLAMOUR?

Reality television is very much to the fore within the new discipline of celebrity studies, partly because it has stripped the word *celebrity* of its original meaning. There are the shows that create celebrities from those who were formerly unknown: there are now other, very popular shows which deploy these same figures in a different capacity: *Dancing with the Stars/Strictly Come Dancing; Celebrity Duets; I'm a Celebrity— Get Me Out of Here!* Shows in this mini-genre use the new reality celebrities, together with soap opera stars, game show hosts, retired sportsmen and women and others who are sinking within their chosen sphere of activity. This tele-genre puts them in new and challenging situations, testing them, making them learn new skills and demanding that they compete against each other, the elements or both. Lastly, there are those reality shows where we follow the lives of real people as if they themselves were the stars of a soap opera: *The Osbournes; At Home with the Kardashians; Katie and Peter—The Next Chapter; What Katie Did Next.*

The stars of reality television shows are not necessarily influential icons of style. However, some can and do influence female audiences unmoved by high fashion who would like to be glamorous rather than fashionable, if we deploy here the binary system set out in the first chapter.

Certainly Jordan's wealth is dependent on her televisual past and present, while the Kardashians owe their very fame to their show. Where these stars possess influence, as is true of both the Kardashians and Jordan, it is for their continuing development of this glamorous look. Heidi Montag, former star of *The Hills,* was so concerned about her failure to meet the ever-rising standards of perfection that, as she subsequently admitted, she had no less than ten operations, or 'procedures', in one single day during 2009. Today's stars, including those who have found fame through reality shows, also make DVDs in which they show off their workout routines; it can be illuminating to find these remaindered, or languishing in what Miranda Priestly would call 'some clearance bin'.

Perhaps the reality shows and their popularity have helped to make the hitherto-extreme glamorous look—deep tan, thick mane, prominent bosom and heavy makeup—more widespread on an everyday level. Thick foundation and obviously false eyelashes might formerly have been reserved for evening. A Norwegian journalist, Aga Veslemøy, was so baffled by the appearance of this phenomenon in Scandinavia that she devoted an article to exploring its origins, contacting myself in the process. The article, *Hverdags Glamour* ('Everyday Glamour'), formed the cover feature of D2, the weekly supplement of the *Norwegian Business Daily* (*Dagens Næringsliv*) on 6 August 2010. The writer profiled four women, one of whom claimed to be an academic, all of whom expressed their desire to be taken 'seriously'. One, Tine Valle, was the winner of a Norwegian reality TV show, *Paradise Hotel;* another described herself as an 'heiress'.

Figure 25   Television shows often bring with them a moment on the red carpet—Stacey Solomon, runner-up in *The X Factor* 2009. Photograph by Anne-Marie Michel.

Lastly, there are the programmes that try *directly* to deal with ways in which ordinary people can become either glamorous or fashionable. In the traditional makeover shows, the ordinary women who put themselves forward are told how to become more conventionally attractive; the participants are given new hairstyles, becoming

Figure 26 From small screen to fashion's front row—Nicky Hambleton-Jones from *Ten Years Younger* and Nicola Roberts of Girls Aloud. Photograph by Anne-Marie Michel.

makeup and flattering clothes. But the newer, more radical shows within this genre involve invasive surgery, cosmetic dentistry, facial peels and lengthy, drastic dieting. These shows include *Nip and Tuck, The Swan, Extreme Makeover* and *Ten Years Younger* (Heller 2007; Palmer 2008; Weber 2009; McRobbie 2004, 2009).

Possibly, with the increasing emphasis on the value of appearance within our celebrity-driven climate, these shows are becoming more directly influential. Certainly cosmetic surgery is on the increase, while injections of Botox and facial filler are now on offer at many high street dentists. Brenda Weber (2005), writing of *Extreme Makeover,* talks of the 'pressure' that is now almost a 'duty' to make extraordinary and expensive efforts. For those who are selected for the programme, these efforts must be continued long after the programme is finished and the transformed participant triumphantly revealed to family and friends. The facelift will need to be redone after a few years, the fillers replaced yearly and the dietary regime, presumably, maintained forever. She also describes the show as a 'gendered gateway' to the pleasures enjoyed by those who conform to heteronormative ideals of beauty, although, as she suggests:

> The programme allows for multiple viewing positions and highly complicated notions of looker and looked-at, thus opening up new spaces for spectatorial surveillance and pleasure. (Weber 2005)

However, what the show really offers is an 'economy of sameness', an appearance conforming to very specific notions of beauty. To achieve this sameness, drastic, costly and endless procedures and prescriptions must be followed and obeyed: it is a lifelong commitment made to this very 'sameness' (Weber 2005).

This programme and others like it are, nevertheless, 'extreme'. But infinitely less drastic programmes, which simply try to make ordinary women better dressed and perhaps more fashionable, can still be problematic since they involve the imposition of presumed good or better taste. Angela McRobbie (2004: 1) has written on *What Not to Wear* and, using the work of Bourdieu and Judith Butler, has shown exactly how that particular programme uses class, privilege and power: 'What emerges is a new régime of more sharply polarised class positions, shabby failure or well-groomed success.'

In fact, the programme *What Not to Wear* was eventually dropped, despite its initial success and the spin-off publications, which were issued to coincide with Christmas and which were relatively successful. There were increasing complaints about the 'bossiness' of its two women presenters; they certainly exploited their presumed authority, whether or not it was dependent on a politics of caste, by being quite ruthlessly critical of their hapless participants and their appearance, before the exercise of the presenters' taste created the necessary changes. Lessons have obviously been learned; the new series *Frock Me* is more democratic in every way. It is sponsored by retailers T. J. Maxx, a discount chain where the prices are extremely low, where end-of-line garments by well-known designers may occasionally be found and where the premises are cruelly lit, bare and basic. The presenters here are the designer Henry Holland, very proud of his working-class northern roots, and Alexa Chung, who started her own career on a music programme. And again in sharp contrast to Trinny and Susannah, who frightened so many on *What Not to Wear,* there is, too, the firmly established gay male presenter Gok Wan, who, in his programmes such as *How to Look Good Naked,* tries to enthuse with and inspire his contestants, rather than be imperious or dismissive.

Certain fashion makeover programmes appeal to a presumed gay sensibility and gay fashion awareness, and this is the basis for the series *Queer Eye for the Straight Guy.* However, in this chapter, as throughout the book, I have concentrated on the younger female viewer who wishes to use fashionable celebrity as model of style. I have suggested that this is central to the workings of this new phenomenon: to quote from Tim Edwards's chapter on the topic, celebrity culture is 'a profoundly gendered construction' (2011: 156).

There are indeed arguments to be made around the male viewer and his perceived, or assumed, attitudes to fashion, often seen as linked to his sexuality. *Queer Eye for the Straight Guy* could be seen as progressive or as mere tokenism; there is work to be done here, but it exceeds the confines of this book (see Harris 2009; Di Mattia 2007; Becker 2006).

Lastly, if music programmes showing live bands and singers have always showcased fashion, now there are music programmes where the ordinary seek fame and the female judges can show off their clothes—shows such as *Pop Idol, American Idol, The X Factor* and their ilk. It might be fitting to close this chapter with contestant Susan Boyle's *partial* makeover, and with Cheryl Cole's new status as celebrity fashion icon, achieved only when she became a judge on *The X Factor* in the UK (from 2008 onwards).

The 48-year-old Susan Boyle was a contestant on the show *Britain's Got Talent.* When she appeared onstage, microphone in hand, small, dumpy, and wearing an unbecoming yellow dress, the expression on the face of Simon Cowell, celebrity talent spotter, was highly sceptical. When she started to sing, and it was obvious that she had a good voice, Cowell's expression softened. The video of this performance was one of the 'most-watched' on YouTube that year (Bunz 2009); the following weeks saw an excessive prying into the life of this shy woman with learning difficulties. More significantly, it saw attempts to glamorize her. First, her hair was trimmed and dyed, then her eyebrows were plucked; this was reminiscent of Bette Davis in *Now Voyager* (see Cavell 1996; Jeffers McDonald 2010). Becoming clothes were selected for her, though there was no magical transformation, no dramatic loss of weight, no momentary failure of recognition. She looked immeasurably smarter, but the total transformation so familiar from Hollywood film did not occur: the 'reveal' moment from *Extreme Makeover* (Weber 2005) can often provoke cries of disbelief. The fact is that the size of her frame and the breadth of her shoulders meant that such a change was not a possibility, even were she to be forcibly starved for weeks. She signed a profitable contact, and she has sold a staggering number of CDs; she was later selected to sing for the Pope on his visit to England in 2010. But possibly because the makeover was not quite the magical feat demanded by popular expectation—she was not reduced to half her former size, nor did she suddenly look magically much younger than her calendar years—there could, perhaps, be difficulties in sustaining her celebrity status indefinitely, even though sales of her recordings are so far extraordinarily strong.

Cheryl Cole, however, has been most successfully transformed while still managing to maintain her ordinary status. Originally selected for a prefabricated girl group, Girls Aloud, she arguably achieved her success as solo artist because of her television presence and popularity. Her public appeal seems predicated not only on her engaging appearance, but once again on the fact of this perceived ordinariness. She has constantly talked of her upbringing on a council estate in the North-East of England, and the problems her brother has had with the law, thus reinforcing her 'wrong side of the tracks' narrative.

When she married Chelsea and England football player Ashley Cole, she gained publicity as one half of a new celebrity couple; an extraordinary Photoshopped image had them posed as if standing on the clouds, possibly on Mount Olympus. But it was her role as a judge on *The X Factor,* with its enormous viewing figures, that cemented her popularity. She seemed genuinely fond of her young protégées and was constantly on the verge of—or in—tears. The show became fashion parade, Cole vying with the other female judge, Dannii Minogue, to show off ever more newsworthy dresses. Cole proceeded to employ a stylist, Victoria Adcock, who had in the past worked with Victoria Beckham and Christina Aguilera. Adcock approached young and hitherto unknown British designer Hannah Marshall, as well as used clothes by the more established Paris couturier, Stephane Rolland, who dresses Queen Rania of Jordan.

When Cole wore a David Koma dress, only available from the rather exclusive shop Browns in London, it sold out rapidly (Day 2010). Given that this dress cost £1,500, this raises questions around those who follow her celebrity style. They are certainly not the girls from similar backgrounds to her own, who would have to content themselves with a pair of her Girls Aloud false eyelashes, on sale everywhere at low cost. Or if they were willing to splash out, they could purchase a pair of Wolford 'Bondage' tights, as worn by Cole in her video for *Promise This* (Abraham 2010).

The acceptance of this young woman by the world of high fashion came quite early; while Victoria Beckham had to wait several years for her first *Vogue* cover, Cole appeared on her first in 2009, another in September 2010. She also landed the more commercial, but highly lucrative and much-coveted, L'Oréal contract, though a disclaimer had to be printed across the bottom of the advertisements explaining that her hair was actually augmented by extensions. Although unlike Beckham she did *not* completely abjure her glamour image and move carefully into proper high fashion mode, when she wore an Alexander McQueen dress for a birthday outing in 2009, this highly critical designer made no objection to her choice.

The subsequent disintegration of her marriage in a welter of allegations about Ashley Cole's infidelity and the lewd text messages he had apparently sent to his mistress

Figure 27 Singer and now television personality Cheryl Cole. Photograph by Anne-Marie Michel/London Entertainment.

only increased her popularity. She was tearful but not accusing. The footballer was seen as villain, his wife as innocent victim. Since then, she has contracted malaria, rather badly, and been hospitalized. This, of course, is part of the celebrity tradition of illness bravely fought—as with Marilyn and Liz Taylor. She has not abandoned her trademark Geordie accent and is close to her family—her mother formerly lived with the young couple in the luxury of their marital home. All these actions, presumably, struck a chord with her ordinary followers, but it is still interesting to speculate who exactly bought those dresses from Browns.

Cole is one of the few 'musicians' to occupy as much Internet and magazine space as other top celebrities. But although she wears high fashion designers, she always combines them with very high heels and her trademark hair extensions. In fact, she remains closer to the glamorous image of the first chapter than to the fashionable one; she may wear trousers, but always accompanied by these towering heels, and she is rarely seen without heavy makeup.

I end the chapter with a brief consideration of these two contrasting figures, since they are relevant to a highly tentative hypothesis around celebrity and the *fallibility* of fairy tales, to which I shall return at the very end of the book. Cole is definitely the beneficiary of a fairy godmother, though her sleek looks have been no guarantee of happiness, whilst poor SuBo, as Boyle was swiftly rechristened, seems somehow to be trapped mid-transformation.

Musicians who operate in rather different ways will form the subject of the following chapter: both music and television are similar in that they are continually evolving, complex, diffuse industries, very difficult to compress into a shape suitable to discuss in a single short chapter.

–9–

Music and Fashion Forge Links

We were reaching people in all parts of town, all different types of people. The groups were getting all mixed up with one another—dance, music, art, fashion, media. (Warhol and Hackett 1991: 162)

When I interviewed the writer and music critic Dave Laing in 2008, who has published extensively on music both as academic and journalist since the 1970s, I asked him about the current state of the music industry and how it might best be understood. He suggested that one of the many difficulties today is the complete heterogeneity, the fragmentation and fissuring of both music itself and of its audiences. In the 1950s and 1960s, the leading bands and the solo performers within the new genre of 'popular music' on both sides of the Atlantic were well known to everyone, not simply to their fans and followers. Elvis and the Beatles, of course, were common property, instantly recognizable, household names.

There are few contemporary equivalents, but inevitably the names of Madonna and Lady Gaga suggest themselves here. Given the fact that both have cropped up earlier in these pages and both are indisputably celebrities who have connections to fashion in their own very different ways, it might be wise to start with a brief consideration of these two women and possibly proffer some points of comparison. I realize that there is a veritable library of literature available on the subject of Madonna (see amongst others Miklitsch 1998; Robertson 1996); however, although I have so far found some work that analyses the relationship between what she wears and the high street (see Kellner 1995; Voller 1999; Clerk 2002), there seems to be no academic discussion around her new place within the pantheon of high fashion.

It is difficult to imagine anyone today who reads a newspaper, uses the Internet or watches television managing to remain totally unaware of the existence and appearance of Lady Gaga. In September 2010, she ensured her own continued notoriety by wearing an extraordinary variety of outfits to MTV's Video Music Awards (VMAs) ceremonies; they included a controversial outfit made up of pieces of raw meat (Topping 2010c). Although she won no less than seven awards and changed costume several times—two of her other outfits were designed by Armani—these facts were driven off the pages and the screens by the 'meat dress'. She also wore it when she posed for the cover of Japanese *Vogue Hommes.*

Obviously this is not likely to set a fashion trend, but it did raise questions that are important here; what, if any, was its intended significance, were there deliberate historical or cultural references, and what might this outfit tell us about her image?

The dress made some commentators invoke the name of Schiaparelli, and there were mentions of a compilation album released by the Undertones in 1983 which had on its cover a woman dressed in pink-patterned vinyl—on close inspection, the pattern there was designed to resemble rashers of bacon, and the necklace worn by this anonymous model was made from a string of raw sausages. Another source was possibly the artwork 'Flesh Dress for an Albino Anorexic', created by Jana Sterbak for an installation and performance in 1987. A copy of the dress is now in the permanent collection of the Walker Art Gallery; the original was created from sixty pounds of steak. Her 1987 performance, 'Vanitas', was intended to provide a 'commentary on consumption, on decay, and on the ways in which women are expected to look and behave' (Knight 2010; Cochrane, K. 2010).

Although Lady Gaga and Madonna before her have both challenged the ways in which women are expected to look and behave, Gaga has never wished, unlike Madonna, to operate within or near the accepted parameters of what is considered to be sexually attractive. When Gaga appears in revealing garments—leotard, fishnets, whatever—they are invariably confrontational rather than come-hither. She presents herself not as woman but as *construct,* and those who criticize her for this, as Camille Paglia has done (Paglia 2010), seem to miss the point. For whereas Madonna, even without her makeup, is still instantly recognizable to the public, the singer Stefani Germanotta could pass undetected in the street. The 'Lady Gaga' persona is inextricably bound up with her extraordinary costumes, most of which are carapace rather than clothing (also see Goodman 2010).

She has frequently claimed that she is influenced by Warhol in various ways. Perhaps, however, she is more politically aware than Andy (Petridis 2010). For her, the meaning of the meat dress seemed to be connected somehow to the presence at the awards ceremony of her own guests, four ex-members of the American armed forces apparently expelled from its ranks over their overt homosexuality and lesbianism; like Madonna, Lady Gaga is both gay icon and champion of gay rights. In fact, at the awards she announced: 'If we don't fight for our rights, we're no more than the meat on our bones' (Cochrane, K. 2010).

However, she then followed this up by announcing 'I'm not a piece of meat', which seemed rather to invoke the symbolism of the earlier artwork, 'Vanitas'. She has completely divided commentators, some of whom have criticized her music itself, complaining that it is peripheral to the performances or simply disappointing by comparison. Others have championed her for her desire to provoke thought and to shock, rather than simply to entertain or titillate. Kira Cochrane defended her on the day after the VMA awards, arguing that a woman who sits on a lavatory seat during a performance, as Gaga did in her live appearance on *The X Factor,* or who ends up beside a smoking corpse, as at the end of the video for *Bad Romance,* is surely pushing back boundaries in some way (Cochrane, K. 2010). In the same piece, Hadley Freeman accused her of elitism, of consistently emphasizing her own intelligence. Camille Paglia called her a 'ruthless recycler' (Paglia 2010): Paglia has, however, always championed Madonna, who has consistently relied on intertextual references during her long career, whether dressing as Dietrich or referencing Monroe. To Paglia, Lady Gaga is a 'plasticised android'. But to be perceived as such is surely one of her objectives.

Madonna, however extreme her attire, has always presented herself as sexual being, while from the very beginning her costumes have often possessed an element of marketing potential. Her very first incarnation in fishnets, lace, rubber crucifixes and belts provoked widespread emulation at mass market level. Some queried the 'Boytoy' belt; Madonna insisted it was 'just a joke'. It was reproduced and put on sale by the high street store H&M; the young girls who wore it may, or may not, have thought of it as a joke. Interestingly, it was H&M with whom, much later, Madonna collaborated on a range of clothing which was not particularly successful.

Since the 1980s, there has surely been enough written about Madonna to create a whole new sub-discipline within cultural studies. I would like simply to pick up on one element, the enduring fashion potential of Madonna. Georges-Claude Guilbert proposes that 'Madonna not only makes fashion, she is fashion' (2002: 37). This claim was further endorsed by US *Vogue* editor Anna Wintour:

> She's a perfect example of how popular culture and street style now influence the world of fashion. Over the years, Madonna has been one of the most potent style setters of our time. She—just as much as Karl Lagerfeld—makes fashion happen. (Wintour cited in Guilbert 2002: 37)

There have been poor career moves: her unsuccessful films, the risible *Sex* book, the horribly expensive Kabbalah water and her strange flirtation with her imagined idea of an English lady's lifestyle, which involved living in what was once Cecil Beaton's country house; learning how to ride, shoot and fish; making sure that the hoi polloi kept off her land; and wearing the most unconvincing tea dresses. Despite these aberrations, Madonna has not only managed consistently to resurrect her musical career, but also to remain a durable fashion icon at different market levels. She 'designed' for H&M; Tom Ford used her to relaunch and 'sex up' the venerable but ailing House of Gucci in the 1990s, while in 2009, at the age of fifty, she was the face, or rather the body, of Louis Vuitton in their spring/summer campaign.

But, as suggested in chapter 1, Gaga has a different relationship with the fashion industry; the theatricality of her costuming and its performative qualities are something she shared with the late Alexander McQueen, who, as described earlier, presented her with the 'hoof shoes' from his Atlantis collection, since they were designed for performance rather than to be put on sale. On-stage and off, however, she has also wielded or worn accessories by more conventional designers: 'Hermes, Chanel, Yves St Laurent, Nina Ricci, Armani, Noritaka Tatehana, Nasir Mazhar' and those of her 'very close friend McQueen' (Robinson 2010: 139). These have been seen on her person, whether or not overshadowed by her more extreme accessories and attire; sunglasses made from razor blades and cigarettes, hats made from telephone handsets and from lobsters, the Muppet coat. Established designers are happy to join the young and the experimental in the creation of her stage costumes; these clothes may have no after-life, but they guarantee extraordinary publicity, given her record-breaking presence on YouTube and Facebook.

The theatricality of Gaga is an interesting contrast to Madonna's energetic, continued diversification. She has written children's stories and is now moving into filmmaking; like Tom Ford, she can use her celebrity status to cross career boundaries. And while there is nothing ordinary about a woman who has maintained a presence in a male-dominated industry for over twenty-five years, nevertheless, the facts of Madonna's blue-collar background are firmly within the public domain. Gaga, however, seems to want it known that she comes from a middle-class family and did not scotch a rumour that she studied at Julliard, the highly competitive academy in New York which accepts only the most talented musicians.

BRANDING AND BEYOND?

Janice Miller's recent book *Music and Fashion* (2011) is a fascinating and long-overdue study of the relationship outlined in the title. What is interesting is that no one had formerly set out to explore the subject in depth, apart from the odd article here and there (see Miller 2011; McLaughlin 2000, 2011) and Stan Hawkins, who focuses in his book upon masculinity and the British pop dandy (2009). Not all of the musicians Miller discusses in her text could be called celebrities; in fact, many of them would shy away from the word and all its implications. But she does look at certain contemporary performers who fall within the remit of this book; she also devotes a chapter to the vexed subject of branding.

The increasingly complex and ever more commercial relationship between fashion, celebrity and music has, of course, meant that those who want to be considered authentic have often had to take drastic measures to retain their autonomy. There seem certain ironies in Mulberry's naming of an expensive handbag as a tribute to the fashionable young television presenter Alexa Chung, often a magazine cover girl (see Hintz-Zambrano 2010). At the time of its launch, she was also the girlfriend of a successful musician, a member of the British band the Arctic Monkeys. This band tried in their early days to operate *outside* the system, acquiring a huge following online—the increasing commercialization of the music industry, its perception as something to be avoided, seems important here. In the current age of celebrity, the relationship between rather more compliant musical partners and the increasingly active fashion industry has become ever more freighted with commercial baggage. But as this chapter will try to show, the patterns were already in place, the templates laid down, when the new age of celebrity dawned. There were early links created between musicians and designers; performers were used to showcase the work of established designers. What is new in the current climate, however, is an additional player within the scenario: the luxury brand.

David LaChapelle's 'Celebrities' photographs include a series of images of Lil' Kim (www.lachapellestudio.com). In one image, Lil' Kim, one of the few black woman rappers, appears devoid of her clothes but stamped all over her body with the Louis Vuitton logo. This image—used for *Interview*—would have delighted Andy himself, not least because of the problems it creates. Firstly, there is the use of a rap singer; rap is a genre where authenticity is central, and the use of bling is seen as totally within the control of the singer, being his (occasionally her) way of showing off hard-won economic capital in a white-dominated world. Here, however, the rapper is primarily a means of advertising, in the most sensational way imaginable, the logo of the luxury brand. Secondly, there are problems around gender, as well as ethnicity; a woman working in a notably misogynistic area of music is stripped of her clothes, her power, and, quite literally, 'branded', just like a heifer. It could be tentatively argued that those who create the advertising campaigns for Louis Vuitton seem adept in selecting the authentic and subsequently disempowering it; Miller (2011) describes in detail the Louis Vuitton advertisement of 2008 showing Keith Richards sitting in a hotel room at night, a Louis Vuitton guitar case on the table beside him.

For years, Richards had seemed the only member of the ageing band to cling onto his blues antecedents and anti-establishment credentials—that is, until the recent 'leaking' of his letter of support for Tony Blair on the invasion of Iraq, in which he told the then prime minister to 'keep on rocking'. This is something that Richards does not mention in his otherwise very candid autobiography, *Life* (2010). While his songwriting partner, Jagger, happily accepted a knighthood, acquired a box at Lord's Cricket Ground and hobnobbed with fashion designers, Richards moved on from the drug-fuelled years described so honestly in his book to acquire his library in Connecticut—and to make a series on the history of the blues for BBC Radio 3. Now, despite the careful ironies in the advertising image to which Miller directs our attention—the bone china teacup rather than a whisky bottle or a spliff, a tea tray on the sofa, a book with a magnifying glass lying on the open page to emphasize the presbyopia that has come with age, and the disclaimer announcing clearly within the advertisement itself that any monies earned go to Gore's climate-change foundation—I would argue that the singer seems, like Lil' Kim, to have been denuded somehow. It is also interesting to speculate still further and ask about the provenance of the scarf that Richards—or the stylist on the shoot—has draped over a table lamp; it does look, perhaps, as if it might be an

Alexander McQueen skull-print scarf. Even Richards seems to have been unable to control fashion exploitation and brand excess.

AMATEURS AND PROFESSIONALS: A HISTORICAL OVERVIEW

Richards is important here, partly because of the very longevity of his career in an industry supposedly charged by youth, but secondly because his girlfriend of the late 1960s and early 1970s, Anita Pallenberg, helped to create the band's image, yet has never received any credit for it. The early career of the Stones is a perfect example of successful amateur styling, later to be chased away by the professionals.

As this chapter will show, it was increasingly the fashion designers of the 1960s and 1970s who benefited from the new music, not the talented amateurs. Proof of Pallenberg's contribution to the image of the band that filtered through into mainstream fashion—the eclectic, raid-the-dressing-up box, rich hippy style—can be found in Marianne Faithfull's autobiography (1994). She writes in detail about the flat that Pallenberg shared in the early 1960s with Brian Jones, her first boyfriend within the band and, with Richards, its co-founder; she lists the theatrical props used as furnishings and describes the huge leather trunk full of silk scarves, embroidered waistcoats, bolts of velvet and floppy hats with which she adorned herself, Jones and anyone else happy to join in (Faithfull 1994: 9). This look would come to dominate the second half of the decade just as the Beatle haircut dominated the early 1960s. That, too, was the work of a girlfriend, Astrid Kirchner, a German artist and girlfriend of original band member Stu Sutcliffe, who cut the hair of all the Beatles into their distinctive fringes back in their Hamburg days (Goldman 2001). Later, their new manager, Brian Epstein, would take the credit for their image; he also tidied them up, getting them out of their battered leather jackets and into matching collarless suits, designed by Ted Lapidus (see Chenoune 1993: 277–8).

In the previous decade, Elvis, too, had been smartened up by 'the Colonel', who got rid of the clothes he originally wore, the brightly coloured suits with their peg-top trousers, directly descended from zoot suits (see Goldman 1981). It is interesting that both managers seemed unaware of the fact that it was precisely the subversive qualities of dress that made their protégés so attractive to the enormous numbers of newly affluent young people who formed their audiences. This chapter should look *back,* at this juncture, since it was the influence of popular music on fashion at this very specific socio-historical juncture which created the patterns to be emulated in our much more cynical climate. Popular music, associated as it is with youth and sometimes subversion, has always been of interest to those who sell and create fashion; they have consistently borrowed, stolen and exploited.

Today, these relationships have the potential to stifle the spontaneity of music, and, in our complicated commercial arena, the authentic, sought by the young and music

Figure 28 Paul McCartney today, still fond of a collarless jacket and a floral-patterned shirt. Photograph by Anne-Marie Michel.

writers alike (McLaughlin 2000; Miller 2011) coexists with the consciously prefabricated as never before. Today's boy bands and girl groups begin not with friends meeting up after school to make music, but with advertisements in the trade press for singers and dancers.

Figure 29 Girl band style. Photograph by Anne-Marie Michel.

Although the music-inspired fashions of the 1950s and 1960s were worn only by the young and helped, in some cases, to make their subcultural loyalties clear, the demographic patterns which brought about the 'youthquake' of the 1960s meant that, from now on, fashion would always be youth-led (see Breward 1995,

2004; Ewing 1997; Melly 1970). The impact of the new music meant that the media, and the fashion retailers, had to adjust quickly. Not only were television programmes and magazines speedily created and launched, but establishment fashion magazines on both sides of the Atlantic such as *Vogue* and its ilk featured the new musicians in their pages (see Church Gibson 2006a). In 'Swinging London', the young girl singers of the period—Marianne Faithfull, Sandie Shaw, Lulu, Dusty Springfield—were swiftly identified as the new fashion leaders and taken up by designers and retailers.

Here we should consider the activities of designers Mary Quant and Barbara Hulanicki, both of whom capitalized on the new demographics and the new market; the unheralded women who helped to create and style the musicians of that period have been written out of history. Quant may have claimed in her autobiography that she dressed 'dockers' daughters and duke's daughters' (Quant 1966: 75), but her first designs, for her King's Road shop, Bazaar, were in fact far too expensive for the majority of young women. Hulanicki was far more democratic in that her clothes were very cheap and furthermore could be purchased by mail order, thus making the new fashions easily accessible to those outside the metropolis (see Hulanicki 1983). Yet too many fashion histories are inclined to agree with Quant's self-mythologizing, as seen in her claim that she 'invented' the miniskirt (see Breward et al. 2004). The miniskirt arguably had its origins in the Courrèges space age collection and the tunics of Paco Rabanne; the miniskirt took off at mass market level because of the famous photographs of Jean Shrimpton at the Melbourne Gold Cup in December 1966.

Quant found young girl singers who suited her style and dressed them (Quant 1966); meanwhile, the underground grapevine led others among them to the Biba shops and the Hulanicki look (Hulanicki 1983). Quant, far more financially aware, joined the promotional tour of the United States in 1966 that was set up for the new British bands, and she forged a profitable deal with the mass market retailer J. C. Penney (Quant 1966; Sheridan 2010). Quant and Hulanicki were seen as celebrities in their own right, photographed, profiled and interviewed.

As the decade progressed, male musicians became increasingly more innovative in their self-presentation; the hippie styles that they adopted later, originating on the West Coast of the United States, have never really disappeared. Now, 'bubble-up' joined 'trickle-down' in the shaping of the 'fashion system' (Simmel 1904; Polhemus 1994).

The dressing of musicians was something that many wanted to do—but they were not always prompted merely by the profit motive. Leading young designer Betsey Johnson was very friendly with Warhol and heavily involved with the Factory; she dressed the band that Warhol helped to form, the Velvet Underground, and in fact married the bass player. She had a small shop, Paraphernalia, in New York, which became, like

Biba, a 1960s site of pilgrimage for all those interested in the new fashions (Francis and King 1997).

This form of synergy continued into the next decade. Malcolm McLaren and his then-partner, Vivienne Westwood, opened a shop on King's Road in 1971 to sell her designs. The shop, which changed its name frequently (these names included, simply, Sex), attracted those involved—or wanting to be involved—with the new punk movement that came from New York and which fascinated McLaren, who had been briefly involved with both the Ramones and the New York Dolls, precursors and prototypes of punk. After McLaren's earlier ventures into music management in New York, he put together an English band he christened the Sex Pistols. John Lydon, recreated by McLaren as 'Johnny Rotten', was simply a customer who happened to be visiting the shop; McLaren, very taken with his green hair, employed him as the lead singer. The band were then dressed in the clothes Westwood created for the shop in the mid-1970s, when she deliberately deployed the taboo and the fetishistic. She took fabrics and images associated with bondage and pornography—rubber, bindings, buckles, lacing, PVC, dog collars, the swastika (Harrison and Martin 1995; Frith and Horne 1987; Muggleton 2000). After the initial heyday of punk, many of these ideas were co-opted by mainstream fashion (see Steele 1996) so that they eventually lost their power to shock.

In the early 1980s, the duo moved on to dressing singer Adam Ant and later Annabella of Bow Wow Wow in the more flamboyant and theatrical clothes from her Pirates collection. These tied in perfectly with the dressing up involved in the short-lived New Romantic movement of the early 1980s (Elms 1995).

Designers were not averse to copying the styles of musicians for their collections, however perverse the marriage might be. In the early years of rap, Karl Lagerfeld copied Run DMC's distinctive style for a show in which models trotted along the catwalk weighed down by gold chains and wearing quilted 'bumbags' that cost several hundred pounds. For a comprehensive account of what they call 'the branding of black culture' during this period and, indeed, subsequently, see Chandler and Chandler-Smith (2005: 238–41).

This rather breathless canter through recent social history has its purpose: to show how the links between music, fashion and celebrity gradually became both stronger and far more contrived—spontaneity, like authenticity, is difficult to protect. In recent years, however, musical celebrities have *themselves* assumed control over designs supposedly inspired by their image; the patterning around music, fashion and celebrity has changed completely.

Musicians like Beyoncé, P. Diddy, Jennifer Lopez and Gwen Stefani, whose label L.A.M.B. has been praised by Anna Wintour, have their own extremely successful, professionally promoted ranges (see Miller 2011). There is some attempt in London to replicate this kind of professionalism. Singer Lily Allen had her very own style, a mixture of 1950s-style prom frocks and trainers; she was quickly taken up, asked to design her own range for Topshop and somehow lost her spontaneity. She wrote on

Figure 30 Although Beth Ditto has been taken up by the fashion world, her eye makeup shows her loyalty to Siouxsie Sioux of the Banshees—and perhaps to Clara Bow. Photograph by Anne-Marie Michel.

her blog of her unhappiness with her own body and her wish to flee from the music business. It is somehow hard to imagine Janis Joplin, the Slits or Joan Jett and the Runaways launching their own ranges, bringing us back to the questions around authenticity, so difficult to sustain in the twenty-first century.

Figure 31   Celebrity performer and fashion icon Jennifer Lopez, with all the relevant red-carpet trappings. Photograph by Anne-Marie Michel.

Singer Beth Ditto of Gossip, very much a size 'twenty-something', was taken up by stylist Katie Grand and featured naked on the cover of her ultra-fashionable magazine *POP.* She was then fêted and photographed in the company of other celebrities such as Kate Moss. Subsequently, she was asked to design a range for Evans, the chain of British shops which serves larger customers. More significantly, Karl Lagerfeld welcomed her personally to a Chanel runway show and dressed her for it in Chanel outfits, which of course had to be specially created.

Although there is a gulf between this seeming acceptance by a supposed inner circle and the selling of Girls Aloud false eyelashes, this chapter has tried to sketch out a brief overview and to suggest that the creation and courting of celebrity are

Figure 32   Part of the fashion in-crowd and very happy about it, Beth Ditto of Gossip. Photograph by Anne-Marie Michel/London Entertainment.

Figure 33 To suggest that she has rock-chick credentials Alice Dellal deliberately dresses down for a fashion show. Photograph by Anne-Marie Michel.

problematic within the music industry. There has been a mingling of musicians with other celebrities on both sides of the Atlantic; they have joined their peers in the front rows of fashion shows and crop up in the photo spreads, online, wherever. Marilyn Manson, so demonized by middle America, happily attended fashion shows while married to burlesque dancer Dita von Teese. But the truly authentic and their audiences have kept their distance.

–10–

Artists, Celebrity and Fashion: From Wilde and Warhol to Taylor-Wood

The LVMH group, where the *L* and the *V* stand for Louis Vuitton, now owns Givenchy, Marc Jacobs, Donna Karan, Dior Parfums and the venerable House of Guerlain; they have also taken over the oldest department store in Paris, Bon Marché, founded in 1852. Their rivals, the PPR (Pinault-Printemps-Redoute) group, have in their turn assumed control of Gucci, Balenciaga, McQueen, Yves St Laurent and Stella McCartney.

The hypothesis advanced throughout is that art is increasingly deployed to lend respectability not only to fashion and to celebrities, but also to the newly dominant luxury brands themselves; these two rival houses of LVMH and PPR increasingly sponsor the art world in different ways, as does designer Miuccia Prada. One of the biggest shows LVMH have so far bankrolled, a tremendous financial success at the Grand Palais in Paris in 2009, was, by a pleasing irony, Warhol's Wide World. In the new art world, brand influence and activity are not confined to sponsorship; they extend, as we will see, to the commissioning of art works and beyond.

Here, we must consider the most recent developments around the artist-as-celebrity and the changing relationship between this figure and the world of fashion. The phenomenon is not, of course, novel in any way; perhaps it becomes more apparent in the period of early modernity (see Burckhardt 1860/2002). The romantic poets, later lumped rather carelessly together within literary history, were not all encircled within the celebrity aura of Byron and Shelley (Gilmour 2003; Abrams 1975; Poplawski 2007; Bennett 1999). But they were united, like the pre-Raphaelite Brethren later in the nineteenth century, by a loathing of the new world of commerce and industry; many of them tried to live apart from or even outside it. However, other nineteenth-century artists saw useful opportunities in their celebrity status. The painter Lord Leighton, more worldly and commercially minded than many of his peers, opened his 'beautiful home' to the public more than a hundred years before *Hello!* magazine was published (Dakers 1999).

Oscar Wilde was also involved in the world, and very aware, too, of fashion. He was the editor of a women's magazine, *Woman's World* (Clayworth and Wilde 2004) and well known for his own sartorial style, the 'artistic dress' that he and others adopted to convey their opposition to late-Victorian mores (Bayles Kortsch 2009; Breward et al.

2004). The writer Marcel Proust was also interested in the complex powers of fashion; the novel sequence *À La Recherche du Temps Perdu*—published in seven volumes between 1913 and 1927—is infused throughout with detailed descriptions of dress. The Italian designer Fortuny is specifically mentioned throughout; his elegant gowns, which evoke his Venetian ancestry, appeal to Marcel. He purchases several for his lover, Albertine, and they are described in detail when they are worn by the elegant Oriane, Duchesse de Guermantes. After Wilde's arrest, conviction and exile, Proust abandoned his own more extravagant excesses of personal style and self-presentation; he was afraid of being similarly stigmatized for his homosexuality.

Both Wilde and Proust loved the beau monde and frequented the fashionable salons of Paris. However, they were welcomed there for their wit and talent, rather than for any perceived celebrity status. The salons of late-nineteenth-century Paris bore no resemblance whatsoever to the celebrity-filled, commercially sponsored openings and parties which characterize today's art world and which we will examine within this chapter.

Vivienne Westwood announced, as the last millennium drew to a close, that she herself wanted to set up a salon and that she hoped to see, in London, the return of the salon in its traditional form as a gathering place and a forum for intellectual activity. Whether or not Westwood did, in fact, start to host regular evenings of the kind she envisaged is not known; there have certainly been no reports in the press—or in glossy magazines—and there is always an interest in the latest activities of this newsworthy woman. However, although the salons of the past have not been reconstituted, there have been new socio-economic developments, but perhaps not quite those Westwood might have had in mind.

Many of today's artists, in common with fashion designers, actively court celebrity status and enjoy the fact that they are frequently photographed at social gatherings, wearing designer clothes and chatting to celebrities from other spheres of activity. However, by virtue of the strange flattening-out process, mentioned elsewhere in this text, which now seems to dominate contemporary visual culture, their creative activities often seem to take second place to their celebrity status. This contemporary situation was, of course, preceded by Andy Warhol's own infatuation with social status and celebrity; his diaries chronicle in detail the endless evenings he spent at the Studio 54 disco with models and musicians (Warhol and Hackett 1991).

We have already mentioned Warhol's lifelong interest in and active involvement with the world of fashion and the way in which he created new connections between art, fashion and celebrity, in so many different ways. His muse and the star of his films, Edie Sedgwick, was photographed for *Life* magazine in a very short tunic, a full two years before the miniskirt became widely popular (26 November 1965), and as *The Girl in the Black Tights* she was fêted in the London press, and put on the cover of the brand-new colour supplement of the *Sunday Times Magazine* (13 February 1966). She also appeared—as herself—in the pages of glossy magazines. She was always photographed in her own clothes; she wore and popularized leopard print, widely hooped stripes and fishnet tights, and these are still fashion staples almost fifty years later (see Weisman and Painter 2007; Finkelstein and Dalton 2006; Stein and Plimpton 2006). Possibly she and Warhol could be credited with making black desirable for urban daywear. Another 1960s Warhol muse, Nico, worked with Factory star Gerald Malanga and Warhol himself on the floor in the low-key department store, Abraham and Strauss, creating and putting on sale a range of paper dresses; Andy believed in making both art and fashion widely accessible.

Yet once Warhol founded *Interview* magazine, for which celebrities in one field interviewed practitioners in another—for example Bianca Jagger's interview with Yves St Laurent and Diana Vreeland's account of her meetings with Chanel—there was a strong element of elitism. He came under fire for having a new interest in *any* kind of celebrity, for abandoning any pretence at good judgment or what we might now call 'political correctness'. He himself interviewed Imelda Marcos, Nancy Reagan and the Shah of Iran for the magazine; in fact, he frequently dined with the Reagans in the 1980s. These developments prompted a vicious and very funny parody of Warhol's interview technique by journalist Alexander Cockburn. Here, Andy is interviewing Hitler for the magazine, using his traditional *Interview*-type questions:

> *Andy*: Did you enjoy being Führer? Is there still pressure on you to think of your image, and act in a certain way?
> *Hitler*: I don't think of image so much any more, I really don't. (Cockburn 1987: 278–81)

After this little exchange, Andy tells him how 'pretty' Berchtesgaden must have been with its 'twinkling lights', which he'd really like to have seen. Yet despite Warhol's growing interest in the 'wrong' kind of celebrity, when he and the magazine simply concentrated on contemporary fashion, interesting work emerged. A number of significant contemporary fashion photographers—Bruce Weber, Herb Ritts, Mario Testino, David LaChapelle and Ellen von Unwerth—began their careers working for *Interview*.

Warhol's highly commercial activities in the greed-is-good decade of the 1980s prompted Christopher Hitchens to attack his 'corrupt, amoral nihilism' (1997); Andy's reputation was saved from further onslaughts by his death in 1987. The subsequent discovery and display of his enormous collection of memorabilia showed exactly how far Warhol was fascinated by the mixture of fashion and celebrity; his extensive Hollywood holdings included not only endless photographs but many garments and *objets,* including a pair of Clark Gable's shoes. Critic Amy Taubin, who had herself posed for one of his 'screen tests', suggests that if Andy 'were alive today, he'd be trawling the internet' (Taubin 1997: 29).

Arguably his compatriot and contemporary, the writer Truman Capote, the author of *Breakfast at Tiffany's,* was in the end destroyed by his infatuation with celebrity. Warhol had idolized Capote when the latter was young, slim and good-looking, even stalking him for a time. The two of them shared a fascination with celebrity, and for fashionable celebrity in particular. Like Warhol, this ultimately damaged his artistic output, but here, a much slighter talent was completely sabotaged. Capote insinuated himself cleverly and carefully into the world of the Upper East Side couture-wearing mavens, for whom he acted as a 'walker'. These women, who had all married money and 'name', who were dressed by the leading designers in Paris, Milan and New York itself, were amused by Capote and confided in him; he christened them his 'Swans' (Plimpton 1998; Capote 1994). He also enjoyed a close friendship with *Vogue* editor Diana Vreeland; in the celebrity documentary *Bailey on Beaton* (1973), he is seen, perched on a stool at the foot of Vreeland's sofa in her legendary 'red room', making intimate and spiteful observations about hitherto-unknown moments in Cecil Beaton's life. His famous Black and White Ball of 1966 brought together every strand within Manhattan high society. For Capote, the most important guests were not the film stars and actresses but the socialites, the fashion leaders of the time, in their Parisian evening gowns (Davis 2010).

For the last ten years of his life, Capote published nothing, though he socialized excessively, and he always claimed to be writing a neo-Proustian novel sequence. When he allowed a short story, supposedly intended to form a part of this novel sequence, to be published in the *New Yorker,* it caused a scandal. In the story, 'La Côte Basque', which described a lunch at the fashionable restaurant of the same name, some characters appeared as themselves—Jackie Kennedy and her sister Lee Radziwill for example, who were described as a 'couple of American geisha girls' (Capote 1994: 153). Others, friends of Capote who had confided in him, found themselves on the page, thinly disguised, all their secrets revealed and every sexual peccadillo publicized. It has been suggested that the novelist was finally taking revenge on the world of fashionable society for his own mother's disastrous career and her ultimate expulsion. Whatever the facts, the publication of this story meant his own exclusion; most of his former friends never spoke to him again.

After his death, the Proustian sequence of novels was found to consist of a few fragmentary pieces, too brief even to count as short stories. These were published posthumously as *Answered Prayers* (1994). Sadly, these stories are not even particularly well written; the prose is so suffused with bile and the desire to damage anyone famous, whether socialite, writer, musician or filmmaker, that narrative and characterization suffer in consequence. The characters are, however, very well dressed—here, as elsewhere, designers are namechecked.

Today, artist Tracey Emin, like Warhol and Capote, also keeps a 'diary'. For a while, she was paid to do so by the *Independent* newspaper, and it was published on a weekly basis (Emin 2007)—we will return to these diary entries later. The broadsheets and the glossy magazines regularly feature photographs of Emin herself and her fellow artist Sam Taylor-Wood, who famously created an installation for the National Portrait Gallery of 'Beckham Sleeping'. Emin, who is dressed by Westwood, seems important to this text, together with Taylor-Wood, who was once half of the leading celebrity couple within the London art world and has now reinvented herself as a filmmaker.

In the new millennium, certain art galleries in New York and London which cater to the rich and famous have become ultra-fashionable, even arguably luxury brands in their own right, while private views are now quite simply *parties* and photo opportunities within our new and obsessive celebrity culture. An article in the *New Yorker* described the way in which newly established hedge-fund managers could assure themselves that they had arrived once they had set up a relationship with the White Cube Gallery and were able to hang its latest offerings on the walls of their offices (Tomkins 2007). Many of the rich on both sides of the Atlantic treat White Cube, with its branches in London and New York, just as they would any other luxury brand outlet, trusting the owner's judgment and making their purchases as if in any exclusive high-end shop.

The art gallery has become a showcase for fashion in so many different ways. At openings, of course, the art works on show are usually obscured by the fashionable faces around them. British model Agyness Deyn was photographed as she stood in front of a painting at a White Cube exhibition (in May 2008). It was her presence there, not the artworks, that interested the journalists and the readers of *Tatler,* who were given her image to scrutinize rather than that of the canvas she obscured—in fact, the magazine did not think to provide any information about the artist.

Jay Jopling, owner and founder of the White Cube, and his then-wife, Taylor-Wood, were photographed endlessly as they moved from party to fashionable party in the early years of the new millennium. Taylor-Wood, whose work includes video installations of celebrities from other spheres of activity, has been interviewed by journalists working for glossy magazines such as *Harper's Bazaar* and *Tatler* who ask her about her clothes, makeup and hair in as much depth and detail as they question her about her artwork. Now that she and Jopling are divorced, they still fascinate the celebrity watchers and have some links to fashion, but in very different ways. Jopling took up briefly with young singer Lily Allen, a very different celebrity, who had already one fashion collaboration, a rather unsuccessful range for New Look (Addley 2007). Taylor-Wood made her first feature film, *Nowhere Boy,* in 2009. It portrays the early life of John Lennon and shows a new interest in, and careful handling of, period detail; she then married its nineteen-year-old star.

On both sides of the Atlantic, the new interweaving of art, fashion and celebrity has been scrutinized and studied. There are concerned art historians, particularly Julian Stallabrass of the Courtauld Institute of Art, who have consistently denounced the corporate takeover of artists, museums and galleries in journals such as *New Left*

Review and *Art Monthly;* there are also one or two academics working within the field of cultural studies. Stallabrass has carefully chronicled the changing relationship between art, fashion and corporate capitalism, linking it to the current cultural obsession with youth and the press coverage of, involvement with and even the very construction of the new *spectacle* that is the contemporary art world:

> Art stars have long been celebrities, but now the art scene as a whole is treated much like fashion or pop, and even its minor players appear in the organs devoting to tracking the intersecting orbits of the celestial bodies. In particular art and fashion have increasingly been seen hand in hand, as the cult of youth that has enveloped culture as a whole has also swept through the art world. (Stallabrass 2004: 14–15)

The new academic debates around celebrity culture which have rather neglected its close relationship with contemporary fashion do not perhaps pay enough attention to the phenomenon of the artist as celebrity. But it is, in fact, the interface and the *network* of celebrities that link the worlds of art, fashion and what Rojek (2001) has called 'ascribed celebrity', which is both central to and which constructs the new dynamic between art and fashion.

In the Holmes and Redmond anthology, *Framing Celebrity* (2006), Catherine Fowler wrote on Taylor-Wood but concentrated on the video portrait of David Beckham commissioned by the National Portrait Gallery in 2004. The chapter, 'Spending Time with (a) Celebrity', locates her work as 'directly connecting with Andy Warhol's repetitive use of Hollywood stardom in his Pop Art friezes and his factory of B-celebrity non-personalities—the Velvet Underground, Nico, and Viva who feature in his films' (Fowler 2006: 243). She goes on to describe Taylor-Wood's centrality within the contemporary London art world, her then-dual role as her half of a power couple through her marriage to Jopling and 'her individual membership' of the YBAs (Young British Artists), the group centred around Damien Hirst and Tracey Emin and known for its 'provocative sensationalism often...mediated aesthetically by the high-visual impact strategies of advertising' (Bush 2004: 103).

Fowler mentions the installation Taylor-Wood created in collaboration with the leading London department store, Selfridges, in 2000. Called '15 Seconds', it consisted of obliterating the entire store with an enormous photographic mural of celebrities, whilst extensive building works were being carried out. She also gives space to another significant installation work, 'Third Party', created in 1999, and mentions the singer Marianne Faithfull, one of those whom Taylor-Wood selected to take part.

I feel that there is perhaps a little more to say about this second work, for this installation is almost a trope in itself; certainly it should be part of any consideration of the reconfigured relationship between art and celebrity. For it contains within it all of the constituent elements of the new network around art, celebrity and fashion, all the central components of the new topography of contemporary culture, where 'the party' is the arena in which art, fashion and celebrity converge in quite a different way from that which Westwood, presumably, envisaged. The central figure within the vast black cube which made up the installation 'Third Party', and the largest of the images projected there, was that of Faithfull. She was, of course, a successful singer in the 1960s, but, far more significantly, she was also a prototype 'dolly bird' of the era, the girlfriend of singer Mick Jagger, one half of a celebrity couple and a fashion icon who featured frequently in the pages of glossy magazines. Lastly, she was part of a tabloid scandal around sex and drugs that kept the British press occupied for weeks.

There are six cameras in the installation, set up so that the viewer feels that he or she is actually present at this fashionable party, watching along with Faithfull as a young married woman, played by actress Saskia Reeves, flirts in front of her husband—the actor Ray Winstone—with a younger man, played by actor Adrian Dunbar (also see Frankel 2000). Amongst the guests we glimpse Pauline, the real-life photogenic assistant to celebrity gallery-owner Sadie Coles, and Sadie Frost, famous for being friendly with Kate Moss, for her former marriage to film star Jude Law and for her subsequent fashion range Frost/French (an early victim of the 2008 'credit crunch').

The party, which has replaced the more sedate 'private view', is of course acknowledged as central to the new commodified, fashion-friendly, corporate-driven art world, described in the anthology *Art, Money, Parties,* edited by Jonathan Harris for the Tate Liverpool Critical Forum in 2004. The book contains an interview with Sadie Coles, the gallery owner who employs Pauline and who is fashionable in two ways; her gallery is a chic meeting place and invitations to its private views attract a crowd of celebrities, while she herself is always stylishly dressed and of interest in her own right. She comments during the interview that 'one of the great strengths of London is the sense of community in the art world...people do literally hang out with each other and that's a very special thing'. She adds that her relationship with Sarah Lucas, one of the YBAs whom she represents, began when 'I met her at a party' (2004: 124).

Gallery openings are no longer for the buyers, of course, just as art magazines are no longer just concerned with art and fashion magazines do not confine themselves to fashion in its narrowest sense but now profile of-the-moment painters, chic galleries and certain new shows. Throughout the 1990s, art and fashion became increasingly intertwined; new magazines like *Tank* and *Purple* were genuine hybrids, while fashion photographers like Juergen Teller and Corinne Day produced art books and showed their new work in galleries. In 2001, the Tate Liverpool curated an exhibition called, simply, 'Shopping', where artist Sylvie Fleury gilded shopping trolleys and put them on display; in the same exhibition, she created an installation from fashionable carrier bags. Previously, in 1991, she had created another installation from a hundred bottles of the Chanel aftershave, Egoiste, at the Frankfurt Art Fair; all one hundred bottles were swiftly stolen. The leading fashion firm who sponsored one of her solo shows, Hugo Boss, produced this statement for the catalogue:

> Art and fashion have always gone hand in hand. Sometimes radical and shocking, sometimes traditional and conservative, both are judged according to subjective standards of taste. Each represents in its own way the mood and spirits of the times. They stimulate the senses and create objects of desire as fetishes of an affluent society and legacies of culture. (anonymous, quoted in Stallabrass 2004: 83)

Perhaps because of her ability to create objects of desire or perhaps because of the excellent publicity she had already given to Egoiste, Fleury was among those invited to create an installation for the new 'Mobile Art' touring exhibition created and funded by Chanel; it seems important now for luxury brands not only to be seen as sponsoring exhibitions, but to create gallery space, or to use their shop spaces to show off objets d'art. The Fondation Cartier, designed by Nouvel, famous for his involvement with Mitterand's *projets,* opened in 1994; perhaps it was the publicity for the exhibition 'Pain Couture', curated or created by Jean-Paul Gaultier and in which he fashioned loaves of bread into garments, that prompted other fashion houses to follow. For the Chanel touring exhibition, which first opened in the Hong Kong store in 2008 and which is housed in a special pavilion designed by architect Zaha Hadid, Fleury chose to make a giant replica of the famous quilted Chanel 2.55 handbag, with its famous chain. It contained a vast Chanel compact, among other things. However, the statements that Fleury wished to make here, it seems, may have been dwarfed by the iconic power of this bag—and the advertising potential of her installation. Certainly much of the attendant publicity ignored whatever other things might be on view inside this bag (Murphy 2008; Porter 2009; Tyrnauer 2008).

When the new Louis Vuitton store on the Champs-Elysée opened in 2006, an installation for its interior gallery space, Espace Louis Vuitton, was specially commissioned from artist Vanessa Beecroft. She used naked fashion models, both black- and white-skinned women, all wearing clown wigs, to spell out the letters *LV* as they lay on a floor; they were then photographed, and thirteen of these images constituted her installation, 'Alphabet'. For the store's opening there was a three-hour performance. Here, Beecroft placed thirty further black and white models, all naked but for G-strings and high heels, on the shelves of the store (Beecroft and Polier 2007; Heinick 2006). Seemingly, she wished to make a political statement about exploitation, gender and ethnicity. Sadly, most of the fashionable guests simply saw it as an ultra-chic monochrome arrangement, even a triumph for elegant soft-porn, for the bindings she had arranged around the models' ankles and arms were created by Louis Vuitton belts and the straps of Vuitton purses. As with the work of Fleury, there is a problem around the depiction or the use of fashionable objects; they may simply be taken at face value, particularly given the success of Murakami's animated film *Superflat Monogram,* made three years earlier.

Murakami's work is in fact *intended* to advertise Louis Vuitton products; the successor to *Superflat Monogram* was another animated film, which appeared in 2009—*Superflat First Love.* It was carefully created from the spring colours used in that year's Vuitton collection, especially designed to show off the scope of the new brand palette ('Louis Vuitton, Murakami' 2009).

For if artworks can now be seen in the luxury brand shops, on sale along with the luxury brand objects, some of the fashion merchandise may also now be a part of the art-fashion collaboration. It has, of course, extended into the sphere of commercial activity, moving out of the galleries and into the retail environment; the indefatigable Murakami has himself designed handbags for Louis Vuitton since 2003, as well as the bottles for Marc Jacobs described earlier in the book—so, too, has fellow artist Martin Prince. And not only can celebrity artists now create either artwork or fashion object; fashionable celebrities can themselves, as we have seen with the work of Taylor-Wood, form an integral *part* of the artworks, or make up their subject matter. However, Taylor-Wood has been outstripped here by the Italian artist Francesco Vezzoli, whose collaboration with Lady Gaga was described in chapter 1.

Vezzoli, whose artistic trademark is to use live or filmed celebrities as the text within each of his artworks, often combined with needlework in some way, increasingly attracts a celebrity audience for his staged events. He has been sponsored and dressed by Miuccia Prada since 2004; he has said, 'Mrs Prada is very generous, and I am very vain' (Blanks 2008). This is rather reminiscent of some medieval vassal wearing the livery of his liege lord.

Vezzoli's career perhaps took off when he used the 1960s supermodel Verushka to form part of his installation 'Joan Crawford was an Embroiderer' for the Whitney Biennial in 2001. She sat, composedly sewing, amidst various collages. He has created a 'pilot' for a (nonexistent) reality television show with Comizi di Non-Amore in 2004, where the celebrities he cast were Catherine Deneuve, Marianne Faithfull and Jeanne Moreau; he went on to make the promotional trailer for a nonexistent *film,* shown at the Venice Biennale in 2005. It was entitled 'Trailer for a Remake of Gore Vidal's *Caligula*' and featured Courtney Love, Helen Mirren and Milla Jovovich, among others.

In New York, a piece of performance art he created and staged in 2007 at the Guggenheim Museum involved various luminaries. By now, according to *New York Magazine,* Vezzoli was 'at the centre of the art-celebrity-fashion nexus that is controversially defining the art world today'. The *New York Times* added 'whatever that is' in its own review of the event, 'Where Art Meets Celebrity Meets Hype' (Trebay 2007). This piece involved the reading of a Pirandello play, *Right You Are (If You Think You Are),* by various well-known actor/celebrities, including Cate Blanchett and Natalie Portman, while Anita Ekberg, star of seminal fashion film *La Dolce Vita* (1959), perched silently on a replica of Dali's Mae West sofa. The one-night-only performance was delayed while Ekberg's hair extensions were woven in so that hundreds of the merely rich-and-famous had to wait along with the very famous and very fashionable, including Miuccia Prada, André Leon Talley and the Olsen twins, for two hours. The *New York Times* told its readers that some of the guests clomped away angrily 'in their Louboutins and their Jimmy Choos' (Trebay 2007).

In 2008, the art-commerce-fashion boundaries were blurred still further by the Art Basel Miami Beach event at the Museum of Contemporary Art in North Miami; it included an opening party held in the Ralph Lauren Polo store in Miami and the launch of special, limited-edition Jimmy Choo handbags (Cook 2008).

Stallabrass, reviewing *Art, Money, Parties* for *Art Monthly,* suggested that 'the circuits of art and the money that flows with it are also circuits of discourse between the favoured members of an élite—those events...where they talk and circulate...are avenues for the creation and confirmation of a hierarchy' (2005). But it is not just the creation of this hierarchy nor the endless parties that Stallabrass deplores. What he sees as inevitable is the way in which the corporate sponsors and the luxury brands can and do dictate the actual *content* of the exhibitions they sponsor, the very nature of the artworks to be included. Stallabrass suggests that the corporate backers want 'art that is accessible, which reproduces well on magazine covers, appeals to the young and wealthy, is newsworthy and connected with celebrities' (2005: 23).

He should have added, 'connected, for maximum appeal, with the world of fashion'. Successful contemporary artists, as Stallabrass points out, have themselves become brands—Hirst and Emin are the best-known—so that their artworks are simply 'self-conscious side-effects of their celebrity' (Stallabrass 2005). Here, he is surely describing the same flattening-out effect that I mention throughout, whereby every cultural product is given similar value. In fact, the restaurant that Damien Hirst opened in London, the Pharmacy, seemed for some to have similar *material* value to his art installations; when it closed down, its contents—just the fixtures and fittings of the restaurant itself—were auctioned off for £11 million.

Emin is now also paid for the adjuncts to her work, for her status as celebrity. The diary in the *Independent* is often deliberately sensational: 'I Tend to Think about Sex a Lot' was the headline for 11 April 2008. It also verges on self-parody: 'Tomorrow I Shall Be in New York Having Tea with Louise Bourgeois' (December 2007). Sadly, neither headline was ironic. When she resumed the diary, in October 2008, the front page was emblazoned 'In Bed with Tracey'.

Interviewed in *Harper's Bazaar* before she went to participate in the Venice Biennale in 2007 and grumbling about the weight she had gained, she declared, 'I've asked Vivienne to make me some new dresses.' This was possibly not the stuff of the salon parlance Westwood had envisaged.

In a further paradox, a gallery which opened in a subway beneath Edgware Road in London and was intended to provide an alternative exhibition space for impoverished young artists itself became highly fashionable. It was used for fashion shoots, and established artists declared their own interest in the space. There was even, by a terrible irony, the offer of commercial sponsorship from vodka brand Vladivar (Hazel 2007).

Meanwhile, a number of international celebrities continue to display their cultural capital through their ostentatious collecting of art, again reminiscent of Veblen (1899). Robbie Coltrane and Jack Nicholson collect Jack Vettriano, commercially viable but critically vilified (Braid 1999); others play it safe and go for the original 'celebrity artist' himself. Hugh Grant and Jane Fonda both collect Andy Warhol (Forrest 2008).

We should not forget that Italy is central in the new world order of art, fashion and celebrity. The Palazzo Grassi in Venice now contains a gallery created by the Gucci group. In 2008, Miuccia Prada announced her plans to turn a former distillery in Milan into a new museum. It was intended to house the five hundred pieces of contemporary art that she and her husband have collected since they first set up the Prada Foundation, to foster and display what she calls 'the most radical intellectual changes in contemporary art and culture'. Since its inception, she has commissioned two installation-based shows a year, with work from artists including Louise Bourgeois, Anish Kapoor and Dan Flavin. And, in the autumn of 2008, the 'Prada Congo Bar' opened in New York, a four-month installation project of two bars, one African, one European, with an 'in-between area' where, it was hoped, 'fashion …could meet…globalisation in the hedonistic metropolis' (Aspden 2008).

Nevertheless, although she has herself played such a pivotal role, she is now troubled by the proliferating links between art and fashion, the fact that the art world has now become so 'fashionable and trendy'. Interestingly, she revealed in this interview that when she first set up the foundation, she wanted to keep fashion and art separate from one another; she originally had a 'sense of shame' because she was working in fashion, which she secretly felt was 'stupid and superficial'. Although her shame is a thing of the past, part of her new ambivalence is the growing commercialism of the art world—'artists have become much more involved with money now, which came as a big relief to me—*they* have the problems now' (Aspden 2008). This relief, however, is tempered by her belief that we continue to have 'such high hopes for morality in art'; these hopes, by implication, are threatened within our overly materialistic society. Late capitalism does not tend to produce morality in art but simply rather encourages the commercial practice of, say, Damien Hirst, who sold much of his work at Sotheby's in London in 2008 for record sums. In this new form of salesmanship, he went directly to the collectors and bypassed the galleries; while the auction was in progress, he was photographed playing snooker at the Groucho Club, while those working for him collected his millions (Barker and Jury 2008).

Miuccia Prada insists that she would never leave fashion to become a cultural entrepreneur, for 'fashion is the place where I have learned what is going on in the world' (Aspden 2008). In the new networks and relationships which I have been trying to portray here, designers seem to want and value the integrity and the radicalism associated with artists, just as artists today want the cachet of high fashion and the backing of the luxury brands. The different worlds meet and mingle at the parties, the endless social gatherings in both galleries and shops which are—alas—the real metropolitan salons of the new millennium.

CODA

An installation at the Venice Biennale of 2009 set out to provide a picture of, or commentary on, the contemporary art world. But it proved, in retrospect, as problematic as trying to portray or parody fashion on film. The Dutch and Nordic pavilions were twinned that year, to display linked installations created by Michael Elmgreen and Ingar Dragset, two artists whose installation 'The Collectors' was intended, presumably, to illuminate the activity of that species. The Dutch Pavilion was created to look as if it were a house put up for sale, a house that had formerly belonged to a fictional and dysfunctional family where the father was a collector. An actor, impersonating a real estate agent, took visitors round and told them of the sad goings-on. The Nordic pavilion was set out as if it were the home of a rich bachelor with a hedonistic, even promiscuous, gay lifestyle. 'Mr B' favoured stylish Scandinavian furniture, and his collection included work by well-known gay artists such as Wolfgang Tillmans, together with the erotic drawings made by Tom of Finland and a display case which contained the underpants of former lovers, pinned to a board like so many butterflies. Most notable, however, was the swimming pool—in which 'Mr B' floated, face downwards, dead.

Meanwhile, the hustlers he had employed were wandering about, in various stages of déshabillé. On the opening night, the real-life celebrities—including Naomi Campbell—descended on the house and made themselves at home, inspecting his artworks. Campbell was photographed sitting in an armchair just as if she were a real guest. There were also goody bags on offer, as at a fashion show. The catalogue was presented as a collectable artwork; some interpreted the drowned man as metaphor for the state of the art world (Velasco 2009).

However, the opening of Maison Louis Vuitton, the brand's new London megastore in the following year, seemed inadvertently to outmanoeuvre 'The Collectors'. The new space was designed by Peter Marino, who worked with Warhol and has also designed the latest Dior flagship store. It is intended to resemble a home rather than a shop; it has a library and plenty of places to sit comfortably, while an apartment on the top floor is for the use of favoured customers, who may make their selection in its seclusion. The features of the Maison include sliding panels which contain Vuitton scarves; they are also to be seen placed within frames, hung and presented like works of art. There is a bag boutique that resembles a gallery space and real artworks on display throughout. There are the 'artists' notebooks' of Gary Hume and Anish Kapoor, while the apartment houses the work of Gilbert and George, Jeff Koons and Basquiat, among others. The work of Damien Hirst is, unsurprisingly, on display, while artist Michael Landy, who famously destroyed all his possessions in a then-empty London store space that is now a branch of Primark, has designed a machine for cutting up credit cards. Apparently it does, in fact, work (Cartner-Morley 2010d).

There are also handbags and shoes for sale, specially designed by Jacobs's close friend, film director Sofia Coppola. The opening night saw Marc Jacobs photographed between Gwyneth Paltrow and Kirsten Dunst; everyone who thinks of him- or herself as a fashion celebrity seemed to be on the premises (Bull 2010b). Jacobs and others are publicizing the Louis Vuitton Young Arts Program (Fox 2010), obviously trying to stake their own claim to art patronage. Meanwhile, an *Evening Standard* article had already asked 'Is Miuccia Prada the New Peggy Guggenheim?' (Field 2009). The disturbing parallels and paradoxes that link the 'houses' of the 'collectors' with the Maison of Louis Vuitton do not need to be laboriously spelt out. But two last thoughts will link this chapter to one which follows in the concluding section of this book. Firstly, in Tokyo, it is now thought that more than 90 per cent of young women own something created by Louis Vuitton—and that would be fashion merchandise, not artwork (Carter 2008; Hata 2008). Meanwhile, Antoine Arnault, the communications director for LVMH, has recently moved into the creation of filmed commercials for the brand. The first, translated into thirteen languages, asks 'Where Will Life Take You?'

Plate 1 Fashion icon Alexa Chung, relaxed and at home in the front row, was given an award for her personal style by the British Fashion Council. Photograph by Anne-Marie Michel.

Plate 2 The 'celebrity look' emulated by the high street—the glitter, the cling and the inevitable vertiginous heels. Photograph by Anne-Marie Michel.

Plate 3 Embodying the possible origins of the glamour look—star of 'adult movies' Jenna Jameson dressed for an appearance at the Las Vegas Film Festival. Photograph by Anne-Marie Michel.

Plate 4 How to negotiate a crash barrier with style—the elegant and truly glamorous Dita von Teese. Photograph by Anne-Marie Michel.

Plate 5 Constantly chided for her bohemian style, English actress Helena Bonham-Carter resists pressure to change and sticks with Dame Vivienne Westwood, her favourite designer. Photograph by Anne-Marie Michel.

Plate 6 One of the all-original supermodels, Naomi Campbell. Photograph by Anne-Marie Michel/London Entertainment.

Plate 7 Paris Hilton at the World Music Awards—celebrity guest rather than nominee. Photograph by Anne-Marie Michel/London Entertainment.

Plate 8 The celebrity as designer—Lauren Conrad accepts the applause. Photograph by Anne-Marie Michel.

Plate 9 The designer as celebrity—Donatella Versace. Photograph by Anne-Marie Michel.

Plate 10 Celebrity and director Sofia Coppola's new film is matched in billboard size and space by the commercial sponsors of the festival where it was first screened. Photograph by Anne-Marie Michel.

Plate 11 The fans wait for the star at the premiere of *Salt*. Photograph by Anne-Marie Michel.

Plate 12 The star does not disappoint them—Angelina Jolie's trademark look. Photograph by Anne-Marie Michel/London Entertainment.

Plate 13 Johnny Depp, as befits the star who created Captain Jack Sparrow, dresses down with style, his spectacle frames colour-coded to match his suit. Photograph by Anne-Marie Michel/London Entertainment.

Plate 14   A celebrity couple are always on show—here they confront lenses, lights and their own vast image. Photograph by Anne-Marie Michel.

Plate 15 George Clooney eschews the 'black tie' dress code and shows off his suit, perhaps to play up parallels with Cary Grant. Photograph by Anne-Marie Michel/London Entertainment.

Plate 16 Leading lady of Hindi cinema, star and mega-celebrity Aishwarya Rai. Photograph by Anne-Marie Michel.

Plate 17 Harry Potter heroine and a face for luxury brand Burberry, Emma Watson shows off her fashion credentials, designer dress and controversial gamine crop. Photograph by Anne-Marie Michel/London Entertainment.

Plate 18 Rock style meets celebrity style—Fergie and the Black-Eyed Peas. Photograph by Anne-Marie Michel.

Plate 19 Pole dancing seems to have taken off as part of the celebrity-music bag of tricks—here, Britney Spears shows her skills. Photograph by Anne-Marie Michel/London Entertainment.

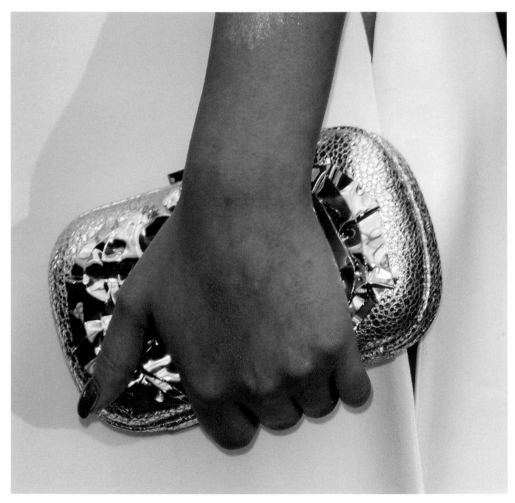

Plate 20 The Chanel nail varnish and a designer clutch bag catch the photographer's eye here, rather than the celebrity herself. Photograph by Anne-Marie Michel.

Plate 21 Skilfully deployed designer accessories are wielded to attract the eye. Photograph by Anne-Marie Michel.

Plate 22 Even an anonymous reveller at the Cannes Lifeball sports his monogrammed accessory. Photograph by Anne-Marie Michel/London Entertainment.

Plate 23 Fandom, a headpiece known as a fascinator and franchise frenzy. Photograph by Anne-Marie Michel.

Plate 24 Fashion icon par excellence: *Vogue* editor Anna Wintour's characteristic style— sharp bob, sunglasses, knee-length dress, Blahnik shoes. Photograph by Anne-Marie Michel.

PART III

Fashion Gone Global

–11–

Designers and Models Become Brands

When Cristobal Balenciaga closed the doors of his couture house forever in 1968, he explained that he was doing so because, as he put it, there was no one left to dress (Drake 2006: 110; Blau 1999: 121). This was interpreted as a symbol of the old order quietly ceding to the new. The 1960s had seen the takeover of fashion by youth, the new domination of inexpensive, affordable fashion and arguably the replacement of the 'trickle-down' theory of fashion, as articulated by Simmel (1904), with the beginnings of what has since been described as the 'bubble-up' system (Polhemus 1994). Now, it is suggested, trends start on the streets and are then subsequently copied by designers or retailers. Certainly, the Ballets Russes collection that Yves St Laurent showed in 1969 was inspired by the hippy fashions he saw around him, the then-new tendency to raid the dressing-up box of the past while simultaneously looking to India, Afghanistan and Morocco for inspiration. This look has ever since been described as 'ethnic', despite the misappropriation involved.

Fashion historians and cultural commentators saw the decision of Balenciaga to close his atelier as an acknowledgement of the rapidly waning power of couture. Yet more than forty years later, couture is still with us; there may have been casualties (Lacroix, for example), but the more commercially minded designers have learned how to adapt and survive, which includes not only a reliance on ready-to-wear and 'diffusion lines', but a growing dependency on scent, makeup and accessories. Most recently, the new economic power of celebrity culture has effectively been harnessed.

The 2010 documentary film *Valentino: The Last Emperor* (dir. Matt Tyrhauer), which takes as its subject matter the life and long career of the Italian designer, contains within its very title an elegiac quality. It implies that Valentino, who dressed Jackie Kennedy, Liz Taylor and Princess Margaret, is the very last representative of an ancien régime. In fact, Valentino, who resigned in 2007, was one of the first and most successful designers to use the new forms of celebrity; he swiftly embraced the new money and the new markets. Unlike Balenciaga, who abdicated lest he be compelled to compromise, Valentino stayed in post to dress Victoria Beckham, along with countless Oscar-nominated actresses, together with those whose function on the red carpet is purely decorative. He does not, as the film shows, have the hauteur of the abdicated grandee. He shares with his celebrity clients a liking for the sun, asking his partner of forty years, as he returns from yet another holiday, if he is too tanned; he often shares his hospitality with certain of his celebrity clientele. The film's narrative is punctuated by lavish parties, the first held at Valentino's very own château in France and the last a three-day bonanza in Rome to celebrate his forty-year career. The guests we see at these events are those familiar within this narrative—Elizabeth Hurley, Gwyneth Paltrow, Elton John, Mick Jagger, Joan Collins—all of whom, it seems, are his close personal friends.

In fact, most designers now seem quite happy to dress anybody who can afford their prices, and they have learned to exploit the new economic power of celebrity in a variety of ways. Firstly, they can ensure maximum publicity for their business through the careful cultivation of their own personal image and a trademark mode of self-presentation. We saw earlier exactly how successful this strategy can be in the discussion around Tom Ford, whose acknowledged celebrity status as designer allowed him to embark on his new career within cinema whilst enhancing the popularity of his designs.

Secondly, designers can elect to use the ever-expanding cast of celebrities in their advertising campaigns, both in magazines and on screen. They may also adopt particular celebrities to act as ambassadors for their brand, such as Chanel's 'special girls', and dress them for all occasions. They may choose a model associated with their look but nevertheless possessed of her own cultural—and erotic—capital (Koda and Yohannan 2009). Marc Jacobs, for instance, enjoyed a long and mutually profitable liaison with the young film director Sofia Coppola, who embodied his notion of a look that was edgy and cool (Wiseman 2008; Gehlhar 2008: 60; Okonkwo 2007: 166). Very aware of the new structures of desire and demand, Jacobs has taken the relationship between design and celebrity in other directions. His perfume, Daisy, launched in 2007, was presented for sale in a bottle designed by the artist Takashi Murakami, who created large plastic daisies to adorn the caps of the scent bottles. Fashion journalists picked up on this feature with delight, talking of a 'covetable' fragrance proffered in a 'collectable' bottle. The art-fashion-celebrity nexus, as always, benefited everybody; sales figures for the first year were high (Chevalier and Mazzalovo 2008: 52) and continue to be healthy.

Through the continued, changing choice of models for his magazine campaigns, Jacobs has demonstrated a clear understanding of the multi-faceted, complex celebrity-fashion relationship. His collaboration with Coppola was perhaps intended to suggest their creative similarities. But other of his campaigns have played with less positive notions of fame and infamy. After actress Winona Ryder was famously arrested for a shoplifting spree involving, inevitably, designer clothes, Jacobs instantly signed her up for his next campaign (La Ferla 2003; Wiseman 2008), which showed her sitting on a bed in what looked like a hotel room surrounded by carrier bags. So, too, in a later campaign, he chose to use Victoria Beckham *before* her final induction into fashion's inner circle; he placed her *inside* a large carrier bag, out of which she seemed to be struggling (see Freeman 2007a). This showed an awareness of Beckham's enormous potential purchasing power, combined with a sly sense of her seeming inability at that time to make the right choices. She herself presumably saw the humour, not least because the advertisement tended to counter the very presumptions it also exploited.

Jacobs now tells us he is 'bored with celebrities' (Donnelly 2010)—meaning, perhaps, that he is bored by the more obvious representatives of their kind. The very next Marc Jacobs campaign to appear after this pronouncement featured British choreographer and dancer Michael Clark, whose ballets have included nude scenes; in one of his ballets, performance artist and cross-dresser Leigh Bowery rampaged across the stage wielding a chainsaw whilst wearing platform boots with eight-inch heels (Barber 2009; O'Mahony 2003). Clark is associated not with fashion but with the artistic avant-garde; Jacobs has attempted to change the game by introducing signifiers of cultural capital. He has since employed photographer Annie Leibovitz—who famously portrays celebrities—and the dancer Mikhail Baryshnikov in his advertisements for Louis Vuitton (Lippert 2010). He has also used *himself*—in place of a less fashionable and more 'boring' celebrity, perhaps. He appears completely naked in the advertisement for his cologne, Bang, a massive faux-flaçon between his splayed thighs. Now tanned and muscular, Jacobs has totally transformed his own appearance; in the early 1990s, the grunge era, he was pallid and slender, as was then de rigeur. It is odd to think that this now super-sleek designer, now so successfully employed by Louis Vuitton, once lost his job after the defiantly subversive 'grunge' collection that he created for Perry Ellis (as was widely reported in the media, including Vogue.com and NYMag.com).

He is not alone in professing to despise aspects of celebrity. Susannah Frankel wrote an article provocatively headlined: 'New Model Army: Why Fashion Has Fallen out of Love with Its A-list Clotheshorses' (2010). However, although she references Keira Knightley for Chanel, the other designers she discussed and whom she quoted were Jacobs and Miuccia Prada, whose designs are not worn by the more popular, glamorous celebrities, while Prada advertising campaigns have consistently, consciously refrained from the use of the celebrity face. The autumn 2010 campaign, a clear reference to the television series *Mad Men,* uses three models who include a supposedly retired supermodel, Christy Turlington.

Karl Lagerfeld was also mentioned in the article, but this seemed simply to reflect his dislike of the 'wrong' celebrities—those lower down the celebrity hierarchy who aspire to the glamorous rather than the fashionable look. As we have seen, he is quite happy to be associated with the 'right' kind of celebrity. He has gone so far as to lend a dress for the Cotillion Ball in Paris to the Texan debutante Jane Aldridge, best known for her blog Sea of Shoes (seaofshoes.typepad.com), which other bloggers regard as overly narcissistic and designer-dependent (interviews, Church Gibson 2008–2010). Lagerfeld was therefore seen *himself,* as he posed with Jane in her borrowed ball gown, in the most stylish inner circles of the blogosphere (Mullen Gordon 2009; 'All Abode' 2010).

Today, it seems, designers themselves are in fact expected to feature in the public domain. The new fashion-literate public wants to know about the *person,* here as in every other sphere. In the past, of course, highly influential designers like Balenciaga succeeded in their wish to keep themselves, rather than their creations, out of the public eye. The man usually described as the first Paris couturier, Charles Worth, was the prototype for the unobtrusive, talented designers who would follow him. He dressed the Empress Eugénie, famed for her elegance, who sat for her portrait by Winterhalter in a Worth gown. But he did not seek openly to prosper by this association. He did, however, present himself carefully and consciously as artist rather than dressmaker; photographs show him wearing the floppy beret and cravats that characterized the 'artistic dress' of the period (Pendergast et al. 2004; Tungate 2008).

The couturiers who followed him, Creed and Redfern, who created the 'tailor-mades' of the early twentieth century, were similarly self-effacing (Taylor 2002: 114; Buckley and Fawcett 2002). Until quite recently, if they wished, designers could still remain remote, even reclusive, figures whose own appearance was not important and who might pass unrecognized in a crowd, though there were, of course, always others more extrovert in temperament, more flamboyant in appearance or who simply understood and courted publicity.

Given the new centrality of fashion and the cult of the designer, today a diffident couturier might find it impossible to remain anonymous and to stay in the background. Yves St Laurent's shyness was legendary (see Drake 2006: 372) despite his famous naked photo shoot to publicize his cologne for men, Pour Homme, in 1971 (see Maisa 2010). But today he might find the press far more intrusive, and his life in general harder.

Alber Elbaz has resurrected the House of Lanvin, and his elegant, unusual clothes are worn by Joan Burstein, owner of Browns in London, and by quirky actress Tilda Swinton (Levy 2009a; Solway 2008); in October 2010, he embarked on a profitable collaboration with high street manufacturer H&M (Stenvinkel 2010). Elbaz himself is short, plump and rather shy (see Levy 2009a). Nevertheless, he now has to give interviews and pose for portraits in order to maintain the high profile of the 'new' Lanvin. It is interesting to consider some of the photographs for which he has posed. In a shoot for Tim Ward, to accompany a profile in the *New Yorker* (Levy 2009b), he is shown wading waist-deep in the sea, fully dressed and holding an open umbrella above his head, perhaps an attempt to highlight the absurdity of photographing *him* rather than the draped, asymmetric gowns and innovative costume jewellery with which he is now associated (Levy 2009b). In another Ward photograph, he has donned a headdress of rabbits' ears made by an even more radical designer, Shona Heath, and looks rueful, uneasily aware of the comic figure he cuts.

Although, like most designers today, Elbaz has a signature outfit—tuxedo jacket, cropped trousers, round-toed shoes and large floppy bow tie—unlike some of his contemporaries, he has resisted any pressure to lose weight. Karl Lagerfeld, however, famously shed at least two stone; he subsequently scorned the 'fat women eating chips' (Paterson 2009) whom he somewhat cavalierly assumed were the moving force behind the public objection to overly slender catwalk models. He also objected to the publication of a radical and one-off edition of French *Elle* in April 2010 which used plus-size women throughout, claiming to find it distasteful and an abject capitulation (McVeigh 2010). However, it would appear that Lagerfeld later changed his approach when he used plus-size models in a shoot for *V* magazine in January 2010.

Christian Dior, famously one of the most influential of all designers, was also far from slim. However, few who admired his designs during his heyday in the 1940s and 1950s would have had any idea of what Dior himself actually looked like; his couture clients, of course, would have known, but not the vast numbers who purchased high street copies of the New Look (1947) and the H-line (1954). Far from the rarefied ether of couture and even from the world of fashion, most people would nevertheless have known his name, given the dramatic effect of his New Look on every high street. The 1947 show—possibly the most significant Paris collection of all time—provoked a frenzy of criticism and led to questions being asked in the Houses of Parliament in London. Harold Wilson, then a Labour underling but later prime minister, made his first appearance in the public eye when he spoke out against the disgraceful waste of fabric involved in the designs and the problems thus created at one remove for a Britain where rationing was in force. All the same, the New Look was enthusiastically adopted by other designers and gradually filtered down to the high streets. It was given a longer shelf life by Hollywood costume designers, who helped prolong it over the next decade. In Alfred Hitchcock's *The Birds*—a film made as late as 1960—Tippi Hedren wears a green suit with a nipped-in waist and narrow skirt designed by Edith Head, perhaps the last cinematic flourish of the New Look. With a mink coat draped over her shoulders, she carries a tiny formal bag and wears very high heels for her fateful trip to the small town of Bodega Bay. Also encumbered by a large birdcage, she seems to epitomize the impracticality of the original, over-accessorized style and the way in which it deliberately impeded women's freedom of movement, making them urban, imprisoned and dependent, just as the lovebirds she carries with her are themselves trapped within their own over-ornate cage.

In the 1950s, the House of Dior became famous for its fragrances and its silk stockings. Dior, a shy man, was avidly courted by the Parisian elite, and his home was photographed for magazine features. Dior understood the need for publicity, and he dressed Hollywood stars, including Ava Gardner and Sophia Loren, both on screen and off, but he was by nature retiring—it was his designs that he wished to be photographed and recognized (see Pochna 1996, 2005; Okawa 2008; Chenoune and

Hamani 2007; Hawthorne 1996). In 1956, Andy Warhol nastily put his own drawing of Dior's plump profile into a window display which he created for Bergdorf Goodman to showcase *Miss Dior*. The unwitting designer's rather pudgy features were woven cruelly into a *Miss Dior* montage, thus creating an early example of 'outing' which displayed Warhol's ruthlessness, at the same time demonstrating the degree of anonymity still possible at that time. Most passers-by and window-shoppers on Fifth Avenue did not recognize the man depicted in the sketch.

Although this chapter is concerned with changes in the self-presentation of the fashion designer in the era of celebrity culture, they are not to be confused with the use and frequently the *syndication* of the *name* of the designer. Pierre Cardin was one of the first to license the use of his name to appear as a logo on objects that he had not himself designed and with which the House of Cardin had no connection whatsoever— ties, cigarette lighters, shirts (Okonkwo 2007; Langle 2005). Cardin himself, champion of progress in the 1960s, designed car interiors, uniforms for air hostesses and costumes for the US version of the successful television series *The Avengers* (1964).

Diversification has continued, for today it is necessary for survival. With a tiny number of couture clients remaining, designers are now financially dependent on their new fragrances, their classic scents and their ranges of makeup. The so-called designer handbags, usually with the logo highly visible, have latterly been extraordinarily profitable (Agins 2000; Chadha and Husband 2006). Here, the designers retain some control and continue to have an input. Their awareness of the centrality of celebrity has also led to some houses abandoning their appeal to their more traditional couture customers and creating younger designs to please the newer clientele who now have the privileged front-row seats.

CHANEL, FIRST CELEBRITY DESIGNER?

In 1921, Gabrielle 'Coco' Chanel launched one of the most successful scents of all time (Groom 1997: 21). The iconic oblong bottle for Chanel No. 5, still revered, was carefully designed to her own very strict specifications, and she selected its contents from several versions created by parfumier Ernest Béaux (Charles-Roux 2009). Meanwhile, once established as a designer, she herself also became a fashion leader; she was constantly photographed and always mindful of publicity, whether it was in popularizing her own cardigan suits and costume jewellery, 'creating' the little black dress or assuming (supposedly sole) responsibility for the new fashionability of the suntan. The designer was photographed in 1925 as she stepped off the Duke of Westminster's yacht in a garment which revealed her deeply suntanned back and arms, thus making that look instantly desirable. Today's celebrities also endlessly seem to have as part of their trademark a set of eminently bronzed limbs. However, in the 1920s, the suntan was unknown in the upper echelons of society. It was thought of as a sign of outdoor work and manual labour, and therefore as distinctly proletarian. Once Chanel displayed her sun-baked body, by contrast, tans became objects of almost frenzied desire. They also became tokens of privilege, of the wherewithal and the opportunity to holiday on the Riviera (though real tans were likewise available in Margate or on the beaches of New Jersey).

Chanel's power is indicated by the fact that she was the only fashion designer to feature in *Time* magazine's list of the Hundred Most Creative People of the Twentieth Century. Meanwhile, the facts of her life have been copiously set down. Designers have certainly been the subject of documentary films, but Chanel is the only one to have inspired not one but two feature films and, indeed, to have been recreated as the heroine of a stage musical (*Coco* starred Katherine Hepburn when it opened on Broadway in 1956). The media interest in Chanel's persona appears to be as intense as ever; the more unpalatable facts of her life seem increasingly to be glossed over as time passes.

However, Chanel was not the first female designer to be aware of aristocratic status, power and myth making. In a very different era, Rose Bertin, dressmaker to Marie Antoinette, used her relationship with the queen to build up her business before and after the French Revolution. Ladies flocked to the little shop she opened in Paris, knowing of her royal connections as well as her often radical designs. Marie Antoinette's clothes were invariably innovative, and the new designs she popularized were achieved with Bertin's help. Caroline Weber's *Queen of Fashion: What Marie Antoinette Wore to the Revolution* (2008) bizarrely suggests that her most radical ideas actually prefigured the Revolution, most notably in the case of Marie Antoinette's adoption of a modified male jacket for riding and the loose flowing muslin dresses, the *chemises à la reine,* which she originally wore in the Petit Trianon at Versailles and which were a forerunner of the high-waisted gowns of the Directoire (Weber 2008: 149–50, 185–6). According to Weber, it was not so much Marie Antoinette's notorious extravagance as the 'revolutionary' nature of the actual styles she adopted that precipitated the events of 1789. One might feel that the historical and political thought at stake in this assertion is worthy of a Lagerfeld. But Bertin's exploitation of her celebrity clientele was not lacking in shrewdness. Like Chanel, she knew exactly how to succeed and survive; she did not go to the guillotine with the elegant ladies she had clothed. Instead, she survived to open another fashion business and to prosper through her well-known former association with the French court (Weber 2008: 181–3).

Chanel was the first woman to achieve real renown in the world of haute couture, and her achievements must be acknowledged. In the interwar years, when Chanel's creations and her own characteristic style of dress were discussed, emulated and endlessly photographed, her fame finally led to her being singled out by Sam Goldwyn of MGM (see chapter 3 and also Gaines 1990; Bruzzi 1997); he lured her to Hollywood with a highly tempting contract. This experiment, intended to combine Parisian chic and Hollywood glamour, was not a success, and Chanel left after completing only one film of a projected dozen.

But there is a worrying tendency in the mythologizing of Chanel; she is presented as playing a central part in the gradual process of women's liberation. It is often argued that not only did she provide women with new, comfortable, relaxed garments, but she herself, it is often suggested, was an inspiring role model (see Madsen 1990; Charles-Roux 2009). The endlessly chronicled facts of Chanel's life—her upbringing in an orphanage, the early work as seamstress and singer, the rich and aristocratic lovers—not only compose an archetypal rags-to-riches story, but also display a ruthlessness that is not, necessarily, admirable. Worse still, her straightforward sexual exploitation of these well-connected lovers, who included two dukes, was followed by her notorious wartime liaison with a Gestapo officer. This enabled her to spend the war years in the comfort and elegance of the Ritz hotel.

When Chanel was arrested after the liberation of Paris, she was not brought to trial, arguably because of her aristocratic connections in Britain (Charles-Roux 2009; Madsen 1990), but she did have to go into exile in Switzerland. Her biographers sometimes skate over this; one even suggests that her imperious dismissal of the official questioning her about her Gestapo lover's nationality and affiliations showed her famous independence of spirit and that she was in some degree justified in hating de Gaulle for trying to bring her to book (see Madsen 1990).

Interestingly, the fact of the Nazi lover may have led to a decade in exile and a much smaller market for her clothes in France when she returned, but it has not prevented her transmogrification into a national heroine. Her contemporary, Edith Piaf, another woman who has been mythologized, actually worked for the French Resistance during the Second World War: her contribution was honoured with a decoration.

But the myth-making around Chanel seems if anything to have intensified. Two feature films were made in 2009, *Coco avant Chanel* and *Chanel and Stravinsky*. However, the most interesting 'Chanel film' is perhaps the four-minute commercial for Chanel No. 5 discussed in chapter 5 and directed by Jean-Pierre Jeunet. For it offers a much clearer image of Chanel clothes and style in its four minutes than either film achieves in two hours. The fact that the House of Chanel employed this art-house director to make their commercial and gave him a vast budget indicates what we have already seen—the new relationship between film and fashion and the new ways in which designers can deploy different modes of celebrity. Audrey Tatou, who played Chanel in *Coco avant Chanel*, was also the heroine of the commercial: she wears different Chanel outfits in each scene of the mini-film.

The House of Dior attempted to rival this achievement by evoking, however indirectly, the other French national heroine, Edith Piaf. Following the success of the biographical film *La vie en Rose*, and using the star of that film, the Oscar-winning Marion Cotillard,

Figure 34 Casual style for rich girls—Tamara Palmer-Tomkinson, sunglasses on head and Chanel jacket paired with jeans. Photograph by Anne-Marie Michel.

the Hollywood director David Lynch, as discussed in chapter 5, was employed to make four mini-films, using some of the visual motifs associated with film noir to publicize the new Lady Dior bag; these were heavily showcased in magazines and trailered in cyberspace. In doing so, he managed to combine Cotillard's status as Oscar-winning actress, invoke the spectre of the iconic singer and deploy the chic legacy of film noir.

Narrative films tend to be less successful in evoking the legacy and image of couture. While presented as a love story, *Coco avant Chanel* was actually part commercial; it was heavily subsidized by the House of Chanel, who gave the costume designer unrestricted access to their archives. The contents are put on display to great effect in the across-the-decades fashion show which ends the film. Here, Tatou sits at the top of the famous stairs in the Rue du Cambon, reflected in the repeated mirrors, wearing a 1960s cream bouclé suit and the classic two-tone Chanel pumps, while her models parade up and down past her. They wear Chanel outfits from every decade. Interestingly, there is one glimpse of a recent Karl Lagerfeld reworking of the classic Chanel motifs: a trouser suit worn with a white shirt and a hat tied beneath the chin gaucho-style.

This ties in with our brief sighting in the film of the Chanel trademark of the white camellia, and we are offered a suggestion of its possible provenance; it is displayed on the lapel of Chanel's great love, Boy Capel, played by Alessandro Nivola; the camera lingers briefly on the flower while the two dine together for the very last time, the night before his fatal car crash. In *Chanel and Stravinsky,* we see the designer hard at work, here creating Chanel No. 5; the film implies that this is an act on a par with the musical compositions of Stravinsky. It is surely significant that the re-mythologizing of Chanel should take place at this particular socio-historic juncture. The creator of the very first luxury brand thus appears as a force for liberation rather than enslavement.

BACK TO THE FUTURE: BRANDING THE DESIGNER

Arguably the current designer-as-celebrity era began with the publicity created for Vivienne Westwood by Malcolm McLaren during the so-called birth of punk, described in the previous chapter. Westwood has since reinvented her own persona, and her celebrity status has been ensured by her various subsequent activities, which include posing for *Tatler* magazine dressed to impersonate Prime Minister Margaret Thatcher and collecting an award from Buckingham Palace while wearing a revealing dress without any underwear (Frankel 2004). Westwood's career is an interesting way of understanding the changes in the industry and across visual culture which inform this book (also see Wilcox 2005; McRobbie 1998; Vermorel 1996; Mulvagh 1998).

For the 1980s—supposedly the designer decade—saw her flounder briefly. Eventually, she found her financial footing, and the former self-elected subversive saw the Japanese, in particular, embrace her designs. Her career really burgeoned in the 1980s, with her publicity-courting runway shows; she used the curvaceous Sarah Stockbridge as a model and ensured that her embonpoint was photographed. So, too, was Naomi Campbell's catwalk tumble off a very high pair of snakeskin platform shoes in 1993. The shoes are now in the V&A Costume Court, while Westwood has been made an OBE (Order of the British Empire). She may have become a part of the fashion establishment, but through her own extraordinary attire, she nevertheless parodies the dress of the English lady and thus maintains her own self-consciously eccentric persona. She sets out, it seems, to look arresting, unusual and bizarre rather than conventionally stylish; she has famously used artist Tracey Emin and former *Baywatch* star Pamela Anderson, rather than conventional models or celebrities, in her advertising campaigns. Unlike Sonia Rykiel, Rei Kawakubo and even Victor and Rolf, Westwood has spurned financially profitable collaborations with the high street. She rides an old-fashioned bicycle and is obviously determined to retain her individuality.

As we have seen, Karl Lagerfeld has certainly not spurned the advances of the high street, nor rejected any opportunities to generate publicity; he has, however, also made the House of Chanel incredibly rich by his reworkings of classic styles and motifs. Twenty years ago, he created for *himself* a signature outfit, which at first involved a ponytail, dark glasses, tight trousers and a fan (Pendergast 1997). The fan has latterly been replaced by extraordinary leather fingerless gloves, and the collars are now very high and starched; but the other elements of the trademark costume remain unchanged.

John Galliano's own image is as theatrical as his couture garments; Galliano has made of himself a creation as extraordinary and eclectic as his own designs. In his collections he mixes up historical and geographical references, famously putting Naomi Campbell in a ballgown reminiscent of the Belle Époque, but then adorning her face and hair with paint and feathers evocative of a Native American (McDowell 2001; O'Byrne 2009). So, too, in his own appearance he combines the dress of the traditional dandy with the piratical and the tribal through his inventive hairstyling and bold stripes of makeup.

Before his dismissal from Dior in 2011, he had already made one appalling error of taste. His 'Homeless' collection of 2001 was perceived by many as totally crass (Benbow-Pfalzgraf 2002: 256). It nevertheless generated a still wider awareness of his name, as did Rei Kawakubo's infamous collection which included two models wearing striped pyjamas, who were sent down the catwalk with close-cropped hair, at the time of the fiftieth anniversary of the liberation of the concentration camps in 1995. Kawakubo professed her complete ignorance of the occasion and the significance of the clothes, claiming that she had been inspired by the idea of young boys at boarding school, and she went on to withdraw the offending outfits (*Independent,* 10 February 1995; Evans 2007: 19).

The designer-as-celebrity does not simply mean that designers now have a trademark appearance as well as a house style; it also leads to press photographs of the designers themselves being featured as widely as those taken at their collections.

They are now featured constantly in magazines, newspapers and on the Internet as celebrities in their own right. Some designers are now so high-profile that not only are they asked to design *clothes* for the high street, but also to design china, bed linen,

Figure 35 Casual street style for low-key designer Henry Holland. Photograph by Anne-Marie Michel.

bath towels and scented candles. Calvin Klein and Ralph Lauren are household names in the States, and they themselves—not just their products—appear regularly on the pages of the glossy magazines, photographed at social events in their own right. Lauren had an eight-page feature and photo spread, *Ralph Lauren—Fashion Czar,* in US *Harper's Bazaar* (December 2007) to celebrate his forty-year career in fashion and his visit to Russia to open his first shops there.

Lauren, interestingly, is very popular in Japan for his own personal style—the cowboy boots, the leather belt, the jeans. It is as if, on his own person, he is reworking the American heritage of the West. There is a Japanese subcultural group who dress in exactly this way, hunting down different versions of vintage Levis online; Lauren and Steve McQueen are featured regularly on the covers of their magazine-cum-catalogue, *Easy.* His designs, however, rework different versions of heritage—he famously creates classic, timeless, often English-inspired looks and sells them to Europeans most profitably. In 2010, he opened a vast emporium in Paris. Like all his shops, and his concessions within department stores, it is carefully designed to evoke a past of country-house living through the preponderance of dark wood, leather armchairs and even mock bookcases. But he has also mined other pasts, using Navajo blankets to great effect as long skirts, and pairing them with buckskin jackets, turquoise jewellery and cowboy hats, so mixing the American West of the pioneers with that of the original occupants of the desert (see McDowell 2001; Lauren 2007; Gross 2004).

Isaac Mizrahi, Karl Lagerfeld, Ozwald Boateng, Giorgio Armani and Yohji Yamamoto have all been the subject of feature-length documentary films made for, and screened in, cinemas. Oscar-winner and Hollywood regular Martin Scorsese directed *Made in Milan,* a film about the work of Giorgio Armani. Jean-Paul Gaultier famously fronted the successful television programme *Eurotrash* in the 1990s. Lagerfeld, with a walk-on part in *Valentino: The Last Emperor,* has also been the subject of his very own documentary, *Lagerfeld Confidential.*

Perhaps the most telling image from the Valentino film, which stresses throughout the quality of his workmanship, involves one of his many seamstresses, for no sewing machines are ever used in the creation of Valentino gowns. After a difficult day, when we have seen tempers fraying, an elderly seamstress slumps wretchedly against a wall, believing herself unseen. It is difficult not to compare this with other moments in the film: Valentino on his private plane with his five pugs, Valentino entertaining at his French chateau, Valentino skiing off-piste in Gstaad carefully monitored by the pilot of his own personal helicopter, which hovers above him. There is a popular belief that to work in the atelier of a great couturier is rewarding although anonymous. The image of this stocky woman, her head thrown back, abandoning herself to exhaustion, somehow belies this notion (also see Tyrnauer 2004).

Today, then, the designer has often become as familiar as the clothes designed, a recognizable brand. The most financially successful designer in England today, Paul Smith, has twenty-four shops in Japan alone and yet does not seem to court publicity. However, his particular form of English identity—proudly Northern, bicycle riding, publicity shunning—is surely an intrinsic part of his appeal outside his own country. And in Japan, his impeccable mod credentials, in his own persona as well as his designs, surely form a part of his appeal; the young Japanese seem fascinated by the Britain of the 1960s (Crewe and Goodrum 2000; Violette 2003).

What some, if not all, designers may share is the desire to be perceived as artists. Since the Romantic period and its mythologizing of the creative genius, artists have been regarded by many—including themselves—as in some way superior to designers. The romantic notion of the artist was, as we have seen, that of a special being, not bound by the normal rules governing human conduct, who might well be unappreciated and starve, who could even, like the poet Chatterton, *die* in a garret, but who was incalculably different, even sublime in some way. Designers, by contrast, were perhaps more earthbound, working with their hands to complete commissions, rather than awaiting spiritual inspiration. And there was—certainly in the past—some unspoken consensus whereby the fashion designer occupied a rather lowly place within the design hierarchy, forever associated with the frivolous and feminine. Today, this may have changed; what has certainly remained is a certain level of mythologizing around art. As we have seen, designers, through their new celebrity status and their involvement in or patronage of the art world, have sought to become involved and similarly mythologized. Now we should look at the changed role of models, without whom the fashion world could not function, but whose careers are usually so much shorter than that of these designers.

MODELS TAKE CENTRE STAGE?

Over the decades, the model has moved from a completely anonymous figure whose job was to show off clothes to best effect, at first on small catwalks and then in photographs, to becoming—in some cases, at least—a well-known public figure. The extraordinary *Vogue* image in which the model Lisa Fonssagrives clings perilously to the Eiffel Tower, published in May 1939, only credited the photographer involved, Erwin Blumenfeld. Interestingly, this particular iconic image has been recreated twice by the contemporary fashion photographer Pete Lindbergh: once in 1989 with a little-known model, Mathilde, and, more significantly for this book, in a shoot with film star Marion Cotillard to advertise the Lady Dior handbag, which appeared in 2008.

But during the 1950s, photographic models began to acquire recognizable personalities and become identifiable by name. The 1960s meant the creation of a celebrity persona, but only for a very few. Today, a very small number have arguably acquired a brand identity. The models who have attained most celebrity status are, in fact, those who are seen as most accessible, as extraordinarily 'ordinary' in Dyer's sense. His ideas around stardom have certainly seemed the most useful in attempting to make sense of the current climate. Significantly, his notion of the 'ordinary' was largely argued through case studies of particular stars, Joan Crawford and Marilyn Monroe among them, who were admired by their fans partly for their transcendence (see Stacey 1994) of their inauspicious origins and their achievement of fame against heavily stacked odds. The potency and continuation of the class-crossing myths around celebrity do seem particularly pertinent here.

Modelling in the 1950s, of course, was a respectable job for a girl of good family on both sides of the Atlantic. Some models went on to make famous and profitable liaisons, Fiona Campbell-Walter marrying Baron von Thyssen and Lisa Fonssagrives becoming the wife of Irving Penn. But Campbell-Walter was, in fact, born an admiral's daughter. However, with the social upheavals of the 1960s, very different models were to become popular. Society and fashion model both became, it seemed, more democratic. The haughty models of the 1950s who gazed out from the pages of *Vogue* and *Harper's Bazaar* on both sides of the Atlantic were young in years, but styled to look like elegant women. The images created for US *Vogue* by Irving Penn and Richard Avedon show off long necks, plucked eyebrows, extravagant hats and couture gowns (see Jobling 1999).

In the 1960s, even before the recognized effect of the 'youthquake' identified by US *Vogue* editor Diana Vreeland, models had changed in appearance and demeanour. They were, or seemed to be, physically smaller and looked very much younger. They might be photographed with rumpled hair, and certainly they were girls, rather than women. They were often photographed in movement, as in the famous British *Vogue* shoot of April 1962, where Jean Shrimpton crosses the streets and walks along the sidewalks of Manhattan, accompanied in one of the images by a teddy bear (see Radner 2000). Twiggy, the only model who was really a true celebrity in the way that we now understand the term, was quickly dubbed 'the Face of 1966' by leading fashion writer Felicity Green. She was much smaller than Shrimpton and far more androgynous, a crop-haired child rather than a girl. An iconic image created by Ronald Traeger shows her grinning widely as she whizzes downhill on a moped (1966); Cecil Beaton famously photographed her for British *Vogue* climbing across the furniture of a large drawing room (1967). Before her discovery, she worked in a hairdressing salon; later, she continued to live at home with her parents in their council house in the unfashionable area of Neasden and was delighted to be photographed standing in the doorway with her mother (see Church Gibson 2006a).

Twiggy, in fact, was the first model who lent her name to a range of products, and so the very first true model-as-designer. In 1966, there was a range of Twiggy dresses, and Twiggy shoes followed swiftly. Although she has recently returned to modelling, persuaded to do so for Marks and Spencer by one of its directors, Stuart Rose, she had actually retired while still only nineteen. She was very young when she became famous; in fact, the distinctive look which made her so popular was in fact created by her boyfriend, manager and Svengali figure, Nigel Davies, who had rechristened himself Justin de Villeneuve. It was he who nicknamed her Twiggy and devised her eye makeup, copied everywhere. He had a Victorian doll with underlashes painted onto its cheeks, which he used for inspiration (see Lawson and Denning 1997). The other

Figure 36   Slim elegance is still desirable—top model Erin O'Connor. Photograph by Anne-Marie Michel.

feature of Twiggy's radical style was the drastic cropped haircut; this was the creation of top London hairdresser Leonard, a friend of 'Justin'. The other components of her look derived partly from the way she had dressed when she went out dancing as a mod, before her job as a 'Saturday girl' brought her to the notice of her mentor (see Lawson and Denning 1997; DeLibero 1994).

Jean Shrimpton, interestingly, however iconic her image, licensed nothing; there was a half-hearted quasi-collaboration with Quant (see Sheridan 2010), but that was all, and eventually she fled from the world of fashion and parties. She was a farmer's daughter from Berkshire, rather than an embryonic hairdresser like Twiggy, who had been sent to the Lucie Clayton School of Modelling, where young girls were still taught deportment as they had been since the school was founded thirty years earlier. Shrimpton had high-profile relationships, firstly with David Bailey, the photographer of the moment who discovered her, and then with film actor Terence Stamp, also a favourite of the press. Tiring of the publicity and the pressure, she escaped to a commune in Wales and is now a hotel owner in Cornwall. She has since said in her autobiography that 'for most of the decade, I was a waif astray' (Shrimpton with Hall 1990: 5).

She was not alone in her wish to flee. One of the most celebrated photographs of the decade was a poster created for the shop now seen as synonymous with 'Swinging London', Biba, by photographer Sarah Moon. It showed a close-up of model Ingrid Boulting, her face half-covered by veiling, her eyes huge and thoughtful. Boulting is now a yoga teacher on the West Coast of the United States, in the small town of Ojai, where the author found herself in one of her classes.

Now models had names and even personalities, though their images, of course, changed from decade to decade. The waiflike girls of the 1960s were replaced by the largely anonymous, healthy-looking women of the 1970s. Jerry Hall, who would later become the partner of Mick Jagger and is still very much in the public eye, is the exception here; she was very friendly with Warhol and later acted as a host for his Factory-style TV show, *Andy Warhol's TV.* Far better known—and very much in the public eye—were the strong-featured supermodels of the 1980s and early 1990s. They were all tall, broad-shouldered and had perceptible curves. They gave some impression, at least, of independence and were interesting, it seemed, en masse. At one point, there was even a short-lived magazine, *Supermodel,* which charted their activities, described their latest looks and publicized their beauty tips. Some of these women have had careers of unusual longevity, like Linda Evangelista, who continued modelling into her forties. Others used their celebrity status to create new careers—Christy Turlington lent her name to a range of yoga wear Nuala, which finally ceased trading in 2007, while Cindy Crawford launched her own line of skincare. But it is perhaps only the range of lingerie 'designed' by Elle MacPherson, Intimates, that has remained a contender within the marketplace. Nevertheless, the women who comprised the supermodels are still photographed, still recognized, part of the new visual culture around celebrity.

Although the supermodel look and physique were challenged by the waif look of the early 1990s, epitomized by Kate Moss and celebrated by photographers like Juergen Teller and Corinne Day, this style would triumphantly reappear. Gisele Bündchen earned $33 million in 2007 while Moss, as the runner-up, earned only nine (*Forbes*). Gisele has long, tanned limbs, a mane of glossy blondish hair—and breasts of which she is inordinately proud, often referring proudly to these assets in interview. She has

Figure 37 Supermodel party style exemplified by Claudia Schiffer. Photograph by Anne-Marie Michel.

not only supermodel but also celebrity status; she is now on magazine covers as a celebrity in her own right, rather than mere photographic model, and was hounded by paparazzi during her four-year relationship with film star Leonardo di Caprio. But she does not seem to inspire great warmth, nor to have the popularity with young women of Kate Moss. Gisele also provoked anger by posing for a controversial Annie Leibovitz cover for *Vogue,* together with African Caribbean basketball star James LeBron, in April 2008. The picture was seen as compounding the most offensive racial stereotypes (see Jeffries 2008). For in it, the athlete, half-naked, has his arm around Gisele in her evening gown, seeming to lift her off the ground; their pose, it was suggested, was deliberately created to evoke the familiar image of King Kong abducting Faye Wray.

Kate Moss, Superstar

Perhaps the only model to achieve real, long-lasting and genuinely popular celebrity status, Kate Moss has been the subject of an academic analysis by Jennifer Craik (2009: 233–7) and has had her image dissected by Angela Buttolph in a book, *Kate Moss: Style* (2008b). She has become one of the best-known women in Britain, and her private life has been successfully used to sell tabloid newspapers. She has 'designed' her own range for Topshop and 'created' fragrances; arguably she is now herself a brand. It seems, perhaps, that the fashion industry has become so celebrity-driven that branding may need to be reconceptualized.

The ultimate 'Moss moment' surely came at a Chanel show in 2009; hopefully it ties together the strands that underpin this book. At the show, she was guest of honour; beside her sat her then boyfriend, later husband, Jamie Hince of The Kills, and her friend and mentor, Philip Green, who had enticed her into creating her own range for high street retailer Topshop. The photographers left their posts and their pit; they swarmed out onto the catwalk itself to photograph Moss and her companions. The new celebrity front row had finally been acknowledged as of more significance than the actual fashion show. It took nearly half an hour to clear the runway and allow that show to begin.

Earlier, in May 2008, the coveted English award for Dress of the Year was bestowed on a relatively inexpensive 'Kate Moss' dress which formed part of her most recent range for Topshop; their lucrative partnership, which began in 2006, finally made possible both the opening and the success of Topshop in New York.

Interestingly, this dress was twinned, on display, with the Chanel star-patterned jumpsuit Moss had worn to her birthday party the previous summer. So Moss-as-celebrity was celebrated along with Moss-as-designer. And in a further interesting illustration of the true power of celebrity culture, the museum approached journalist Paula Reed of *Grazia* magazine to make the selection. All this was an unprecedented move for the prestigious Museum of Costume in Bath; since the award was set up, it had always been presented to recognized, trained designers, whether high fashion or high street (Shields 2009).

Just as with the star styles described by Patty Fox (1995), Angela Buttolph's book *Kate Moss: Style* (2008b) deconstructs and teases out the constituent elements of her look. It actually draws up a numbered list of the key components of this look, from vintage evening dresses through waistcoats and leather jackets. Books like *Audrey Style,* however, are a gaze into a mythical closet, to admire what cannot really be purchased. But with the Moss book, the author seems to encourage some form of

DIY emulation; this is surely proof of her supposed accessibility, of her perceived 'ordinariness' (see Buttolph 2008a). Elliott Smedley, writing for *Fashion Cultures* (Bruzzi
and Church Gibson 2000), argues that the controversial early shoots on which she
worked with photographer Corinne Day and which established her *extraordinary* career
were in no way sexual, but rather served to emphasize her *ordinary* appeal and even
her humble social background. The first shoot, the 'Third Summer of Love', the cover
and main fashion feature for *The Face* in 1990, saw Moss grinning happily and romp-
ing topless on Camber Sands in Essex, wearing a feathered headdress and looking
like the very young girl that she was—only fifteen at the time. A later shoot with Day
provoked far more negative public reaction; it was not in an alternative publication like
The Face but within the pages of British *Vogue* in 1993. Here, Day photographed Moss
in what was in fact Moss's very own sparsely furnished flat. The shoot was for underwear, much of which came from the high street; the sight of the very slender Moss,
wearing nylon knickers and a thin cotton vest, leaning against an old-fashioned industrial radiator and outlined by a string of cheap Christmas tree lights, was seen by some
as highly offensive. It was suggested by some commentators at the time that not only
did these images glorify anorexia, but that there was a problem with her extreme youth
(see Smedley 2000, for a detailed discussion of the furore). *Vogue* editor Alexandra
Shulman, in fact, made a public statement defending the publication of the pictures.

The controversy did not disappear, and the continued use of young, ultra-slim models combined with the 'dirty realism' style of photography adopted and favoured by Day,
Juergen Teller and David Sims created further concern around what President Clinton
christened 'heroin chic' (again, see Smedley 2000). This was seen as being reflected
in the grunge fashions of the time, seemingly Seattle-inspired, which were picked up
and put on the catwalk by some designers, most notably the young Marc Jacobs.

Moss went on to work for Calvin Klein; her controversial campaigns for Obsession
and, more significantly, CK One led to yet more anger, still more publicity. She nevertheless endeared herself not only to fashion editors, photographers and designers,
but also more and more to the general public.

Efforts to dethrone Moss, particularly the tabloid 'Cocaine Kate' scandal of 2005,
have so far been singularly unsuccessful. She lost some contracts but gained more;
she also saw Alexander McQueen stride onto the catwalk after his show that season
wearing a T-shirt emblazoned with the message WE LOVE YOU KATE (Cartner-Morley
2010a). Pictures of this particular moment were as popular, if not more, than the original images of Moss with rolled-up banknote and incriminating white powder.

It will be interesting to see what Moss does eventually; she is still in constant demand as a model but has talked about moving into another role within the industry.
The interesting difference between Moss and Twiggy is that Moss does seem to be *in
control,* if only of her image; even in the infamous Pete Doherty phase, there was no
sense that a man was pulling the strings, that a stylist was choosing her every outfit.

Although Moss may have been influenced by some stylists, in particular Katie Grand, she has assimilated their knowledge; in fact, she is so frequently caught off-guard that we can assume that her look is now indeed all her own work. Whereas Twiggy looked childlike, Moss looks *young*—an important difference.

Both Moss and Twiggy, significantly, not only embody Dyer's ideas about 'ordinariness', but both remind us frequently of their origins, Twiggy's childhood in the council house and Moss's life with her single mother in Croydon. The discovery factor may be a part of Moss's appeal to young women, the idea that any pretty girl in a check-in queue at an airport can be sighted and scouted, as she was at JFK in 1992. Unlike Twiggy, who abdicated and was later lured back, Moss continued to model across two decades. The celebrity magazines love her; so do the broadsheets. She has been used, interestingly, for mass-market, inexpensive, 'ordinary' campaigns, such as Rimmel cosmetics, as well as for couture images.

In 2010, she entered yet another liaison—this time to design with, or for, the long-established but rather staid French firm Longchamp, who make serviceable, stylish but not celebrity handbags. The first advertising campaign showed Moss stark naked in the back of a limousine but concealing all with a strategically placed bag from the new collection.

Meanwhile, fashion photographer Mario Testino published a limited-edition book (fifteen hundred signed copies), charting his relationship with Moss across two decades (Testino 2010). Originally retailing in August 2010 at a cost of £300, within two months four copies were being offered on Amazon for £725–£800. Testino has photographed all the leading models of the past two decades and many of the celebrities, including his famous collaboration with Princess Diana (Testino 2006). In fact, her former husband Charles later commissioned Testino to create a series of portraits showing off his way of life at his country home, Highgrove; he obviously thought that Testino could make him—or at least his lifestyle—attractive and desirable (Alderson and Edwardes 2002). Testino could now photograph anyone he chose for a coffee-table book; but to ensure that it would sell out, he selected Moss.

However, not long after the publication of the Testino book, it was announced that Moss and Topshop were to part company. There were rumours that Philip Green wanted to replace her with his own daughter and other, unkind suggestions that her range had lost its original appeal. Whatever the truth, Moss herself remains visually omnipresent; she has more front-cover credits than any other model. Her extracurricular activities, even without Topshop, include her own line of fragrances and her role as 'ambassador' for Dior.

The papers had hardly finished analysing the reasons for Moss's departure from Topshop when they found it once again necessary to put her picture on their front pages. Singer Bryan Ferry had chosen Moss for the cover of his new album, *Olympia* (Bull 2010a). Both the title of Ferry's album and the subsequent styling of Moss for its cover came from the Manet painting 'Olympe', which hangs now in the Musée d'Orsay in Paris. The painting caused a scandal when it was first unveiled. The courtesan depicted lies on her bed, naked but for a ribbon around her neck and her elegant slippers; most disturbingly, she gazes coolly out of the frame to meet and challenge the gaze of the spectator. Ferry suggested that she was perhaps 'the first pin-up girl' and that Moss was the clear choice to impersonate her. Perhaps she should not worry about the cancelled Topshop contract. She has also been co-opted by the world of fine art, having been sculpted in bronze by Marc Quinn and painted by Lucian Freud. And now—a second coda is needed.

Naomi Campbell—A Difficult Narrative

This chapter cannot end without emphasizing the continuing and wholly extraordinary *whiteness* of the modelling world, where nearly all the current faces are still white. Women of colour are certainly on the books of modelling agencies worldwide. They have been used on the Parisian catwalks since the 1960s (see Newby 1962: 239). Pierre Cardin was perhaps the first to give non-white women star status; he famously took a Japanese model, Hiroko, had her hair cut into the Vidal Sassoon 'five-point' bob of the early 1960s and used her to open his shows. Models of colour are still, sadly, used in this same way—seemingly employed in order that their 'otherness' may be somehow fetishized (Dyer 1993, 1997). This began with the use of the black model Donyale Luna in the 1960s. Originally discovered by Warhol in his 'screen tests', she was always posed and styled so as to look extraordinary and other-worldly (see her frequent use in the radical publication *Nova*), and this creation of exoticism continues unchecked.

A perfect example of this is the August 2008 edition of *Vogue Italia.* Insensitively dubbed 'the Black Issue', it sold out within a very short time; it also provoked a good deal of justifiable controversy. The critics pointed out that all the models were styled so as to emphasize otherness, to look exotic or even tribal. Headdresses, extraordinary braided and towering coiffures, animal skins and weapons, oiled limbs—the issue was, perhaps, reprehensible rather than in any way 'progressive' (Mower 2008).

Naomi Campbell, who like Moss was discovered as a schoolgirl and who has remained in the public eye ever since, has consistently talked in public of the racial discrimination at work within the world of fashion. She has specifically mentioned the difficulty for women of colour in the securing of cosmetic advertising contracts—these, rather than the fashion editorial shoots, are the source of real financial profit for models (Crilly 2007; Pool 2007). They are certainly employed in advertising shoots for hair and makeup products specifically created for women of colour. But only one African-Caribbean woman has been chosen for the infamous 'Because You're Worth It' campaign run for so long by L'Oréal. However, the woman in question, Beyoncé, as we saw earlier, had her hair straightened and was said to have had her skin visibly lightened, a claim which L'Oréal denied (Glaister 2008).

Campbell's role as spokesperson is invaluable; but sadly her public profile and current celebrity status today are shaped by her erratic behaviour, her fits of anger and sensational incidents which serve to demonize her further. In 2008, she was in the news, accused of hitting out at aircrew who had lost a piece of her Louis Vuitton luggage, and she was also accused of attacking her chauffeur; these incidents took place long after her highly publicized trial for attacking her housekeeper with a mobile telephone, which led to a short sentence and anger management classes (Siddique 2008).

The 'blood diamond' trial of 2010 provided yet more notoriety, casting her as the callous recipient of an unsavoury gift from a very dubious admirer, a man accused of appalling war crimes. Campbell's testimony to the international tribunal at the Hague was not only front-page news; it was televised in its entirety. There were unpleasant sniggers when she explained that she'd never heard of Liberia before, and her choice of words was unfortunate when she stressed that the trial was 'a massive inconvenience' for her (Plunkett 2010; Weaver 2010).

I have mentioned Campbell's career as a conclusion to this chapter since it raises certain questions not only around ethnicity, but also about life in the public eye and the fashion world for young and vulnerable girls. Campbell was only sixteen when, at a fashion show in Paris, a reporter breathlessly enthused: 'She just skipped down the catwalk—she had slung a pair of boxing gloves belonging to her boyfriend Mike Tyson around her neck; she looked innocent and delightful' (*Elle* magazine report on the spring/summer collections, 1988).

This seems ominous now when we know of the subsequent adventures of both parties. It also raises various questions, not least as to why everygirl Moss should have her misdemeanours pardoned, while Campbell must remain the victim of her very own 'troubled diva' narrative.

Other Continents, Other Celebrities, Other Fashions

There are, of course, celebrities across the world who influence fashions in their countries of origin; the question for this book, perhaps, is how they relate to the global dominance of Anglo-American celebrities. Possibly non-Western celebrity has to function rather differently, since it must balance its interest in its own homegrown fashion icons with the reception of Western stars. There are celebrity-led fashions which do not travel beyond their countries of origin—for example, the short-lived trend in South Korea for outlining eyes in carmine after the success of the film *Lady Vengeance* (dir. Chan-Wook Park, 2005). The Hindi film industry, based in Mumbai, is the largest in the world: its stars have enormous power as fashion leaders both within India and in diasporic communities worldwide. Any new modifications in traditional dress will find their origin in the costuming of a particular star, a particular film; cinema is used here for tie-ins, just as in the heyday of Hollywood (see Dwyer 2000). Sadly, the Hindi film *Aisha* (2010, dir. Rajshree Ojha) shows a worrying development: the shopping montage is used here to sell Western luxury brands, and we see sixteen Dior dresses. This film, like *Clueless,* is loosely based on Jane Austen's novel *Emma.* The heroine who remodels her new best friend of inferior social status here wears Western designer clothes; the humbler character is originally dressed in traditional garb.

The magazines *Grazia* and *Vogue* have both been syndicated in India for its newly affluent bourgeoisie. *Vogue India*'s first cover, in October 2007, provoked controversy; the white Australian model Gemma Ward was photographed flanked by five young Indian women, all stars of Hindi cinema, thus giving the impression of a princess surrounded by her handmaidens (see Brook 2007). This extraordinary neocolonialist group was a reworking of the very first cover of Chinese *Vogue* in August 2005, which featured Ward in a similar pose with five Chinese models. One particular fashion spread in Indian *Vogue,* in August 2008, prompted yet more criticism. Models in expensive designer clothes were photographed on location in a Rajasthan village, alongside and amongst those in traditional clothes and in abject poverty. Some of the villagers were provided with designer accessories for the duration of the shoot: a grandmother proudly holds a baby wearing a Fendi bib, an old man wields a Burberry umbrella and the wife seen perched with her son and husband on the family motorbike is clutching a Hermès Birkin bag (Timmons 2008; Cartner-Morley 2008).

This 'poverty chic' ties in with what film-maker Nik Mijovic immortally called 'poverty porn' in dialogue with the author when discussing the Oscar-garlanded film *Slumdog Millionaire* (UK, dir. Danny Boyle, 2008). This film is relevant here since its narrative is constructed around the finding of fame and fortune through the familiar medium of the television game show. It is also highly disturbing in ways simply never discussed in the extant reviews. A small boy, locked into a public latrine by his older brother, may miss the chance to secure an autograph from one of the best-known Hindi film stars; consequently, he throws himself into the cesspit behind him and emerges, completely covered with human excrement, to greet his hero. This seems to have a metaphorical resonance relevant in this particular text; a later scene, where a kidnapped street boy is blinded by his captors so that he may earn more as a beggar, seems better suited to the context of a film like Bunuel's *Los Olvidados* (1950) than to a film which would subsequently be marketed as a feel-good film and which made a fashion celebrity of its star, Freida Pinto. She was seen in the front row at couture shows in the season following the film's success; in 2010, she was signed by L'Oréal for the seemingly endless 'Because I'm Worth It' campaign.

Across the world, dark skin is whitened through the use of creams and lotions, and there are other ways of emulating whiteness and a Western appearance. Susie Orbach tells us that an estimated 50 per cent of Korean women have a 'surgical procedure' to create a Western eyelid (2009: 81). She also describes how 'poorer girls and women in Chinese cities are creating sticky plasters to tape on their eyelids to duplicate the look of an open, western eye . . . a young woman may carry several makeshift eyelid openers and go to the bathroom mirror hourly to replace her makeshift remedy' (Orbach 2009: 82–3). Increased global imperialism within beauty and fashion is presumably one of the repercussions of the new dominance of Western celebrity alongside the existing indigenous variants. However, the extraordinary economic growth of China and the corollary invasion of Western fashion-related products meant that the vast American firm of Estée Lauder signed leading Chinese model Liu Wen in 2010. Her first campaign for them, in that year, was, however, confined to Chinese magazines.

Here, I have chosen to engage in a dialogue, rather than work with focus groups; for an outsider such as myself, gleaning in-depth information might be very difficult. But a music producer, DJ and much more, Terre Thaemlitz, who shares many of my concerns about celebrity culture and its global impact, has lived and worked for the last ten years in Japan. An interview with him around the issues central to this text will therefore follow: he is uniquely positioned to explore these questions of cultural imperialism. This interview was conducted partly on the telephone, and partly in cyberspace. Terre describes himself as 'a transgendered and queer-identified cross-genre media producer who attempts daily to culture-jam the market-places of music, activism, higher education and daily consumerism.'

INTERVIEW WITH TERRE THAEMLITZ: CELEBRITY CULTURE IN JAPAN?

TT: Perhaps it might be helpful to start by clarifying my relation to celebrity culture is antagonistic, to say the least. Also, although I keep an eye on dominant trends to a certain degree from a critical distance, I do not study up on celebrities. If someone starts a sentence with, 'Tom Cruise's wife . . . ', I never want to waste brain space knowing whom they are talking about. Being able to identify Tom Cruise is waste enough. In Japan, I cannot name a single member of AKB48. But I feel having an informed opinion about the cultural and industry mechanism behind such things does not necessarily require a detailed knowledge of the product itself. For your sake, I hope so, at least. I suppose it's the difference between analyzing the mechanics of an assembly line, and analyzing the products generated by the factory . . . you could say I'm more interested in the engineering, since the variation of products seems both endless and perhaps expendable in many ways.

PCG: So, what is going on in Japan?

TT: In Japanese, people use the term *serebu*—a phonetic attempt at *celeb*—when talking about celebrity culture. In general, Japanese people do not associate the notion of celebrity with fame. This is a radical difference in approach from the West—if not a blatant misunderstanding. Over here, *serebu* simply refers to lifestyles of luxury, typically focussing on Western forms of excess. Anonymous yet filthy-rich housewives are the epitome of *serebu*. *Serebu* can be easily spotted by their excessively expensive brand clothes and handbags, overpriced jewellery and watches, spa treatments, bizarre diets, art collections, toy dogs, expecting servitude from others and other indications of a general lack of common sense and inter-human connection.

I believe one reason the Japanese concept of *serebu* does not usually incorporate Western notions of fame, nor the celebrity as an individual or character on display (a true Japanese *serebu* exists in a world so removed from the norm that they cease to be seen by the 'little people'), is that Japanese culture traditionally places very little value upon the 'individual'. In this way, the entire psychological foundation of Western celebrity culture is replaced by something else—something that has no need to understand the Western concept. It is not a conscious or conspiring replacement, but an omission by the arrogance of power—in this case, more specifically an omission by the *serebu*'s belief in the propriety of one's own definition of celebrity. (Of course, we can find this sort of ignorance and misunderstanding born of wealth in all cultures.)

I think about a story told by a close friend here who used to work in a traditional restaurant during college. The lunch menu consisted of various bento—prepared lunches delivered in hard, lacquered boxes of a fixed size. They were priced at ¥1,000, ¥2,000 and ¥3,000 each, based on varying quantities and qualities of ingredients. Every now and then, wealthy customers would request a ¥5,000 or ¥10,000 bento, which caused the chef trouble since there was really no way to cram more than ¥3,000 worth of food into a bento box. But, of course, the customers were insistent—they would rather go elsewhere than eat a ¥3,000 bento—so the chef would resort to pointless decorations such as gold leaf flakes. The solution was not a change or increase in contents—which was, on a material level, impossible—but to employ bizarre aesthetics. In the end, there really aren't that many things of value in the world to match the excessive and disproportionate wealth of the fortunate few. Yet the rich are such believers in their own values *having* value, and so detached from the reality of how little it costs for a human to survive on a basic level, that they demand the world produce things of impossible value. And I think this is a key reason for the tackiness of so much brand culture. The aesthetics of glamour are rooted in an unrealistic demand—more like an infantile tantrum—for something possessing a degree of value that does not exist, and cannot exist.

Of course, these aesthetics appeal to the lower classes as well. In Tokyo, it is all about brand bags and wallets. No matter how poor you are, no matter your gender, everyone must wear a combination of something cheap with something expensive. Louis Vuitton is the brand of choice among the non-*serebu*. A 500 Euro wallet holding the equivalent of 50 Euros. You know the routine. There are also Japanese brands specifically developed for sale to this market of dreamers, such as Samantha Thavasa. But this dictation of Japanese fashion is, again, not only to be understood through a Western lens of 'the poor aspiring to be rich', but more importantly through the traditional Japanese attempt to camouflage class differences.

If both the poor and wealthy are essentially dressed the same, it becomes impossible to identify what class a person comes from. Meanwhile, as I said, the true *serebu*—or super-rich—are unseen, transported to another world by their bizarre and insular lifestyles.

While this may appear all well and good to the tourist visiting Japan who is impressed by how 'nice' everyone looks, from a standpoint of political organization the reluctance for class identification among the Japanese becomes a major roadblock. This also means that the signs of Western fashion, as they relate to historical developments and class struggles, are sadly of no interest or value here. We know there has been a great deal of cultural appropriation from the poor by couture culture in the West. In a bizarre inversion, rich people now wear tattered jeans bearing the marks of labor and manual action, whereas poor people can only afford unfaded and stiff new jeans. And as someone born in the American Midwest who wore second-hand clothing my entire life, I feel the violence of this on a gut level. I feel robbed. Still, I think in the West fashion can still be framed in relation to a history of domination (as typified by the act of theft itself)—even if that history appears to no longer be felt by the masses. However, in Japan (and particularly Tokyo), where Western fashion is simply an import, the very notion of 'political fashion' is all but impossible. It is simply color without meaning, or late-phase Dada. Outside of Tokyo, some of these dynamics are weakened, and you see a bit more diversity of fashion. For example, in Osaka and Kyoto you may actually find people in clubs or such going out of their way to dress differently. I think one reason is that these areas have a stronger relation to communist thinking, partly because there are many Korean-Japanese with cultural ties (although not necessarily political ties) to North Korea and who continue to resist certain forms of assimilation into Japanese culture as a result of their parents or grandparents having been brought to Japan under conditions of slavery and servitude prior to and during World War II. And, of course, the presence of people openly resisting assimilation affects the entire community, including fashion. Kyoto also has a history of leftist resistance, but it is tied up with Japanese nationalism, so the mood is a bit different from Osaka.

But generally speaking, you will be hard pressed to find Japanese people who can read political or class struggle into Western fashion (other than saying something looks expensive or cheap). In the world of music, this means you have Japanese bands with one member dressed as a punk, another as a B-boy, a third as a glam rocker, a fourth as a biker, a fifth as a royal prince from the land of fairy tales...and their sound is simply straight-up, fluffy, pop-rock boy band. It's a major mind-f**k for a person like myself, for whom the connections between fashion, music, class and identity were so explicitly and deliberately interwoven.

It seems music is one form of celebrity culture that Japan is trying to export. Not the actual Japanese musicians, but to sell specific band formats as franchises in other countries. AKB48, a group of forty-eight teenage girls in sailor-style Catholic school uniforms, is the current example. They are a product launched by Akimoto Yasushi, who produced the similar girl group Onyanko Club ['Kitty Club'] during the 1980s. I believe France (another bizarrely insular culture) is one of the countries who is buying an AKB48 franchise, which will consist of French girls. But I doubt it will really take off worldwide. Perhaps in South America—I could imagine that.

An important part of J-Pop (Japanese Pop music) is that the stars cannot be good singers. Their stars must not shine too brightly...all of which is very different from K-Pop (Korean Pop), Canton-Pop from Hong Kong, Mandarin-Pop from Taiwan, where they try to emulate on-pitch US and UK wailing diva stylings. And again, the Japanese approach is structured around a denial of individuality. If a singer were too talented, they would stand apart from the rest of society and become an individual. This is unappealing and unmarketable to Japanese sensibilities. (Conversely, you can understand why Japan is unable to generate trends with serious and longstanding appeal for the West.)

In the land of karaoke, the biggest pop stars are those who sound like completely regular people trying their best at a sing-along...but not quite getting it right. Their appeal lies in their failure as talents—their impossibility to become that which the West would demand of them. And this is, I feel, very Japanese. It is very much about a refusal to globally integrate that emerges from a particularly xenophobic relationship to the rest of the world—one in which Japan is both colonized and colonizing. I can think of no other international superpower that is so non-international on a cultural and political level (this extends to a lack of internal diversity, immigration difficulties, border controls on people and products and so on...Current debates in the US about foreign residents carrying identification cards make no sense here, since I must carry one every day).

But in the end, it's hard to tell from Japanese media what is really happening around global celebrity culture. Television is filled with success stories about Japanese trends taking hold in various countries, but as an 'international performer' myself I know these to be distortions. Just because some Japanese artist had an exhibition in some small closet of a gallery in New York, or a singer gave a show in some unknown club in the EU, that does not make them an international sensation. In fact, my entire career is based on debunking this fiction—and the fact that probably less than 1 per cent of your readers have ever heard any of my music despite my having released more than fifteen solo albums is testimony to this process of 'visible anonymity'. Of course, these distortions and misrepresentations are also a key part of how the West sees Japan, since the artists, performers and other celebrities that 'make it' overseas are generally unknown within Japan itself. (This is also my experience as an American who never gets work in the US.) Or, if they are known here, they are often known as something else. For example, most Japanese people have never seen the hard-edged films by internationally renowned director Kitano Takeshi, who simply exists in Japan as the television comedian 'Beat' Takeshi. I know that sounds impossible, but I have never met a Japanese person who has seen his movies. Another thing to keep in mind is that Japanese people who live permanently overseas tend to be an unusual lot, and in the same way it would be a mistake for anyone to look to me as a representative of the US (despite my undeniable Americanness in many ways), so it is a mistake to think one knows about Japan simply because they have a Japanese friend, roommate or partner. Pride may make it hard to admit this—by which I refer to both the pride of the non-Japanese person as well as their Japanese friend. But this is why I feel I have to talk more about the perspective through which we attempt to interpret Japanese culture, rather than simply portray scenes of Japan to a non-Japanese audience and pretend my fingerprints are not all over those images.

PCG: As I've been writing the book, it's become increasingly obvious that the celebrity/consume push *seems* to be all one way—from West to East? The West sends over images/products but doesn't want any back—am I right?

TT: Clearly you're right if you look at the direction of the global marketplace—on a mathematical level the signs of the West outnumber all others, and that obviously expresses power and cultural imperialism. And of course, the arrogance of power almost always excludes outside influences, if only because power and wealth tend to foster a belief in the elite's supremacy as they are—the delusion that power and wealth are natural expressions of being the best in the world. So that's your short answer right there.

I think that on a cultural level, there is an ethnocentrism that emerges from wealth—not the wealth of individuals, but of nations (whose peoples include the impoverished)—which finds expression in the desire to consume one's own reflection. Of course, part of this is simply a basic desire to consume what is familiar and practical—people in England are more likely to buy silverware before chopsticks (whereas Japanese are likely to buy both). But there is also certainly a dynamic of nationalism within that bizarre thing called 'consumer pride', and I think this desire to consume the self is certainly a part of both the construction of celebrity culture, and its consumption by celebrities and non-celebrities. Perhaps a state of 'celebrity' could be described as nationalism filtered through psychoanalysis—nationalism as narcissism?

If I can let out the Marxist in me for a moment, this consumer pride is an expected part of consumption within a field of reification (by which value and meaning are perceived as existing within the thing rather than derived from a contextual perception of acts of production), and is necessary to capitalist processes of selling identity. Women's fashion strikes me as the most elaborate and overdeveloped system for selling identity, cultic in its depth. I think celebrity culture is in many ways a subset of feminine expressions of power—including male celebrities, in the same way one could say wealthy men of Victorian fashion also incorporated a kind of femininity into their identities (as opposed to dry, Protestant humility).

Celebrity includes a notion of over-the-topness, which is also about aspiration. Celebrities generally present themselves in ways that exceed their material realities, showing themselves as the celebrities they themselves aspire to be (see the M. C. Hammer mansion). And through the lens of history, I think for a culture as a whole to share in this moment of self-aspiration is a rather recent advent of Western humanism—for the wealthy to allow the poor to entertain the very notion of aspiration within their lifetime, rather than only conceptualizing of comfort in the hereafter. It's quite an odd concept through which to perpetuate systems of domination, actually, and presents a radical cultural shift away from people simply 'knowing one's place'. And this specifically Western ideological root of celebrity culture is also perhaps why its imagery is so likely to take on Western forms. Given that fashion is contextual, it is less likely that cultures not rooted in humanism would be actively generating many 'traditional' or 'non-Western' trends that fit within contemporary celebrity markets. It seems fairly predetermined that non-Western celebrity culture will largely be a regurgitation of Western influences.

Ideological context, more than wealth, strikes me as the key difference between celebrity culture in the West, and those in Japan and other non-Western cultures. Like in the West, Japanese celebrities live not as themselves, but as the celebrities they aspire to be (here I am speaking about 'celebrities' as public 'stars', not as anonymous *serebu*). However, unlike in the West, the narcissism of Japanese celebrity culture is not rooted in a consumption of a familiar or conventionally nationalist image of the self. It revolves around a non-Westerner consuming the Western. I think the Kano Sisters (who are actually not sisters) are an easy example of Japanese celebrities who consume Western celebrity life—they have never publicly admitted to surgical alteration. Their grotesqueness is apparent to the Japanese public, and is in fact a part of their popularity—much as people in the West love celebrities who make asses out of themselves.

I think the cultural specificity of celebrity culture—regardless of its global appeal, that it expresses culturally specific Western ideological functions that limit its international reach—is an important complication to the 'export only' dynamics you ask about—not as a counter to problems of imperialism, but as another layer of shit on top of those problems. In some ways it begs the question if other cultures should be bothered to actively contribute to celebrity nonsense in unique ways. Perhaps that's too much for the West to ask. It raises the question if uniqueness has any value in non-Western cultures, as well as if a Western desire to consume something uniquely Japanese would simply be just one more senseless expression of individualist desires steeped in humanism (i.e., completely unrelatable from a Japanese perspective)? Surely the Kano Sisters transformed themselves into something unique—but unique in a Western sense. Their uniqueness is a reflection of micro-social 'individuality', as opposed to non-individualist and macro-social concepts of the unique found in clan or nationalist pride (the former is more openly linked to processes of alienation, the latter is more about homogenized clustering). Their uniqueness now prohibits them from functioning in Japanese society at large, and is not a uniqueness to be envied by the majority. Their artificiality in body is a material expression of their artificiality as 'constructed individuals' (as opposed to the alienation experienced by Western celebrities being associated with innate character flaws). For me, the popularity of the Kano Sisters represents the Japanese inability to conceive of the individual on a humanist level—that the individual is but a parody of freedom within systems of domination. And I think, in some ways, they are right in doing so.

There is perhaps something liberating—culturally liberating—to be found in one's inability to recognize a 'traditional' or 'natural' reflection of the self in the consumption of one's identity—not out of a quest for uniqueness, but as the least violating of options when considering the internalization of the self through the marketplace. Sometimes I'd like to imagine Japan's way of consuming that which remains clearly foreign/outside/other (even in the absence of being able to define the 'self') is maybe in some ways a step closer to denaturalizing those identities that have been so thoroughly reified and naturalized under capitalism. Or, at least by failing to place the 'indigenous' within the global marketplace, it could be a way for non-Western cultures to preserve something culturally other-than the imposed faces of imperialism. And perhaps to not return things to the West—even if only at the unconscious level of being unable to return things that appeal to the West by simply 'not getting' the West—is in itself a form of cultural self-defense, if not resistance.

Okay, I'm pushing it, and you know I'm not good at playing the optimist to begin with, but maybe you get my point. It affects the way in which one might approach the issues raised by your question—your concern about imperialism and domination. I think one way to counter the dynamics of the one-way/export-only domination you are talking about is not to worry about how to 'balance the marketplace' through imports, but to identify intercultural dynamics that are counter-intuitive to the prioritization of Western desire. I think to strip domination of desire—and discussions about domination generally tend to secretly prioritize the desires of the oppressor—helps us start talking instead about processes of brutality (physical, ideological, economic...).

PCG: And the more I think about the celebrity images the more pernicious it all becomes—fashion hijacked on the one hand by the luxury brands and on the other by the rock-bottom outfits who clean up by selling cheap clothes made by children—so much for debates around agency, no? There's the whole body thing in every strand of visual culture and the 'celebrification' of popular music in the US and UK...your opinions?

TT: Right, without even getting to celebrity culture, agency is not to be provided through the market place. Agency is not on the table within that realm—exploitation is a fundamental of profit-based economics. It is a requirement. Imbalance is a requirement. There is no profit without something—or someone—being undervalued. To pretend for an instance that our little pockets of 'democracy' and First World ways of life are possible without international imbalances that extend to slavery is, again, bringing us back to the arrogance of power. And of course, that blatant hypocrisy as seen from other sides is what breeds anti-Western hatred—I believe more than the imbalances of power in and of itself. It's the hypocrisy. Democratic-identified nations lack a kind of honesty about power and brutality.

Japan presents a very difficult case when talking about issues of agency and anti-imperialism, since it is so xenophobic and homogeneous. So much so that I have to wonder if the diversity found within contemporary Western cultures (ethnic, racial, religious) offers more of a solution to your first question than anything Japan might export to the West. I think there is a way in which the West is continually importing from the 'other within'.

PCG: What celebrities do people in Japan copy?

TT: Do you mean Japanese people in general? I think they copy the usual suspects—Japanese models, musicians, actors and actresses, and occasionally politicians or royalty...Those are usually the types of characters who might be described on television as 'fashion leaders'. If you're asking what Western celebrities are copied by Japanese celebrities (not anonymous *serebu,* but public stars), I'm sure there are examples of Japanese celebrities who 'sincerely' copy the looks and actions of celebrities from other cultures. But I have to say the majority of examples I can think of come from Japan's popular celebrity-impersonating comedians. For example, Naomi Watanabe is known as 'Beyoncé', Notchi-san (Nozomu Sato) of the comedian group Dangerous is called 'Obama', and Terusan (Teruichi Kikuchi) of the comedian group Do-yo is known as 'De Niro'. Such stars' resemblance of the celebrities they copy is always tenuous, and their impersonation skills tend to sway between totally absent (such as Notchi-san) or an unlikely contrast between appearance and talent (such as the rather overweight Watanabe's good dancing). Unlike Western comedy impersonators, they do not present the audience with a range of impersonations—they simply keep appearing like fifth-generation damaged clones of their one 'original' Western icon.

While the majority of these comedians and impersonators have a very short shelf life, I have noticed an interesting trend among the few one-trick-pony impersonators who manage to stick around. Basically, after months of nothing but the one impersonation, they slowly start appearing on shows out of character. Or, rather, they emerge as a new character—their 'true selves', dressed in casual street wear. As with Japanese music celebrities who cultivate talentlessness, so do these (and other) actors present a 'true self' that is generally down-to-earth, plain, not particularly skilled at anything and not particularly interesting...just 'friends' in your living room.

I do think there is something about Japanese concepts of the body to be read into these impersonator celebrities, in that they always invoke a notion of Japanese 'otherness' and the absurdity of identifying 'the foreign' within Japanese bodies ('How insane to think a Japanese person looks like Obama,' etc.). I think Watanabe is particularly interesting in that she is always received as both ridiculous and erotic. From a Japanese Pop perspective she is ridiculous (or more properly, ridiculed) because of her weight and curves in a culture that idolizes women with Twiggy-style figures—frail, bony frames with little body fat or muscle tone. But the ridicule always comes coupled with a concession that—despite her 'Western figure'—she certainly represents something sexual on a 'global' level, bringing out reactions of confusion as to whether it is possible or appropriate for Japanese commentators to consider her symbolic of a different type of sexual ideal...and can 'Japanese people' (as a self-constructed 'different species' of human born of xenophobia) get aroused by it? Basically, Watanabe allows Japanese people to discuss the same sexual confusion they feel around the actual Beyoncé (or any 'voluptuous' body). 'Is Beyoncé sexy?' Of course, this is a common trash tabloid question heard in the West as well—but within a Japanese cultural context I believe this question leads us to a very difficult and specific subtext that is in perpetual flux between what Westerners might identify as both Japanese 'anti-imperialist cultural resistance' and Japanese 'racism'.

There is a danger when using Western concepts of race and racism to interpret Japanese cultural observations. Whereas the language of Western race politics evolved out of contexts of multi-racialism and multi-culturalism (as imbalanced as those contexts have been and continue to be), Japan is still primarily a homogenous culture. The majority of immigrants are Korean and Chinese, many of which manage to physically/linguistically/culturally pass as Japanese (although not always). The rest of us are clearly 'not Japanese' from the start, presumed to be temporary visitors who will eventually 'go home'. Therefore, as I said, the primary form of Japanese discrimination is not in the form of 'racism', but rather in expressions of xenophobia. These are two very different things, since the current language of 'race' tends to focus on humanist concepts of all people having a 'body in common', whereas xenophobia remains focussed on issues of bloodline clan differentiation—the 'body uncommon'. (The recent history of US immigration policy is always tying these two very different concepts into a knot, best summarized as the xenophobia of a nation of once-outsider-immigrants obsessed with racial profiling.) The myth of interconnectivity felt by most 'real Japanese', including their inability to understand or be understood by 'outsiders' (*gaijin*), supersedes all issues of race. Discussions of race as it applies to intra-cultural diversity (say, race as an issue existing within a single culture) are no longer possible nor relevant, since the presumed inseparability between Japanese bodies and Japanese culture completely obliterates the concept of, say, a 'true' black Japanese person—regardless of whether such person was native-born. Like in Germany, 'true' Japanese nationality is both culturally and legally bestowed by bloodline, and not place of birth. Whereas a country like the US grants nationality to anyone born within its borders, being born and raised here in Japan is not enough. This, of course, can be a very dangerous position, and it results in numerous forms of discrimination. However, it also means there are times when Japanese culture's inability to conceive of race (as it relates to the Western 'human condition') stops it from participating in the Western language of representation around 'racialized bodies'. For example, the fact that Watanabe, Notchisan and Teru-san all impersonate non-Asians (and more specifically, American whites or blacks) is irrelevant to the Japanese audience. All that is relevant is the fact that they impersonate people who are non-Japanese. And it is this moment of identifying—on a physical level—some trait of the non-Japanese within the comedians' 'Japanese bodies' that presents the impulse of humor, the actual target of which is the 'Japanese body'. If white people did (and do) 'black-face' as a parody of disenfranchisement, Japanese 'black-face'/'white-face' becomes about the absurdity of Japan attempting to be something other than itself (however mythical that 'self' certainly is). Whereas Americans might have debated if Al Jolson or Elvis, as whites in a position of racial privilege, were belittling or paying homage to African American culture, in Japan the debate is only about how the impersonator belittles or pays homage to the Japanese 'self'.

Aside from impersonators, the other type of pop-level celebrity emulation that comes to mind is about the 'celebrity' as phenomenon or buzzword, as opposed to an actual person. A recent example is the Japanese film *Beck,* the poster for which looks more like an advertisement for a musician's concert or album than for a movie—yet it has nothing to do with the indie musician Beck whom we are all familiar with. It is common practice in Japanese advertising (and I think Asian advertising in general) to take a foreign word, name or catch phrase that is already associated with the genre of one's product (such as music, video, food, beverages), and use that name to sell one's own product. However, as with *Beck* (which is a film based on a series of manga comics about struggling teen rockers), the point of the seller is not to deceitfully present oneself as the person whose name has been stolen, but rather simply to highjack that person's 'aura' and sell it as a feeling. In this situation, it is actually better that the audience is not overly familiar with the person named, but rather that they can interact with the famous name's invocation in a vague and imprecise way. 'Beck' becomes an ethereal symbol of indie music, and no longer a sign of the artist Beck. It's a fine line that has no legal justification according to Western copyright rules, and I think as a branding strategy it expresses a lot of poor judgment when done by major corporations that simultaneously enforce their own copyrights, but I can also see how it emerges organically within a 'global marketplace' that exports Western names, words and images to countries like Japan. The Asian tendency to use Western words when selling Western-oriented products to their own markets—despite their own markets not understanding the words on a fundamental linguistic level—is prone to bear strange fruits. And I think, culturally, the West provides the seeds.

PCG: Is there a good deal of surgical intervention to achieve different celebrity looks?

TT: No. There is rampant plastic surgery in other Asian countries—particularly in Korea, where nose jobs and other cosmetic surgery for women are extremely commonplace (I just saw a Japanese program with the frightening statistics that over 61 per cent of female Korean university students said they had undergone cosmetic surgery, and over 82 per cent said their procedures were absolutely necessary)—but not so much in Japan. In fact, many Japanese women still don't pierce their ears (although this is changing with people under twenty-five or so). I'm told the main reason for this is a general belief that the body given by one's parents should not be cut or mutilated. But beyond that, schools also have prohibitions on accessories and piercings. Some high school girls go ahead and get their ears pierced anyway, without much repercussion, but in general people reach adulthood without piercings, so they just go on that way it seems. I see a few more tattoos on young people lately, but not significantly. Most public baths and hot spring *onsen* continue to ban people with tattoos from entering, which comes from the fact that tattoos were traditionally worn by criminals and *yakuza,* so these kinds of mindsets around preserving the body 'as-is' are still rather rampant. Although orthodontics and braces are catching on, crooked teeth can still have sex appeal here. Breast implants are extremely rare. The Western porn look is totally out. Even when Japanese women shave their bikini line, they usually just shave the V-line and never think to trim the length of their remaining pubic hair shorter, so I think something as radical as plastic surgery remains off the radar for the majority here. Even within the realm of sexual reassignment surgery (SRS), one might expect great things of a technologically advanced nation such as Japan, yet the number of SRS procedures in Japan pale when compared to the world leaders Thailand and Iran. There is one kind of physical intervention that comes to mind, although it is not specifically related to celebrity culture. It is, however, related to peer pressure and copying en masse. A lot of teenage girls and young women put tremendous effort into walking pigeon-toed and palsied, which comes from the 'frail and helpless' school of sex appeal that can be seen in the tiny footsteps and toes-in standing positions of geishas. It can be quite disturbing to foreign eyes who might interpret it as a sign of health problems such as polio or rickets, which are typically associated with more impoverished countries and can be seen in the elderly here. In fact, I have known many foreigners to observe this 'traditional' way of walking, and express heartfelt concern and bafflement over how a country of Japan's stature could have such health problems. I admit, I also find this walking style incredibly hard to watch, especially when thinking about the long-term health problems that surely arise from such postures which, over time, become so habitual that they can no longer be reversed. Then again, I also find Western high heels to be a comparable form of female debilitation...I avoid high heels in my own drag whenever possible, not only for their lack of comfort but for their metaphorical implications. I have a theory that the degree of women's oppression in a given culture can be measured by the height of their heels—that footwear's physical immobilization of the female body is an outgrowth of women's social immobility in general.

PCG: What about Japanese street style/youth cultures? To an outsider they do *seem* to be both extraordinary and inventive...with something like goth, say...Tell me the truth.

TT: I thought goth was a British/EU thing. When I was a kid, the goths were all copying the singer from the Cure. Is Japan known for goth now? I'm so out of it. Maybe you mean the *Lolicon* (short for 'Lolita complex') black frilly skirts with kittens, skulls and nurse bandages, or something? I think this fashion is perhaps more inspired by girls' animation and manga—which has always had a highly Victorian edge—than by traditional goth culture. There is a lot of this fashion around, and it seems to be particularly adapted as a new beauty aesthetic among heavyset girls here (which I think is also the case in the West?). Before the black clothing came into style, *Lolis* wore similar frilly styles in pastel. The traditional *Lolis* strike me as much more hard-core, since you might see women in their thirties, forties, or even fifties wearing visually extreme and financially punishing outfits. These women—particularly the elders—absolutely continue to constitute an antisocial and impenetrable caste of misfits detached from reality. It's quite tragic, really. On the other hand, most of the black *Lolis* I see today are in their twenties, and seem a bit less socially insular. They are considered more 'trendy' than 'crazy', and the clothes are available in every shopping mall.

It's very difficult for me to associate the term 'inventive' with Japanese fashion—as campy as it may be at times—if only because it is so rigidly corporate driven. It relies on mass-distributed, accessible, polished, finished product. It also relies on non-differentiation—either all the kids wear it, or none do. There is not much room for a counter-cultural moment in Japanese fashion.

As a teen growing up in the rural American Midwest in the early 1980s, I was a new wave gender-bender. For myself, the act of directly constructing not only one's outfit, but one's clothes themselves, was very important. I say 'constructing', but this often meant 'destroying' clothes, recycling things, making odd combinations and juxtapositions that caused discomfort in those around me. I think at that time street styles had much more to do with a resistance to wearing the uniforms society handed us, unlike today's youth cultures which are about straightforward consumption. It makes me wonder, if people my age once fantasized about a world in which 'we had the power' to dictate fashion, do today's youth somehow feel a sense of conquest when purchasing off-the-rack clothes inspired by our once-destructive gestures? Do they feel the victory we naively longed for? I don't think so. I don't think there is any effort put into it by the wearers (other than possibly financial effort?), and in that sense I feel it lacks any semblance of 'inventiveness'. Maybe that is just my personal inability to reconcile the ideological contradiction presented by off-the-rack alternative fashion.

So when I see a teenager wearing ¥60,000 tattered bondage pants, with a ¥20,000 ripped T-shirt and ¥80,000 in hair extensions—all of which have no fading or signs of actual wear—I literally want to vomit. And again, like I mentioned earlier about Japanese music groups with each member wearing a different genre of clothing, I find no sense of direction or agenda among Japan's various youth cultures. In fact, if you listen to the CDs bought by these most funky of fashion extroverts, it is often straight up pop. So, whereas you say, 'to an outsider they seem very inventive', I feel (as an outsider of various ilk) that they seem radically classist and conservative. Aggressively so. We can see this in the EU and US as well, of course. You heard my talk at the 'Out of Order' symposium in Bremen in 2010, so you know this is a very touchy subject for me. It just strikes me as mass-manufactured, and culturally isolated (shockingly disconnected from other cultural movements, such as music, politics, alternative information systems of resistance, etc.). Which makes it trite. And standard. And an expression of dominant culture systems. All of which is incredibly confusing and sad from my perspective.

PCG: Could you take us out with something about the impact or function of branding in Japan?

TT: I spoke earlier about Louis Vuitton as an almost mandatory accessory in Japan, particularly in the Tokyo region. I personally know one tragic Tokyo-ite who, while on vacation in Paris, used to stand on line in front of the Vuitton store and sweet-talk men passing by, ultimately asking them to stand with her for over an hour just to buy handbags with cash she would pass them upon entering the store, as a way around the store's two-bag per customer limit. Talk about your iconic stereotypes—these stories are a dime a dozen, and their amusement factor usually outweighs their capacity for cultural insight.

I prefer to tell you a different story about a dear friend's mother, who was raised in rural Iwate Prefecture in Northern Honshu. I say rural, but this was also an area with a history of labor organizing, and you could best sum up the mother's social outlook as quasi-anarchistic with leftist inklings. When she first visited Tokyo in the early 1970s, she was surprised to see everyone's bags and attaché cases having the same markings—she didn't know what they were at the time, but they were standard brown Vuitton bags with the L.V. logo. At first she thought all of those people must be working for the same company...or perhaps they were supporters of a local sports team she was unfamiliar with. When she finally figured out they were high-end fashion bags, she was shocked, 'Those ugly, cheap things are considered *fashionable*? And they cost *how much*? Ridiculous!'

I like this story because it shows that not all Japanese women are brand-queens, and that a lot of the ideas people overseas get about Japan are perhaps regional to Tokyo, or to a particular tourist class. I also like it because, as someone who grew up in the rural American Midwest, I can completely relate. When I was young, Vuitton used to make me think of some old clunky railroad trunk in some grandmother's attic, completely boring and 'old country' in design, no visual indications of unusual value, utterly uncool, and therefore only conceivably desirable for its camp potential and unquestionable squareness. When I found out it was not only an expensive brand, but considered *chic*...well, I've still never quite absorbed that idea.

In any case, getting back to Japan, and more specifically the homogenizing fashion movements in Tokyo, I think it is easy to understand how branding finds support in (and gives support to) social structures rooted in assimilation and non-differentiation. Unlike in the West, where it is a faux pas to be publicly caught in the same outfit as the person next to you, here in Japan it is commonplace to see groups of women friends dressed identically from hair to shoes—particularly among women in their twenties. This presumably has the function of eliminating jealousy and rivalry between friends, yet any such balance is hypocritically achieved by imposing tremendous pressure to keep up with the group at all costs.

Also, like the West, Japan is at a stage of economic growth under global capitalism in which we see the first generations of children who were raised with brands (Adidas, Levis, Nike, whatever...) having children of their own. So these cultural codings around consumer-based self-worth are coming to full bloom here as in the West. In this sense, branding is not simply about passing trends, but is a logistical development of global capitalism. Of course, we know there is a contradiction presented by global fashion brands in that they somehow manage to package their products of mass manufacture with an aura of rarity. In fact, the products themselves are usually not rare at all in terms of quantity or availability. Their rarity is not about supply and demand. Rather, it is about accessibility. Any rarity emerges from the difficulty of paying the unjustifiably hyper-inflated price tag on an average person's income. Ultimately, to purchase brand clothing is to pass through a rite of initiation. In the West, brand fashion is usually associated with initiation into a higher class (however real or illusory). But perhaps in a city like Tokyo, where class differentiation among citizens is so often deliberately camouflaged, branding is about a more general feeling of initiation into the Japanese status quo. The brand object becomes about lateral social mobility—not upward mobility. It is a sign of normalcy and being a team player.

And in that sense, perhaps my friend's mother was correct in her initial reading of Vuitton bags, and the function of brands in general—that it all boils down to the most banal images of business and sportsmanship…two of the three things I detest most in this world. The third thing, which I detest most of all, is epitomized by the cultic way in which people follow brands: religiosity.

–13–

Concluding Thoughts:
Folklore, Fallibility, the Future

The complex relationship between celebrity and social class, particularly in Britain, continues; the pattern in the United States seems slightly less rigid. In Britain, barriers around social class, and also around ethnicity, have remained difficult to negotiate or transcend. In the United States, Oprah Winfrey has become one of the richest women in the country, and arguably one of the most influential, while we have already discussed the iconic status of Michelle Obama; in England and Europe, it is still, sadly, quite inconceivable that a person of colour might become prime minister. Diane Abbott entered the contest for leader of the Labour Party in 2010, knowing that she would attract very few votes. However, she believed that it was vital for her to stand simply because she was both a woman and of African Caribbean ethnicity. This was at a moment when the composition of the English Cabinet had become more rigid—male, white and middle class. Presumably the extreme right-wing white populist Sarah Palin is popular with her following in 2010 because she offers a bizarre challenge to a perceived elite, to the traditionally well-educated and often privileged rulers of America on Capitol Hill.

If in the United Kingdom during the 1960s, there really was some belief in social mobility and the eventual breaking down of class barriers, it was challenged and even dispelled, first by the recession and unemployment of the 1970s, then by 'Reaganomics' in its British manifestation and the Thatcherite economic boom of the 1980s. The aspirational nature of that decade was decisive. Many of the young upwardly mobile men on either side of the Atlantic who were the beneficiaries of this new wealth creation wanted to show off their new status through fresh forms of conspicuous consumption. The portrait of Sheldon, the Wall Street banker and self-styled 'Master of the Universe' in Tom Wolfe's *Bonfire of the Vanities* (1987), is both illuminating and horribly prophetic. Wolfe depicts the excesses of the moneyed Manhattan in which many would like to live and which lingers on and on within popular culture—see Mr Big in *Sex and the City,* or most of the cinematic characters in a Nancy Meyers 'comedy'.

Popular fictions, their content and their construction, are important in a consideration of celebrity and its links to fashion, though it is only within the odd novel that both have been explored directly. Bret Easton Ellis, who famously depicted the dark underside of

Figure 38 Every modern celebrity needs a limousine to attract the photographers. Photograph by Anne-Marie Michel.

the 1980s in *American Psycho* (1991) and wove into that novel the new obsession with designer names that emerged during the decade, followed this up with the curiously underexplored and equally disturbing novel *Glamorama* (1999). Here, he depicts the late 1990s obsession with fashionable celebrities. Victor, the narrator, a successful fashion model, is hired to host a new club in Manhattan; the guest list for the opening night which he reels off is a 'who's who' of stylish Manhattan for 1999 (Easton Ellis 1999: 8). His later two-page description of the aftermath of a plane crash near Charles de Gaulle Airport sees the landscape strewn, not only with corpses, but with garments and accessories that bear brand names and a fashionable lineage (441).

As the gulf between rich and poor widened, it created a highly receptive climate for the reality television shows that could and did make the humblest person briefly famous, if not rich. In Britain, some of the new celebrities created in this way managed to sustain some sort of subsequent career, while the new talent-hunting programmes created working-class-and-proud-of-it celebrities. America has its own rags-to-riches celebrities, of course, but this is an intrinsic trope within American popular mythology. What is interesting is that there seems to be rather less possibility of succeeding in the United States without some discernible talent or charisma. Perhaps the uncoupling of celebrity from talent—like the obsession with class—is a particularly British phenomenon.

Figure 39   Ivana Trump, part of a New York dynasty, faces the problem of how to leave that limousine. Photograph by Anne-Marie Michel.

However, in the United Kingdom during the 1990s, possibly the most interesting icons for the now-trapped working classes were the newly wealthy Premiership footballers. For the first time, these sportsmen became fashion-aware (see Bruzzi 2000). Their extraordinary new purchasing power was extended to their wives and girlfriends,

Figure 40   Fantasies of a celebrity lifestyle often involve poolside relaxation and a luxury hotel. Photograph by Anne-Marie Michel.

the WAGs described earlier, who became role models for thousands of young girls. Coleen McLoughlin, brought up on a council estate in Liverpool, amassed an enormous fortune and following simply through her relationship with Wayne Rooney of Manchester United and England. She acquired two weekly magazine columns, a celebrity fragrance contract, became the face of George at Asda, a profitable supermarket fashion line, and later made a television commercial for Littlewood's Catalogues, aimed at a similar demographic. Whether or not the footballers' wives boom continues in England, it dominated the first decade of the new century. It may or may not be part of the reason for the worrying national statistic of a trillion pounds in unsecured personal loans.

If the Beckhams, as we have observed, used this very opportunity to make of themselves a global brand, it should be remembered that Victoria was, as a Spice Girl, much richer and better known when they first joined forces. David moved first to Madrid and then to Los Angeles to play for a US team; their life in the United States was then followed on a daily basis. They seem to have successfully established themselves as celebrities in their new home, and Victoria's high design has been accepted. Yet part of David's appeal, perhaps, is that despite his star status—he shared his

thirtieth birthday party with George Clooney and the host was the ubiquitous Valentino—
he has retained strong ties with his parents and family of origin; he is openly proud of
his working-class roots. He is also attractive to many for other reasons, including his
obvious devotion to his children and his attempts to overcome homophobia in British
football, where it is still sadly rampant (see Church Gibson 2004b, 2008; Edwards
2011: 154). He has in the new millennium a vast income, a fashionable wife and a
sartorially sharp image.

I would suggest here that David, famously depicted by photographer Annie Leibovitz
as Prince Charming within the pages of *Vanity Fair,* can certainly be likened to a character from fairy tale and folklore, but not to that particular prince. Rather, David is the
boy in the fairy tales who transcends his humble origins, who profits through his physical bravery and his willingness to seize an opportunity; he might be the soldier from
Hans Christian Andersen's *The Tinder Box.*

Rojek (2001) likens celebrities to modern-day inhabitants of Mount Olympus;
certainly Greek gods and goddesses do squabble, fall out with one another, stray and
generally create havoc, so betraying their weaknesses as well as their power. I would
venture to suggest that we might also investigate the contemporary power of what
might be called the *flawed* fairy tale, examining its potency—and its dependence upon
the workings of fashion—within particular celebrity histories. The work of Russian critic
Vladimir Propp on the morphology of the folk tale was deployed in film scholarship in
the 1970s. But unlike cinematic narratives, most celebrity stories lack closure and be-
tray imperfection. Paradoxically, however, it may be the very *imperfection* of certain fashionable celebrities which gives them maximum resonance within contemporary culture.

I would suggest that David is one of these flawed folk heroes, as was the late Princess Diana. I am, of course, only too aware that the term *fairy tale* has been endlessly
invoked in previous discussions of these two celebrities; what has not been properly
investigated is the particular role played within their histories by *fashion.* Given the
continuing popularity of stories around transformation, together with the new centrality of the 'How to get their look' feature within contemporary fashion media, I would
suggest that both these figures are supremely relevant here. I would therefore like to
end this exploration of fashion and celebrity by looking at the similarities between their
two narratives, since both stories feature fashion as central figure and show transformation in progress.

Both Diana and David found their footing and fashion sense while already in the public eye, and for both there were much-publicized experiments and the odd fashion faux
pas. Early pictures of the two show us pleasant young people with short, nondescript
brown hair; both would seemingly transform *themselves* into blondes who managed to
combine glamour and fashion. What David and Diana share in the public perception
are good looks, coupled with a seeming authenticity. Neither Diana nor David were, in
fact, ordinary in any way. Diana was hardly a girl from the block; David was a supremely

talented footballer. Nevertheless, the secret of their extraordinary status and the affection both inspired is based on their apparently sudden rise to fame, fortune, and *fashionability,* together with the fact that both were nevertheless perceived as what Lumby, writing of Diana, called 'accessible' (Lumby, quoted in Turner et al. 2000: 9).

Diana was already the daughter of an earl before she became betrothed to a prince, but the press were quick to seize on and present the simpler, more ordinary facts of her life. She had a job in a nursery school, drove a small red Austin Metro and shared a flat with three school friends. Again, the fact that she did not actually need to work, and that she *owned* this large flat in an expensive area of London, were carefully overlooked by both the press and her followers. There was a seeming determination to present her as a typical young girl, in her first job, away from home for the first time. Her apparent shyness, her natural looks and behaviour, were what first endeared her to the British press and then ensured her global appeal. As she changed, under the media and public gaze, so her popularity could only increase. Her status as fashion icon, as well as über-celebrity, is intimately bound up with the fact that, like David, Diana finally found her fashionability, but in a process that could be followed, step by step, in the public eye.

At first, she did not dress well for public occasions—she chose an ill-fitting and rather matronly Cojana suit for her engagement photograph. Her off-duty clothes were more becoming, and the high street began to copy them—her sheep-patterned sweaters and her Laura Ashley blouses with the infamous pie-frilled collars became popular. In 1981, she wore a very low-cut black evening dress for her first evening engagement as the fiancée of Prince Charles; David's equivalent disaster was the sarong topped by a black T-shirt, worn as evening wear in the summer of 1998, on holiday in the south of France with his Spice Girl. Both outfits provoked caustic criticism: leading fashion writers, including Ernestine Carter, were publicly critical of Diana, while the sarong had a wider public profile, seen as further proof of David's sins after his well-deserved World Cup sending-off for his petulance in the match against Argentina. The sarong was used to adorn a puppet strung up from a lamppost and was further lampooned in the tabloids (see Bruzzi 2000).

However, both outfits set trends, but did so at different market levels. David's own sarong was actually designed by Jean-Paul Gaultier, but copies of it swiftly went on sale in Topshop and were snapped up by young men eager to go clubbing on their own holidays in the sun. Diana's black dress was made for her by the Emmanuels, a young British couple whom she then entrusted with the creation of her wedding dress. Big taffeta ball gowns and overly ornate wedding dresses characterized the decade to follow. Diana and David also engaged in experiments with new hairstyles; these, too, were carefully followed and widely publicized (see Church Gibson 2008).

Diana began to receive professional advice on her style, but she went on making the odd mistake. The more serious mistakes, however, had to do with her choice of

Figure 41 The theatrical white dress, now emblematic of the red carpet rather than a vast public wedding. Photograph by Anne-Marie Michel.

men rather than frocks: the ultimate Cinderella whose Prince Charming turned out to be an adulterous frog, her subsequent lovers all let her down in different ways. This only enhanced the public's sympathy for their heroine; her constantly changing body image, the struggles with her weight loss, the admission of bulimia, all these gained her more followers as the deceived princess became a global superstar, dressed by international designers and featured on the covers of leading fashion magazines. Most significantly, her public disputes with the royal family only served to garner still more sympathy for the Princess, once recounted in the infamous Martin Bashir interview. Like Beckham at a later date, she swiftly became public property, but whereas Diana was Virtue Deceived, David was Virtue Triumphant. Whatever rumours and scandals circulated, he managed by one expedient or another to rout them and remain the Good Father, the Ultimate Provider, while retaining the potency of the handsome hero who gazed down from billboards across the world. He fascinates writers on fashion as well as those who deal only with celebrity (see Cashman 2006; Rahman 2006; Edwards 2011). It may be, of course, that a scandal or tragedy will upset or catastrophically disrupt the Beckham narrative; at the time of writing, the production is still in progress.

Although Diana has been dead for over ten years, her story retains its potency, and she cannot escape scrutiny; leading journalist Tina Brown, who so enjoys investigating celebrities, published an uncharitable book, *The Diana Chronicles,* in 2007. There will certainly be more journalistic speculation about Beckham in the years to come.

The other common factor within the David/Diana stories that ensures their continued potency are the myths they somehow perpetuate around social class. Class here is seen as no longer a constraint; boundaries can be crossed or hopped across, in either direction—Diana hugged old ladies, David adorns the walls of the National Portrait Gallery. Interestingly, Jordan—who knows that boundaries are fixed, and who is not held in any reverence—has repeatedly likened herself to a 'latter-day Diana' (*Guardian,* 17 November 2008). After her death, Steven Fry famously called the British star of reality television Jade Goody 'a kind of Princess Di from the other side of the tracks' (Weaver 2009). Goody—like all successful celebrities—had briefly endorsed a scent; the advertisements for it actually played with ideas around class, origin and status, showing Jade resplendent on a red carpet but bearing the tagline 'Straight from Essex'.

At the time of the 2006 World Cup, the *Sun* tabloid newspaper used Beckham, then the captain of the national team, to help celebrate the queen's birthday. She featured on its front page with the headline 'Happy Birthday, Your Majesty', while Beckham dominated the back page, the sports page, with a vast caption, 'His Majesty: God Bless Him'. While these two contrasted kingdoms both provide different forms of lavish public spectacle, Premiership football surely answers more basic needs and arguably provokes far more passion.

Diana and David, the two putative folk heroes whom I have tentatively pushed forward as in some degree paradigmatic, who combine fashion with celebrity in their construction and in their appeal, are both English, but they are not in the slightest degree parochial; both achieved global popularity.

We should end as we began, by thinking of Warhol, both creator and construct of fashion and celebrity, and wonder where he, too, would fit within modern folklore. He

Figure 42   Silver shoes—but Cinderella did not have matching painted toenails. Photograph by Anne-Marie Michel.

would surely be cast by many as a wicked uncle; others might see him as the supreme magician. There is the intriguing fact that the Freud Museum in Vienna showed his film *Couch* in 2006, as part of the exhibition 'Thinking in Repose'. A series of photographs from the 1960s now remain there; they were on display in December 2010 and depict the infamous Factory couch with various of his 'superstars' in situ. One reading, overly simplistic, perhaps, of this public juxtapositioning—Andy's couch outside Freud's sanctum—might be that so many of Warhol's couch incumbents were destined for disaster, while those who left Freud's consulting room were, supposedly, well-equipped to confront them. But possibly the thinking behind the installation was,

Figure 43   These may be the 'red shoes' of contemporary fairy tales—Amy Adams in her red-soled Christian Louboutin stilettos. Photograph by Anne-Marie Michel.

rather, to present Warhol as the man uniquely equipped to understand the unconscious drives of the later twentieth century.

Whatever the rationale, he retains his powers. Most celebrities have a short lifespan and fall sadly short of mythic status. The desire to find successors to David and Diana, too, is palpable; even now, the luxury brands, who have sometimes looked like the arch-villains of this particular story, may be concocting their very own contributions to fashion folklore, hoping by those means to exorcise their possible demonic status.

There are dynastic possibilities in place; in 2010, at the age of eight, David Beckham's son Romeo launched his own range of designer sunglasses. He then appeared in *GQ* magazine's annual list of the World's Most Stylish Men. Meanwhile, in 2011, a new princess has appeared on stage; Kate Middleton, now married to Diana's son and currently the Duchess of Cambridge, has the self-same long locks and tanned limbs that are part of the celebrity style analysed in these pages. Presented with Diana's very own engagement ring, the dresses that she has worn for all public appearances have been widely discussed, the ready to wear ones sold out; these very same stories might continue with a new young cast. Or perhaps not—as young people took to the street again in what seemed to be a resurgence of political activity in England, protesting against the draconian cuts of the new regime, a resplendent Rolls Royce carrying the heir apparent was the target of a small but vociferous group. Possibly in London as once at Versailles, the display of publicly funded opulence may serve to stir increasing resentment, rather than to provoke admiration.

Bibliography

Abraham, Tamara (2010), 'Fancy Leg Work: Cheryl Cole Sends Sales of Luxury Tights Soaring as Women Splash Out £30 per Pair', *Daily Mail* (24 September), <www.daily mail.co.uk/femail/article-1314592/Cheryl-Cole-sends-sales-luxury-tights-soaring-women-splash-30-pair.html#ixzz10x2QOVZz> accessed 29 September 2010.

Abraham, Tamara (2009), 'Alexander McQueen's Tall Order: Towering 12-inch Boots on Paris Catwalk That Were NOT Made for Walking...', *Daily Mail* (8 October), <www.dailymail.co.uk/femail/article-1218802/Alexander-McQueens-tall-order-Towering-12-inch-boots-Paris-catwalk-walking-.html#ixzz0wONG1VXD> accessed 8 August 2010.

Abrams, Corrine (2009), 'Stylist Rachel Zoe Answers Timesfashion Twitter Questions', *Times Online* (19 May), <women.timesonline.co.uk/tol/life_and_style/women/fashion/article6319788.ece> accessed 29 September 2010.

Abrams, Meyer Howard (ed.) (1975), *English Romantic Poets: Modern Essays in Criticism,* Oxford: Oxford University Press.

Addley, Esther (2007), 'After Moss and Madonna, Lily Allen Tries to Make the High Street Smile', *Guardian* (20 February), <www.guardian.co.uk/business/2007/feb/20/retail.musicnews> accessed 16 October 2010.

Addison, Heather (2006), 'Must the Players Keep Young?: Early Hollywood's Cult of Youth', *Cinema Journal,* 45/4 (Summer): 3–25.

Addison, Heather (2000), 'Hollywood, Consumer Culture, and the Rise of Body Shaping', in David Desser and Garth Jowett (eds), *Hollywood Goes Shopping,* Minneapolis: University of Minnesota Press.

Adolescent (2008), 'Profile in Style: Chloe Sevigny', Women's Fashion Spring 2008, *New York Times,* <www.nytimes.com/indexes/2008/02/24/style/t/index.html#pageName=24hgood> accessed 7 August 2010.

'After the Blob, an Enthusiastic Jack Nicholson Shows Us the Twist' (2009), *Daily Mail* (4 August), <www.dailymail.co.uk/tvshowbiz/article-1204016/Jack-Nicholson-life-party-shows-moves-dance-floor.html> accessed 12 September 2010.

Agins, Teri (2000), *The End of Fashion: How Marketing Changed the Clothing Business Forever,* New York: Quill.

Akass, Kim, and McCabe, Janet (eds) (2004), *Reading Sex and the City,* London: IB Tauris.

Akerlund, Jonas (2010), 'Ballet Russes Italian Style', film trailer on 'Rah-rah-ah-ah-ah! Lady Gaga at MOCA', *New York Times Style Magazine* blog (12 February), <tmagazine. blogs.nytimes.com/2010/02/12/rah-rah-ah-ah-ah-lady-gaga-at-moca/> accessed 8 August 2010.

Alderson, Andrew, and Edwardes, Charlotte (2002), 'Prince of Wales Does Vogue Shoot with Diana's Favourite Photographer—Mario Testino Has Photographed Prince Charles for the Fashion Magazine', *Sunday Telegraph* (6 January).

Alexander, Hilary (2010), 'New York Fashion Week: Tom Ford's Fashion Comeback', *Telegraph* (13 September), <fashion.telegraph.co.uk/columns/hilary-alexander/TMG7999519/New-York-Fashion-Week-Tom-Fords-fashion-comeback.html> accessed 25 September 2010.

Alexander, Hilary (2009), 'British Fashion Awards: Christopher Bailey Named Designer of the Year', *Telegraph* (9 December), <www.telegraph.co.uk/fashion/fashionnews/6772705/British-Fashion-Awards-Christopher-Bailey-named-designer-of-the-year.html> accessed 7 August 2010.

'All Abode: Sea of Shoes: Mother-Daughter Bloggers Judy and Jane Aldridge Invite Nowness into Their Dallas Home' (2010), *Nowness* (27 July), <www.nowness.com/day/2010/7/27/801/all-abode-sea-of-shoes> accessed 25 September 2010.

Anger, Kenneth (1975), *Hollywood Babylon,* 1981 edition, New York: Dell.

Appadurai, A. (ed.) (1986), *The Social Life of Things: Commodities in Cultural Perspective,* Cambridge: Cambridge University Press.

Armani on Screen (2003), BBC, documentary aired BBC4 (30 December), programme synopsis/promotion by Caroline Frost, <www.bbc.co.uk/bbcfour/documentaries/profile/armani.shtml> accessed 8 August 2010.

Armstrong, Lisa (2009), 'Grace Coddington: The *Vogue* Visionary', *Times* (16 December), <women.timesonline.co.uk/tol/life_and_style/women/fashion/article6957921.ece> accessed 7 August 2010.

Armstrong, L. (2008), 'Victoria Beckham Presents Her Debut Fashion Collection', *Times* (9 September), <women.timesonline.co.uk/tol/life_and_style/women/fashion/article4711607.ece> accessed 23 July 2010.

Armstrong, L., and Leich, L. (2010), 'New York Fashion: Victoria Beckham's Triumph', *Times* (15 February), <women.timesonline.co.uk/tol/life_and_style/women/fashion/article7026849.ece#cid=OTC-RSS&attr=5745502> accessed 12 January 2011.

Arnold, Eve (2005), *Marilyn Monroe: An Appreciation,* 2nd new edition, New York: Harry N. Abrams.

Arnold, Rebecca (2009), *Fashion: A Very Short Introduction,* Oxford: Oxford University Press.

Aspden, Peter (2008), 'A Contemporary Marriage', *Financial Times* (26 April).

Austin, T., and Barker, M. (eds) (2003), *Contemporary Hollywood Stardom,* London: Arnold.

Babington, Bruce, Davies, Anne, and Powrie, Phil (eds) (2004), *The Trouble with Men: Masculinity and Contemporary Cinema,* London: Wallflower Books.

Badiou, Alain (2004), *Circonstances: Irak, Foulard, Allemagne / France,* Paris: Editions Leo Scheer.

Bagley, Christopher, and Klein, Steven (2005), 'Domestic Bliss', *W* (July), <www.wmagazine.com/celebrities/archive/brad_pitt_angelina_jolie#slide=1> accessed 19 September 2010.

Bamigboye, Baz (2006), 'Marie Antoinette Booed as Critics Call for Director's Head', *Daily Mail* (24 May), <www.dailymail.co.uk/tvshowbiz/article-387593/Marie-Antoinette-booed-critics-directors-head.html> accessed 7 August 2010.

Bankowsky, Jack, Gingeras, Alison, and Wood, Catherine (2010), *Pop Life: Art in a Material World,* London: Tate Publishing.

Barber, Lynn (2009), 'The Interview: Michael Clark', *Observer* (9 August), <www.guardian.co.uk/stage/2009/aug/09/interview-michael-clark-ballet-dancer> accessed 25 September 2010.

Barker, Godfrey, and Jury, Louise (2008), 'Even His Fag Ends Sell as Hirst Art Auction Hits £100 Million', *This Is London* (16 September), <www.thisislondon.co.uk/standard/article-23556081-even-his-fag-ends-sell-as-hirst-art-auction-hits-100-million.do> accessed 17 October 2010.

Barnett, Leisa (2008), 'Comme Des Garçons for H&M', *Vogue.com* (3 April), <www.vogue.co.uk/news/daily/2008–04/080403-comme-des-garçons-for-handm.aspx> accessed 8 August 2010.

Barrett, Elizabeth (2010), 'Fashion World Pays Tribute to Alexander McQueen', *Independent* (19 February), <www.independent.co.uk/life-style/fashion/news/fashion-world-pays-tribute-to-alexander-mcqueen-1904849.html> accessed August 2010.

Barron, James (1999), 'Marilyn Monroe Auction Is an Icon's Best Friend', *New York Times* (28 October), <www.nytimes.com/1999/10/28/nyregion/marilyn-monroe-auction-is-an-icon-s-best-friend.html> accessed August 2010.

Barron, Lee (2009), 'An Actress Compelled to Act: Angelina Jolie's Notes from My Travels as Celebrity Activist/Travel Narrative', *Postcolonial Studies,* 12/2: 211–28.

Barron, Lee (2007), 'The Habitus of Elizabeth Hurley: Celebrity, Fashion and Identity Branding', *Fashion Theory: The Journal of Dress, Body and Culture,* 11/4 (December): 443–61.

Barron, Lee (2006), 'Elizabeth Hurley Is More Than a Model: Stars and Career Diversification in Contemporary Media', *Journal of Popular Culture,* 39/4.

Barthel, Diane (1992), 'When Men Put on Appearances: Advertising and the Social Construction of Masculinity', in Steve Craig, *Men, Masculinity and the Media,* London: Sage Publications.

Barthes, Roland (1967), *The Fashion System,* 1990 edition, Berkeley: University of California Press.

Bartky, Sandra Lee (1988), 'Feminism, Foucault and the Modernisation of Patriarchal Power', in I. Diamond and L. Quimby (eds), *Feminism and Foucault: Reflections on Resistance,* Boston: Northeastern University Press.

Bashir, Martin (1995), 'The Panorama Interview', transcript of the BBC1 Panorama interview with the Princess of Wales, broadcast in November 1995, <www.bbc.co.uk/politics97/diana/panorama.html> accessed 19 September 2010.

Battle, Bella (2006), 'WAGs: How They Spend It', *Sun Woman Online* (22 June), <www.thesun.co.uk/sol/homepage/woman/52938/WAGs-How-they-spend-it.html> accessed May 2009.

Baudelaire, Charles-Pierre (1863), *The Painter of Modern Life,* reprinted 2010, London: Penguin Books.

Baudrillard, Jean (1981), *Simulacra and Simulation,* 1994 edition, Ann Arbor: University of Michigan Press.

Baudrillard, Jean (1970), *The Consumer Society: Myths and Structures,* 1998 edition, London: Sage.

Baudrillard, Jean (1968), *The System of Objects,* 2005 edition, London: Verso.

Baudry, Leo (1986), *The Frenzy of Renown: Fame and Its History,* Oxford: Oxford University Press.

Bayles Kortsch, Christine (2009), *Dress Culture in Late Victorian Women's Fiction: Literacy, Textiles and Activism,* London: Ashgate Publishing.

Becker, Ron (2006), *Gay TV and Straight America,* Rutgers, New Jersey: Rutgers University Press.

Beecroft, Vanessa, and Polier, Alexandra (2007), *Vanessa Beecroft: VB LV,* New York: Charta.

Bell, Emma (2010), 'Book Review: *Fame* by Mark Rowlands', *Celebrity Studies,* 1/1 (March): 126–9.

Benbow-Pflalzgraf, Taryn (2002), *Contemporary Fashion,* Farmington Hills, Michigan: St James Press.

Benjamin, Walter (2002), *Selected Writings,* vol. 3, *1935–8,* ed. Howard Eiland and Michael W. Jennings, trans. Edmund Jephcott and Howard Eiland, Cambridge, Massachusetts: Belknapp Press at Harvard University Press.

Benjamin, Walter, and Tiedemann, Rolf (1999), *The Arcades Project,* Cambridge, Massachusetts: Harvard University Press.

Bennett, Andrew (1999), *Romantic Poets and the Culture of Posterity,* Cambridge: Cambridge University Press.

Benwell, Bethan (ed.) (2003), *Masculinity and Men's Magazines,* Oxford: Blackwell Publishing.

Berger, John (1972), *Ways of Seeing,* London: Penguin Books.

Bergin, Olivia (2009), 'Emma Watson as the New Face of Burberry', *Telegraph* (9 June), <www.telegraph.co.uk/fashion/fashionnews/5484342/Emma-Watson-as-the-new-face-of-Burberry.html> accessed 9 August 2010.

Berman, Marshall (1980), Baudelaire: Modernism and the Streets', in Arthur Berger (ed.), *Television as an Instrument of Terror: Essays on Media, Popular Culture, and Everyday Life,* New Brunswick, New Jersey: Transaction.

Berry, Sarah (2000a), 'Hollywood Exoticism: Cosmetics and Colour in the 1930s', in David Desser and Garth Jowett (eds), *Hollywood Goes Shopping,* Minneapolis: University of Minnesota Press.

Berry, Sarah (2000b), *Screen Style: Fashion and Femininity in 1930s Hollywood,* Minneapolis: University of Minnesota Press.

Black, Rosemary (2010), 'Men Get Their Own Super Skinny Mannequins—and a Host of New Body Issues', *New York Daily News* (6 May), <www.nydailynews.com/lifestyle/health/2010/05/06/2010–05–06_men_get_their_own_superskinny_mannequins__and_a_host_of_new_body_issues.html> accessed August 2010.

'Blake Lively: Anna Wintour Took Me to the Chanel and Dior Shows' (2010), *Huffington Post* (3 September), <www.huffingtonpost.com/2010/09/03/blake-lively-anna-wintour_n_704885.html> accessed 29 September 2010.

Blanks, Tim (2009), 'How Tom Ford Became the Toast of Hollywood', *Independent* (22 December), <www.independent.co.uk/arts-entertainment/films/features/how-tom-ford-became-the-toast-of-hollywood-1847009.html> accessed 24 September 2010.

Blanks, Tim (2008), 'Interview with Francesco Vezzoli', *Fantastic Man,* 8 (Autumn/Winter).

Blau, Herbert (1999), *Nothing in Itself: Complexions of Fashion,* Bloomington: Indiana University Press.

Block, M. (2009), 'R. J. Cutler—Spending "September" with Anna Wintour', *NPR* (27 August), <www.npr.org/templates/story/story.php?storyId=112291340> accessed 14 July 2011.

Boorstin, Daniel (1961), *The Image: A Guide to Pseudo-events in America,* 1992 edition, New York: Vintage Books.

Bourdieu, Pierre (1984), *Distinction: A Social Critique of the Judgement of Taste,* London: Routledge.

Brabant, Malcolm (2009), 'Mamma Mia Island Bucks Tourism Trend', *BBC News* (31 August), <news.bbc.co.uk/1/hi/business/8230781.stm> accessed 24 September 2010.

Brady, Shirley (2010), 'Madonna Sued over Material Girl Collection', *Brandchannel News* (23 August), <www.brandchannel.com/home/post/2010/08/23/Madonna-Faces-Material-Girl-Suit.aspx> accessed 25 August 2010.

Braid, Mary (1999), 'Jack Nicholson Loves Him. The Public Adores Him. His Erotic Art Has Made Him Millions and his Posters Outsell Van Gogh and *Star Wars.* So Why Is Jack Vettriano So Bitter?' *Independent* (23 July), <www.independent.co.uk/arts-entertainment/jack-nicholson-loves-him-the-public-adores-him-his-erotic-art-has-made-him-millions-and-his-posters-outsell-van-gogh-and-star-wars-so-why-is-jack-vettriano-so-bitter-1107992.html> accessed 17 October 2010.

Brando, Marlon (1995), *Songs My Mother Taught Me,* New York: Arrow Books.

Breward, Christopher (2004), *Fashioning London: Clothing and the Modern Metropolis,* Oxford: Berg.

Breward, Christopher (2000), 'The Dandy Laid Bare: Embodying Practices and Fashion for Men', in Stella Bruzzi and Pamela Church Gibson (eds), *Fashion Cultures: Theories, Explorations and Analysis,* London and New York: Routledge.

Breward, Christopher (1999), *The Hidden Consumer: Masculinities, Fashion and City Life 1860–1914,* Manchester: Manchester University Press.

Breward, Christopher (1995), *The Culture of Fashion: A New History of Fashionable Dress,* Manchester: Manchester University Press.

Breward, C., Evans, C., and Ehrman, E. (2004), *The London Look: Fashion from Street to Catwalk,* New Haven, Connecticut: Yale University Press.

Brook, Stephen (2007), 'Vogue Thinks Big for Indian Launch', *Guardian* (20 September), <www.guardian.co.uk/media/2007/sep/20/pressandpublishing.fashion> accessed 17 October 2010.

Brooke, Iris, and Laver, James (2000), *English Costume from the Seventeenth through the Nineteenth Centuries,* reprint, London: Courier Dover Publications.

Brooks, Libby (2009), 'Kate Moss Deserves a Picture Postcard, instead of the Bitter Glare of Heat', *Guardian* (20 August), <www.guardian.co.uk/commentisfree/2009/aug/20/kate-moss-beauty-supermodels> accessed 9 August 2010.

Brown, David, Gray, Sadie, and Pitel, Laura (2010), 'Alexander McQueen in Apparent Suicide after the Death of His Mother', *Times* (12 February), <women.timesonline.co.uk/tol/life_and_style/women/fashion/article7024163.ece> accessed 8 August 2010.

Brown, Kelly (2007), *Florence Lawrence, The Biograph Girl: America's First Movie Star,* New York: McFarland.

Brown, Laura (2007), 'Partners in Crime', *Harper's Bazaar* (June), <www.harpersbazaar.com/magazine/cover/paris-nicole-feature-0607> accessed 29 September 2010.

Brown, Tina (2007), *The Diana Chronicles,* London: Century Books.

Bruzzi, Stella (2000), 'The Italian Job: Football, Fashion and That Sarong', in Stella Bruzzi and Pamela Church Gibson (eds) (2000), *Fashion Cultures: Theories, Explorations and Analysis,* London and New York: Routledge.

Bruzzi, Stella (1997), *Undressing Cinema: Clothing and Identity in the Movies,* London and New York: Routledge.

Bruzzi, Stella, and Church Gibson, Pamela (2004), 'Fashion Is the Fifth Character: Fashion, Costume and Character in Sex and the City', in Kim Akass and Janet McCabe (eds), *Reading Sex and the City,* London: IB Tauris.

Bruzzi, Stella, and Church Gibson, Pamela (eds) (2000), *Fashion Cultures: Theories, Explorations and Analysis,* London and New York: Routledge.

Buckley, Cheryl, and Fawcett, Hilary (2002), *Fashioning the Feminine: Representation and Women's Fashion from the Fin de Siècle to the Present,* London and New York: IB Tauris.

Bull, Sarah (2010a), '"Femme Fatale" Kate Moss Is a Cover Girl Once Again as She Poses for Front of Bryan Ferry's New Album Olympia', *Daily Mail* (10 September), <www.dailymail.co.uk/tvshowbiz/article-1310438/Kate-Moss-poses-cover-Bryan-Ferrys-album-Olympia.html#ixzz10rMNPaeS> accessed 28 September 2010.

Bull, Sarah (2010b), 'Gwyneth Paltrow Puts In a Hair-raising Display with Swept Back Locks and a Daring Keyhole Dress at Louis Vuitton Party', *Daily Mail* (27 May), <www.dailymail.co.uk/tvshowbiz/article-1281406/Louis-Vuitton-Maison-launch-Gwyneth-Paltrow-belle-ball-new-hair-daring-keyhole-dress.html#ixzz12dnGRRSq> accessed 17 October 2010.

Bumpus, J. (2010), 'Angelina Out', *Vogue* (11 January), <www.vogue.co.uk/news/2010/01/11/karen-elson-for-st-john> accessed 19 March 2010.

Bumpus, Jessica (2009), 'Ungaro Upset', *Vogue* (12 November), <www.vogue.co.uk/news/daily/091112-emanuel-ungaro-on-lindsay-lohan.aspx> accessed 8 August 2010.

Bunz, Mercedes (2009), 'Susan Boyle on Britain's Got Talent is YouTube's Top Video of 2009', *Guardian* (16 December), <www.guardian.co.uk/media/pda/2009/dec/16/susan-boyle-britains-got-talent-youtube> accessed 29 September 2010.

Burckhardt, Jacob (1860), *The Civilization of the Renaissance in Italy,* 2002 reprint, New York: Random House.

Burt, Jason (2010), 'World Cup 2010: David Beckham to Act as Player Liaison for Fabio Capello', *Telegraph* (4 June), <www.telegraph.co.uk/sport/football/world-cup-2010/teams/england/7801797/World-Cup-2010-David-Beckham-to-act-as-player-liaison-for-Fabio-Capello.html> accessed 6 August 2010.

Bush, Kate (2004), 'Young British Art: Kate Bush on the YBA Sensation', *Art Forum* (October).

Bushnell, Candice (2010), *The Carrie Diaries,* New York: Harper Collins Children's Books.

Bushnell, Candice (2008), *One Fifth Avenue,* New York: Little, Brown.

Bushnell, Candice (2005), *Lipstick Jungle,* New York: Little, Brown.

Bushnell, Candice (2003), *Trading Up,* New York: Little, Brown.

Bushnell, Candice (2000), *Four Blondes,* New York: Little, Brown.

Bushnell, Candice (1996), *Sex and the City,* New York: Little, Brown.

Buttolph, Angela (2008a) 'How to Dress Like Kate Moss', *Guardian* (10 October), <www.guardian.co.uk/lifeandstyle/2008/oct/10/fashion> accessed 7 August 2010.

Buttolph, Angela (2008b), *Kate Moss: Style,* London: Century.

Byrne, Charlie (2010), 'Grace Coddington', *Running in Heels* (8 February), <runninginheels.co.uk/articles/grace-coddington/> accessed 7 August 2010.

Calistro, Paddy (2004), 'Edith Head', in Susan Ware and Stacey Braukman (eds), *Notable Women: A Biographical Dictionary Completing the Twentieth Century,* Harvard: Harvard University Press.

Camber, Rebecca, and Nathan, Sara (2010), 'British Fashion Icon Alexander McQueen Commits Suicide Days after Death of His Beloved Mother', *Daily Mail* (12 February),

<www.dailymail.co.uk/news/article-1250249/Alexander-McQueen-commits-suicide.html#ixzz0w2CXp900> accessed August 2010.

Campbell, Alastair (2007), *The Blair Years: Extracts from the Alastair Campbell Diaries,* London: Hutchinson.

Campbell, C. (2005), *The Romantic Ethic and the Spirit of Modern Consumerism,* 3rd ed., Oxford: Alcuin Academics.

Cannatà, Teresa (2010), 'Stars, Celebs, Models: Manolo Blahnik', *Italian Vogue* (25 March), <www.vogue.it/en/vogue-starscelebsmodels/vogue-masters/2010/03/manolo-blahnik> accessed 7 August 2010.

Capote, Truman (1994), *Answered Prayers: The Unpublished Novel,* London and New York: Vintage Books.

Carter, Dominic (2008), 'The Decline of Luxury Brands in Japan?' *Japan.inc* (31 August), <www.japaninc.com/mgz_september_2008_decline-of-luxury-brands-in-japan> accessed 17 October 2010.

Cartner-Morley, Jess (2010a), 'Alexander McQueen: A Genius Is Lost and Darkness Has Won', *Guardian* (11 February) <www.guardian.co.uk/lifeandstyle/2010/feb/11/alexander-mcqueen-death-cartner-morley> accessed 16 October 2010.

Cartner-Morley, Jess (2010b), 'The Measure', *Guardian* (18 September), <www.guardian.co.uk/lifeandstyle/2010/sep/18/mulberry-tote-aviator-boots-tights> accessed 29 September 2010.

Cartner-Morley, Jess (2010c), 'Victoria Beckham at New York Fashion Week: Catwalk Curiosity to New Ticket', *Guardian* (12 September), <www.guardian.co.uk/lifeandstyle/2010/sep/12/victoria-beckham-new-york-fashion-week> accessed 16 December 2010.

Cartner-Morley, Jess (2010d), 'Welcome to the House of Vuitton', *Guardian* (25 May), <www.guardian.co.uk/lifeandstyle/2010/may/25/welcome-house-louis-vuitton> accessed 17 October 2010.

Cartner-Morley, Jess (2010e), 'Why WAG Fashion Is Still Where it Is At', *Guardian* (12 May), <www.guardian.co.uk/lifeandstyle/2010/may/12/wags-world-cup> accessed 8 August 2010.

Cartner-Morley, Jess (2009), 'Eyes Front: Forget About the Clothes and the Catwalk Models. The Big Fashion Shows Are All About the Front Row', *Guardian* (13 March), <www.guardian.co.uk/lifeandstyle/2009/mar/13/fashion-shows-front-row> accessed January 2009.

Cartner-Morley, Jess (2008), 'Is This the Most Tasteless Fashion Shoot Ever?' *Guardian* (4 September), <www.guardian.co.uk/lifeandstyle/2008/sep/04/fashion.pressandpublishing> accessed 17 October 2010.

Casciato, Paul (2009), 'Dolce & Gabbana Launch Luxury Make-up Line', *Reuters* (4 March), <www.reuters.com/article/idUSTRE5235BP20090304> accessed 8 August 2010.

Cashmore, Ellis (2006), *Celebrity Culture,* London and New York: Routledge.

Cashmore, Ellis (2004), *Beckham,* fully revised and updated, Cambridge: Polity Press.

Cashmore, E., and Parker, A. (2003):, 'One David Beckham? Celebrity, Masculinity, and the Soccerati', *Sociology of Sport Journal,* 20(3): 214–31.

Castle, Terry (1993), *The Apparitional Lesbian: Female Homosexuality and Modern Culture,* New York: Columbia University Press.

Cavell, Stanley (1996), *Contesting Tears: The Hollywood Melodrama of the Unknown Woman,* Chicago: University of Chicago Press.

Caws, Mary Ann (2003), *Vita Sackville-West: Selected Writings,* London: Palgrave Macmillan.

Celant, Germano, and Koda, Harold (2000), *Giorgio Armani: Guggenheim Museum Publications* [exhibition catalogue], New York: Harry N. Abrams.

Chaban, Matt (2009), 'Gaga for Gehry', *Architect's Newspaper* blog (4 December), <blog.archpaper.com/wordpress/archives/5456> accessed 7 August 2010.

Chadha, Radha, and Husband, Paul (2006), *The Cult of the Luxury Brand: Inside Asia's Love Affair with Luxury,* London: Nicholas Brealey Publishing.

Chandler, Robin M., and Chandler Smith, Nuri (2005), 'Flava in Ya Gear: Transgressive Politics and the Influence of Hip-Hop on Contemporary Fashion', in Linda Welters and Patricia A. Cunningham (eds), *Twentieth-Century American Fashion,* Oxford: Berg.

Charles, Jeffrey, and Watts, Jill (2000), '(Un)real Estate: Marketing Hollywood in the 1910s and 1920s', in David Desser and Garth Jowett (eds), *Hollywood Goes Shopping,* Minneapolis: University of Minnesota Press.

Charles-Roux, Edmonde (2009), *Chanel: Her Life, Her World, and the Woman behind the Legend She Herself Created,* London: Quercus.

Chenoune, Farid (1993), *A History of Men's Fashion,* London: Flammarion.

Chenoune, Farid, and Hamani, Laziz (2007), *Dior,* New York: Assouline.

Chevalier, Michel, and Mazzalovo, Gerald (2008) *Luxury Brand Management: A World of Privilege,* Chichester and Armes, Iowa: John Wiley and Sons.

Chierichetti, David (2004), *Edith Head: The Life and Times of Hollywood's Celebrated Costume Designer,* New York: Harper Collins.

Child, Ben (2010), 'Sex and the City 2 Disappointment Could Lead to Prequel', *Guardian* (4 June), <www.guardian.co.uk/film/2010/jun/04/sex-and-the-city-prequel> accessed 24 September 2010.

Child, Julia (2001), *Mastering the Art of French Cooking,* New York: Alfred A. Knopf.

Chilvers, Simon (2010), 'Brits Fashion: Let's Hear It for the Lads', *Guardian* (17 February), <www.guardian.co.uk/lifeandstyle/2010/feb/17/brit-awards-fashion> accessed 6 August 2010.

Church Gibson, Pamela (2008–2010), *Interviews: Celebrity, Fashion and Consumption,* based at London College of Fashion.

Church Gibson, Pamela (2008), 'Concerning Blondeness: Gender, Ethnicity, Spectacle and Footballers' Waves', in Geraldine Biddle-Perry and Sarah Cheang, *Hair: Styling, Culture and Fashion,* Oxford: Berg.

Church Gibson, Pamela (2007), '"Is That What They Think a Real Man Looks Like?": Hollywood, Gender and Consumption', in Frank Kelleter and Daniel Stein (eds), *American Studies as Media Studies*, Heidelberg: Universitätsverlag Winter.

Church Gibson, Pamela (2006a), 'Myths of the Swinging City: London in the Media', in Christopher Breward, David Gilbert and Jenny Lister (eds), *The Swinging Sixties,* London: V&A Publications.

Church Gibson, Pamela (2006b), 'New Stars, New Fashions and the Female Audience: Cinema, Consumption and Cities 1953–1966', in Christopher Breward and David Gilbert (eds), *Fashion's World Cities,* Oxford: Berg.

Church Gibson, Pamela (2005a), 'Brad Pitt and George Clooney, the Rough and the Smooth: Male Costuming in Contemporary Hollywood', in Rachel Moseley (ed.), *Fashioning Film Stars: Dress, Culture and Identity,* London: BFI Publishing.

Church Gibson, Pamela (2005b), 'Fashion, Fetish and Spectacle: The Matrix Dresses Up—and Down', in Stacy Gillis (ed.), *The Matrix Trilogy: Cyberpunk Reloaded,* London: Wallflower Press.

Church Gibson, Pamela (2004a), 'Otherness, Transgression and the Postcolonial Perspective: Patricia Rozema's *Mansfield Park*', in Eckart Voigts-Verchow (ed.), *Janespotting and Beyond: The British Heritage Film since the Mid-Nineties,* Germany: Gunter Narr Verlag.

Church Gibson, Pamela (2004b), 'Queer Looks, Male Gazes, Taut Torsos and Designer Labels: Contemporary Cinema, Consumption and Masculinity', in Bruce Babington, Ann Davies and Phil Powrie (eds), *The Trouble with Men: Masculinity and Contemporary Cinema,* London: Wallflower Books.

Church Gibson, Pamela (2000), 'Redressing the Balance: Patriarchy, Postmodernism and Feminism', in Stella Bruzzi and Pamela Church Gibson (eds), *Fashion Cultures: Theories, Explorations and Analysis,* London and New York: Routledge.

Church Gibson, Pamela (1998), 'Film Costume', in John Hill and Pamela Church Gibson (eds), *The Oxford Guide to Film Studies,* Oxford: Oxford University Press.

Clark, Roger (2010), 'His Dark Material', *Sight and Sound* (March).

Clayworth, Anya, and Wilde, Oscar (2004), *Oscar Wilde: Selected Journalism,* Oxford: Oxford University Press.

Clerk, Carol (2002), *Madonnastyle,* London: Omnibus Press.

Cochrane, Kira (2010), 'Is Lady Gaga a Feminist Icon?' *Guardian* (17 September), <www.guardian.co.uk/music/2010/sep/17/lady-gaga-feminist-icon> accessed 29 September 2010.

Cochrane, Lauren (2010), 'Not So Ugly Betty—Meet TV's Fashion Stars', *Guardian* (11 August), <www.guardian.co.uk/tv-and-radio/tvandradioblog/2010/aug/11/ugly-betty-fashion-tv> accessed 29 September 2010.

Cockburn, Alexander (1987), *The Corruptions of Empire,* New York: Verso.

Cohen, Louise (2009), 'Whitney Port on Having Her Life Exposed in The City and The Hills', *Times* (14 October), <entertainment.timesonline.co.uk/tol/arts_and_entertainment/tv_and_radio/article6873050.ece> accessed 7 August 2010.

Cole, Shaun (2010), interview with Pamela Church Gibson.

Collins, Joan (2009), 'Joan Collins: What Happened to Hollywood's Icons of Style?' *Times* (21 August), <entertainment.timesonline.co.uk/tol/arts_and_entertainment/film/article6804425.ece> accessed 19 September 2010.

Colman, Davis (2010), 'Manorexic Mannequins', *New York Magazine* (2 May), <nymag.com/news/intelligencer/topic/65753/> accessed August 2010.

Cook, Pam (2008), *Sofia Coppola's Marie Antoinette: A Fashionable History,* University of Nottingham Ningbo, China, 23 October, <www.nottingham.edu.cn/resources/documents/Pam%20CookNingboPaper%20PDF.pdf> accessed 15 May 2009.

Cook, Pam (1996), *Fashioning the Nation: Costume and Identity in British Cinema,* London: BFI Publishing.

Cook, Xerxes (2008), 'Miami Diary 1: The Art of Upstaging', *Guardian* (4 December), <www.guardian.co.uk/artanddesign/2008/dec/04/art-basel-miami-beach-fair> accessed 17 October 2010.

Cooke, Rachel, et al. (2009), 'Yes Michelle Obama Can', *Observer* (3 May), <www.guardian.co.uk/lifeandstyle/2009/may/03/michelle-obama> accessed 12 September 2010.

Couldry, Nick, and Markham, Tim (2007), 'Celebrity Culture and the Public Connection: Bridge or Chasm?' *International Journal of Cultural Studies,* 10/4 (December): 403–21.

Cox, Caroline, and Widdows, Lee (2005), *Hair and Fashion,* London: V&A Publishing.

Cozens, Claire (2003), 'Close Shave for Gucci Ad', *Guardian* (26 February), <www.guardian.co.uk/media/2003/feb/26/advertising> accessed 24 September 2010.

Craik, Jennifer (2009), *Fashion: The Key Concepts,* Oxford: Berg.

Crane, Diana (2001), *Fashion and Its Social Agendas: Class, Gender and Identity,* Chicago: University of Chicago Press.

Craughwell-Varda, Kathleen (1999), *Looking for Jackie: American Fashion Icons,* New York: Hearst Publishing.

Crewe, Louise, and Goodrum, Alison (2000), 'Fashioning New Forms of Consumption: The Case of Paul Smith', in Stella Bruzzi and Pamela Church Gibson (eds), *Fashion Cultures: Theories, Explorations and Analysis,* London and New York: Routledge.

Crilly, Rob (2007), 'Campbell Rails at Vogue for Models with White Skins', *Times* (20 August), <www.timesonline.co.uk/tol/news/world/africa/article2289097.ece> accessed 16 October 2010

Cunningham, Patricia, Mangine, Heather and Reilly, Andrew (2005), 'Television and Fashion in the 1980s', in Linda Welters and Patricia Cunningham (eds), *Twentieth Century Fashion,* Oxford: Berg.

Dana, Rebecca (2010), 'Best Shoes Ever: How Alexander McQueen's "Armadillo Boots" Charmed Lady Gaga, Daphne Guinness, and Barbie', *Daily Beast* (4 February), <www.thedailybeast.com/blogs-and-stories/2010–02–04/best-shoes-ever/> accessed 7 August 2010.

Dakers, Caroline (1999), *The Holland Park Circle: Artists and Victorian Society,* New Haven, Connecticut: Yale University Press.

Davey, Jenny (2007), 'Primark Oldie's Golden Touch', *Sunday Times* (22 April), <business.timesonline.co.uk/tol/business/industry_sectors/retailing/article1687148.ece> accessed 7 August 2010.

Davis, Deborah (2010), *Party of the Century: The Fabulous Story of Truman Capote and His Black and White Ball,* Chichester and Armes, Iowa: John Wiley and Sons.

Davis, S. (2008), 'What Men REALLY Think About…Helen Mirren in a Bikini at 62', *Daily Mail* (21 July), <www.dailymail.co.uk/femail/article-1036785/What-men-REALLY-think–Helen-Mirren-bikini-62.html#ixzz1Rz99pE58> accessed 12 September 2010.

Day, Elizabeth (2010), 'Cheryl Cole's Favourite Designers Are the Real Winners of X Factor', *Observer* (29 August), <www.guardian.co.uk/culture/2010/aug/29/cheryl-cole-x-factor-british-designers> accessed 29 September 2010.

Debord, Guy (1968), *Society of the Spectacle,* 2002 edition, Detroit, Michigan: Black and Red.

DeCordova, Richard (2001), *Picture Personalities: The Emergence of the Star System in America,* Urbana: University of Illinois Press.

DeLibero, Linda Benn (1994), 'This Year's Girl: A Personal/Critical History of Twiggy', in Shari Benstock and Suzanne Ferriss (eds), *On Fashion,* Rutgers, New Jersey: Rutgers University Press.

Denby, David (2006), 'Dressed to Kill: The Devil Wears Prada', *New Yorker* (10 July), <www.newyorker.com/archive/2006/07/10/060710crci_cinema> accessed 24 September 2010.

DeSimmone, Andrea (2010), 'Sneak Peek: Mary-Kate and Ashley Olsen's Brit-Inspired Olsenboye Fall Collection', *People StyleWatch* (12 July), <stylenews.peoplestylewatch.com/2010/07/12/sneak-peek-mary-kate-and-ashley-olsens-brit-inspired-olsenboye-fall-collection/> accessed 7 August 2010.

Desser, David, and Jowett, Garth (eds) (2000), *Hollywood Goes Shopping,* Minneapolis: University of Minnesota Press.

Di Mattia, Joanna (2007), 'The Gentle Art of Manscaping: Lessons in Hetero-Masculinity from the Queer Eye Guys', in Dana Heller (ed.), *Makeover Television: Realities Remodelled,* London: IB Tauris.

Doane, Mary Ann (1982), 'Film and the Masquerade: Theorising the Female Spectator', reprinted in Thornham, Sue (ed.) (1999), *Feminist Film Theory: A Reader,* Edinburgh: Edinburgh University Press.

Donnelly, Erin (2010), 'Marc Jacobs Says No to Celebrities at His Fall 2010 Show', *StyleList* (10 February), <www.stylelist.com/2010/02/10/marc-jacobs-says-no-celebrities-at-his-fall-2010-fashion-show/> accessed 25 September 2010.

'Don't Call Kim Cattrall a Cougar!' (2010), *Extra TV,* <extratv.warnerbros.com/2010/05/dont_call_kim_cattrall_a_cougar.php> accessed 24 September 2010.

Douglas, M., and Isherwood, B. (1996), *The World of Goods: Towards and Anthropology of Consumption,* London: Routledge.

Drake, Alicia (2006), *The Beautiful Fall: Fashion, Genius, and Glorious Excess in 1970s Paris,* London: Bloomsbury.

Duff, Mike (2009), 'Wal-Mart Launches Miley Cyrus Apparel Connected to Tour and Youth Strategy', *Bnet* (3 June), <www.bnet.com/blog/retail-business/wal-mart-launches-miley-cyrus-apparel-connected-to-tour-and-youth-strategy/1585> accessed 8 August 2010.

Dwyer, Rachel (2000), 'Bombay Ishtyle', in Stella Bruzzi and Pamela Church Gibson (eds), *Fashion Cultures: Theories, Explorations and Analysis,* London and New York: Routledge.

Dyer, Richard (1997), *White,* London and New York: Routledge.

Dyer, Richard (1994), 'Feeling English', *Sight and Sound,* 4/3 (March).

Dyer, Richard (1993), 'White', in Richard Dyer, *The Matter of Images: Essays on Representation,* London: Routledge.

Dyer, Richard (1986), *Heavenly Bodies: Film Stars and Society,* 2nd revised and updated edition, 2004, London and New York: Routledge.

Dyer, Richard (1978), *Stars,* new revised edition, 1998, London: BFI Publishing.

Dyhouse, Carol (2010), *Glamour: Women, History, Feminism,* London: Zed Books.

Easton Ellis, Brett (1999), *Glamorama,* New York: Picador.

Easton Ellis, Brett (1991), *American Psycho,* New York: Picador.

Eckert, C. (1978), 'The Carole Lombard in Macy's Window', in Jane Gaines and Charlotte Herzog, *Fabrications: Costume and the Female Body,* 1990 edition, London: Routledge.

Edwards, E. (2009), 'Hair, Devotion and Trade in India', in G. Biddle-Perry and S. Cheang, *Hair: Styling, Culture and Fashion,* Oxford: Berg.

Edwards, Tim (2011), *Fashion in Focus,* London and New York: Routledge.

Edwards, Tim (2006), *Cultures of Masculinity,* London and New York: Routledge.

Edwards, Tim (1997), *Men in the Mirror: Men's Fashion, Masculinity and Consumer Society,* London: Continuum.

Ellis, Rosemary (2010), 'Michelle Obama at Home in the White House', *Good Housekeeping* (July), <www.goodhousekeeping.com/family/celebrity/michelle-obama-interview-white-house> accessed 12 September 2010.

Elliott, Stuart (2010a), 'Mad Men Dolls in a Barbie World, but the Cocktails Must Stay Behind', *New York Times* (9 March), <www.nytimes.com/2010/03/10/business/

media/10adco.html?_r=1&adxnnl=1&adxnnlx=1285765500-EZhqOQQqGiQ92P/ vWWs/FA> accessed 29 September 2010.

Elliott, Stuart (2010b), 'What Next, the Official Salad Dressing of 'Sex and the City 2'?' *New York Times* (20 April), <mediadecoder.blogs.nytimes.com/2010/04/20/ what-next-the-official-salad-dressing-of-sex-and-the-city-2/> accessed 24 September 2010.

Elms, Robert (1995), *The Way We Wore: A Life In Threads,* London: Picador.

Elsworth, Catherine (2010), 'Mad Men Costume Designer Reveals Secret to Joan Holloway Look', *Telegraph* (10 October), <www.telegraph.co.uk/news/newstopics/ celebritynews/8053267/Mad-Men-costume-designer-reveals-secret-to-Joan-Hollo­way-look.html> accessed 16 October 2010.

'Emanuel Ungaro RTW Fall 2010' (2010), *Women's Wear Daily* (8 March), <www. wwd.com/fashion-week/fall-ready-to-wear-2010/review/emanuel-ungaro-rtw-fall-2010–2533835> accessed 8 August 2010.

Emin, Tracey (2007), 'My Life in a Column', *Independent,* <www.independent.co.uk/ opinion/columnists/tracey-emin/tracey-emin-my-life-in-a-column-396701.html> accessed 16 October 2010.

'End of an Era—Carrie and Co Hang Up Their Manolos as Sex and the City Comes to an End' (2010), *Mail Online* (29 June), <www.dailymail.co.uk/tvshowbiz/article-1290602/Sex-And-The-City-comes-end—Carrie-hang-Manolos.html#ixzz10ajeQRfj> accessed August 2010.

Engelmeier, Regine, and Engelmeier, Peter W. (1984), *Fashion in Film,* 2nd revised edition, 1997, London: Prestel.

Ennis, Betsy (2000), 'Giorgio Armani', Guggenheim Press Release Archive (25 September), <www.guggenheim.org/new-york/press-room/releases/press-release-archive/2000/698-september-25-giorgio-armani> accessed 8 August 2010.

Epstein, Rebecca (2000), 'Sharon Stone in a Gap Turtleneck', in David Desser and Garth Jowett (eds), *Hollywood Goes Shopping,* Minneapolis: University of Minnesota Press.

Esquevin, Christian (2008), *Adrian: Silver Screen to Custom Label,* New York: Monacelli Press.

Evans, Caroline (2007), *Fashion at the Edge: Spectacle, Modernity and Deathliness,* New Haven, Connecticut: Yale University Press.

Ewing, Elizabeth (1997), *History of 20th Century Fashion,* London: Quite Specific Media Group.

Fairclough, Kirsty (2008), 'Fame Is a Losing Game: Celebrity Gossip Blogging, Bitch Culture and Post-feminism', in *Going Cheap? Female Celebrity in Reality, Tabloid and Scandal Genres,* special issue of *Genders,* 48, <www.genders.org/lockss/ Genders2008.html> accessed 28 October 2010

Faithfull, Marianne (1994), *Faithfull,* London: Penguin Books.

Falcone, Michael (2008), 'Obama Gets "Celebrity Treatment" in New McCain Ad', *The Caucus: The Politics and Government Blog of the Times,* <thecaucus.blogs.nytimes.com/2008/07/30/obama-gets-celebrity-treatment-in-new-mccain-ad/> accessed 12 September 2010.

Feasey, Rebecca (2008), 'Reading Heat: The Meanings and Pleasures of Star Fashions and Celebrity Gossip', *Continuum: Journal of Media and Cultural Studies,* 22/5 (October): 687–99.

Feasey, Rebecca (2006), 'Get a Famous Body: Star Styles and Celebrity Gossip in Heat Magazine', in Su Holmes and Sean Redmond (eds), *Framing Celebrity: New Directions in Celebrity Culture,* London and New York: Routledge.

Ferguson, Marjorie (1983), *Forever Feminine: Women's Magazines and the Cult of Femininity,* London: Heinemann.

Ferragamo, Salvatore (1987), *Salvatore Ferragamo: The Art of the Shoe, 1927–1960,* London: V&A Publishing.

Field, Marcus (2009), 'Is Miuccia Prada the Next Peggy Guggenheim', *London Evening Standard* (14 August), <www.thisislondon.co.uk/lifestyle/article-23732163-is-miuccia-prada-the-next-peggy-guggenheim.do> accessed 17 October 2010.

Field, Patricia (2010), 'Patricia Field's Guide to the Many Looks of Sex and the City 2', *New York Magazine* (26 May), <nymag.com/daily/entertainment/2010/05/satc_2_stills.html#photo=1> accessed 25 September 2010.

Fifield, Dominic (2010), 'Tearful David Beckham Sees World Cup Dream Dashed by Milan Injury', *Guardian* (15 March), <www.guardian.co.uk/football/2010/mar/15/david-beckham-world-cup-injury> accessed 6 August 2010.

Finel Honigman, Ana (2007), 'Alison Jackson in Conversation with Ana Finel Honigman', *Saatchi Online* (19 December), <www.saatchi-gallery.co.uk/blogon/art_news/alison_jackson_in_conversation_with_ana_finel_honigman/3930> accessed 6 August 2010.

Finkelstein, Nat, and Dalton, David (2006), *Edie: Factory Girl,* New York: VH1 Press.

Fiske, John (1993), *Television Culture,* London and New York: Routledge.

Fiske, John (1989a), *Reading the Popular,* London and New York: Routledge.

Fiske, John (1989b), *Understanding Popular Culture,* London and New York: Routledge.

Flint, Hanna (2009), 'Joan Collins: I Shop at Primark', *Now* (17 October), <www.nowmagazine.co.uk/celebrity-news/401216/joan-collins-i-shop-at-primark/1/> accessed 7 August 2010.

Foreman, Amanda (1999), *Georgiana: Duchess of Devonshire,* London: Harper Collins.

Forrest, Nicholas (2008), 'Opinion: Celebrity Art Collectors Revealed', *Digital Journal* (17 August), <www.digitaljournal.com/article/258710> accessed 17 October 2010.

Fortini, Amanda (2008), 'Lindsay Lohan as Marilyn Monroe in "The Last Sitting"', *New York* (February), <nymag.com/fashion/08/spring/44247/> accessed December 2009.

Foster, Hal (2001), 'Death in America', in Benjamin Buchloh and Annette Michelson (eds), *Andy Warhol,* Cambridge, Massachusetts: MIT Press.

Foucault, Michel (1979), *Disciple and Punish,* London: Vintage Books.

Fowler, Catherine (2006), 'Spending Time with (a) Celebrity: Sam Taylor Wood's Video Portrait of David Beckham', in Su Holmes and Sean Redmond (eds), *Framing Celebrity—New Directions in Celebrity Culture,* London and New York: Routledge.

Fox, Imogen (2010), 'Louis Vuitton Launches Young Arts Project', *Guardian* (12 May), <www.guardian.co.uk/lifeandstyle/2010/may/12/louis-vuitton-young-arts-project> accessed 17 October 2010.

Fox, Imogen (2008), 'Carla Bruni-Sarkozy: Style by Stealth', *Guardian* (28 March), <www.guardian.co.uk/lifeandhealth/gallery/2008/mar/28/fashion> accessed 20 September 2010.

Fox, Patty (1995), *Star Style: Hollywood Legends as Fashion Icons,* Los Angeles: Angel City Press.

Francis, Mark, and King, Margery (1997), *The Warhol Look: Glamour Style Fashion,* Pittsburgh, Pennsylvania: Andy Warhol Museum.

Frankel, David (2000), 'Sam Taylor Wood', *Artforum,* 23/2 (May): 177.

Frankel, Susannah (2010), 'New Model Army: Why Fashion Has Fallen out of Love with Its A-list Clothes Horses', *Independent* (29 July), <www.independent.co.uk/life-style/fashion/features/new-model-army-why-fashion-has-fallen-out-of-love-with-its-alist-clotheshorses-2037770.html> accessed 25 September 2010.

Frankel, Susannah (2004), 'Vivenne Westwood: And Long May She Reign…', *Independent* (15 March), <www.independent.co.uk/news/people/profiles/vivienne-westwood-and-long-may-she-reign-566381.html> accessed 1 October 2010.

Fraser, Antonia (2010), *Must You Go? My Life with Harold Pinter,* London: Weidenfeld & Nicholson.

Fraser, Antonia (2001), *Marie Antoinette: The Journey,* London: Weidenfeld & Nicolson.

Freeman, Hadley (2010), 'The Death of Sex and the City', *Guardian* (24 May), <www.guardian.co.uk/film/2010/may/23/sex-and-the-city-film-terrible> accessed 24 September 2010.

Freeman, Hadley (2008), 'The Making of an Icon', *Guardian* (18 December), <www.guardian.co.uk/lifeandstyle/2008/dec/18/victoria-beckham-fashion> accessed 29 September 2010.

Freeman, Hadley (2007a), 'Marc Jacobs Hires Victoria Beckham and the Universe Implodes', *Guardian,* Lost in Showbiz blog (29 November), <www.guardian.co.uk/lifeandstyle/lostinshowbiz/2007/nov/29/marcjacobshiresvictoriabec> accessed 25 September 2010.

Freeman, Hadley (2007b), 'Primark's £8 Jeans and £2 Bikinis Cause a Stampede', *Guardian* (6 April), <www.guardian.co.uk/uk/2007/apr/06/fashion.topstories3> accessed 12 September 2010.

French, Philip (2010), 'Sex and the City 2', *Observer* (30 May), <www.guardian.co.uk/film/2010/may/30/philip-french-sex-and-city-2-review> accessed 25 September 2010.

Friedlander, Ruthie (2010), 'Fashion Wars: Whitney Port vs. Olivia Palermo', *Stylite* (2 April), <www.styleite.com/media/whitney-port-style/> accessed 7 August 2010.

Frith, Mark (2008), *The Celeb Diaries: The Sensational Inside Story of the Celebrity Decade,* London: Ebury Press.

Frith, Simon, and Horne, Howard (1987), *Art into Pop,* London: Taylor and Francis.

Fuller, Bonnie (2008), 'What the Creators of 'Sex and the City' Know about Marketing That You Don't', *Advertising Age* (9 June), <adage.com/madisonandvine/article?article_id=127610> accessed 16 October 2010.

Gaines, Jane (1990), 'Costume and Narrative: How Dress Tells the Woman's Story', in Jane Gaines and Charlotte Herzog (eds), *Fabrications: Costume and the Female Body,* London and New York: Routledge/AFI Film Readers.

Gaines, Jane, and Herzog, Charlotte (eds) (1990), *Fabrications: Costume and the Female Body,* London and New York: Routledge/AFI Film Readers.

Gamman, Lorraine, and Marshment, Margaret (1988), *The Female Gaze: Women as Viewers of Popular Culture,* London: Women's Press.

Gehlhar, Mary (2008), *The Fashion Designer Survival Guide: Start and Run Your Own Fashion Business,* New York: Kaplan Publishing.

Gelder, Ken, and Thornton, Sarah (eds) (1997), *The Subcultures Reader,* London and New York: Routledge.

Genz, Stephanie, and Brabon, Benjamin (2009), *Post Feminism: Cultural Texts and Theories,* Edinburgh: Edinburgh University Press.

Geraghty, Christine (2000), 'Re-examining Stardom. Questions of Texts, Bodies and Performance', in C. Gledhill and L. Williams (eds), *Reinventing Film Studies,* London: Hodder Arnold.

Gibson, Cristina (2009), '*Lipstick Jungle* is Really, Truly Cancelled', *E Online!* (27 March), <uk.eonline.com/uberblog/hwood_party_girl/b106477_lipstick_jungle_really_truly_canceled.html> accessed 24 September 2010.

Gilligan, Sarah (2010a), 'Branding the New Bond: Daniel Craig and Designer Fashion', in Rob Weiner and Jack Becker (eds), *James Bond, History and Popular Culture: The Films are Not Enough,* Newcastle-Upon-Tyne: Cambridge Scholars Publishing.

Gilligan, Sarah (2010b), 'Fashioning Masculinity and Desire in *Torchwood*', in Andrew Ireland (ed.), *Illuminating Torchwood: Essays on Narrative, Character and Sexuality in the BBC Series,* Critical Explorations in Science Fiction and Fantasy, London: McFarland.

Gilligan, Sarah (2009a), 'Becoming Neo: Costume and Transforming Masculinity in the *Matrix* Films', in Peter McNeil, Vicki Karaminas and Catherine Cole (eds), *Fashion in Fiction: Text and Clothing in Literature, Film and Television,* Oxford: Berg.

Gilligan, Sarah (2009b), 'Get Me an Exit: Mobile Phones and Transforming Masculinity in the *Matrix* Trilogy', in Ruby Cheung and David Fleming (eds), *Cinema, Identities and Beyond,* Newcastle-Upon-Tyne: Cambridge Scholars Publishing.

Gilligan, Sarah (2000), 'Gwyneth Paltrow', in Stella Bruzzi and Pamela Church Gibson (eds), *Fashion Cultures: Theories, Explorations and Analysis,* London and New York: Routledge.

Gilman, Sander (2000), *Making the Body Beautiful: A Cultural History of Aesthetic Surgery,* Princeton, New Jersey: Princeton University Press.

Gilman, Sander (1997), *Creating Beauty to Cure the Soul: Race and Psychology in the Shaping of Aesthetic Surgery,* Durham, North Carolina: Duke University Press.

Gilmour, Ian (2003), *The Making of the Poets: Byron and Shelley in Their Time,* New York: Carroll and Graf Publishers.

'The Girl with the Black Tights' (1965), *Life* (26 November), available online via Google books.

Glaister, Dan (2008), 'L'Oreal Denies "Whitening" Beyoncé Knowles' Skin in Cosmetics Ad', *Guardian* (8 August), <www.guardian.co.uk/media/2008/aug/08/advertising.usa1> accessed 16 October 2010.

Gledhill, Christine (ed.) (1991), *Stardom: Industry of Desire,* London and New York: Routledge.

'Glossy Karlie . . . Vogue and Lucky Launch Partnerships . . . New Gravy Train . . .' (2010), *Women's Wear Daily* (7 January), <www.wwd.com/media-news/?module=tn#/article/media-news/fashion-memopad/glossy-karlie-vogue-and-lucky-launch-partnerships-new-gravy-train-2405375?full=true> accessed 19 September 2010.

Glover, Eleanor, and Smith, Lizzie (2009), 'As She Falls out of Yet ANOTHER Revealing Outfit, Would You Take Style Advice from Katie Price?' *Daily Mail* (16 October), <www.dailymail.co.uk/femail/article-1220566/Standing-Out-wrong-reasons-Would-style-advice-Katie-Price.html#ixzz0w7RMYSZa> accessed December 2009.

Goldman, A. (2001), *The Lives of John Lennon,* Chicago: Chicago Reviews Press.

Goldman, Albert (1981), *Elvis,* New York: McGraw Hill.

Goodman, Elizabeth (2010), *Lady Gaga: Extreme Style,* London and New York: Harper Collins.

Goodyear, Dana (2009), 'Celebromatic', *New Yorker* (30 November), <www.newyorker.com/talk/2009/11/30/091130ta_talk_Goodyear> accessed 7 August 2010.

Gough-Yates, Anna (2003), *Understanding Women's Magazines: Publishing, Markets and Readerships,* London and New York: Routledge.

Greer, Germaine (2008), 'We Like Our Venuses Young', *Guardian* (30 April), <www.guardian.co.uk/artanddesign/2008/apr/30/photography.women> accessed 16 October 2010.

Groom, Avril (2010), 'How Deep Is Your Luxe?' *Financial Times: How to Spend It?* (8 March), <www.howtospendit.com/#/articles/1303-ethical-luxury-how-deep-is-your-luxe> accessed 24 September 2010.

Groom, Nigel (1997), *The New Perfume Handbook,* New York: Springer.

Gross, Michael (2004), *Genuine Authentic: The Real Life of Ralph Lauren,* New York: Perennial.

Gundle, Stephen (2008), *Glamour: A History,* Oxford: Oxford University Press.

Gurley Brown, Helen (1962), *Sex and the Single Girl,* New York: Random House.

Gutner, Howard (2001), *Gowns by Adrian,* New York: Harry N. Abrams.

Gyben, E. (2011), 'Olivia Palermo in the Limelight,' *Fashion etc.,* <fashionetc.com/news/fashion/1551-olivia-palermo-limelight-photo-shoot> accessed 13 July 2011.

Hall, Stuart, and Jefferson, Tony (1993), *Resistance through Rituals: Youth Subcultures in Post-war Britain,* London and New York: Routledge.

Handy, Bruce (2008), 'Miley Knows Best', *Vanity Fair* (June), <www.vanityfair.com/culture/features/2008/06/miley200806> accessed August 2010.

Hardy, Bert (1985), *Bert Hardy: My Life,* London: Gordon Fraser Gallery.

Harris, Jonathan (ed.) (2004), *Art, Money, Parties: New Institutions in the Political Economy of Contemporary Art,* Liverpool: Tate Publishing.

Harris, Mark (2010), 'What's Wrong with the Summer's Movies?' *Entertainment Weekly* (11 June), <www.ew.com/ew/article/0,20393064,00.html> accessed 25 September 2010.

Harris, William (2009), *Queer Externalities: Hazardous Encounters in American Culture,* New York: SUNY Press.

Harrison, Richard, and Martin, Richard (1995), *Contemporary Fashion,* Farmington Hills, Michigan: St James Press.

Hata, Kyojiro (2004), *Louis Vuitton Japan: The Building of Luxury,* New York: Assouline.

Haughland, H. Kristina (2010), *Grace Kelly Style,* London: V&A Publishing.

Hawkins, Stan (2009), *The British Pop Dandy: Masculinity, Popular Music and Culture,* London: Ashgate Publishing.

Hawthorne, Nigel (1996), *The New Look: The Dior Revolution,* London: Hamlyn.

Haywood, Paul (2010), 'Fabio Capello Has Become English Football's Answer to Nick Clegg', *Guardian* (16 May), <www.guardian.co.uk/football/blog/2010/may/16/fabio-capello-england-world-cup-squad> accessed 6 August 2010.

Hazel (2007), 'The Black Wall at the Subway Gallery', *Londonist* (30 January), <londonist.com/2007/01/the_black_wall.php> accessed 17 October 2010.

Head, E. (1959), *The Dress Doctor,* New York: Little, Brown.

Hebdige, Dick (1979), *Subculture: The Meaning of Style,* London: Taylor Francis.

Heinick, Angelika (2006), 'Alive among the Trophies of Luxury: Vanessa Beecroft at Espace Louis Vuitton', *Frankfurter Allgemeine* (28 February), English translation available online (via Google Translate) <www.faz.net/s/RubBC09F7BF72A2405A

96718ECBFB68FBFE/Doc~E6322DE7FA819442F93A60D7078913420~ATpl~Ec ommon~Scontent.html> accessed 17 October 2010.

'Helen Mirren the Bikini Queen Reigns Supreme at 63' (2008), *Daily Mail* (21 July), <www.dailymail.co.uk/tvshowbiz/article-1035510/Helen-Mirren-bikini-queen-reigns-supreme-63.html> accessed 12 September 2010.

Heller, Dana (2007), *Makeover Television: Realities Remodelled,* London: IB Tauris.

Hermes, Joke (1995), *Reading Women's Magazines: An Analysis of Everyday Media Use,* London: Polity Press.

Heyes, C., and Jones, M. (2009), *Cosmetic Surgery: A Feminist Primer,* Farnham: Ashgate.

Hickman, Martin (2006), 'Britons in Debt to the Tune of £1.13 Trillion', *Independent* (3 January), <www.independent.co.uk/news/uk/this-britain/britons-in-debt-to-the-tune-of-163113-trillion-521489.html> accessed December 2009.

Hill, Andrew (2005), 'People Dress So Badly Nowadays: Fashion and Late Modernity', in Christopher Breward and Caroline Evans (eds), *Fashion and Modernity,* Oxford: Berg.

Hintz-Zambrano, Katie (2010), 'Alexa Chung Inspires Mulberry Alexa Bag', *StyleList* (7 January), <www.stylelist.com/2010/01/07/alexa-chung-inspires-mulberry-alexa-bag/> accessed 29 September 2010.

Hirschberg, Lynn (1996), "Next. Next. What's Next?" *New York Times* (7 April), <www.nytimes.com/1996/04/07/magazine/next-next-what-s-next.html?pagewanted=1> accessed 7 August 2010.

Hitchens, Christopher (1997), 'The Importance of Being Andy: The "Warhol's World" Keynote Lecture 1995', in Colin MacCabe et al. (eds), *Who Is Andy Warhol?* London: British Film Institute.

Hollows, Joanne (2000), *Feminism, Femininity and Popular Culture,* Manchester: Manchester University Press.

Hollows, Joanne, and Moseley, Rachel (eds) (2006), *Feminism in Popular Culture,* Oxford: Berg.

Hollywood Records (2009), 'Miley Cyrus—"Party in the USA"—Official Music Video', YouTube, <www.youtube.com/watch?v=M11SvDtPBhA> accessed 8 August 2010.

Holmes, Su, and Negra, Diane (2008), Call for papers for Going Cheap?: Female Celebrity in the Tabloid, Reality and Scandal Genres, conference at University of East Anglia, United Kingdom, 25 June 2008, <www.h-net.org/announce/show .cgi?ID=161151, accessed 7 August 2010.

Holmes, Su, and Redmond, Sean (2010), 'A Journal in Celebrity Studies', *Celebrity Studies Journal,* 1/1 (2010), <www.informaworld.com/smpp/title~db=all~conten t=g919931240> accessed 6 August 2010.

Holmes, Su, and Redmond, Sean (eds) (2006), *Framing Celebrity: New Directions in Celebrity Culture,* London and New York: Routledge.

Horyn, Cathy (2010), 'Alexander McQueen's Final Bow', *New York Times* (2 April), <www.nytimes.com/2010/04/04/fashion/04mcqueen.html?_r=1> accessed 8 August 2010.

Hudovernik, Robert (2006), *Jazz Age Beauties: The Lost Collection of Ziegfeld Photographer Alfred Cheney Johnston,* New York: Universe.

Hughes, Kathryn (2008), 'Zeal and Softness', *Guardian* (20 December), <www.guardian.co.uk/books/2008/dec/20/women-pressandpublishing> accessed 27 September 2010.

Hulanicki, Barbara (1983), *From A to Biba,* London: Hutchinson.

Hyde, Marina (2006), 'Come on You Wags!' *Guardian* (23 June), <www.guardian.co.uk/lifeandstyle/2006/jun/23/fashion.worldcup2006> accessed 8 August 2010.

'"I'll Never Be Like Jordan...Pamela Anderson's My Heroine," Reveals I'm A Celeb Nicola McLean' (2008), *Daily Mail* (10 December), <www.dailymail.co.uk/tvshowbiz/celebrity/article-1093222/Ill-like-Jordan—Pamela-Andersons-heroine-reveals-Im-A-Celeb-Nicola-McLean.html#ixzz0w7OIBEWC> accessed December 2008.

Isherwood, Christopher (1964), *A Single Man,* 2010 reprint, London: Vintage Books, Random House.

Jackson, Alison (2007), *Confidential. What You See in This Book Is Not "Real"* ', London: Taschen GmbH.

Jackson, Alison (2003), *Private,* London: Michael Joseph.

Jackson, Tim, and Shaw, David (2006), *The Fashion Handbook,* London and New York: Routledge.

Jacobson, Harlan (2006), 'Coppola's Movie Booed at Cannes: Was Something Lost in Translation?' *USA Today* (24 May), <www.usatoday.com/life/movies/news/2006–05–24-marie-antoinette-cannes_x.htm> accessed 7 August 2010.

'Japan Unveils Chocolate Beckham' (2002), *BBC News* (17 December), <news.bbc.co.uk/1/hi/world/asia-pacific/2582349.stm> accessed 6 August 2010.

Jeffers McDonald, Tamar (2010), *Hollywood Catwalk: Exploring Costume and Transformation in American Film,* London: IB Tauris.

Jeffries, Stuart (2008), 'Caught Up in the Moment: Why Stars Love to Pose for Annie Leibovitz', *Guardian* (30 April), <www.guardian.co.uk/artanddesign/2008/apr/30/photography.women> accessed 16 October 2010.

Jenkyn Jones, Sue (2002), *Fashion Design,* London: Laurence King Publishing.

Jermyn, Deborah (2009), *Sex and the City: TV Milestones,* Detroit, Michigan: Wayne State University Press.

Jermyn, Deborah (2006), 'Bringing Out the * in You: SJP, Carrie Bradshaw and the Evolution of Television Stardom', in Su Holmes and Sean Redmond (eds), *Framing Celebrity: New Directions in Celebrity Culture,* London and New York: Routledge.

Jermyn, Deborah (2004), 'In Love with Sarah Jessica Parker: Celebrating Female Fandom and Friendship in *Sex and the City*', in Kim Akass and Janet McCabe (eds), *Reading Sex and the City,* London: IB Tauris.

Jobling, Paul (1999), *Fashion Spreads: Word and Image in Fashion Photography since 1980,* Oxford: Berg.

Johnson, Chris (2009), 'Put It Away Madonna! Heavily Airbrushed Singer Strikes Raunchiest Pose ever in Latest Louis Vuitton Ad', *Daily Mail* (6 January), <www.dailymail.co.uk/tvshowbiz/article-1106024/Put-away-Madonna-Singer-strikes-raunchiest-pose-Louis-Vuitton-ad-campaign.html> accessed 7 August 2010.

Johnson, Lee (2008), 'Alison Jackson at the Liverpool Biennial', *White Hot* (October), <whitehotmagazine.com/articles/2008-alison-jackson-liverpool-biennial/1639> accessed 6 August 2010.

Jones, Chris, and Novak, Tony (1999), *Poverty, Welfare and the Disciplinary State,* London and New York: Routledge.

Jones, Liz (2010), 'Looking Polished and Approachable, Samantha Cameron Is the Winner in the Wives' Style Stakes', *Daily Mail* (7 May), <www.dailymail.co.uk/femail/article-1274129/UK-ELECTION-2010-Samantha-Cameron-winner-wives-style-stakes.html#ixzz0zKSMDIPx> accessed 12 September 2010.

Junor, P. (1983), *Diana: Princess of Wales,* London: Doubleday.

'Karl Lagerfeld for H&M in Store November 12' (2004), H&M, press release (28 October), <www.hm.com/us/press/pressreleases/__prfashion.nhtml?pressreleaseid=342> accessed 8 August 2010.

Kellner, Douglas (1995), 'Madonna, Fashion and Image', in Douglas Kellner, *Media Culture: Cultural Studies, Identity, and Politics between the Modern and the Postmodern,* London and New York: Routledge.

Kelly, Ian (2007), *Beau Brummell: The Ultimate Man of Style,* London: Simon & Schuster.

Khan, Nathalie (2000), 'Catwalk Politics', in Stella Bruzzi and Pamela Church Gibson, *Fashion Cultures: Theories, Explorations and Analysis,* London and New York: Routledge.

Kinsella, Sophie (2009), *Shopaholic Abroad,* New York: Little, Brown.

Kinsella, Sophie (2004), *Shopaholic Ties the Knot,* New York: Little, Brown.

Kinsella, Sophie (2002), *Shopaholic Takes Manhattan,* New York: Little, Brown.

Kinsella, Sophie (2001), *Confessions of a Shopaholic,* New York: Little, Brown.

Knight, Christopher (2010), 'Lady Gaga, Meat Jana Sterbak', *LA Times* blogs (13 September), <latimesblogs.latimes.com/culturemonster/2010/09/lady-gaga-meat-dress-recycled.html> accessed 29 September 2010.

Knox, Kristen (2010), *Alexander McQueen, Genius of a Generation,* London: A & C Black.

Koda, Harold, and Yohannan, Kohle (2009), *The Model as Muse: Embodying Fashion,* New Haven, Connecticut: Yale University Press.

Koenig, R. (1973), *The Restless Image,* London: George Allen and Unwin.

La Ferla, Ruth (2007), 'My So-called Gossipy Life', *New York Times* (16 September), <www.nytimes.com/2007/09/16/fashion/16gossip.html> accessed 29 September 2010.

La Ferla, Ruth (2003), 'Front Row', *New York Times* (4 February), <www.nytimes.com/2003/02/04/nyregion/front-row.html?ref=winona_ryder> accessed 25 September 2010.

'Lagerfeld's High Street Split' (2004), *Vogue* (18 November), <www.vogue.co.uk/news/daily/2004–11/041118-lagerfelds-high-street-split.aspx> accessed 8 August 2010.

Landay, Lori (2002), 'The Flapper Film: Comedy Dance and Jazz Age Kinaesthetics', in Jennifer Bean and Diane Negra (eds), *A Feminist Reader in Early Cinema,* Durham, North Carolina: Duke University Press.

Langle, Elisabeth (2005), *Pierre Cardin: Fifty Years of Fashion,* New York: Vendôme Press.

Lauren, Ralph (2007), *Ralph Lauren,* New York: Rizzoli International Publications.

Lawson, Twiggy, and Denning, Penelope (1997), *Twiggy in Black and White,* London: Simon and Schuster.

Leavis, F. R (1930), *Mass Civilisation and Minority Culture,* Cambridge: Minority Press.

Lee, Joyce (2010), 'Dr. Frank Ryan, Heidi Montag's Plastic Surgeon, Killed in Car Crash', *CBS News* (17 August), <www.cbsnews.com/8301–31749_162–20013877–10391698.html> accessed 29 September 2010.

Lehu, Jean-Marc (2007), *Branded Entertainment: Product Placement and Brand Strategy in the Entertainment Business,* London: Kogan Page Business.

Leight, Michele (2000), 'Beyond the Neutral Rush and the Stereotyped Monochromism: Giorgio Armani at the Solomon R. Guggenheim Museum', *City Review* (27 October), <www.thecityreview.com/armani.html> accessed 8 August 2010.

Levy, Ariel (2009a), 'I wish I Knew How to Enjoy It More: Overweight, Uncompromising, Plagued by Self-doubt, Alber Elbaz Is an Unlikely Fashion Icon', *Observer* (17 May), <www.guardian.co.uk/lifeandstyle/2009/may/17/alber-elbaz-lanvin-fashion-designer> accessed 25 September 2010.

Levy, Ariel (2009b), 'Ladies Man', *New Yorker* (16 March), <www.newyorker.com/reporting/2009/03/16/090316fa_fact_levy> accessed 25 September 2010.

Lewis, Peter (1978), *The Fifties,* London: Lippincott, Williams and Wilkins.

Lippert, Barbara (2010), 'Louis Vuitton and Annie Leibovitz', *Adweek* (31 March), <www.adweek.com/aw/content_display/special-issues/media-hot-list/e3ie9fc421daf51cf8244464b1879c8cc59> accessed 25 September 2010.

Lloyd, Fran (1993), 'The Changing Images of Madonna', in Fran Lloyd (ed.), *Deconstructing Madonna,* London: Batsford.

Lomrantz, Tracey (2010), 'Who Needs Diamonds? Johnny Depp Bought His Girl . . . Marilyn Monroe's Shoes!' *Glamour,* Slaves to Fashion Daily Style blog (12 July), <www.glamour.com/fashion/blogs/slaves-to-fashion/2010/07/who-needs-diamonds-johnny-depp.html> accessed 18 September 2010.

'Louis Vuitton, Murakami Celebrate Six Years with "Super Flat First Love" Anime Short' (2009), *Fashionologie* (10 June), <www.fashionologie.com/Louis-Vuitton-Murakami-Celebrate-Six-Years-Superflat-First-Love-Anime-Short-3281006> accessed 17 October 2010.

Macartney, Jane (2010), 'Chinese Websurfers Go Gaga for English Buzz Phrases', *Times* (22 April), <www.timesonline.co.uk/tol/news/world/asia/article7103634.ece> accessed 7 August 2010.

Mackenzie Stuart, Amanda (2007), *Consuelo and Alva Vanderbilt: The Story of a Daughter and a Mother in the Gilded Age,* reprint edition, London: Harper Perennial.

'Madonna's "Material Girl" Designs Clothing Range' (2010), video clip, *BBC News* (31 March), <news.bbc.co.uk/1/hi/entertainment/8596604.stm> accessed 7 August 2010.

Madsen, Axel (1990), *Coco Chanel: A Biography,* London, Berlin and New York: Bloomsbury.

Maisa, Isa (2010), 'Yves Saint Laurent Retrospective at the Petit Palais Paris', *Benjamin Kanarek Blog* (13 September), <www.benjaminkanarekblog.com/2010/09/13/yvessaintlaurentretrospectivepetitpalaisparis/> accessed 25 September 2010.

Malkin, Marc (2010), 'Who's Ready for Sex and the City: The Teen Years?' *E Online* (2 June), <uk.eonline.com/uberblog/marc_malkin/b183931_whos_ready_sex_city_teen_years.html#ixzz0pnijQtCq> accessed 24 September 2010.

Mann, William (2001), *The Biograph Girl,* New York: Kensington.

Mansour, David (2005), *From ABBA to Zoom: A Pop Culture Encyclopedia of the Late 20th Century,* Kansas City, Missouri: Andrews McMeel Publishing.

Marcuse, Herbert (1964), *One Dimensional Man: Studies in the Ideology of Advanced Industrial Society,* London and New York: Routledge.

Marshall, P. David (1997), *Celebrity and Power: Fame in Contemporary Culture,* Minneapolis: University of Minnesota Press.

Marshall, P. David (ed.) (2006), *The Celebrity Culture Reader,* London: Routledge.

Martin, Nicole (2008), 'Hannah Montana Star Miley Cyrus: Vanity Fair Shoot Was One Dumb Decision', *Telegraph* (10 October), <www.telegraph.co.uk/news/newstopics/celebritynews/3174259/Hannah-Montana-star-Miley-Cyrus-Vanity-Fair-shoot-was-one-dumb-decision.html> accessed 19 September 2010.

Marx, Karl (1844), 'Economic and Philosophical Manuscripts of 1844', in Karl Marx and Fredrick Engels (1844/1988), *Economic and Philosophical Manuscripts of 1844 and The Communist Manifesto,* translated by Martin Milligan, New York: Prometheus Books.

Massey, Anne (2000), *Hollywood beyond the Screen: Design and Material Culture,* Oxford: Berg.

'Material Girl' (2010), Macy's, promotional website, <www.macys.com/campaign/social?campaign_id=154&channel_id=1> accessed 7 August 2010.

Mayer, Ruth (2002), *Artificial Africas: Colonial Images in the Times of Globalisation,* Lebanon, NHUPNE.

McCann, Graham (1998), *Marilyn Monroe,* Rutgers, New Jersey: Rutgers University Press.

McDowell, Colin (2001), *Galliano,* London: Cassell Paperbacks.

McElvoy, Anne (2010), 'Manifesto Mannequins: What the Election Wives are Wearing', *London Evening Standard* (14 April), <www.thisislondon.co.uk/standard/politics/

article-23824385-manifesto-mannequins-what-the-election-wives-are-wearing.do> accessed 12 September 2010.

McFadden, Robert, and Macropoulous, Angela (2008), 'Wal-mart Employee Trampled to Death', *New York Times* (28 November), <www.nytimes.com/2008/11/29/business/29walmart.html> accessed 12 September 2010.

McLaughlin, N. (2011), 'Rattling out of Control: A Comparison of U2 and Joy Division on Film', *Film, Fashion and Consumption,* 1/1 (February): 101–20.

McLaughlin, Noel (2000), 'Rock, Fashion and Performativity', in Stella Bruzzi and Pamela Church Gibson (eds), *Fashion Cultures: Theories, Explanations and Analysis,* New York and London: Routledge.

McLuhan, Marshall (1964), *Understanding Media: The Extensions of Man,* reprinted 1994, Cambridge, Massachusetts: MIT Press.

McNeil, Peter (2010), 'Conference Report: The Future of Fashion Studies', *Fashion Theory: The Journal of Dress, Body and Culture,* 14/1 (March): 105–10.

McNeil, Peter (2008), *Critical and Primary Sources in Fashion,* 4 volumes, Oxford: Berg.

McNeil, Peter, Karaminas, Vicki, and Cole, Catherine (eds) (2009), *Fashion in Fiction: Texts and Clothing in Literature, Film and Television,* Oxford: Berg.

McRobbie, Angela (2009), *The Aftermath of Feminism: Gender, Culture and Social Change,* London: Sage.

McRobbie, Angela (2004), 'Notes on What Not to Wear and Post-feminist Symbolic Violence', in L. Adkins and B. Skeggs (eds), *Feminism after Bourdieu,* Oxford: Blackwell.

McRobbie, Angela (1998), *British Fashion Design: Rag Trade or Image Industry?* London and New York: Routledge.

McRobbie, Angela (1997), 'More! New Sexualities in Girls' and Women's Magazines', in Angela McRobbie (ed.), *Back to Reality?: Social Experience and Cultural Studies,* Manchester: Manchester University Press.

McRobbie, Angela (1991), *Feminism and Youth Culture: From 'Jackie' to 'Just Seventeen',* Boston: Unwin Hyman.

McVeigh, Tracy (2010), 'Elle Magazine Breaks Fashion's Last Taboo: Plus Size Models on the Cover', *Observer* (28 March), <www.guardian.co.uk/lifeandstyle/2010/mar/28/elle-models-france-plus-size> accessed 25 September 2010.

Melly, George (1970), *Revolt into Style: The Pop Arts in Britain,* London: Allen Lane.

Merck, Mandy (2004), 'Sexuality in the City', in Kim Akass and Janet McCabe (eds), *Reading Sex and the City,* London and New York: IB Tauris.

Michelson, A. (2001), *Andy Warhol (October Files),* Cambridge, Massachusetts: MIT Press.

Miklitsch, Robert (1998), *From Hegel to Madonna: Towards a General Economy of 'Commodity Fetishism',* New York: SUNY Press.

Miles, S. (1998), *Consumerism—as a Way of Life,* London: Sage.

Miller, Daniel (2001), *The Dialectics of Shopping,* Chicago and London: University of Chicago Press.

Miller, Daniel (1998), *A Theory of Shopping,* London: Polity.

Miller, Janice (2011), *Fashion and Music,* Oxford: Berg.

Milligan, Andy (2010), *Brand It Like Beckham: The Story of How Brand Beckham Was Built,* London: Marshall Cavendish.

Mitchell, Claudia, and Reid-Walsh, Jacqueline (2008), *Girl Culture: Studying Girl Culture,* Westport, Connecticut: Greenwood Publishing.

Mitchell, Leslie (2003), *Bulwer Lytton: The Rise and Fall of a Victorian Man,* London: Continuum International Publishing Group.

Mitford, Nancy (1945), *The Pursuit of Love,* 2000 edition, London: Penguin Books.

Moir, Jan (2008), 'Mamma Mia! Island's Star Turn', *Telegraph* (5 July), <www.telegraph.co.uk/news/newstopics/celebritynews/2253947/Mamma-Mia-islands-star-turn.html> accessed 24 September 2010.

Moodie, Clemmie (2006), 'WAGs' £1m Shopping Spree Boosts Sleepy Town', *Daily Mail* (10 July), <www.dailymail.co.uk/tvshowbiz/article-395024/WAGs-1m-shopping-spree-boosts-sleepy-town.html> accessed 8 August 2010.

Moodie, Clemmie, and Lawler, Danielle (2010), 'Bittersweet Brits Triumph for Lady GaGa as She Dedicated Three Awards to Late Pal Alexander McQueen', *Mirror* (16 February), <www.mirror.co.uk/celebs/news/2010/02/17/bittersweet-brist-triumph-for-lady-gaga-as-she-dedicated-three-awards-to-late-pal-alexander-mcqueen-115875–22048563/>, accessed 6 August 2010.

Moore, Booth (2010), 'Madonna, Daughter Lourdes Partner on Junior Fashion Line', *LATimes* (23 June), <articles.latimes.com/2010/jun/23/entertainment/la-et-madonna-20100623> accessed 7 August 2010.

Morgan, K. P. (2009), 'Women and the Knife: Cosmetic Surgery and the Colonization of Women's Bodies', in C. Heyes and N. Jones (eds), *Cosmetic Surgery: A Feminist Primer,* Farnham: Ashgate.

Mort, Frank (1996), *Cultures of Consumption: Masculinity and Social Space in Late 20th Century Britain,* London and New York: Routledge.

Morton, A. (1998), *Diana: Her True Story in Her Own Words,* New York: Simon and Schuster.

Moseley, Rachel (ed.) (2005), *Fashioning Film Stars,* London: BFI Publishing.

Moseley, Rachel (2002), *Growing Up with Audrey Hepburn,* Manchester: Manchester University Press.

Moseley, Rachel (2001), 'Respectability All Sewn Up: Dressmaking and Film Star Style in the Fifties and Sixties', *European Journal of Cultural Studies,* 4/4 (November).

Möttölä, Anna (2007), 'Style Star—Admiring Audrey Hepburn in the 1950s', in Kari Kallioniemi, Kimi Kärki, Janne Mäkelä and Hannu Salmi (eds), *History of Stardom Reconsidered,* edited by International Institute for Popular Culture, <iipc.utu.fi/reconsidered/>.

Mower, Sarah (2009), 'D-Day: Carla Bruni-Sarkozy and Michelle Obama—The First Ladies of Fashion', *Telegraph* (6 June), <www.telegraph.co.uk/news/worldnews/

northamerica/usa/michelle-obama/5463518/D-Day-Carla-Bruni-Sarkozy-and-Michelle-Obama-the-first-ladies-of-fashion.html> accessed 24 September 2010.

Mower, Sarah (2008), 'Fashion World Stunned by Vogue for Black', *Guardian* (27 July), <www.guardian.co.uk/lifeandstyle/2008/jul/27/fashion.pressandpublishing> accessed 16 October 2010.

Muggleton, David (2000), *Inside Subculture: The Postmodern Meaning of Style,* Oxford: Berg.

Mullen Gordon, Julia (2009), 'Meet Jane: How a Teenager from Trophy Club Became an "It Girl"', *Texas Monthly* (March), <www.texasmonthly.com/2009–03–01/webextra6.php> accessed August 2010.

Mulvagh, Jane (1998), *Vivienne Westwood: An Unfashionable Life,* London: Harper Collins.

Mulvey, Laura (1975), 'Visual Pleasure and Narrative Cinema', *Screen* 16/3: 6–18.

Murphy, Robert (2008), 'Chanel Cancels Mobile Art Tour', *Women's Wear Daily* (19 December), <www.wwd.com/eyescoop/chanel-cancels-mobile-art-tour-1899292/?src=nl/newsAlert/20081219> accessed 17 October 2010.

Negra, Diane, and Holmes, Su (2008), 'Introduction', *Going Cheap? Female Celebrity in Reality, Tabloid and Scandal Genres,* special issue of *Genders,* 48, <www.genders.org/g48/g48_negraholmes.html> accessed 28 October 2010.

Newby, Eric (1962), *Something Wholesale: My Life and Times in the Rag Trade,* 1985 reprint, London: Picador.

Nicholl, Katie (2010), 'Is Victoria Beckham's American Dream about to Come True?' *Mail Online* (25 September), <www.dailymail.co.uk/tvshowbiz/article-1315269/Victoria-Beckham-Is-American-dream-come-true.html#ixzz10rgn3BjD> accessed 28 September 2010.

Nicholl, K. (2009), 'Victoria Beckham Says She's Not Fur Turning with New Louis Vuitton Handbag', *Daily Mail* (22 November), <www.dailymail.co.uk/tvshowbiz/article-1229863/KATIE-NICHOLL-Victoria-Beckham-says-shes-fur-turning-new-Louis-Vuitton-handbag.html> accessed 23 July 2010.

Nixon, Sean (1996), *Hard Looks—Masculinities, Spectatorship and Contemporary Consumption,* London: UCL Press/Palgrave Macmillan.

Norris, Herbert, and Curtis, Oswold (1998), *Nineteenth Century Costume and Fashion,* London: Dover Publications.

O'Byrne, Robert (2009), *Style City: How London Became a Fashion Capital,* London: Frances Lincoln.

Odell, Amy (2009a), 'Lindsay Lohan's Ungaro Debut Deemed Disastrous', *New York* (5 October), <nymag.com/daily/fashion/2009/10/lindsay_lohans_ungaro_debut_de.html> accessed 8 August 2010.

Odell, Amy (2009b), 'We Are Not Surprised *Vogue* Photoshopped Sienna Miller's Head onto a Different Body', *New York,* <nymag.com/daily/fashion/2009/01/we_are_not_suprised_vogue_phot.html> accessed September 2010.

'Offensive Opium Posters to be Removed' (2000), *Guardian* (19 December), <www.guardian.co.uk/media/2000/dec/19/advertising.uknews> accessed 24 September 2010.

Okawa, Tomoko (2008), 'Licencing Practices at Maison Christian Dior', in Regina Lee Blaszczyk (ed.), *Producing Fashion: Commerce, Culture and Consumers,* Philadelphia: University of Pennsylvania Press.

Okonkwo, Uche (2007), *Luxury Fashion Branding: Trends, Tactics, Techniques,* London: Palgrave Macmillan.

Olins, Alice (2009), 'The Sartorialist Scott Schuman: What Makes Someone Stylish', *Times* (14 October), <women.timesonline.co.uk/tol/life_and_style/women/fashion/article6873270.ece> accessed 28 September 2010.

Oliver, Hatty (2007), 'Masquerade of Living Dolls: Is There a "Real" Woman behind Exaggerated Performances of Femininity Enacted by Kylie and Jordan?' *Times Higher Education Supplement* (2 February), <www.timeshighereducation.co.uk/story.asp?storycode=207696> accessed January 2008.

Olsen, Mary-Kate, and Olsen, Ashley (2008), *Influence,* London: Michael Joseph.

Olsen, Mary-Kate, and Olsen, Ashley (2006), *Mary-Kate and Ashley Style Secrets: What to Wear and How to Wear It,* New York: Harper Collins Children's Books.

O'Mahony, John (2003), 'My Past Is Kind of Obscene', *Guardian* (22 April), <www.guardian.co.uk/stage/2003/apr/22/dance.artsfeatures> accessed 25 September 2010.

Orbach, Susie (2009), *Bodies,* London: Profile Books.

O'Sullivan, Jack (1998), 'What Is Middle England?' *Independent* (29 September), <www.independent.co.uk/news/what-is-middle-england-1201255.html> accessed 12 September 2010.

Owens, Susan (2007), 'High Time for Paris' Great Tearooms', *Los Angeles Times* (19 July), <travel.latimes.com/articles/la-trw-paris22jul22> accessed 7 August 2010.

Oxbury, Eve (2010), 'PPR's Profits Soar 162% in First Half', *Drapers* (30 July), <www.drapersonline.com/news/womenswear/news/pprs-profits-soar-162-in-first-half/5015774.article> accessed 7 August 2010.

Paglia, Camille (2010), 'Lady Gaga and the Death of Sex', *Sunday Times Magazine* (12 September), <www.thesundaytimes.co.uk/sto/public/magazine/article389697.ece?CMP=KNGvvp1-camille%20paglia%20lady%20gaga> accessed 29 September 2010.

Palermo, Olivia (2010), 'Olivia Palermo: Today I'm Wearing', *Vogue.com* photo blog (April), <www.vogue.co.uk/photo-blogs/olivia-palermo/100401-olivia-palermo-day-1b-.aspx> accessed 7 August 2010.

Palmer, Gareth (ed.) (2008), *Exposing Lifestyle Television: The Big Reveal,* London: Ashgate Publishing.

Parkins, Wendy (2004), 'Celebrity Knitting and the Temporality of Postmodernity', *Fashion Theory: The Journal of Dress, Body and Culture,* 8/4 (December): 425–41.

Paterson, Tony (2009), 'Lagerfeld Slams Fat, Jealous Mummies', *Independent* (13 October), <www.independent.co.uk/life-style/fashion/news/lagerfeld-slams-fat-jealous-mummies-1801773.html> accessed 25 September 2010.

Pedersen, Stephanie (2005), *Shoes: What Every Woman Should Know,* Newton Abbott, Devon: David and Charles.

Pendergast, Sara et al. (2004), *Fashion, Costume and Culture: Clothing, Headwear, Body Decorations and Footwear through the Ages,* Detroit, Michigan: UXL.

Pendergast, Sara (1997), *Contemporary Designers,* Farmington Hills, Michigan: St James Press.

Petridis, Alexis (2010), 'Lady Gaga's Direct Line to Andy Warhol', *Guardian,* Lost in Showbiz blog (9 September), <www.guardian.co.uk/lifeandstyle/lostinshowbiz/2010/sep/09/lady-gaga-andy-warhol> accessed 29 September 2010.

Picardie, Justine (2010), *Coco Chanel: The Legend and the Life,* London: Harper Collins.

Plimpton, George (1998), *Truman Capote: In Which Various Friends, Enemies and Acquaintances and Detractors Recall His Turbulent Career,* New York: Anchor Books.

Plunkett, John (2010), 'Naomi Campbell: Media Adviser Says Hague Tribunal Is Big PR Winner', *Guardian* (12 August), <www.guardian.co.uk/media/2010/aug/12/naomi-campbell-war-crimes-tribunal> accessed 16 October 2010.

Pochna, Marie-France (2005), *Dior,* New York: Assouline.

Pochna, Marie-France (1996), *Christian Dior: The Man Who Made the World Look New,* New York: Arcade Publishing.

Polhemus, Ted (1994), *Streetstyle: From Sidewalk to Catwalk,* London: Thames and Hudson/V&A Museum.

Pomerantz, Dorothy, and Rose, Lacey (2009), 'Special Report: The Celebrity 100', *Forbes* (22 June), <www.forbes.com/2010/06/22/lady-gaga-oprah-winfrey-business-entertainment-celeb-100–10_land.html> accessed 19 September 2010.

Pool, Hannah (2007), 'Campbell's Coup: Vogue Magazine Has Run Just Twelve Covers Featuring Black Models in Its 91-year History. Maybe Naomi Campbell Has a Point about Racism in Fashion', *Guardian* (21 August), <www.guardian.co.uk/commentisfree/2007/aug/21/campbellscoup> accessed 16 October 2010.

Poplawski, Paul (ed.) (2007), *English Literature in Context,* Cambridge: Cambridge University Press.

Porter, Charlie (2009), 'Blood on the Catwalk as Cutbacks Bite', *Observer* (4 January), <www.guardian.co.uk/lifeandstyle/2009/jan/04/fashion-recession-chanel-job-losses> accessed 17 October 2010.

Postle, Martin et al. (2005), *Joshua Reynolds: The Creation of Celebrity,* London: Tate.

Price, Katie (2009), *Standing Out: My Look, My Style, My Life,* London: Century.

Price, Katie (2007), *Jordan: A Whole New World,* London: Arrow.

Price, Katie (2006), *Being Jordan: My Autobiography,* London: John Blake.

Price, Richard (2010), 'As Lourdes Launches Her Own Risqué Fashion Range, How Madonna Is Grooming Her Daughter to Eclipse Her Stardom', *Daily Mail* (5 August), <www.dailymail.co.uk/femail/article-1300460/As-Lourdes-launches-risqué-fashion-range-Madonna-grooming-daughter-eclipse-stardom.html> accessed 7 August 2010.

Power, Katherine, and Kerr, Hillary (2010), 'Girl of the Month Olivia Palermo', *Who, What, Wear,* <www.whowhatwear.com/website/full-article/girlthe-month-olivia-palermo/> accessed 7 August 2010.

Primark (2010), 'Primark in Our Own Words', corporate video, <www.primark.co.uk/page.aspx?pointerid=2f6909e623754e70b9ec58c1c8593ded> accessed 7 August 2010.

'Primark Goes Posh Victoria Beckham Copycat Jacket Is Best Seller' (2007), *Now* (9 March), <www.nowmagazine.co.uk/celebrity-news/235361/primark-goes-posh/1/> accessed 7 August 2010.

Pullin, Graham (2009), *Design Meets Disability,* Cambridge, Massachusetts: MIT Press.

Pulver, Andrew (2010), 'Tom Ford: A Single Man and His Address Book', *Guardian* (28 January), <www.guardian.co.uk/film/2010/jan/28/tom-ford-a-single-man> accessed September 2010.

Purohit, Raj (2008), *Beckham and the Conquest of America,* Bloomington, Indiana: iUniverse.

Quant, Mary (1966), *Quant by Quant,* London: Cassell.

Radner, Hilary (2000), 'On the Move: Fashion Photography and the Single Girl in the 1960s', in Stella Bruzzi and Pamela Church Gibson (eds), *Fashion Cultures: Theories, Explorations and Analysis,* London and New York: Routledge.

Radner, Hilary (1995), *Shopping Around: Feminine Culture and the Pursuit of Pleasure,* London: Routledge.

Radner, Hilary, and Luckett, Moya (1999), *Swinging Single: Representing Sexuality in the 1960s,* Minneapolis: University of Minnesota Press.

Rahman, Momin (2006), 'Is Straight the New Queer? David Beckham and the Dialectics of Celebrity', in P. David Marshall (ed.), *The Celebrity Culture Reader,* London: Routledge.

Rappaport, H. (2004), *Queen Victoria: A Bibliographic Companion,* Santa Barbara, California: ABC-CLIO.

Rawi, Maysa (2010), 'Material Girl: Madonna Set to Design Junior Clothing Range Inspired by Daughter Lourdes', *Daily Mail* (12 March), <www.dailymail.co.uk/femail/article-1257237/Material-Girl-Madonna-set-design-junior-clothing-range-inspired-daughter-Lourdes.html#ixzz0vvgG3skN> accessed 7 August 2010.

Rawi, Maysa (2009), 'Move over Geldof Girls: Meet Tavi, 13, the "Tiny" Blogger with the Fashion Industry at Her Feet', *Mail Online* (23 September), <www.dailymail.co.uk/femail/article-1215048/Meet-Tavi-Gevinson-13-tiny-blogger-fashion-industry-feet.html#ixzz10rlii5Vm> accessed 28 September 2010.

Redmond, Sean, and Holmes, Su (eds) (2007), *Stardom and Celebrity: A Reader,* London: Sage.

Reich, Jacqueline (2004), *Beyond the Latin Lover: Marcello Mastroanni, Masculinity and Italian Cinema,* Bloomington: Indiana University Press.

Reslen, Eileen (2010), 'Madonna's Material Girl Clothing Line Launches at Macy's in New York City', *MTV News* (3 August), <hollywoodcrush.mtv.com/2010/08/03/madonna-material-girl-macys-launch/> accessed 7 August 2010.

Richards, Jeffrey (1973), *Visions of Yesterday,* London and New York: Routledge.

Richards, Keith, with James Fox (2010), *Life,* London: Weidenfeld and Nicolson.

Roberts, Andrew (2010), 'LVMH Profit Beats Estimates on Rising Fashion Sales', *Bloomberg Business Week* (27 July), <www.businessweek.com/news/2010–07–27/lvmh-profit-beats-estimates-on-rising-fashion-sales.html> accessed 7 August 2010.

Roberts, Laura (2010), 'Colin Firth Nearly Turned Down the Part that Won Him a Best Actor BAFTA', *Telegraph* (22 February), <www.telegraph.co.uk/culture/film/baftas/7287770/Colin-Firth-nearly-turned-down-the-part-that-won-him-a-best-actor-Bafta.html> accessed 24 September 2010.

Roberts, Laura (2008), 'Legendary Photographer Annie Leibovitz Apologises for Taking Topless Shots of 15-year-old Hannah Montana Star Miley Cyrus', *Daily Mail* (29 April), <www.dailymail.co.uk/tvshowbiz/article-562548/Legendary-photographer-Annie-Leibovitz-apologises-taking-topless-shots-15-year-old-Hannah-Montana-star-Miley-Cyrus.html#ixzz1013KPDJZ> accessed 19 September 2010.

Robertson, Pamela (1996), *Guilty Pleasures: Feminist Camp from Mae West to Madonna,* Durham, North Carolina: Duke University Press.

Robinson, Lisa (2010), 'Lady Gaga's Cultural Revolution', *Vanity Fair* (September).

Rocamora, Agnes, and Djurdja, Bartlett (forthcoming), 'Fashion Blogging: The New Fashion Journalism', in Sandy Black (ed.), *The Eco Fashion Book,* London: Thames and Hudson.

Rocamora, Agnes, and O' Neill, Alistair (2008), 'Fashioning the Street: Images of the Street in the Fashion Media', in Shinkle (ed.), *Fashion as Photograph: Viewing and Reviewing Images of Fashion,* London: IB Tauris.

Rodriguez, Narciso (2009), 'Hamish Bowles', *Interview,* <www.interviewmagazine.com/fashion/hamish-bowles/> accessed 8 August 2010.

Rojek, Chris (2001), *Celebrity,* London: Reaktion Books.

Ross, Sara (2000), 'The Hollywood Flapper and the Culture of Media Consumption', in David Desser and Garth Jowett (eds), *Hollywood Goes Shopping,* Minneapolis: University of Minnesota Press.

'RPattz Waxwork Wows Screaming Fans' (2010), *ITN News* (25 March), <itn.co.uk/69a88f52f2895dc551b560818d8c958c.html> accessed 19 September 2010.

Ryan, Nicky (2007), 'Prada and the Art of Patronage', *Fashion Theory: The Journal of Dress, Body and Culture,* 11/1 (March): 7–23.

Sabbagh, Dan (2007), 'Katie Price Settles Row with Heat Magazine over Her Disabled Son', *Times Online* (4 December), <women.timesonline.co.uk/tol/life_and_style/ women/celebrity/article3000126.ece> accessed 29 September 2010.

Sackville-West, Vita (1930), *The Edwardians,* new edition, with an introduction by Victoria Glendinning, 1983, London: Virago Press.

Samuel, Henry (2010), 'Carla Bruni-Sarkozy and Michelle Obama at Odds, Book Claims', *Telegraph* (15 September), <www.telegraph.co.uk/news/worldnews/europe/ france/8004848/Carla-Bruni-Sarkozy-and-Michelle-Obama-at-odds-book-claims. html> accessed 24 September 2010.

Savage, J. (2007), *Teenage: The Creation of Youth Culture,* London: Chatto and Windus.

Sedgwick, Eve Kosofsky (1985), *Between Men: English Literature and Male Homosocial Desire,* New York: Columbia University Press.

Sedgwick, Eve Kosofsky (1990), *Epistemology of the Closet* Berkeley : University of California Press

Sedgwick, Eve Kosofsky (1993), *Tendencies* London : Routledge

Segal, Lynne (1999), *Why Feminism? Gender, Psychology, Politics,* New York: Columbia University Press.

Sells, Emma (2010), 'Sarah Jessica Parker to Join Halston', *Elle* (14 January), <www. elleuk.com/news/Star-style-News/sarah-jessica-parker-to-join-halston> accessed 25 September 2010.

'Sex and the City: A Product Placement Roundup' (2008), *Vanity Fair Daily* (30 May).

Sharkey, Alix (2000), 'How the Man in Black Conquered the World', *Independent* (20 January), <www.independent.co.uk/news/people/profiles/how-the-man-in-black-conquered-the-world-728220.html> accessed 7 August 2010.

Sheilds, Rachel (2010), 'Debt Is a Feminist Issue: Huge Leap in Bankruptcy among Women', *Independent* (25 July), <www.independent.co.uk/news/uk/home-news/ debt-is-a-feminist-issue-huge-leap-in-bankruptcy-among-women-2034991.html> accessed 24 September 2010.

Shields, Rachel (2009), 'Moss's £60 High Street Frock Is Named Dress of the Year', *Independent* (3 May), <www.independent.co.uk/life-style/fashion/news/mosss-16360-high-street-frock-is-named-dress-of-the-year-1678123.html> accessed 16 October 2010.

Sheridan, Jayne (2010), *Fashion, Media, Promotion: The New Black Magic,* Chichester: Wiley- Blackwell.

Sherrow, Victoria (2006), *Encyclopedia of Hair: A Cultural History,* Westport, Connecticut: Greenwood Publishing.

Shrimpton, Jean, and Hall, Unity (1990), *Jean Shrimpton: An Autobiography,* London: Ebury Press.

Siddique, Haroon (2008), 'Naomi Campbell Faces Five Charges after Heathrow Terminal 5 Incident', *Guardian* (29 May), <www.guardian.co.uk/uk/2008/may/29/ ukcrime2> accessed 16 October 2010.

Simmel, George (1904), 'Fashion', in *On Individuality and Social Forms,* Chicago: University of Chicago Press.

Simms, Joseph (1974), 'Adrian, American Artist and Designer', *Costume: The Journal of the Costume Society,* 8.

Simpson, Mark (1994a), 'Here Come the Mirror Men', *Independent* (15 November), <www.marksimpson.com/pages/journalism/mirror_men.html> accessed 10 May 2009.

Simpson, Mark (1994b), *Male Impersonators: Gay Men Performing Masculinity,* London and New York: Routledge.

Singh, Anita (2009), 'Madonna in New Louis Vuitton Advertising Campaign', *Telegraph* (6 January), <www.telegraph.co.uk/fashion/4140704/Madonna-in-new-Louis-Vuitton-advertising-campaign.html> accessed 7 August 2010.

'SKYY Vodka(R) Reprises Role in New Line Cinema's Sex and the City 2 Movie' (2010), *PR Newswire* (16 February), <www.prnewswire.com/news-releases/skyy-vodkar-reprises-role-in-new-line-cinemas-sex-and-the-city-2-movie-84470032.html> accessed August 2010.

Smedley, Elliott (2000), 'Escaping to Reality: Fashion Photography in the 1990s', in Stella Bruzzi and Pamela Church Gibson (eds), *Fashion Cultures: Theories, Explorations and Analysis,* London and New York: Routledge.

Sohn, Amy (2004), *Sex and the City: Kiss and Tell,* New York: Pocket Books.

Solway, Diane (2008), 'Helmut Lang', *W* (October), <www.wmagazine.com/artdesign/2008/10/helmut_lang> accessed 8 August 2010.

'Source: Jolie-Pitt Baby Pics Fetch $14 Million' (2008), *Associated Press* (1 August), <today.msnbc.msn.com/id/25967334> accessed 19 September 2010.

Slater, Don (1997), *Consumer Culture and Modernity,* London: Polity.

Solway, Diane (2008), 'Tilda Swinton', *W* (September), <www.wmagazine.com/celebrities/2008/09/tilda_swinton> accessed 25 September 2010.

Spigel, Lynn (2008), *TV by Design: Modern Art and the Rise of Network Television,* Chicago: University of Chicago Press.

Springer, Claudia (2007), *James Dean Transfigured: The Many Faces of Rebel Iconography,* Austin: University of Texas Press.

Stables, Kate (2008), review of Sex and the City: The Movie, *Sight and Sound,* 18/8 (August).

Stacey, Jackie (1994), *Star Gazing: Hollywood Cinema and Female Spectatorship,* London and New York: Routledge.

Stallabrass, Julian (2005), 'Partying', *Art Monthly,* 286 (May), <www.courtauld.ac.uk/people/stallabrass_julian/reviews/art-money-parties-revise.pdf> accessed 17 October 2010.

Stallabrass, Julian (2004), *Art Incorporated: The Story of Contemporary Art,* Oxford: Oxford University Press.

Stebbins, Meredith (2010a), 'Speaking with The Sartorialist', *Vanity Fair Daily* (20 February), <www.vanityfair.com/online/daily/2010/02/speaking-with-the-sartorialist. html> accessed 29 September 2010.

Stebbins, Meredith (2010b), 'Who Sits Where at Fashion Week and Why', *Vanity Fair Daily* (10 February), <www.vanityfair.com/online/daily/2010/02/who-sits-where-at-fashion-week-and-why.html> accessed 9 August 2010.

Steele, Valerie (1996), *Fetish: Fashion, Sex and Power,* Oxford: Oxford University Press.

Steele, Valerie (1991), 'The F Word', *Lingua Franca: The Review of Academic Life* (April).

Stein, Jean, and Plimpton, George (2006), *Edie: An American Biography,* London: Pimlico.

Stenvinkel, Kristina (2010), 'Lanvin to Design Exclusive Collection for H&M this Autumn', H&M, press release (2 September), <www.hm.com/sk/__prfashion.nhtml? pressreleaseid=1081> accessed 25 September 2010.

Street, Sarah (2001), *Costume and Cinema: Dress Codes in Popular Film,* London: Wallflower.

Swaine, Jon (2008), 'Paris Hilton Hits Back at Jon McCain in Video', *Telegraph* (6 August), <www.telegraph.co.uk/news/newstopics/uselection2008/johnmccain/ 2509767/Paris-Hilton-hits-back-at-John-McCain-in-video.html> accessed 12 September 2010.

Sweeney, Mark (2008), 'Glossy Launch for Candace Bushnell's *Lipstick Jungle* on Living TV', *Guardian* (29 August), <www.guardian.co.uk/media/2008/aug/29/ television.marketingandpr> accessed September 2010.

Sykes, P. (2008), 'Rebel Romance', *Vogue* (21 June), <www.vogue.com/magazine/ article/sarah-jessica-parker-rebel-romance/?mbid=ob_ppc_mag_18> accessed 21 February 2010.

Talarico, Brittany (2010), 'Blake Lively Gets Love from Louboutin!' *OK* (15 September), <www.okmagazine.com/2010/09/blake-lively gets-love-from-louboutin/> accessed 29 September 2010.

Tartakovsky, Maragrita (2010), 'Men, Body Image and Disordered Eating: Q&A with Leigh Cohn', *PSchCentral: Weightless* (April), <blogs.psychcentral.com/weightless/ 2010/04/men-body-image-disordered-eating-qa-with-leigh-cohn/> accessed August 2010.

Taubin, Amy (1997), 'Four Stars', in Colin MacCabe et al. (eds), *Who Is Andy Warhol?* London: British Film Institute.

Taylor, Lou (2002), 'The Wardrobe of Mrs Leonard Messel 1895–1920', in Christopher Breward et al. (eds), *The Englishness of English Dress,* Oxford: Berg.

Testino, Mario (2010), *Kate Moss,* London: Taschen GmbH.

Testino, Mario (2006), *Diana: Princess of Wales*, London: Taschen GmbH.

Thomas, Liz (2010), 'What's Madonna Doing Letting Her Daughter, 13, Pitch This Clothes Range at Young Girls?' *Daily Mail* (4 August), <www.dailymail.co.uk/femail/

article-1300085/Whys-Madonna-letting-Lourdes-pitch-Material-Girl-clothing-range-young-girls.html?ito=feeds-newsxml> accessed September 2010.

Thompson, Kristin, and Bordwell, David (2006), *Film History: An Introduction,* New York: McGraw Hill.

Thompson, M. (2009), 'Victoria Beckham', *Allure.*

'Times Square Mad Men Premiere Review' (2010), *AMC, Talk: Mad Men* (26 July), <blogs.amctv.com/mad-men/talk/2010/07/times-square-ma.php> accessed 29 September 2010.

Timmons, Heather (2008), 'Vogue's Fashion Photos Spark Debate in India', *New York Times* (31 August), <www.nytimes.com/2008/09/01/business/worldbusiness/01vogue.html?_r=2&scp=1&sq=%22vogue%20india%22&st=cse&oref=slogin> accessed 17 October 2010.

Tolkien, Tracy (2002), *Vintage: The Art of Dressing Up,* London: Pavillion.

Tomer, Mary (2009), *Mrs O: The Face of Fashion Democracy,* New York: Center Street.

Tomkins, Calvin (2007), 'A Fool for Art', *New Yorker* (12 November), <www.newyorker.com/reporting/2007/11/12/071112fa_fact_tomkins> accessed 17 October 2010.

Topping, Alexandra (2010a), 'Emma Watson Is Named Hollywood's Highest Paid Female Actor', *Guardian* (5 February), <www.guardian.co.uk/film/2010/feb/05/emma-watson-vanity-fair-rich-list> accessed 8 August 2010.

Topping, Alexandra (2010b), 'Fashion Industry Faces Airbrushing Clampdown', *Guardian* (25 July), <www.guardian.co.uk/lifeandstyle/2010/jul/25/fashion-industry-airbrushing-clampdown> accessed 28 September 2010.

Topping, Alexandra (2010c), 'Lady Gaga's Meat Dress Angers Animal Rights Groups', *Guardian* (13 September), <www.guardian.co.uk/music/2010/sep/13/lady-gaga-meat-dress-vmas> accessed 29 September 2010.

Tran, Mark (2010), 'Fashion Designer Alexander McQueen Dies Aged 40', *Guardian* (11 February), <www.guardian.co.uk/uk/2010/feb/11/alexander-mcqueen-dies-fashion-designer> accessed September 2010.

Trebay, Guy (2007), 'Where Art Meets Fashion Meets Celebrity Meets Hype', *New York Times* (1 November), <www.nytimes.com/2007/11/01/fashion/01vezzoli.html> accessed 17 October 2010.

Tungate, Mark (2008), *Fashion Brands: Branding Style from Armani to Zara,* London: Kogan Page.

Turin, Luca, and Sanchez, Tania (2008), *Perfumes: The Guide,* London: Profile.

Turner, Graeme (2004), *Understanding Celebrity,* London: Sage.

Turner, Graeme, Bonner, Frances, and Marshall, David P. (2000), *Fame Games: The Production of Celebrity in Australia,* Cambridge: Cambridge University Press.

Turim, Maureen (1984), 'Designing Women: The Emergence of the New Sweetheart Line', in Jane Gaines and Charlotte Herzog (eds), *Fabrications: Costume and the Female Body,* London and New York: Routledge/AFI Film Readers.

Tyrnauer, Matt (2008), 'Partnership of the Travelling Bags', *Vanity Fair* (June), <www.vanityfair.com/culture/features/2008/06/chanel200806> accessed 17 October 2010.

Tyrnauer, Matt (2004), 'So Very Valentino', *Vanity Fair* (August), <www.vanityfair.com/culture/features/2004/08/valentino200408> accessed 17 October 2010.

Uhlirova, Marketa (2009), 'In The Bubble', *City,* 63 (April/May): 60.

Veblen, Thorstein (1899), *The Theory of the Leisure Class,* 1994 edition, London and New York: Penguin.

Velasco, David (2009), 'Elmgreen and Dragset', *ArtForum* (1 June), <artforum.com/words/id=23020> accessed 17 October 2010.

Vermorel, Fred (1996), *Vivienne Westwood: Fashion, Perversity and the Sixties Laid Bare,* London: Overlook Press.

Vernon, Polly (2010), 'Thin Is In: In Search of the Perfect Male Body', *Guardian* (27 June), <www.guardian.co.uk/lifeandstyle/2010/jun/27/mens-health-weight> accessed 8 August 2010.

Vernon, Polly (2005), 'The Lure of Thrift Luxe', *Guardian* (10 July), <www.guardian.co.uk/lifeandstyle/2005/jul/10/fashion.shopping> accessed 7 August 2010.

Veslemøy, Aga (2010), 'Hverdags Glamour', *Dagens Næringsliv* (6 August), in Norwegian, prepublication English translation provided by the author.

Vincendeau, Ginette (2005), 'Hot Couture: Brigitte Bardot's Fashion Revolution', in Rachel Moseley (ed.), *Fashioning Film Stars: Dress, Culture, Identity,* London: BFI Publishing.

Vincent, John, and Hill, John S. (2007), 'David Beckham—Major League Soccer's First Crossover Celebrity', <www.sports-media.org/newpedimensionapril2007.htm> accessed 6 August 2010.

Vincent, John, Hill, John S., and Lee, Jason W. (2009), 'The Multiple Brand Personalities of David Beckham: A Case Study of the Beckham Brand', *Sport Marketing Quarterly* (1 September), <www.thefreelibrary.com/The+multiple+brand+personalities+of+David+Beckham%3A+a+case+study+of...-a0216352321> accessed 6 August 2010.

Vinken, Barbara (2005), *Fashion Zeitgeist: Trends and Cycles in the Fashion System,* Oxford: Berg.

Violette, Robert (ed.) (2003), *Paul Smith: You Can Find Inspiration in Everything,* London: Thames and Hudson.

Voller, Debbi (1999), *Madonna: The Style Book,* London: Omnibus Press.

Vreeland, Diana (1984/2003), *D.V.,* New York: Da Capo Press.

Yablonsky, Linda (2009a), 'Lady in Waiting: Los Angeles', *Art Forum* (19 November), <artforum.com/diary/archive=200911> accessed 8 August 2010.

Yablonsky, Linda (2009b), 'Star Turn: Los Angeles', *Art Forum* (20 November), <artforum.com/diary/archive=200911> accessed 8 August 2010.

Yu, Chia-Chen (2005), 'Athlete Endorsement in the International Sports Industry: A Case Study of David Beckham', *International Journal of Sports Marketing & Sponsorship,* 6/3: 189–99.

Wanamaker, Marc (1984), *The Hollywood Reporter Star Profiles,* New York and London: Gallery Books.

Warhol, Andy (1975), *The Philosophy of Andy Warhol,* 2010 reprint, London: Penguin Books.

Warhol, Andy, and Hackett, Pat (1991), *The Andy Warhol Diaries,* New York: Grand Central Publishing.

Warner, Helen (2009), 'Style over Substance? Fashion, Spectacle and Narrative in Contemporary US Television', *Popular Narrative Media,* 2/2.

Warner, Michael (1993), 'The Structural Transformation of the Public Sphere', in Bruce Robbins (ed.), *The Phantom Public,* Minneapolis: University of Minnesota.

Warner, Michael (1992), 'The Mass Public and the Mass Subject', in Craig Calhoun (ed.), *Habermas and the Public Sphere,* Cambridge, Massachusetts: MIT Press.

Warren, Christina (2010), 'Sex and the City Switches from Apple to HP', *Mashable* (21 May), <mashable.com/2010/05/21/sex-and-the-city-hp/> accessed 25 September 2010.

Waters, Darren (2006), 'Coppola's Period Drama Falls Flat', *BBC News,* <news.bbc.co.uk/1/hi/entertainment/5012530.stm> accessed 7 August 2010.

Waugh, Evelyn (1930), *Vile Bodies,* 2000 edition, London: Penguin Modern Classics.

Waugh, Evelyn (1928), *Decline and Fall,* 2003 edition, London: Penguin Modern Classics.

Weber, Brenda (2009), *Makeover TV: Selfhood, Citizenship and Celebrity,* Durham, North Carolina: Duke University Press.

Weber, Brenda R. (2005), 'Beauty, Desire and Anxiety: The Economy of Sameness in ABC's Extreme Makeover', *Genders,* 41, <www.genders.org/g41_weber.html> accessed September 2010.

Weber, Caroline (2008), *Queen of Fashion: What Marie Antoinette Wore to the Revolution,* London: Aurum.

Weintraub, Stanley (2001), *Edward the Caresser: The Playboy Prince Who Became Edward VII,* volume 2001, part 2, London: Free Press.

Weisberger, Lauren (2003), *The Devil Wears Prada,* London and New York: Harper Collins.

Weaver, Matthew (2010), 'Naomi Campbell's "Blood Diamond" Testimony at War Crimes Trial: Live Updates', *Guardian,* News blog (5 August), <www.guardian.co.uk/law/blog/2010/aug/05/naomi-campbell-blood-diamonds> accessed 16 October 2010.

Weaver, Matthew (2009), 'Tributes Pour in for Jade Goody after Reality Star Dies from Cancer, Aged 27', *Guardian* (22 March), <www.guardian.co.uk/media/2009/mar/22/jade-goody-dies-tributes> accessed 17 October 2010.

Weisman, David, and Painter, Melissa (2007), *Edie: Girl on Fire,* New York: Chronicle Books.

West, Naomi (2008), 'Rei Kawakubo of Comme des Garçons designs for H&M', *Telegraph* (26 October), <www.telegraph.co.uk/fashion/3365690/Rei-Kawakubo-of-Comme-des-Garcons-designs-for-HandM.html> accessed 8 August 2010.

Wharton, Edith (1938), *The Buccaneers,* completed by Marion Mainwaring, 1993 edition, London: Fourth Estate.

Wheeler, Rachael (2009), 'Madonna Stars in New Dolce & Gabbana Campaign for Vanity Fair', *Mirror* (17 December), <www.mirror.co.uk/celebs/news/2009/12/17/madonna-stars-in-new-dolce-gabbana-campaign-for-vanity-fair-115875–21904203/> accessed 7 August 2010.

Whitworth, M. (2009), 'Lindsay Lohan's New Fake Tan: Sunshine in a Bottle', *Telegraph* (4 May), <www.telegraph.co.uk/health/5256949/Lindsay-Lohans-new-fake-tan-sunshine-in-a-bottle.html> accessed 23 May 2010.

Wilcox, Claire (2005), *Vivienne Westwood,* London: V&A Publishing.

Williams, Zoe (2010), 'Carrie Bradshaw, You Are Definitely Not a PC', *Guardian* (21 April), <www.guardian.co.uk/film/2010/apr/21/mac-pc-carrie-sex-city> accessed 25 September 2010.

Wilson, Elizabeth (1985), *Adorned in Dreams: Fashion and Modernity,* second revised and updated edition, 2005, London: IB Tauris.

Wilson, Eric, and Horyn, Cathy (2010), 'Alexander McQueen, Designer, Is Dead at 40', *New York Times* (11 February), <www.nytimes.com/2010/02/12/fashion/12mcqueen.html> accessed 8 August 2010.

Winter, Lyn (2009), 'The Museum of Contemporary Art, Los Angeles Celebrates 30 Years with MOCA New 30th Anniversary Gala', MOCA, press release (3 November), <www.moca.org/pdf/press/MOCA_NEW_30th_Anniversary_Gala_Release.pdf> accessed 8 August 2010.

Wiseman, Eva (2009), 'Tavi Gevinson: The 13-year-old Blogger with the Fashion World at Her Feet', *Observer* (20 September), <www.guardian.co.uk/lifeandstyle/2009/sep/20/tavi-gevinson-new-york-fashion> accessed 28 September 2010.

Wiseman, Eva (2008), 'Designer with Bags of Talent', *Observer* (31 August), <www.guardian.co.uk/lifeandstyle/2008/aug/31/fashion.celebrity1> accessed 25 September 2010.

Wolf, Naomi (2002), *The Beauty Myth: How Images of Beauty Are Used against Women,* New York: Perennial.

Wolfe, Tom (1987), *Bonfire of the Vanities,* New York: Farrar, Straus and Giroux.

Woods, Judith (2006), 'When Did Shopping Become a Team Sport?' *Telegraph* (14 June), <www.telegraph.co.uk/fashion/shoppingandfashion/3354291/When-did-shopping-become-a-team-sport.html> accessed 12 September 2010.

Woods, Richard, and Flintoff, John-Paul (2008), 'The Rise of Boden Man', *Sunday Times* (3 August), <www.timesonline.co.uk/tol/news/politics/article4449286.ece> accessed 12 September 2010.

Woodward, Kathleen M. (1991), *Ageing and Its Discontents: Freud and Other Fictions,* Bloomington: Indiana University Press.

Zoe, Rachel (2007), *Style A to Zoe: The Art of Fashion, Beauty, and Everything Glamour,* New York: Grand Central Publishing.

Zweig, Stefan (1933/2002), *Marie Antoinette: The Portrait of an Average Woman,* New York: Grove Press.

Index

Contemporary critical theorists can be found in the bibliography, together with articles from print journalism and Web sites.